Eroticism in Ancient and
Medieval Greek Poetry

EROTICISM

in Ancient and Medieval
Greek Poetry

J.C.B. Petropoulos

Duckworth

First published in 2003 by
Gerald Duckworth & Co. Ltd.
90-93 Cowcross Street, London EC1M 6BF
Tel: 020 7490 7300
Fax: 020 7490 0080
Email: inquiries@duckworth-publishers.co.uk
www.ducknet.co.uk

A catalogue record for this book is available
from the British Library

ISBN 0 7156 2985 9

Typeset by Ray Davies
Printed in Great Britain by
CPI Bath

Contents

Contents

Prologue

The role of popular song in the ancient Greek world and the hypothetical question of its relation to later Greek tradition remain to be studied afresh and from a strictly philological point of view. Here I have set myself a more modest goal: to show that numerous erotic motifs and images have been consistently used with permutations in ancient, medieval and modern Greek popular tradition.

Any study that enquires into the apparent 'continuity' of popular elements can only proceed by documenting specific instances; moreover, even after disposing of a host of procedural obstacles, it must always reckon critically with the twin sources of 'highbrow' and popular inspiration. Accordingly, the subject-matter of this book has been divided into four separate cases of 'continuity', each occupying a chapter. In the first two instances (Chapters II and III), which are conceived as companion test cases, the complex dialectical relationships between learned, literary, sub-literary and popular media are reconstructed. The scheme of transmission put forward in these chapters may be extrapolated to the cases examined in the remaining chapters. Throughout the book the persistence of specific popular features will be argued on the basis of typological analysis, supplemented where necessary by anthropological data bearing on the relevant social or ritual context.

As someone who lives and works in the Balkans and the eastern Mediterranean in the early twenty-first century, I hasten to add a fundamental rider: by 'continuity' I understand the extensive use and enrichment of certain traditional features of love-songs (broadly defined) over time. These features are historically contingent products of human (especially literate) agency; most of them can be reliably documented in Greek sources; but their seeming continuance in the Greek speaking world does not in the least imply an untroubled, seamless or statically 'authentic' tradition.

A word about my main procedural models. Since its publication in 1963, Sir Kenneth Dover's paper 'The poetry of Archilochus' (now reprinted in *Greek and the Greeks: collected papers* [Oxford, 1987], i.97-121) has exemplified the recourse to ethnographic data from preliterate cultures as an analytical tool in approaching the context and other aspects of Archilochus' poems. In a serious sense, this book has grown out of that paper; Chapters II, III and IV presuppose that Sappho's wedding-poems may be regarded essentially as 'songs', and my object here is to account for the apparent coincidences in outline and detail between Sappho and modern Greek folk-songs. The work of two other eminent scholars has also proved influential: Margaret Alexiou's *The ritual lament in Greek tradition* (Cambridge, 1974) and Johannes Kakrides' *Homeric researches* (Skrifter ... Lund, xlv, 1949), *Homer revisited* (Skrifter ... Lund, lxiv, 1971), *Xanagyrizontas ston Omiro* [an expanded version of the latter] (Thessalonica, 1971), and *Ela, Aphroditi, anthostephanômeni* (Athens, 1983). In my largely historical discussion of wedding-songs in Chapters II and III, I try to do what Professor Alexiou undertook in connection with the ritual lament and, following on the late Professor Kakrides' comparative exploration of popular love topics, I have attempted something which, as far as I know, has never been ventured on such a scale in relation to popular Greek eroticism: first, to delineate further the vast penumbra of popular song, especially love-song, which presumably underlay and fertilised many literary genres in antiquity; second, to address the methodological problems involved by a study of continuity; third, to define more precisely the hypothetical corpus of traditional material that makes up the inheritance of medieval and modern folk-poetry in general; and fourth, to add a few new details about the modern songs' form and content. In all these respects this study may, I hope, serve as a pendant or even a supplement to Professor Alexiou's and Professor Kakrides' comparative analyses of Greek tradition.

As a classicist who probed outside his former fields, I cannot but be grateful to certain classical scholars and other specialists for advice: the late Professor Samuel Baud-Bovy, Dr Antonio Corso, Mrs Mary Coulton, Mr Seth Fagan, Professor Wolfram Hörandner, Mr Vangelis Karayiannis, Dr Steven Lambert, Mr Peter Liddel, Professors A.R. Littlewood, Demetrios Loukatos and M. Manusakas; Mrs Helen Psychoyiou, Dr Charles Stewart, Dr Gerasimos Zoras, Madame Popi Zora, and especially Dr H.-C. Günther, Professor P. Mackridge, Mr Antonis Panayiotou, Dr Christiane Sourvinou-Inwood, and Mr Nigel Wilson, F.B.A. Warm thanks are also due to: the head librarian and staff of the Slavonic and Modern Greek Annexe of the Taylor Institution, especially Mr Roger Green; the directors and staff of the Gennadius Library, the Libraries of the American School of Classical Studies and the British School at Athens, Widener Library at Harvard University, and the fabulous library at Dumbarton Oaks. Professor Anna Papamichaël, former Director of the Centre for Folklore Research at the Academy of Athens, is also to be thanked for granting me access to archival material. By her kind permission a large number of folk-songs (some recorded nearly a century ago) appear in this work for the first time.

This work began life as a D.Phil. thesis at the University of Oxford. I am therefore grateful to St Cross College for electing me a scholar during my first three years at Oxford. Lincoln College, where I spent my subsequent postgraduate days, similarly proved to be a most agreeable and humane community in which to live and work, and I am thankful for this.

I wish also to record my gratitude to the Alexander S. Onassis Public Benefit Foundation for awarding me a scholarship for the years 1985-6 and 1987-8. The Center for Hellenic Studies in Washington, D.C. offered me a three-month scholarship and term of residence in 2000, during which I worked, alongside of another major project, on the final recension of this book. I thank the Center's former directors, Professors Kurt Raaflaub and Deborah Boedeker, its current director, Professor Gregory Nagy, and all of the Center's staff for munificent assistance and *philoxenia* at a crucial juncture.

The late Professor Robert Browning and Dr Ruth Padel subjected the thesis version of this book to the most incisive and genuinely helpful cross-examination. In doing this, they not only redeemed me from certain inferential and other errors, but also stimulated further critical thought on the perplexing (and often ill-construed) subject of 'continuity'. Needless to say, neither they nor anyone else should be held accountable for any remaining flaws in this work. I am also pleased to thank Deborah Blake, Duckworth's editorial director, for her encouragement and expert advice in dealing with a daunting bilingual text.

It is to Sir Kenneth Dover that my deepest gratitude goes. He inspired and supervised my doctoral thesis; his erudition and encouragement, indeed his friendship helped to bring the thesis, and hence this book, into being.

While this book was in proof my wife, Angela Tamvaki, died. An art historian who was also trained in prehistoric archaeology, Angela was a rare, generous person, with a versatile, ever-enquiring mind. Her deep love and learning of art embraced multifarious subjects – from Palaeolithic murals, Minoan and Mycenean seals, the masterpieces of Titian, Rubens and Rembrandt, to Ethiopian folk art, cinema posters and modern Greek naive painting. Questions similar to those she frequently encountered when looking at visual images are addressed in this comparative study of popular and literary tradition. This is but one reason – among innumerable others – that this book is dedicated to angelic Angela's memory.

Athens
May 2003

J.C.B. Petropoulos

Note on Abbreviations

Many of the abbreviations used for authors, texts and editors are listed in the Bibliography.

1. Ancient authors and works

Throughout the book ancient Greek authors and texts (including inscriptions) are cited according to the abbreviations employed in the ninth edition of LSJ (= H.G. Liddell and R. Scott, *A Greek-English Lexicon*, revised and augmented by Sir Henry Stuart Jones, and R. McKenzie, with a revised Supplement [Oxford, 1996]), except in a few cases where these may appear impractical or confusing. Quotations of ancient texts are taken from the Oxford editions, unless otherwise stated.

2. Classical periodicals

References to classical periodicals follow the style of *L'Année Philologique*.

3. Christian authors and works

Christian authors and works dating up to the seventh century are cited usually in accordance with the abbreviations employed in G.W.H. Lampe's *A Patristic Greek Lexicon* (Oxford, 1961; rp. 1968, 1972), but with three main departures:

Jo. Chrys. = Chrys. in Lampe
Methodius *Banquet* = Meth. *Symp.* in Lampe
Ps. = Pss. in Lampe

4. Corpora of early Christian and Byzantine texts, including inscriptions, and editions of individual authors

Abbreviations of editions of early Christian texts usually conform to those employed in Lampe above, but with one major exception:

PG = *Patrologiae Cursus, series Graeca*, ed. J.-P. Migne, i-clxi (Paris, 1857-66)

Note on Abbreviations

Details (e.g. abbreviations of series) of editions of Byzantine texts adhere to the style suggested in *Dumbarton Oaks Papers* 27 (1973), 329-39.

5. Other periodicals

(a) Titles of periodicals dealing with Byzantine topics are abbreviated in accordance with the forms suggested in *DOP*, loc. cit. Of the abbreviations not in the *DOP* list the following deserves special attention:

BMGS = Byzantine and Modern Greek Studies

(b) Titles of periodicals dealing with modern Greek topics are abbreviated in accordance with the forms suggested in *DOP*, loc. cit. Abbreviations not in this list are self-explanatory; the following two deserve special notice:

Laogr. = Laographia
Trivolos, i-iii = *Trivolos* (Mytiline, 1931-52; reissued in 3 vols, Athens, 1980)

6. Other

AG = Ancient Greek
MG = Modern Greek

Note on Transliteration

In transliterating ancient and medieval Greek words and phrases I have adhered to standard academic practice, even when (in the cases of most of the Byzantine and all of the early demotic passages and terms here quoted) this is patently anachronistic.

In transliterating modern Greek words and phrases I have made a number of departures from the above convention, namely:

αυ = av, af
ευ = ev, ef
η = i (or ê)
υ = y
β = v
ξ = z
χ = ch (or h)

My translations are intended to guide especially those who may wish to consult the original texts. I have therefore tried in most cases to reproduce as closely as possible the syntax of the Greek.

Acknowledgements

The author wishes to thank Oxford University Press for permission to make extensive use of translations of Menander Rhetor by D.A. Russell and N.G. Wilson (eds), *Menander Rhetor ...* (Oxford, 1981); and the President and Fellows of Harvard College for permission to quote translations by D.A. Campbell (ed.), *Greek Lyric I: Sappho, Alcaeus* (Cambridge, MA & London, England, 1982; rp. with corr. 1990; rp. 1994).

Plates are included by courtesy of the following: 1, 3: National Museum, Athens; 2, 8: British Museum, London; 4, 6, 9, 10: American School of Classical Studies, Athens; 5: J. Paul Getty Museum; 11: DAI Athens; 12: *Ekdotiki Athinon* & Hagios Panteleimon Monastery, Mt Athos; 13: Victoria and Albert Museum, London.

I

Problems, Sources and Strategies

Since the days of St Eustathius of Thessalonica in the twelfth century, classical scholars and other specialists have postulated influences or sought parallels between passages from ancient Greek literary poetry and subsequent folk tradition, particularly folk-song. The aim and method of this book are thus not without precedent.[1] By means of diachronic comparison and analysis I will trace the main historical connections between a number of putatively popular or sub-literary motifs, images and even formal devices which occur in ancient Greek poetry, and seemingly identical or analogous motifs, images and formal devices found in medieval and modern Greek popular poetry. As will soon become evident, such a comparative methodology can prove quite promising, for it tends to confirm the popular affinities of an ancient element, and under the best of circumstances (when historical affiliations and identity of function can be sufficiently established), it may even prompt new and very plausible interpretations of an ancient passage.[2] But the enterprise of drawing comparisons between ancient Greek poetry and popular Greek poetry of later periods immediately raises some basic questions; and from their individual angles the classicist, Byzantinist and modern folklorist are bound to put forward certain theoretical and practical objections.

In the first place, folk-song and generally popular culture of the ancient, medieval and early modern periods are inadequately represented in our texts. By their very nature such forms as folk-song and folk-tale were anonymous and orally transmitted, and, largely because of the ancient upper-class bias in favour of morally and stylistically 'improving' literature, were only rarely thought worthy of preservation in written form.[3] (The amateurish *carmina popularia et convivialia* found in Page and the Aesopic corpus are such rare exceptions.) Therein lies our first problem: other than under modern scientific conditions, popular (oral) poetry[4] is not generally susceptible of diachronic scrutiny, far less of scrutiny on such a wide time-scale as this study proposes. But the existence of popular song particularly in ancient and medieval Greek culture, as in most cultures, is difficult to deny. Certainly in the case of ancient Greece, the richness and sophistication of the literary tradition suggest that there was a vast underground of popular material from which authors could draw ideas and stories, patterns of thought and expression, even rhetorical devices. Highly developed lyric like that of Sappho and Alcaeus, elegy, iambus,[5] comedy and the mime as we know them in their literary versions must all presup-

1

pose a long and widespread tradition of folk-song and popular entertainment in general.[6] It must have always been possible for jokes, comic themes, song and dance to find their way from the more or less extemporaneous entertainment of the streets or the symposium into self-conscious and ambitious literary genres.[7] And, as I shall argue in Chapter II, ancient popular song, which at first inspired and underlay much of sophisticated song, was seldom superseded and swept aside, but as a rule coexisted with and continuously borrowed from literary poetry.

Even if ancient and medieval oral tradition can be sufficiently documented or at any rate confidently reconstructed, we must still demonstrate that a comparative treatment of ancient, medieval and modern Greek popular poetry is justifiable. It may be urged that, especially from the late sixth century onwards – the time of the first Slav invasion – Byzantium suffered an irreparable breach with late antique Greek culture and that, consequently, the question of continuity from this later period is moot.

A review of the complex arguments framing this provocative question cannot be expected here; I shall therefore limit myself to a précis of the solution offered recently by Speros Vryonis, Jr and supplement it with the findings of the late Robert Browning.[8] After refuting the hypothesis that Byzantine culture was basically slavonicised,[9] Vryonis notes that the arguments against continuity usually assume a static, purist and therefore partitive model of culture. For instance, one school of thought equates 'culture' with political ideology; any deviation from the latter criterion is seen as a sign of discontinuity. On Vryonis' view scholars are better equipped to treat the evolution of Byzantine and modern Greek cultural traits by recourse to a dynamic and totalising model, which includes the interplay of erudite and popular levels of influence and leaves aside questions of racial extraction. From the late sixth century onwards Greek prevailed as the language of culture, and Byzantine culture, broadly conceived, was innately traditionalist and syncretic. Byzantine secular and religious education maintained and developed the rich linguistic and intellectual tradition of the Hellenistic and Roman periods;[10] homiletic tradition is perhaps one of the 'middle-brow' influences that percolated through to the wider public. In the popular domain, moreover, the pressure of the physical environment, relative continuity of language, and a high degree of borrowing and syncretism in religious and other practices[11] favoured cultural continuity. (Indeed, some of the preliminary conclusions of this book bear out this part of Vryonis' and Browning's arguments. The appropriation of pagan forms such as the wedding *exemplum*, which is innately magical in function, will be discussed in Chapter II, and we may generally assume that there are few popular ritual activities which exhibit more clearly and more conclusively an unbroken chain of tradition from remotest antiquity to the modern period than the magical arts.) Lack of absolute identity with antique culture need not therefore imply total absence of continuity. Above all, the wider perspective on culture advocated by Vryonis and Browning permits us to analyse Byzantine culture – and, by extension, modern Greek culture – as an enormously complicated, often

2

contradictory, and *sui generis* legacy of post-classical and Christian erudite forms and aesthetic practices, encrusted, as it were, with popular elements that persisted darkly but undeniably under the Orthodox skin of medieval Christendom. The cultural legacy of late antiquity was not, however, merely handed down to passive recipients; historians such as Vryonis and Browning envisage rather a continuous, if uneven, re-handling and even transformation of this formal heritage.[12]

On balance the academic debate over continuity, whether for or against, is not yet settled or even relevant in its more extreme formulations. Nonetheless, the contributions of these scholars in particular have not only decisively altered the tone of the debate, but also, one hopes, dispelled the prejudice that cultural *discontinuity* is a foregone conclusion. Possibly the singular merit of their case lies in the conclusion that Byzantine culture, and to a considerable extent its modern successor, drew from, eventually changed and, in a serious sense, thereby perpetuated two sources of imitation and inspiration, the former of which conceivably coloured the latter: the sophisticated culture of late (rather than Attic and classical) antiquity, and the varied repertory of popular forms and practices, aesthetic, religious and magical, dating at the latest to the Hellenistic and Roman periods.[13] Under carefully circumscribed conditions, then, it is theoretically legitimate to draw comparisons between elements of Greek folk-poetry as evidenced in its three main phases, ancient, medieval and modern.

As already noted, oral poetry is by its nature difficult to document, especially for more remote periods. Yet given the likelihood that higher forms affected lower ones and that at later periods lower forms seem to have affected higher tradition more extensively than before (see immediately below), we can, with due caution, approach the popular song tradition of earlier periods indirectly through the literary specimens to hand. In numerous instances we can postulate the relation of the ancient and medieval literary evidence to social and ritual contexts, and also the relation of such evidence to subsequent popular song; and by means of informed conjecture we can extrapolate the features which appear consistently to be peculiar to popular song tradition. In the remainder of this section it may be helpful to describe the main sources, literary, sub-literary and popular, for the Byzantine and post-Byzantine periods, and to enumerate the overarching limitations which these texts impose upon this enquiry. At the same time we shall consider whether any of these obstacles can be overruled or in any event outweighed by other considerations.

The Byzantine (predominantly literary) evidence is late, if at times highly suggestive

The search for popular erotic motifs and images is frustrated by a combination of three facts. (i) The direct evidence for medieval folk-songs is exiguous, comprising little more than one or possibly two fragmentary citations in Constantine Porphyrogenitus' *De Caeremoniis* and an excerpt recorded by St Neophytos Engleistos (1180).[14] (No doubt the tyranny of the high style and the Church's blanket condemnation of secular song – and dance – ensured that no serious attempt was made to preserve folk-songs until the very end of the Byzantine period.)[15] (ii) With the exception of certain epigrams included in the *Cycle* of Agathias and sundry other compositions, straightforward amatory material in general is scarce until the emergence of court poets in the eleventh century.[16] (iii) The literary evidence with any bearing on popular poetry at all is also relatively late, the first specimens dating from the ninth century.[17]

The official spring song[18] in the metre of the *politicos stichos* (see below), which was chanted antiphonally by the demes at Constantinople, and the imperial wedding-song as emended by Kyriakides to the fifteen-syllable metre,[19] are probably the earliest available versions of popular song.[20] The spring song can safely be considered to be earlier than the time of Constantine Porphyrogenitus.[21] Fortunately, the indirect evidence of popular poetry increases from the Comnenian era onwards. At this time we detect a heightened interest in secular and especially amatory topics, as exemplified strikingly in a quartet of erudite romances (three of which are entirely preserved),[22] and a parallel predilection, noticeable even in such 'highbrow' works as Theodore Prodromos' occasional poems, Anna Comnena's *Alexiad* and a *progymnasma* by Eustathius of Thessalonica,[23] for *subsidiärer Realismus* in the matters of narrative detail, psychological plausibility and linguistic register.[24] As we shall see, these learned texts already manifest a number of motifs and formal devices which are shared by folk-song in later centuries. Furthermore, the radical linguistic experiments fostered briefly under John II or Manuel I Comnenos resulted in the first specimens of a literary vernacular, notably the roughly contemporaneous *Ptochoprodromica* and the version which presumably underlies the *chanson de geste* known as the Escorial *Digenis Akrites*.[25] The vernacularisation of literature was resumed and continued apace from the fourteenth century, especially in areas under western domination. The anonymous *Digenis*, then, as well as the Paleologue popular verse romances of chivalry,[26] in particular *Callimachos and Chrysorrhoë, Lybistros and Rhodamnê* and the *Achilleïs*, the thirteenth(?)-century satirical poem *Krasopateras*[27] and the collection of vivacious love-songs known as the *Erôtopaignia* (c. 1450),[28] are all very helpful to our purposes. As I shall have occasion to refer to these later texts throughout this book, it may be appropriate summarily to comment on them.

All but two, the romance *Callimachos and Chrysorrhoë* and the *Erôtopaignia*, exist in different versions, all use a literary vernacular[29] and the *politicos stichos*, all save *Krasopateras* adhere superfically to western models;[30] and in varying degrees all are couched ostensibly in an oral-formulaic style, although none, with the hypothetical exception of the *Erotopaignia*, can be proved to be the product of oral performance.[31] It is important to note that *Callimachos and Chrysorrhoë*, which was composed c. 1310-40 by Andronikos Palaiologos, and the slightly earlier (?) *Achilleïs* are distinguished from the other romances by an especially strong link to fairy-tales and folk-song,[32] and that substantial portions of *Krasopateras* (which has a copious MS. tradition) and of the *Erôtopaignia* in particular were transmitted orally until fairly recently.[33] Inasmuch as the medieval works in the vernacular cited in this study adumbrate the themes and formulae which can be paralleled from the early demotic song tradition, they can be credited as reliable witnesses to the popular song tradition of the late Byzantine period.[34]

Evidence of ancient motifs and images in vernacular poetry from the late Veneto-Cretan period onwards may be illusory, since these works may reflect literary and, in theory, classicising influences from the Renaissance and post-Renaissance west

The next body of vernacular texts to be used in this investigation comprises (1) the (Rhodian?) love-songs of the fifteenth or sixteenth century (edited by Pernot as *Chansons populaires*), which have remote formal connections with Italian poetry,[35] and (2) Cretan literature written under Venetian rule,[36] especially the pastoral poem *I Orea Voscopoula*,[37] Chortatsis' quasi-Senecan tragedy *Erôphili*,[38] the epic romance *Erotocritos*[39] by Vitsentzos Kornaros (in which long, dramatic speeches abound) and the anonymous play *The sacrifice of Abraham*;[40] all but *Voscopoula* use rhyming couplets (on which see below), and their chronology ranges from the late sixteenth to the early seventeenth century.[41] The language of *Erotocritos* and *The sacrifice* may be described as a *Kunstsprache* closely based on the spoken Greek of eastern Crete and relatively innocent of the learned expressions characteristic of the popular poetry of the late Byzantine period and Cretan literary poetry of the fifteenth and sixteenth centuries.[42] Both poems, moreover, draw from Greek vernacular literary tradition, yet the considerable affinities of both works with the style, syntax and content of folk-poetry often suggest an emulation of popular sources carried out to good dramatic effect. Although the debt of Cretan literature in general to western Renaissance models may appear to be restricted only to details of the plot, as has been argued,[43] we should not in principle rule out the possibility of western influence of a profounder kind. The status of the demotic evidence is complicated further by the fact that, during the Turcocratia, chap-book versions of the highly popular *Erôphili* and *Erotocritos* in particular – alongside sporadic translations of late medieval and Renaissance works[44] – were diffused in Crete and other occupied areas. (Chapbooks printed in Venice were in circulation from the early sixteenth century and made available a range of literary works in the demotic such as the *Rimada Alexandrou*, a popular redaction of pseudo-Callisthenes, reprinted repeatedly from 1529 until the nineteenth century, and the romance *Apollonios of Tyre*, a close translation from the Italian into rhyming couplets, first published between 1524 and 1526 and reprinted many times until 1805.)[45] As a result, oral performances of the *Erotocritos* and of a great proportion of folk-songs inspired thereby were likely to depend ultimately upon texts, whether manuscript copies or chap-book

5

versions, of this influential work.[46] The complex derivation of the early modern evidence may indeed give us pause; from the sixteenth century onwards, ancient elements may have entered the repertory of folk-song by way of various learned and popular texts, as this diagram shows:

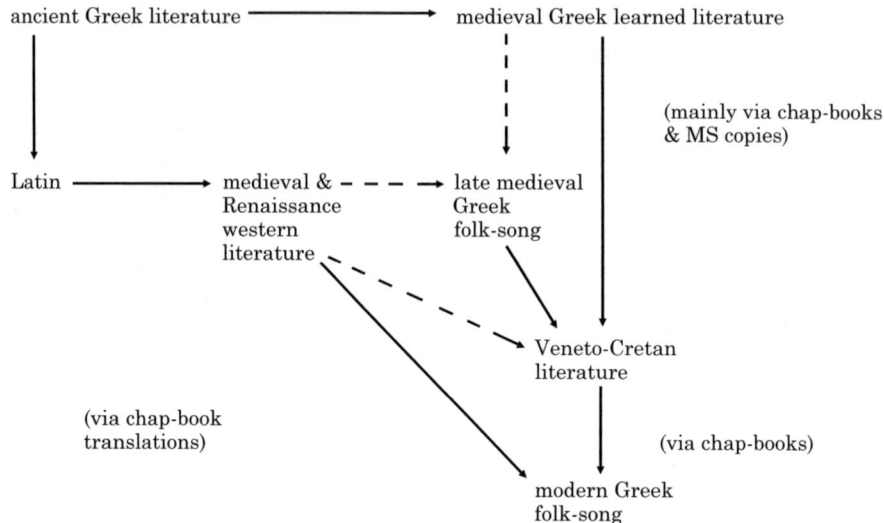

This theoretical derivation cannot be ruled out, but in many specific cases it can be demonstrated that a given motif or image was in use before the advent of extraneous factors such as the fourth crusade or the emergence of Venetian chap-books. This consideration is doubtless a potent argument in favour of a particular instance of continuity.

Allowance must be made for the influence of literary and educated acquaintance with ancient poetry upon modern folk-poetry[47]

This eventuality may be represented thus:

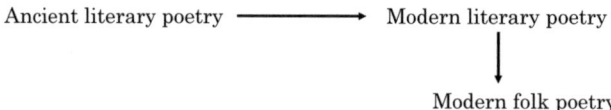

There are obvious and universal motifs and images which are likely to turn up in the erotic poetry of all or most cultures

This objection is liable to beset any enquiry advancing the claim of continuity, especially when erotic material from other neighbouring cultures is not compared. I will therefore attempt to show either that the resemblances between an ancient motif or device and a later one are specific, detailed and, in the light of Thompson's *Motif-Index*, exceptional, or that these resemblances are (simply) specific and detailed. Even if an element attested in ancient and subsequent sources is not unique to Greek tradition, it remains to be demonstrated why spontaneous analogy should be judged *a priori* likelier than historical kinship. (Of course historical kinship may also explain the 'convergence' of popular song traditions, particularly within the Balkan *Sprachbund*; this *may* ultimately implicate Byzantine cultural influence, even if at several removes.)

With respect to the modern folk-songs discussed, attention should be drawn to the bias towards textual analysis and to the complete absence of musicological analysis

Because oral poetry is distinguishable from literary poetry by virtue of the fact that it is performed, it is first and foremost a 'communicative *event*'[48] and only secondarily a stark text. In discussing folk-songs we must therefore examine a range of stylistic and formal attributes which includes musical form and accompaniment and prosodic features, in addition to other data of wider anthropological and sociological relevance, such as the context of the performance, the personality of the performer, the role and reaction of the audience, and so forth. Although I cannot claim to have undertaken a protracted or profound anthropological treatment, I have made every effort to look at the modern folk-songs both 'synchronically' – that is, largely in terms of what is known about their social or ritual context and function – *and* 'diachronically' – that is, in the light of the historical links, verifiable or likely, which many of these songs have to earlier tradition. The combined historical and social anthropological approach to popular song was admirably employed by the late Baud-Bovy[49] and outside the field of modern Greek studies by Hermann Bausinger, in his noteworthy investigation of the mutual influence of high and low media in modern south-west Germany.[50] (Concerning the particular question of the continuity of popular forms, Bausinger and other German scholars have in fact advocated the collaboration of historians and folklorists.)[51]

Incidentally, we may note that, for obvious reasons, the problem of *metrical* continuity cannot be taken up in this thematic enquiry. It may however be useful to register in passing the contribution of Baud-Bovy and others to this question.[52]

The likeliest formal ancestor of the medieval *versus politicus*, which remains in use today, is the catalectic iambic tetrameter characteristic of Aristophanes. The main links in this genealogy are three late antique specimens in catalectic iambic tetrameter, of which the earliest and most striking is found in a sub-literary narrative in prosimetrum from a second century AD papyrus edited by Haslam.[53] As Haslam himself suggests, the *versus politicus* derives 'by direct and as it were underground descent from the verse exemplified in this papyrus'.[54] Indeed, the structural coincidences between the iambic tetrameter and the *politicos stichos* seem too significant to be merely accidental: both ancient and medieval metres have four metra with a break between the two, both have two stresses (two *longa* in the ancient texts) per metron, and both are truncated at the end. Yet how, it may be asked, did the iambic tetrameter survive the prosodical changes in effect by the time of Nonnus at the latest? One strong possibility – which specialists may do well to consider – is that during the transitional period from the Hellenistic era to the sixth century popular singers enjoyed more and more freedom in adapting textual scansion to musical declamation. An alternative possibility is this: from, say, the third century AD, as quantitative distinctions broke down further, the song repertory particularly favoured the iambic tetrameter because it could be adapted more or less to both sets of metrical rules.[55] No doubt violations of the ancient rules were frequent; it must have been difficult for unsophisticated singers invariably to make quantity coincide with dynamic (stress) accent.[56] However that may be, the main rhythms and melodic forms[57] of the modern folk-songs can be traced back through a continuous tradition to the ancient world. The restraints of the *politicos stichos* undoubtedly acted as an *aide-mémoire* to the oral performer and a guide to composition for the literate versifier, and can only have guaranteed the preservation not merely of syntactical paradigms but also, crucially, of archaic linguistic and thematic content.[58]

The allusiveness of imagery of a great many songs makes interpretation and 'motifemic' analysis difficult

Symbolism is a lyrical device *par excellence* and almost certainly a primeval cross-cultural mode.[59] By and large, explicit erotic references are infrequent in most modern Greek folk-songs as they have come down to us until recently,[60] and it would not be fanciful to suspect that numerous songs deal in *double entendre* or even multiple allusion, often employing what may be called a shifting or 'teasing' technique. A noun, a compound epithet, a phrase or a formula constituting an image may be introduced in a song by reason of its sexual implications: once these become clear, however, the singer may consciously shift either to associations of the image at hand which can cause no embarrassment or to a different, altogether safer topic, often at the expense of logical coherence.[61]

A good example of this 'teasing' technique is the following love-song from Roumeli:[62]

I'll come to your garden, my little gardener-girl,
to snatch whatever your mind wants and whatever your soul desires:
cherries from your cherry trees and apples from your apple trees,
along with citron-lemons from your lemon trees.
I don't want racing cars and money, nor splendid palaces,
it's *you* I want, my doll, and your eyes.

As will become clear from the discussion in Chapter IV, the singer has taken up three main ideas and elaborated them in succession through associative imagery: the beloved is termed a gardener-girl (v. 1); that is, her beauty is associated implicitly with that of a garden; then arguably her genitals are conceived of as her 'garden', hence the motif of plucking fruit (vv. 2-4) may signify the man's imaginary advances;[63] finally the addressee is thought of as separate from the garden and is presumed to be sequestered in a *real* garden (vv. 1, 6). This is by no means an isolated example;[64] the beauty of these songs – and a large part of the frustration in analysing them – frequently has to do with their subtle suggestiveness.

To sum up, then. No fewer than eight broad procedural problems should be kept in mind throughout the chapters which follow. As for some of the more *specific* issues which attend a diachronic survey of Greek popular tradition, we may turn to Chapter II.

II

Nuptial Praise

When I praise the wedded couple I'll have to have my
mind tied in chains lest it slip away and I lose it.

> Wedding-song, L.A. MS. 102, p. 9
> (unpublished, Mesolonghi, 1914)

A. Introduction

Because it raises the fundamental questions of method and approach
which generally concern an investigation of 'continuity', the genus of
nuptial praise constitutes an instructive case. By means of the formal
device of the nuptial encomium, praise, frequently of an erotic content,[1] is
applied to the bridal pair either individually or together. The considerable
attestations throughout ancient and medieval tradition replicate a number
of amatory motifs, images and even formal characteristics that are common to modern popular wedding-song. As we shall see, wedding-song in
general and the marriage encomium in particular are functional, forming
an indispensable part of wedding ritual. The scope and competence of this
work, however, do not permit a full examination, interpretation and correlation of ancient and subsequent marriage rituals; the exact relationship
of comparable ritual components, such as the nuptial bath (see below), and
still more relevant, the relation of the modern encomium to specific practices, would only be established by an exhaustive analysis of the symbolic
contexts.[2] I shall rather draw mainly on the evidence of the wedding
encomia themselves, supplementing it with comparative anthropological
material and literary sources.[3] It is the purpose of this chapter to demonstrate, first, the continuous existence of the erotic encomium within the
context of certain Greek wedding practices and, secondly, the correlation
between the literary and sub-literary specimens of the nuptial encomium
in the Greek language. The relevant testimonia are listed below, pp.
89-113.[4-5] Before turning to these, I shall discuss the main problems of
method which concern us in this chapter.

Methodological problems

To begin with, a comparative treatment on such a wide historical scale as
I propose is likely to lead to results of value only if I can decide at the outset
on the procedure by which to test the hypothesis of continuity. It is scarcely

10

sufficient to demonstrate the general survival of the encomiastic mode in Greek wedding-songs. Praise of the bride and bridegroom for some trait, especially the good looks, wealth, skills and virtues of the bride, the good looks, strength, courage (and maybe skills and virtues) of the bridegroom, is bound to occur in any wedding-song in any culture (except perhaps in cultures where it may be feared that such praise will attract bad luck).[6] Agamemnon's evaluation of his mistress Chryseis' attributes, physical and mental, uses Clytemnestra as a standard of comparison and so summarises aptly the range of qualities likely to be sought and praised in a bride in a great many cultures even today: see TA3.[7] Given the inevitability of nuptial praise in general and the almost universal currency of various encomiastic themes (beauty, congratulations, the wish for conjugal happiness and offspring), we are obliged to pursue two lines of enquiry: (1) Assuming that certain popular practices motivated wedding-songs of praise, what is the external evidence bearing on the existence and growth of the ritual wedding-encomium from antiquity to the present day? and (2) What conventions of form, content, and symbolism are particular to popular Greek wedding-praise? A consideration of both external (historical) factors and internal (chiefly morphological) ones will offer an optimum method for tracing the development of popular features. It will be shown in this section, however, that neither line of enquiry can be followed without certain reservations.

Let us take up our first line of enquiry, by considering the evidence bearing on ancient wedding rituals. In addition to passing references in literature, extensive iconographic documentation is available.[8] The vases usually depict an individual playing an instrument and a number of individuals engaged in a ritual action (e.g. the *domum deductio*, i.e. the conveyance of the bride to the bridegroom's house) while presumably singing, but we are unfortunately denied the verbal components of the accompanying songs. It is here that an analogous modern paradigm may help to reconstruct the content of the ancient songs as well as the general significance of the rituals that may have motivated them.

At least three nuptial rituals figured in vase paintings appear to be accompanied by song: the bridal bath (see Plate 1), the toilette (presumably on the day of the wedding, see Plate 2)) and the *agôgê* (i.e. the parading) of the bride to her new home (see Plate 3).[9] Besides the component of music and song, what other formal features did the ancient practices have in common with later analogues? The bridal bath, amply documented in iconographic and literary sources, may provide a good case for comparative treatment: from a synchronic point of view, it may mark a rite of separation – the first stage of a more elaborate rite of passage.[10] It would perhaps be an oversimplification to consider the bath only as a purificatory act. On the analogy of the bathing and the *prothesis* ('laying out') of the corpse which together signal the transitional period between 'death' and the funeral, it may appear, superficially at any rate, that the bride's bath and her ensuing presentation likewise usher in a separation and transition between the impending surrender (or 'death') of maidenhood[11] and the wedding proper, which socially recognises womanhood. Needless to say, both types of bath will also attempt to effect some degree of incorporation.[12] In diachronic terms, moreover, the rite of separation enacted by the bridal bath and indeed by the toilette (on the next day) has obviously remained intact, perhaps reflecting the persistence of the deeper significance of wedding rituals involving external preparation and embellishment.[13] The future bride has consistently been treated as the protagonist[14] in a ritual drama wherein she is destined to move through the three stages of a rite of passage: separation, transition and incorporation. As protagonist she has always been the main object of adornment (bath, toilette) as well as of songs of praise.

At this point we may invoke further data from modern Greece. The majority of current wedding-songs reflect a remarkable (and often doting) interest in details of ornamentation and external appearance. From a random sampling of wedding-songs it is possible to deduce certain pervasive motifs, conveyed in a stylised manner: the attire of the nuptial pair, the filigreed patterns of the embroidered bridal bed-canopy (*sperveri*),[15] the décor of the alcove, the toiletries used in the bride's bath, and invariably the physical description, which can even amount to an *ecphrasis* (i.e. an extended description, as if of a work of art) of the couple. For a description of the bath which also features an *ecphrasis* of the bride see TG1, a Rhodian song.[16] Of course the preoccupation with embellishment is dependent on the actual rituals which the songs accompany; in this sense the songs are truly functional. Thus on Saturday, when the bride is ritually bathed, her female peers and kin sing praises of her beauty;[17] afterwards she is presented to the bridegroom and his company to be admired in song.[18] On Sunday at midnight water is fetched from a local spring and the bridegroom is solemnly shaved; the assembled womenfolk sing, extolling his aspect and breeding.[19] The extensive lauding of the couple, individually and as a unit, with regard to physical attributes, clothing, and so on, in fact occurs at nearly every stage of the week-long rituals that culminate in the wedding on Sunday.[20]

Three salient points emerge so far. First, certain ancient and modern rituals – the bridal bath and toilette – produce a series of formal coincidences. Secondly, as the vases show, songs were performed in the course of these rituals, probably being motivated by them. Thirdly, as our ancient literary testimonia and the modern ritual songs both suggest, these songs were likely to feature (among other types of praise) *erotic* praise of the couple. The foregoing considerations in turn raise a notable implication: wedding rituals in antiquity, formally analogous (when not identical in certain points of detail) to their modern counterparts, engendered songs of a content similar to that of our modern specimens. This pattern of analogies may reflect the stability of the significance of the rituals themselves. What might this be?[21]

In the traditional wedding the sexual act, involving specifically the loss of virginity, is validated both notionally and as a cultural event.[22] One possible interpretation is that the wedding thereby becomes a meaningful

12

negotiation of virginity without which the sexual act would be viewed explicitly as a rape.[23] Perhaps external embellishment is equivalent to the conceptual validation – one might say adornment – and acculturation of the sexual act which underlie the wedding itself.[24] It is this functional relationship between ritual actions and cultural objectives that has in effect assured that verbal analogues of embellishment, namely songs of erotic praise, should be featured continuously in wedding rituals. Further- more, sexual acculturation surely explains the literary epithalamium's thematic interest in defloration and coitus (e.g. possibly Sappho fr. 27.8 f. [LP], TA4, TB1.1-15, Catullus 61.51f., 66f., *et passim*; Menander Rhetor 405.15 [RW] *passim*). Vase-painters, too, showed the same interest: an Attic red-figure *lekythos* or oil and perfume flask (= Oakley & Sinos, figs. 112-14 [discussion, p. 37]) depicts a young woman who is probably the personified/deified Partheneia ('Miss Virginity') energetically flying into the night as Ariadne sleeps contentedly next to Theseus; the young boy sleeping at their feet probably symbolises the anticipated consequence of the bride's defloration.[25] See also Plate 11 and n. 26 immediately below. In the case of ancient and modern traditions alike, the generic *gamos* (i.e. 'wedding') serves as a woman's rite of passage *par excellence*.[26] The initia- tory aspect of the modern wedding is confirmed by the prominence of women in the *drômena* (i.e. ritual actions which include songs)[27] as well as by the Church's minimal involvement therein:[28] until about sixty years ago, many if not most weddings were held in the bride's or bridegroom's house,[29] not the local church. (Only recently has the function of initiation been subordinated to the Church's blessing; and now the possibility of civil marriage *may* slowly displace the Church as a protagonist.) The Church's superfluous and incidental role in fact probably reflects the tenacity of the pre-existing functional paradigm which we may assume for antiquity.

It is conceivable, then, that the wedding's intrinsic function of sexual initiation and acculturation has motivated the popular genre of the sung erotic 'encomium'.[30] But it does not follow from this that various features of ancient popular praise have necessarily reached modern Greece via medieval practice, or that popular (oral) tradition interacted directly with literary examples, ancient and medieval, of nuptial praise without under- going some degree of influence itself. Such a straightforward 'stemmatic' derivation of modern material[31] would leave out of account a ponderable factor: learned influence. It may be possible, by describing more compre- hensively the 'stemmatic' relationships between ancient and subsequent sources, to trace the main conduits of interference between the learned and subliterate spheres.

Let us examine the erotic wedding-encomium in TB2. As has been shown,[32] sophistic (prose) *topoi* had already been extended to poetry and poetic *topoi* to rhetoric by Theocritus' time at least. This process of mutual influence may be traced to the early *progymnasmata*, i.e. preliminary rhetorical exercises, which drew thesis material from poetry (among vari- ous other sources) and in turn affected later poetic practice.[33] The question of influence in Theocritus 18 therefore becomes rather complicated. Sappho need not have been a particular theoretical model, nor Stesichorus for that matter;[34] the poet may have resorted to a diffuse or even a common source. What complicates matters is that Theocritus' wedding-poem as a whole is highly 'rhetoricised', incorporating as it does a sophistic ordering of the topics of praise *as well as* poetical precedents. These multiple influences can in fact be described in terms of two lines that converge: actual wedding-songs and the poetical renditions of these; and traditional epinician customs and their elaboration by Pindar and the fifth-century sophists or their fourth-century successors.[35]

From the Hellenistic era at latest, the poetic epithalamium must have followed a set of rules elaborated by rhetoricians of the fifth and fourth centuries BC. After a lacunose period, during which we are entirely deprived of direct versions of wedding-songs, the genre's theoretical form is attested in Menander Rhetor, while private wedding speeches and poems appear in the period after Menander.[36] His epithalamian schema – and certainly that of pseudo-Dionysius – owes much to the eulogising *basilikos logos* with respect to the disposition of the *topoi* of praise. A full-dress encomium, the *basilikos logos* appeared at public occasions in the classical and Hellenistic periods (whence its deliberately 'rhetoricised' character) and only by the time of Menander were its prescriptions extended to private occasions in the consciously informal *laliai*.[37] On the whole, the 'generic' epithalamium as set forth in Menander[38] was a hybrid of various precedents and stages and therefore was not necessarily representative of the characteristics and aims of the ancient genre. Of course Sappho (who herself drew upon a number of popular motifs in her epithalamia) and actual wedding-songs were likely models for the theoretical epithalamium; but it should not be forgotten that Menander probably also had before him a wider spectrum of literary and sub-literary models for his eclectic recipe.

In the Christian era literary epithalamia, both rhetorical and poetic,[39] were often composed for recitation in the classroom or *theatron*[40] and were inescapably dependent on Menander's rules for epideictic. From early on, rhetoric was reduced to panegyric precept, while Byzantine 'high-brow' literature in general became intensely rhetoricised – a development which was aided by Atticism and mimesis;[41] and this last ensured that ancient specimens of the epithalamium could be imitated directly.[42] The encomium-scheme in fact was expanded to all literary genres, affecting poetry and even religious and later vernacular literature.[43] Libanius and Aphthonius were used as guides in the Early period;[44] from roughly the end of this period (fifth to sixth century AD) the *Corpus Hermogenianum* (which included Aphthonius) and, especially in regard to epideictic, Menander were regarded as canonical.[45] It is not surprising, then, that *epainoi*, especially of an erotic variety, are conspicuous elements of the literary epithalamia which we possess for the Byzantine period. It must be remembered however that the formal mechanism of nuptial praise *per se*, owing to its ritual or functional basis, must also have been a constant in ancient and medieval popular tradition, as it continues to be today.

We may reasonably suppose that sub-literary wedding-song led a parallel existence at this time,[46] using many of the motifs and devices that were concurrently enshrined in the canon of high literature. There is circumstantial evidence,[47] for instance, suggesting that the mythic *exemplum* – an encomiastic feature attested in a range of ancient, medieval and modern sources – has led just this kind of 'double life'. The *exemplum*'s rhetorical function of *amplificatio* corresponds to (and probably stems from) the ritual amplification of the wedding-ceremony. The *exemplum* descends from actual wedding-song – or presumably from folk-song to Homer, Sappho and (whether independently or not of the last two) Aristophanes – and is employed by rhetorical theory in the Imperial period and subsequently by the literary epithalamium. If correct, this hypothesis must suggest that this particular feature, though a resource of elevated poetry from the archaic period onwards, also existed independently of the literary sphere.

At this point we may schematise our findings by constructing a stemma:

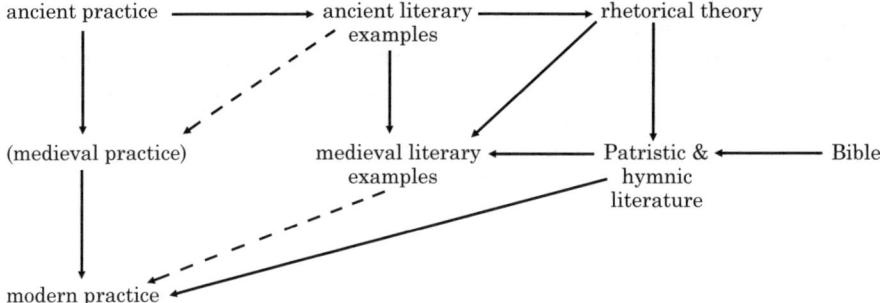

Because of this skein of stemmatic relationships, it must often remain a matter of idle speculation whether a given nuptial motif or image owed its existence to learned or vernacular tradition, or rather, as will be argued shortly, to a vernacular tradition enriched by a long literary past – or even a literary past that has borrowed from popular allusion.

The extent of learned infiltration in popular song is not quantifiable in precise terms; it is rather a question of probabilities. In general, the 'filtering through' of a great number of wedding-song motifs from high culture to popular song is more than likely: it is consistent with actual practice that a sub-literate poet, working within the framework of a literary tradition with ritual (popular) associations e.g. wedding-song or the lament, will draw upon certain literary tropes and devices. (A literate poet may, by the same token, be attracted to folk tradition, if only for the sake of verisimilitude.)[48] Three parallels, one ancient, the other two modern, may help to illustrate the probable degree and direction of literary and sub-literary interaction.

The low-grade epitaphs of antiquity use epic dialect, yet they may be metrically suspect, often bordering on prose. The incompetent use of metre as well as the occasional lapses in epic morphology betray a less literate poet's attempt to assimilate the requirements of high literature.[49] At the modern linguistic level we may compare the ill-disguised assimilation of the formal elements and diction of purist Greek in Makriyiannis' prose, and the general phenomenon of 'popular' purist Greek.[50] As a more recent example we may consider the 'filtering through' of twentieth-century concert-hall music into the background music of films or the integration of high-grade motifs in jazz.[51] In the case of ancient and modern nuptial motifs neither learned nor popular influence can invariably be proven beyond a reasonable doubt; we face the likelihood of a vicious circle of multiple 'contamination'. Furthermore, even if (contrary to anthropological evidence)[52] contamination were unlikely or less likely, we should still have to reckon with a serious difficulty: in the absence of incontestable controls for the periods in question,[53] how do we detect such motifs in a corpus made up largely of literary specimens? Yet even acknowledging this methodological dilemma, we must admit that, as our three comparative examples suggest, the traffic of many motifs has conceivably moved from the 'high' register to the 'low' one; this flow was virtually assured in a culture such as ancient and medieval Greece, which was essentially illiterate, often verging on the semiliterate.[54] As regards the Byzantine period, we cannot overlook the influence particularly of the hymnic and sermonising traditions, both of which may have contributed various motifs to the popular domain.[55] Lastly, with regard to the modern period, we must add to the two latter variables a third factor which may have conduced to the dissemination of archaising and other elements: the paraphrases in middle-low style of hagiographies by Nicodemos Hagioreites (*Synaxaristes*[1], [Venice, 1819]).

B. Form

In the first part of this chapter the complex interaction of traditional epithalamian forms and literary composition has been argued. It has been shown that neither popular belief and practice nor the purely learned sphere has been an airtight compartment, immune to 'contamination' by the other. What is more, such interaction of high and low media, represented as a congeries of 'stemmata', will account for the transmission of encomiastic devices and motifs to the present day. Having established the traditional and rather complicated nature of our material, we can pursue our enquiry more closely by asking: what *particular* kinds of praise of the bride and bridegroom occur regularly in Greek culture? Because 'continuity' does not even remotely imply immutability, but instead continuous if probably uneven re-handling and, in some cases, diversification of various features through time,[56] an analysis such as the present one will serve to delineate the common origins and evolution of a great many morphological traits of the wedding-encomium. Thus in this part of the chapter we shall distinguish formal peculiarities while in Part C we shall deal with the thematic *content* of the nuptial encomium.

II. Nuptial Praise

1. An encomiastic address or exclamation

An encomiastic address or an exclamation made to either party, specifying his or her physical or other qualities, or an observation to simlar effect which is not necessarily addressed to anyone in particular.

Testimonia:
TA5, TA6, TA7, TA18.1722, TA19.1760; also cf. section 7.ii below
TB3
TC4.35f. (*et passim*)
TD2, TD3
TF2.13f. (= TF3.29f.); TF3.36; TF4.48; TF5 a.2, b.1, etc.
TG2, TG2b, TG3

The allusive address, implying a transferred identification, will be discussed in section 3a below. Also cf. *makarismos*, section 6: a typical *hymenaios* consisted of the *Hymenruf* and an *olbismos* or *makarismos* in the form of an address or exclamation e.g. *ô trismakar* ('o thrice-blessed').[57]

2. Simile

Direct comparison (*eikôn*) of either party to a natural object (especially a plant or fruit) or seasonal phenomenon.[58]

Testimonia:
TA8a-b (discussed in Chapter IV, *passim*); TA9.2 (cf. below); the bride apparently was also likened to a rose in Sappho (cf. n. 65 below); TA10.1709f.; TA11.162-8; cf. TA29x below
TC2, TC3
TD4.18-19
TE2a-b
TF3.40f.;[59] TF5c.12f.; TF6.29f.[60]
TG2a, TG4, TG5.1-2, TG6

2a. Simile conveying pre-eminence

This constitutes a special type of simile which *may* be particular to Greek tradition; but cf. n. 62 below. A direct comparison usually to a natural object or phenomenon may establish the physical pre-eminence of the bride or bridegroom. As J. Kakrides notes in connection with TA12[61] (discussed under Content: Mythic *exemplum*), this type of comparison evokes visual and generally aesthetic pre-eminence among related subjects which are themselves already remarkable for some reason (e.g. beauty);[62] this device thus also functions as a hyperbole, presenting an image which is analogous to the superlative expressions, *anax anaktôn, makarôn makartate* ('King of

Kings, most blessed amongst the blessed'), etc.[63] The comparison, often featuring the verb *prepô* ('stand out among'), is on the model:

As A stands out among X (1),
so B stands out among Y (2), where A and X are somehow related, as are B and Y.

Testimonia:
Cf. TA1, TA2.45-9,[64] TA12; Sappho apparently compared the bridegroom to a 'prizewinning steed';[65] also Euripides *Hecuba* 355 *parthenois apobleptos meta*
TB2
TC5.3
TF1.13-14 (discussed below)
TG7, TG8[66]

Gow's reading of TB2 is none too literal-minded. He notes (ad vv. 26-8) that the point of the initial two juxtapositions is not so much Helen's beauty *per se* as its incontestable status vis-à-vis her peers. On the formal structure of the similes in vv. 26f., see Dover (1971) ad loc.; cf. the negative construction of the similes in TA10.1709f. For a list of ancient examples of this type of simile in erotic encomia in general, consult Nisbet & Hubbard i.12.48 (who do not cite Aristophanes *Birds*). The structural coincidence specifically between the similes in Theocritus and the comparison in the popular distichs may suggest that the poet is consciously evoking the sub-literary epithalamium. This supposition seems likelier if it is remembered that simile in general is attested more regularly in contexts that bear closely on sub-literary tradition, i.e. the ritual lament as represented in Homer and the funerary inscriptions; whereas it appears less frequently in tragedy, the hymn and the literary encomium.[67] What is more, the verb *prepô* itself is an element of formal continuity, since the specialised usage in our modern examples (= 'to shine forth, hence be pre-eminent')[68] is surely archaic (poetic) and rarely occurs in standard colloquial Greek today. Cf. the ancient *prepô* = 'to be conspicuous among a number' (LSJ.1). The verb appears to be exclusively poetic, not being attested in ancient prose: cf. e.g. *ekprepês* (TA2.46, etc.), also particular to poetry, which is probably used deliberately as a poetic term in later prose e.g. Plato *Phaedrus* 238a, etc. For the commonplace *prepô* in archaic Greek poetry, see Page (1955), 89-90, n. ad TA1.6; also cf. Calame (1977), i.90-2, on the related motif of being *arignôtê* because of exceptional beauty. The type of simile in question is presumably cross-cultural;[69] cf. Song of Songs 2.3f., etc. for a distant parallel. Even so, it may be argued that certain motifs associated with this device (see section C below) and undoubtedly the verb *prepô* are peculiar to Greek tradition.

II. Nuptial Praise

3. Metaphor

Implicit comparison to a natural object or phenomenon is particular neither to wedding-song nor to the ritual lament nor, for that matter, to Greek culture.[70] In ancient Greek literature it is a 'normal' poetic feature or quality.[71] The unbroken existence of the 'allusive method', as Alexiou calls the metaphoric association of human beings or emotional states with natural objects, especially plants, points to an underlying symbolic system which has periodically been augmented by various learned sources.[72] The symbols which appear to be characteristic of this tradition will be reviewed under Content below. It is worth remarking that metaphor is featured more frequently in modern wedding-song and the lament than simile.[73]

Testimonia:
TA11.154-9; cf. ibid. 162f.; TA11a; also cf. Sappho fr. 34 (LP)
TB4.30-1 (examined below, section C.3)
TD4, TD5, TD6, TD7[74]
TE1.2, 5; TE3.41f.
TF1.13-14, 17; TF3.26; TF4.56-9, etc.; TF6.1-2, etc.; TF7; TF8a.17f.; TF8b.21f.
TG2b; TG5.3-4; TG9, TG10, TG11

3a. Allusive address

The allusive encomistic address consists of a noun (or a noun and adjective) which is used metaphorically of someone. This symbolic mode in particular can be traced to the series of unconnected epithets used in ancient Greek hymns and encomia, and has persisted in medieval and modern popular tradition.[75] It is not attested in the epithalamium before Methodius.

Testimonia:
Cf. *Odyssey* 16.23; 'Plato' i (in Page [1981], 162): Aristophanes *Ecclesiazusae* 973a
Cf. Theocritus 11.39 (not in Alexiou)
TC4.32f., 39 *et passim*
TE3.17, 53, etc.
TF2.16; TF3.44;[76] TF4.25f.; TF5a.23; TF5e.19; TF6.48-9
TG12.3-4

4. Eikasia

Typologically speaking, this is a rhetorical question and answer which together constitute a conjectural (or sometimes fanciful) direct comparison (*eikôn*).[77] The generic *eikasia* was probably a ludicrous comparison in origin and was formalised as the parlour 'guessing game' of *eikasmos*; as such it elaborated a conjecture based (no doubt exaggeratedly) on external resemblance.[78] The *eikasmos* was usually played at symposia throughout ancient

Greece and, as will be noted, appears to have persisted in a recognisable form in popular tradition, although it does not occur in the modern wedding-songs under consideration. Fraenkel was the first to draw attention to the affinity between Sappho's wedding poem TA9 and this popular game, which was also imitated by Plautus.[79] TA11.149-52 is another example of the nuptial *eikasia*. Hague (1983), 132-3, proposes that marriage songs featuring the *eikasdein* formula[80] were the decorous analogues of the sympotic *eikasmos*. In addition, cf. Theocritus 1.86f. (not in Fraenkel but discussed by Dover [1971] in his comments on vv. 86 and 87f.), and further sub-literary testimonia of such 'improbable, almost surrealistic comparisons' in Ph. Kakrides (1974), 158 on *Birds* 804:

(i) Aesop *Vita* G 87(P): 'What a monstrosity he is to look at! Is he a frog, or a scampering hog, or a pot-bellied wine-jar, or a captain of monkeys, or a small flask in likeness (*eikasdomenos*), or a cook's kitchen cabinet, or a bitch in a basket?'

(ii) Satirical couplets in modern Greek folk-song.

(iii) Exchanges between characters in the Greek shadow-theatre (*Karaghiozes*) which flourished from the nineteenth to the mid-twentieth century.

5. Mythic exemplum

In common with items 3a and 4, this device is formally an extension of the generic comparison and occurs in literary and sub-literary versions of wedding-song in the ancient, medieval and modern periods. Its origin may perhaps be sought in its innately auspicious associations. The rehearsal of a divine *exemplum* would establish a comparison or analogy between certain figures of myth and the mortal participants of a wedding;[81] in this sense the mythic analogy operates much as the 'persuasive analogy' which underlies sympathetic magic:[82] a future action is encouraged not by any external (empirical) analogy between A (a god or hero) and B (a mortal), but rather by the belief that a certain ritual procedure (namely the recital of a *hypomnêsis*) will 'persuade' B to correspond to (or in the case of wedding practice to emulate) A in a particular aspect. The *exemplum*'s 'rhetorical' function of *amplificatio* will be discussed under Content below. Praise by mythological allusion is formulated in two ways:

(i) *Direct* comparison (i.e. simile) of either party to a mythical or extraordinary figure:
TA8b; TA11.150f.; TA12, TA13, TA14.5; cf.Il. 9.388-90, discussed in n. 7 above
TC1.1-2; TC5.4, 6;[83] TC6, TC7
TD6.7-8; TD8, TD8a
TE4
TF8d, TF8e[84]
TG13.1-2; TG14.1; TG15.2; TG16

II. Nuptial Praise

(ii) *Implicit* comparison of either or usually both parties to mythical figures, extolling the couple and complimenting the guests as well:
TA15.4-5; TA16, TA17; TA18.1731f., 1748f.; TA19a-b
TC4.20-1, 61-3, 78-9, etc.
TD4.3 (= TD5.4), 9f.; TD5.11f., *et passim*; TD9; TD10.5-6; TD11, TD12
TE3.23, 53; TE5.31f., 43; TE6, TE7, TE8
TF8c, TF8f, TF9
TG12.4; TG13.7-8; TG17

6. Makarismos

Another form of complimentary comparison, albeit an indirect and often a non-erotic one, is the *makarismos* proper, addressed (1) to the bridegroom or bride individually, (2) to the couple, or (3) to the respective families or the guests. The pronouncement of blessedness (denoted by *makar, makaira, olbios, olbia*)[85] confers a god-like status on the person(s) addressed and so serves as an outright compliment. Whether the term was employed in the first instance of gods and applied thereafter to mortals or whether the allusion to a divinity stemmed from a human paradigm remains an open question.[86] Either way the generic *makarismos* operates as an *exemplum*,[87] its force being invariably both auspicious and encomiastic; see Aristophanes *Clouds* 1206f.: Strepsiades' song, which he terms an *enkômion*, begins with a *makarismos* of himself.[88] As one of the main formal devices of ancient wedding-song the *makarismos* is more than probably based on popular models.[89] In TA27a.311f. *makarios ho gametas / makaria d'egô basilikois lektrois* recalls the answering echo of actual wedding-song; so also may the *anadiplosis ôlbisan ôlbisan* in TA20.640 evoke wedding-song.[90]

Testimonia:
(i) *Makarismos* of the bridegroom:
TA11.158-9; TA18.1721-2; TA21.7; TA22.1; TA23, TA24, TA26, TA28, TA29
TB1.16
TC4.13, 21, 56, etc.[91]
TG18[92]

(ii) *Makarismos* of the bride:
TA19a.1760; TA20; TA27b.335f.; TA29x (not in Diggle), TA30, TA31[93]
TC4.103
TD3.36f.[94]
TF5d.1, 24
TG19, TG20

(iii) *Makarismos* of the couple:[95]
TA17.1076-9; TA25; TA27a.310f (discussed in section 12 below); TA32
TE1.4, 6
TG21

21

(iv) *Makarismos* of the families or guests:
TA10.1707; TA11.154-7; TA18.1725-8; TA27b.326-8
TE5.63f.[96]
TG9

7. Parallelism

Parallel structure may be found in folk-songs from diverse cultures and historical periods.[97] It may well be the case that, in common with other formal features, parallelism was adapted from a ritual or at least a functional context (say, magical incantation or work songs) to learned poetry and prose.[98] The mere existence of parallel constructions should not therefore be interpreted uniformly as an index of popular style;[99] each instance must be examined on its own merits. In our specimens we may distinguish three types of parallelism, and we must consider what connections, if any, these specimens may have with folk-song:

(i) General parallelism:
TA10.1709-12; TA33x; TB2.29-30; TB5.32-5[100]
TD5.1-3, 11-13
TF1.4-5, 9-10, 13-14; TF2.2-4, 15; TF3.29-30; TF5.a.17, 19-20[101]

Of the four literary examples above, only Prodromos and, in particular, his imperial epithalamia, may afford a direct formal link to sub-literary sources. Additionally, cf. the parallel structure in his *diegertikon* ('wake-up song') (TF1), especially in the unsophisticated comparison (vv. 13f.), in which we may also observe an *asyndeton*. Assuming that Prodromos and pseudo- (or 'Ptocho-') Prodromos, the putative author of the four 'begging poems', are the same person,[102] or at least that the two writers are contemporaries, it seems rather likely that Prodromos is here resorting to the same fund of vernacular formulae which he – or 'Ptochoprodromos' – copiously draws from in the 'begging poems'.[103]

(ii) The construction known as *kata symplokên antexetastikôs*:
This formal device, first adumbrated in Sappho fr. 112 (LP) = TA22,[104] is deemed obligatory by Menander Rhetor for praise of the erotic (or physical) variety in the epithalamian speech. The device might be correlated with the double-barrelled acclamations of beauty incised on vases;[105] thus cf. B218 (bride and bridegroom in chariot) 'Lysippides is beautiful, Rhodon is beautiful'; R1019 (a youth, a woman and a slave-girl) 'Timodemos is beautiful' and 'The bride is beautiful', all cited by Dover (1978), 115f. Further, as Oakley and Sinos (1993), 45-7 note, some red-figure vase scenes which portray the couple as physically idealised seem to bring out the couple's mutual attraction and physical congruity. In Menander a separate encomium of either party is possible in the case of non-erotic praise (TC3.4f. *idia kai khôris hekastou ... ton epainon epainein*); but erotic or quasi-erotic compliments may only be formulated by 'counter-examina-

tion' (*kata antexetasin*),[106] i.e. by means of a common statement (usually consisting of parallel clauses or sentences) or a series of such statements made of each party on the model: (1) 'A is X, Y, Z. B is X, Y, Z',[107] or (2) 'A is X, B is X; A is Y, B is Y, etc.'.[108]

Testimonia:
TA22; TA33.5f., 11f.(?); cf. the syntax at Asclepiades xxiv.916f. (*HE*), which
    celebrates a well-matched pair of boys or youths: TC5.2-6
TD8x.6-13
TF2.13-19; TF5; TF8a.7f.; TF10
TG22, TG23

Menander's restrictions on physical praise are not followed unfailingly; a number of Byzantine specimens of the epithalamian genre feature separate descriptions and *ecphraseis* proper of either party.[109] Methodius (TC4.11-13), 35-9, 105f.) compliments the couple individually for their attractiveness by means of evocative epithets, several of them compounds. Himerius in the *protheôria* of his *Oratio* 9 prescribes the *ecphrasis* of the bride's beauty for the end of the wedding-speech. Cf. also Leo Magister (TE3.17., 29f., 35f.; TE5.61-8). Prodromos, however, follows the 'counter-examination' structure, often admitting of parallel clauses, as has already been noted.[110]

(iii) Parallelism and *parêchêsis*:
This method, which is first attested in a non-wedding context in Homer,[111] is in fact a variation of the 'counter-examination' method. Here the physical (and often moral) parity of the bridal couple is stressed by the parallel construction of members with the same initial vowel or consonant.[112]

Testimonia:
Cf. Aristotle *Rhetoric* 1412b.28f. 'the worthy man must marry a worthy
    woman'
TD4.6;[113] TD5.9; TD6.24
TF3.32; TF5d.12; TF8a.15f.
TG24

8. Physical description and ecphrasis

A complimentary physical, quasi-erotic or erotic description is a standard mode of nuptial praise, occurring in other contexts and cultures; see, for instance, the Song of Songs[114] and other non-Greek specimens cited in n. 6 above. The wedding encomium is essentially descriptive; the modes of praise reviewed so far, with the possible exception of sections 5 and 6, which do not necessarily elaborate praise of the physical variety, are subsumed by this device. It goes without saying that a description at a wedding does not objectively refer to the actual identities of the couple but is rather a stylised politeness: cf. TA22x, the wedding compliment paid to

Cyclops. In modern Greek folk-song such description is regularly straight-forward and cursory, and it may include deftly applied metaphors.[115] The reserve and seeming objectivity with which physical description is formu-lated in folk-songs recalls the reticence of Homer and certain archaic poets, a fact which in Kakrides' view[116] suggests Homer's indebtedness to popular models: in the majority of folk-songs (including wedding-songs) and Homer alike, the subject is described in general terms from the vantage point of an *anerastos* party,[117] even when direct speech is being quoted.[118] On the other hand, the lengthy and highly suggestive *ecphrasis* which is found in many nuptial songs is probably an oriental feature (cf. Song of Songs, *Thousand and One Nights*), while *ecphrasis* by means of a cumulation of abstract epithets or a catalogue of appealing features is almost certainly due to learned (especially Byzantine) influence.[119]

Testimonia:
TA10.1709-12 (of bridegroom), TA18.1713 & 1723 (of bride); TA22.3f.;
    TA22x; TA29x.3-4; TA33.5; TA34; TA44.4-5; cf. TA6; TA33x (a coarse
    compliment)
TB2.26-31
TC4.11-13, 35-9, 105f.
TD13,[120] TD14
TE3.17, 29-30, 35-6, 41-2
TG25

TA22 is examined in some detail in section C.5 below; see also section B.7 above. In TB2.26f. the epithalamian *ecphrasis* of Helen consists of a series of nature similes, on which see especially sections B.2a above and C.2 below. On Menander Rhetor's restrictive guidelines for physically sugges-tive descriptions, see section B.7.ii above. Rather like Psellos, whose detailed physical description e.g. of the Empress Zoë is hardly erotic, Prodromos, be it noted, eschews evocative physical *ecphrasis*, resorting only to the most general terms in his compliments; as will be shown, he innovatively concentrates rather on the non-physical attributes of the nuptial pair. Lastly, the Cretan song, which is performed at the wedding feast, represents a rhyming popular *ecphrasis* consisting of a catalogue of the bride's alluring features.[121] *Ecphraseis* of the bride or bridegroom occur in modern Greek wedding-songs with varying frequency.[122]

9. Description and ecphrasis of moral qualities

An elaboration of the mental and generally moral aspects of either party has been inevitable in wedding-song from the earliest times. The moral description *per se* is evidenced in Hesiod's prescriptions regarding the choice of a wife (*Works and Days* 699-705) and occurs *in extenso* in Semonides' elaboration of female types (fr. 7[W]). As J. Kakrides has argued on comparative grounds,[123] character analysis of the genealogical kind (which he calls *gynaikogonia apo zôa*) such as is found in Semonides is very probably based on folk *aitia*. It is therefore not unlikely that roughly similar 'character sketches' in our ancient sources also have popular affiliations.[124]

Testimonia:
TA5, possibly TA7[125]
TB5
TC3.26f.; TC4.32f.
TD15
TF2.15, 27; TF3.30-5; TF5a.12-14; cf. op. cit., b.1f., c.1f., etc. TF8c.12f.; TF8e.12f.

TA7 is an exclamation[126] addresssed to the bridegroom which functions to compliment the bride (*païs*) for unspecified attributes, presumably moral ones among others. TA5, owing to its structural similarity to TA7, may be classified with considerable probability as an epithalamium.[127] Praise of 'moral' qualities of either party (e.g. the bride's *semnotês*, *epieikeia*, her manual and musical skills, etc.) was a nuptial *topos* or became one in rhetorical tradition, as may be inferred from Menander Rhetor.[128] The prevalence of moral *ecphraseis* in Prodromos' nuptial compositions, coupled with his virtual suppression of explicit physical description as also of mythological allusion, reveals the extent to which he supersedes and even diverges from conventional rhetorical patterns and Hellenistic and Roman social ideals.[129] This originality in part stems from his idiosyncrasy, in part from the performative context which may be assumed for these compositions.[130] Prodromos' own 'programme' of contemporary social ideals, namely the ideals of war, wealth and nobility of lineage (*eugeneia*, *eukosmia*) prompts him to include in his epithalamia extensive digressions on actual military campaigns and catalogues of ancestors, and still more striking, to formulate *ecphraseis* extolling moral qualities e.g. the *semnotês* of the bridal couple and especially their parity in social and spiritual terms.[131]

10. Antiphonal question and answer

Dialogue and, in particular, the exchange of question and answer, often entailing symmetrical repetition,[132] are probably among the most ancient and least sophisticated elements of Greek poetry. Alternate exchange predates tragedy and conceivably emerged from primitive funeral rituals.[133] This tradition may have evolved continuously from Homer, as M. Alexiou[134] suggests; if so, it was deliberately exploited by tragedy[135] or, just as likely, it was revived (under popular influence?)[136] because of its inherent dramatic effects. In particular, stichomythic questions and answers can be documented in Greek tradition as follows:

TA35a-b: The Homeric passages,[137] questions and answers cast in the form of a priamel, represent the device which J. Kakrides calls the composite 'mistaken question': the question consists of two or more disjunctive propositions, all rather improbable and reflecting the speaker's confused state of mind: the answer (cf. Alcman fr. 16 [Davies]) is made up of a series of connected propositions with parallel members and repeats verbatim the phraseology of the question. It is perhaps significant that the 'mistaken question' does not occur in learned poetry after Homer but is only attested in modern Greek folk-song.[138]

TA36, apparently in antiphonal form.

TA37: These two non-literary verse inscriptions from the archaic period consist of a statement addressed to the passer-by by an individual and an object, respectively; *possibly* these statements (which are not epitaphs) also presuppose a conversation or exchange.[139]

TA38: A question (posed by the dead person) is followed by an address (by the same) in the vocative to the passer-by; cf. *CEG* I 127 (*SEG* XLI 526, *c.* 500 BC?).

TA39: A sequence of brief questions followed by a nearly parallel sequence of answers.

TA40: Catechistic questions and answers in tragic laments.[140]

TA41: A popular song, consisting of a tripartite question followed by a tripartite answer.[141]

TA42: A popular ditty, accompanying the children's game of *khelikhelônê*.[142]

TB6: An address in the vocative (*xene*) + statement by the dead youth; cf. *IG* XII.1 147.4-5.

TC8: The passer-by poses a composite question; the dead woman gives a lengthy, itemised answer. Cf. esp. *SEG* IV 634 (XXX 1396), XV 577, Miranda 95, *SEG* XXXVIII 1224: questions and answers are exchanged between the dead person (or his or her tomb) and the passer-by. See also Peek 755, 1399, *SEG* XIV 619, *ICUR* X 27644, Peek 1887-8; *Epi. Gr.* 120; *MAMA* VI 138; Lattimore (1942), 50, 57; Appendix V below.

The Byzantine and modern testimonia will be discussed shortly.

The specific device of the question and answer probably arose out of a ritual exchange between two groups. The case of the ritual lament is helpful here. Antiphony *in general* is first demonstrated in the laments quoted in Homer,[143] and the device of the question and answer which is found in non-literary funerary inscriptions of roughly the same period[144] can be projected back to the primeval imagined intercourse between the dead person and his or her survivors.[145] The Homeric instances of question and answer (TA35a-b) are unconnected with the lament, suggesting that this type of responsion was an autonomous feature. Full-scale *stichomythia*, usually involving a series of questions and answers which can approach a lugubrious repartee, however, is unexampled in non-literary inscriptions before tragedy (cf. TA40) and conceivably represents a literary intrusion (cf. esp. TC8 v. 18), although *stichomythia* of this kind is itself an elaboration of an arguably popular device.

The reasons for the occurrence of questions and answers in folk-songs of the later period might reasonably be sought in the intervening Byzantine period. It may therefore be as well to discuss summarily the general phenomenon of antiphony in its late-antique and Byzantine context. If *lalountes heautois = l. allêlois* at Ephesians 5:19 (*plêrousthe en Pneumati, lalountes heautois psalmois*), then alternate singing is understood here, as also at Colossians 3:16 (*didaskontes kai nouthetountes heautous psalmois*, etc.).[146] According to both passages, religious songs and hymns were to be sung chiefly at home and in private gatherings for the purpose of mutual edification.[147] Pliny the Younger's report about the Christians in Bithynia, 'carmen Christo quasi Deo dicere secum invicem' (*Letters* x.97), would seem to confirm the early importance of antiphony.[148] On the generally accepted view,[149] alternate singing emerged at Antioch in either the second or the fourth century AD, whence it spread to Caesarea, Constantinople and elsewhere. From the mid-fourth century the alternate performance of the Psalms and other religious canticles was widespread and was introduced at wakes[150] or other events.[151] St John Chrysostom himself traced responsion to ancient Judaic practice.[152] It is important however to remember that responsion, among other formal features, certainly pre-existed in Greek literary tradition and in some cases the existence of antiphony must be due to literary influence, particularly from the Hellenistic realm.[153] Methodius, who wrote before Chrysostom, purposefully integrated archaising features in his hymn, including antiphony: Thecla sings the hymn while a chorus of eight virgins surrounding her deliver the refrain (on which see below). Medieval testimonia are to be found in M. Alexiou (1974), 142-4; 232f. n. 30; for further testimonia from the second and fourth centuries and relevant bibliography, see Pasquato (1976), 274 n. 147; 276 nn. 159-60; Mitsakis (1971). In addition, see Sevcenko (1969-70), 187-228 (206 n. 36), for testimonia (from Romanos onwards) and for a bibliography of the *anaklômenon*, or refrain, which conventionally occurs, with or without variations, at the end of each stanza in a hymn. Constantine Porphyrogenitus quotes in *De Caeremoniis*[154] a spring song in the *koinê* which is executed antiphonally by two demes. From the same period we can document various types of highly developed *anaklômena* in a group of funerary poems written in 'political' verse; these poems probably had an occasional function and seem to have been composed for performance by two choirs, one of them singing the stanzas, the other the refrains and the *versi intercalati*.[155] The precise nature and extent of the formal influence of church music on popular Greek song requires further investigation.[156] For the time being, we can only raise the possibility that the articulation of antiphony in some types of folk-song may be a learned feature emanating from hymnographic tradition.

In wedding-songs too, stichomythic question and answer constitutes a recurrent pattern:

TA4,[157] possibly Sappho frr. 107 (LP) and TA9; cf. fr. 137 (LP), conceivably a wedding poem cast as a dialogue between a man and a woman;[158] TA43; cf. Catullus 62.20-4, 26-30, 39-47, and 49-58, featuring the antithetical response between the chorus of young women and that of young men at a wedding (here the very notion of a singing match between two rival choruses is probably borrowed from Theocritus);[159] cf. TD1: decorous songs in praise of the bride were performed antiphonally, it would appear, by a chorus of virgins and a chorus of married women; *possibly* Choricius (n. 46 above), 11.20f.

TE1

TF6

TG26

M. Alexiou (1974), 139, 146f., on antiphony and dialogue in the modern lament, may be profitably consulted. Here it is advisable however to append a crucial *caveat*. As far as the present-day field evidence goes, most Greek folk-songs (including the lament) are not antiphonal in the strict sense of an exchange between A and B.[160] A soloist or group of singers may sing a strophe (or in some cases a single verse) which is subsequently repeated by the other singers. The singer now proceeds to the next strophe, the others acting in effect as an 'echo' for each strophe. It is considered an insult not to repeat the soloist's lines, as it is assumed that a particular song 'belongs' to a given singer. Nonetheless, dialogue does exist in folk-song in the sense that a performer may take on two different personae conducting an exchange.[161] The circumstances surrounding the performance of the Macedonian song above may now be remarked. On the afternoon before the wedding the bride is seated in her bedroom; the bridegroom's party are in the next room or an ante-chamber. The women comb and braid the bride's hair as they sing 'antiphonally'. The second strophe is probably sung by the same singer or chorus – but never by the bride, whose silence is *de rigueur* – speaking as if from her point of view. (The anxiety about her hair, expressed in the final six verses, has to do with the use of hair in sympathetic magic.)[162]

11. Refrain

The pattern of strophe and refrain is one of the oldest and most stable traits of ritual song and, in function and form alike, arguably has affinities with the magical incantation (*epôdê*) Ancient marriage songs featured a refrain. This formal trait apparently was descended from the ritual cry *Humên* or *Humenaios* which was repeated at some stage of the wedding, conceivably during the *domum deductio* (see e.g. *Iliad* 18.493); the lengthened versions of the *Hymenruf* subsequently became a refrain, often occurring in conjunction with an exclamatory *makarismos* or *olbismos*.[163] Alongside the refrain in the generic wedding-song, it may be instructive to note the parallel phenomenon of the refrain in the lament: all ancient specimens of the latter, whether intended for solo or choral performance, preserve traces of a refrain.[164] In the case of the lament, evidence of this device, as of the antiphonal question and answer, spans the archaic, classical and Hellenistic periods[165] and in later tradition antedates eastern and other influences.[166]

Testimonia:
TA14, TA45, TA20, TA26.227; TA27a.310, 314, 322, 331; TA18.1736a-b,
   1742a-b, 1754; TA28.1334 *et passim*; TA48[167]
TB8[168]
TC9, TC10

The sole attestation of this device in the Byzantine epithalamium occurs in Methodius' hymn; the refrain, repeated throughout after each strophe, is probably derived from earlier literary models.169 Lastly, cf. TG30.[170]

12. Anaphora

Anaphora characterises learned literature as certainly as folk-song.[171] In all the testimonia tabulated below, the incidence of this type of repetition recalls folk-song rather than literate media. Compare Aristotle's observation (*Rhetoric* 1413b.14f.) that repetition is a feature of oral delivery in general.

Testimonia:
TA27a.311-12; TA46-7,[172] TA48, cf. the *anadiplôsis* at TA18.1726 and
   TA20.640[173]
TB9[174]
TD2
TF1.4-5, 7-8, 9-10, 13-14
TG27, TG28, TG29

It is perhaps worth observing that TD2 above is a mock improvisation of a wedding-song; at the end of his epithalamian speech Himerius invokes Aphrodite as a bride. At least the formal features and the tone of the song suggest an awareness of popular style. The three modern *diegertika* ('wake-up songs') are interesting not only because they exemplify the *anaphora* typical of folk-song,[175] but also because, as will be shown, they may serve as parameters for the analysis of vernacular motifs in Prodromos' song (TF1).

13. Salutatio

The formulaic greeting *khaire* with a wish implied (cf. *Odyssey* 8.408, 11.248), and the explicit wish *khairois*, both borrowed from everyday speech, are common features of ancient wedding-song. The earliest greetings are *khaire* and *khairein*; *khaire* in particular, figures in funerary inscriptions from the seventh century onwards.[176] *Khaire* and *khairois* are standard invocations of someone present in person or, if a deity, in a statue; cf. Headlam (1922), 174 on Herodas *Mimes* IV.1-11; and Cunningham also ad op. cit., v. 58. On variations of *khairein* in the sense of hail or goodbye, also cf. Thomson (1966), 49f., 52 on Aeschylus *Agamemnon* 538-9 (= 'hail'), 572 (= 'hail' or 'goodbye').[177] Variants of these formulae also made their way into subsequent epistolography.[178] On the analogy of colloquial usage, we may suppose that some form of greeting was likely to appear in the opening[179] or at the conclusion of a wedding-song.[180] The greeting *per se*, as the congratulations addressed to the couple, is standard in other cultures as well and therefore predictable; but, as will be seen, the medieval and modern variants of the general *khairein* formula – *hara eis ton ~, hara sto(n)*, etc. – undoubtedly represent a specific case of formal continuity.

Testimonia:
TA17.1063f.; TA46,[181] TA47[182]
TB9
TC4.30; TC5, TC11
TD3.36
TE1
TF2.13, 48, etc.; TF6.48-9
TG21

The song preserved in the *De Caeremoniis* (TE1) attracts attention because, perhaps more than any other specimen from the Byzantine period, it bears clear traces of popular tradition. Prescribing it for the wedding of a co-emperor, Porphyrogenitus records the social context: the song is performed in the evening by two rival demes[183] (who play tympana and cymbals) after the bride has been conducted on horseback to the imperial palace.[184] Further, he specifies the *êkhos* or mode, for the song, suggesting that it was actually sung. We may consider the version given by Porphyrogenitus and translate, following Reiske's *CSHB* commentary (*De Caeremoniis*, ii.354): see TE1. The first verse may at first appear puzzling in the mouth of a male chorus; but it is not necessarily unusual, since the line in question is modelled on the Song of Songs.[185] *Rhodoeumorpha* ('as beautiful as roses') and *englukotheata* ('sweet to behold') are neologisms with a literary flavour. The physical praise, the *salutatio*, and the implicit comparison of the couple to roses are just as likely to be rhetorical motifs as they are popular ones. All the same, it must be granted that the particular form of the *salutatio* here (vv. 4, 6) is recognisably popular. In later folk tradition *hara sto(n), sti(n), sto, stous*, etc. is formulaic for a *salutatio* (with a wish implied) which is concurrently a *makarismos*.[186] On this last consideration we may bring to bear the arguments which Kyriakides presented in favour of the song's sub-literary provenance.[187] On the grounds of the known performative context and the relevant musical instructions, Kyriakides supposed that the text was a corrupt rendition or even a paraphrase in prose of a song that must have been sung in the 'popular' fifteen-syllable metre.[188] He noted the incidence, in four positions, of self-contained accentual iambic octosyllables, which correspond to the first hemistich of political verse, and tentatively proposed the following emendation:[189]

(1) *Anthê esôreusa tou agrou | | kai eis ton paston esêba,*
(2) *hêlion eidon sdeugonumphon | | eis khrusentimon klinên,*
(3) *allêla êngalisdonto | | pothêtên pethumian.*
(4) *Khara eis kallê ta terpna, | | ta englukotheata,*
(5)   *kai rhoda ta rhodoeumorpha.*
(6)   *Khara eis sdeugos to khruson.*[190]

C. Content

It may be recalled that the subject-matter of nuptial praise is largely predictable from universal (and mainly western) custom. At modern weddings in the west, and, one would suspect, in a very high proportion of existing cultures, speeches made in honour of the bride and bridegroom are bound necessarily to praise their good looks, skills, virtues, etc. Praise, moreover, is apt generally to be a heavily conventionalised politeness, expressed in various types of images and symbols. With the few exceptions which will be pointed out shortly, it is the object of this part of the chapter to identify those motifs and images informing the wedding-encomium which are *particular* to Greek culture. In at least several instances we must be prepared to admit the probability that the general function and setting of nuptial praise in Greek culture have guaranteed the recurrence of these elements.

1. Exclamation

Apart from the special type of simile discussed earlier,[191] there is another means of conveying the unparalleled excellence of either party: a hyperbolic exclamation to the effect that 'nowadays there is no other person such as the bride or bridegroom'. This motif is first adumbrated in TA11.160f., where it is formulated in the manner of a compliment to a prospective bride (Nausicäa). TA7 is an exclamation addressed to the bridegroom which functions to compliment the bride (*païs*) for unspecified attributes – presumably, among others, her beauty. Muth conjectures that this fragment was sung before the bridal chamber.[192] Cf. TA5, which, owing to its structural similarity to the previous fragment, may be classed as part of an encomiastic epithalamium.[193] (Here however the chorus or soloist directly praises the bride [*parthenon*] as skilful.)[194] TA7 may be compared with the praise of the bride in TB1.20f. *hoia Akhaiiadôn gaian patei oudemi' alla,* etc. ('an Achaean maiden such as who none other walks the earth, etc.'). The chorus' *epainos* need not be exclusively erotic; the import may simply be that Helen is generally 'beyond compare' i.e. pre-eminent. That the statement is meant in a general way may be gathered by considering v. 21 *ê mega ka ti tekoit', ei materi tiktoi homoion* ('and wondrous shall be the child she bears if it be like its mother'), where the neuter *mega*, referring at one remove to Helen, may equally suggest physical as well as another kind of 'greatness'.[195] Furthermore, the general force of the praise in Theocritus loc. cit. may be confirmed by examining its patent model, *Odyssey* 21.107, Telemachus' compliment to his mother, where praise is not intended to be specific: Penelope, after all, is consistently lauded in Homer on both physical and non-physical grounds. Returning to TA7 itself, we may propose two alternative interpretations, based on the force of *nun* ('now'):

(i) 'There is no other bride like her now, i.e. no other bride will *ever* be like her', with the stress being laid on the contrast between the present and the *future*;[196] or

(ii) stressing the contrast between the decadent present and the golden *past*, i.e. 'Nowadays, in this Iron Age, there is no other bride like her'. In either case the bride's putative qualities belong to the here and now and are very likely to be physical as well as moral. If so, the bride embodies a conjunction of positive physical *and* moral attributes which contradicts the mythological record for her gender.

Finally, we may observe that the motif under consideration appears to reflect a popular sentiment. For this reason it is not surprising that the motif is given formulaic expression in modern wedding-songs: cf. TG33-6.

2. Nature imagery

From M. Alexiou's discussion of the 'allusive method' it is plain that a large number of symbols have featured consistently in Greek tradition as follows: (i) harvest and seasonal motifs (e.g. the motifs of the grapes and corn), as well as the symbols of the tree, the apple and the refreshing spring, which are all sporadically attested in ancient literature proper but more widely evidenced in funerary inscriptions and later folk-song, seem to have been transmitted independently through popular tradition;[197] (ii) light imagery, including the encomiastic motif of the sun, occurs in early Byzantine hymns modelled on classical rather than Hebrew or Syriac forms and, moreover, preserves many of its ancient features;[198] (iii) all of the above images antedate the first crusade. This system of imagery may be classified in three groups and analysed accordingly.

2a. Fruits, flowers and plants in general

Stylised symbols of fertility like flowers, flower pots and pairs of broad-leaved plants dominate woven and embroidered bridal textiles in medieval Greek folk art. According to Zora (1994), esp. 226 these naturalistic motifs aim at attracting fecundity.[199] Millennia-old sympathetic symbolism arguably also underlies the complimentary images of fruits, flowers and plants in bridal songs in all phases of Greek culture and to these we now turn.

The comparison, whether implicit or explicit, of the bride or bridegroom to a tree or plant in particular was by Menander Rhetor's day,[200] and very probably earlier, a *locus communis* of epithalamian (and generally erotic) praise.[201] For instance, *phoinikos neon ernos* at TA11.163, deliberately chosen to recall the diction of wedding-songs, is an indirect compliment to Nausicäa as a bride-to-be.[202] The image of the slender sapling in TA9 refers to the bridegroom's physique and stature. At TA11a the quasi-metaphor of the *neazon*, lit. 'young life', conjures up a young plant sequestered against the elements; significantly, Deianeira used this motif to describe the blissful lot of a *parthenos* until the day of her wedding.[203] Theocritus' complimentary use of *kuparittos* in Idyll 18 will be examined in section 2b below. Methodius' hymn, although formally not an epithalamium, is clearly indebted to standard epithalamian conceits,[204] including plant motifs. One of Dioscuros' 'rhetoricised' hexameter epithalamia features the indirect comparison of the bride to a 'honey-sweet cluster from the young bloom of the vine' (TD4.7 *k[u]pris[m]ôn nearôn meliêdea botrun aeireis*). Since Dioscuros was a Christian,[205] it is not unlikely that this specific comparison, hitherto unexampled in ancient Greek literature,[206] was modelled on, say, Song of Songs 1.14f. *botrus kuprinos* (where, however, it refers to the bridegroom) or Psalm 79.9 *ampelon ex Aiguptou metêras*, which resembles Dioscuros' passage even more closely. Yet the distinct possibility that the *botrus*-motif existed simultaneously in the literary or even sub-literary pagan sphere should not be overlooked. In an anonymous two-line epigram (*AP* 5.304) an unresponsive maiden is called outright an *omphax* and a *staphulê* in turn.[207] Romanos the Melodist (fl. 536-56), Dioscuros' contemporary, may perhaps here serve as a 'control'. Cf. his *kontakion* 'On the Nativity' II.16.6-7 (Maas-Trypanis): *O botrus mou, mê ekthlipsôsi se anomoi· / eblastêsa se* (the Virgin Mary to Christ, on hearing of the necessity of the Crucifixion); this unconventional image is applied to a nubile heroine, again in the context of a lament which is quoted, in Eustathius Makrembolites' *Hysminê and Hysminias* X.11.4 (Conca). The metaphor of the *ampelos*, on the other hand, used of the Virgin Mary in Romanos op. cit. 1.1, has an indisputable scriptural pedigree.[208] For compliments which rest on vegetal imagery in general cf. the Marian *Akathist Hymn*, dating from the sixth century and generally ascribed to Romanos: *blastou amarantou klêma, aroura blastanousa, anthos tês aphtharsias, dendron aglaokarpon* and *krinon*[209] are used of Mary; *rhodon to amaranton* and *to mêlon to euosmon*[210] refer to Christ.[211]

The wedding-song preserved in TE1 has plausible links to popular tradition, as has been argued in the section on the *salutatio*: the implied comparison to a rose[212] (discussed immediately below) may be a learned vestige, although it is just as likely to betray a non-literary intrusion. The obligatory comparison to a fruit, plant or tree can be documented in epithalamia from the Middle and Late Byzantine periods. Thus in Prodromos (TF4.57) and Nicetas Choniates (TF8b.21f.) *ampelos*, used of the bride, patently derives from Psalm 79.9 and is probably a rhetorical item.[213] At TF3.41 Prodromos' images of an ivy fastened to a plane tree[214] and a vine-branch embracing a laurel represent erudite allusions of which every detail – from the archaising *sunemprepeis* to the motif of the laurel – has a distinctly literary ancestry: (i) on the archaic (poetic) usage of *prepô* and its compounds see B.2a above; (ii) cf. the simile of the ivy embracing the elm in Euripides *Hecuba* 398; the sensual description of a garden (based on rhetorical *exempla* of mutual attraction) at Achilles Tatius 1.15.3 (Garnaud) '... the ivy spiralled intimately among the pine boughs. This symbiosis provided support for the ivy and ivy wreaths of honour for the tree', tr. Winkler, in Reardon (1989), 186 (Hörandner does not cite these parallels to Prodromos); and the associated similes at TA29x and Paulus Silentiarius *AP* 5.255.13f. (of two lovers, embracing passionately) 'one will more readily disentangle a vine's plaited stems, / twisted and grown interlaced over the years / than them, kissing' (not in Hörandner);[215] (iii) on the comparison to a *klêma* in an epithalamium see Eratosthenes (n. 206 above), and generally for comparisons of a maiden's features to plants and flowers in late antique literature see Rohde (1960), 164 n. 3; (iv) on the significance of the laurel in antiquity see *Der Kleine Pauly*, iii (1969), col. 736f.[216]

It is striking that the selfsame simile of the ivy embracing a tree occurs in modern wedding-songs in Greece: cf. TG4, TG6. As in Prodromos and the ancient examples, the image is intended to suggest the physical intimacy of marriage as well as the strength of the spiritual tie. We may reasonably suppose that sub-literary wedding-songs have led a parallel existence, using many of the motifs and images which were concurrently enshrined in the canon of high literature.[217] Later composers of epithalamia like Prodromos surely must have been aware of this 'underground' tradition. Roughly two centuries after Prodromos, the simile of the ivy was to have a legitimate place in a vernacular romance such as the *Achilleïs*, where it refers to two lovers embracing after coitus: *hôsan kissos eis to dendron etse ton eneplakên*[218] ('like ivy on a tree, so she embraced him'). Moreover, it is no surprise that in an era that was becoming increasingly attuned to vernacular culture[219] Prodromos presented the motif of the ivy in a form which may suggest popular song.

His satirical epithalamium (TF1), technically a *diegertikon* featuring an admixture of both rhetorical and 'lowbrow' ingredients, has considerable suggestive value here. The ancient genre of the *diegertikon* is implied in TB7 and Menander Rhetor 402.2f. (RW) (not in Gow [1952], ii ad TBF7) and referred to in Aeschylus *Danaïds* fr. 43 (*TGrF*, iii [Radt]); TA44 is an actual specimen. Composed within the parameters of this inherently popular genus,[220] Prodromos' song (partly in quantitative anacreontics) occurs in his archaising Lucianic dialogue *Amarantos ê gerontos erôtes*.[221] It is sung by a comic poet, Chaerephon, in honour of the aged philosopher Stratocles and his young bride. The song derives its humorous point from the fact that Chaerephon cites the bridegroom as a *kouros* ('lad') and inflames him so that he (Stratocles) immediately retires with the girl to his bedroom. Verses 1-6 follow Menander's prescription that Aphrodite and the god of marriage (among others) should be extolled in the proemium.[222] On the other hand, the accumulation of various vernacular features – the *anaphoras* (7-8),[223] the parallelism (10-11),[224] and a number of motifs[225] – coupled with the uncouth form of the comparison to a rose (vv. 14-15), which in effect establishes the pre-eminence of the bride in point of beauty,[226] rather strengthen the case that the poet has purposely reproduced a 'folksy' version of a wedding-song. A comparative glance at three modern *diegertika*, TG27-9, may in fact serve to confirm Prodromos' formal and thematic affinities with popular tradition.

In sum, the consistent comparison to a plant, flower, etc. may reflect the underlying symbolic system of vegetal imagery that can be traced in the Greek language from antiquity. Generally speaking, as has been shown in Part A of this chapter, the 'filtering through' of a great many nuptial motifs from high culture to popular song may be assumed.

2b. The cypress motif

In antiquity proper this motif is first attested in a passage in Theocritus which represents the most extensive instance of a fully articulated wedding encomium: TB2.26-31. The image of the cypress is the third in a series of in effect four nature similes which the chorus of maidens uses in order to illustrate their claim (v. 25) that they are physically 'flawed' when compared with the bride Helen. The lesser terms in each statement e.g. night, winter, etc., of course refer implicitly to the maidens. The first two similes hinge on an appearance or epiphany in an astronomical context; cf. v. 28 *hôde ... diephainet' en hamîn*. The next two comparisons have to do with the notion of adornment; cf. v. 31 *hôde ... Lakedaimoni kosmos.*[227]

The cypress motif can be traced especially from late antiquity onwards, in both literary and sub-literary sources:

(i) Aristaenetus I.1.28f. (Mazal) (probably early sixth century AD): of the gait of a woman.

(ii) *Achmetis Oneirocriticon*[228] (Drexl): 'the cypress tree signifies the position of the queen because of the tree's shapeliness and fragrance and because it never fades or sheds its leaves' (108.15); 'the cypress tree [sc. signifies] a princess or noble and beautiful woman' (154.17).

(iii) *Anonymous Dreambook* 97 (Drexl):[229] 'To have seen a cypress tree somewhere represents a noble woman'.

(iv) *Geoponica* XI.4 (Beckh, p. 329 with Fehrle [1920], 9):[230] the aetiological tale stresses the likeness of the tree to a maiden.

(v) Michael Psellos *Epitaphios eis Eirênên kaisarissan*, p. 167.5 (Kurtz and Drexl).

(vi) Pseudo-Lucian *Timarion* 241 (Romano, p. 58): of the stature of a man (early twelfth century).

(vii) Theodore Prodromos funerary epigram XXXIX.5 (Hörandner); epithalamian epigram XLIIIc.2: of the attractiveness of the bridegroom; TF1.1b (refers to the couple's future offspring).

(viii) Comnenian romances: (a) Eustathius Makrembolites *Hysminê and Hysminias* (Conca) V.10.4 (of a maiden); X.11.3 (lament over a maiden); (b)

Nicetas Eugenianos *Drosilla and Charicles* (Conca) I.142 (of the heroine); III.315; (c) Theodore Prodromos *Rhodanthê and Dosicles* (Conca) II.209 (of the heroine's gait); VI.291-2 (lament over heroine, of her stature and beauty); VII.226 (of the heroine's stature).

(ix) Nicolaos Eirenicos epithalamium for the wedding of John III Doukas Vatatzes and Anna-Costanza (mid-thirteenth century)[231] = TF6.1-2.

(x) *Achilleïs* 99 (Naples MS., Hesseling, p. 44): of the slender physique of the hero (early fourteenth century?).

(xi) *Belthandros and Chrysantza* 652f. (Kriaras, p. 114): of a maiden (1310-50).

(xii) *Erôtopaignia* 266 (Hesseling & Pernot): a maiden is addressed as *triantaklonokuparisse* ('cypress with thirty branches').

(xiii) Nineteenth-century Cypriot folk-song, in Papadopoullos (1975), 265, v. 91 (of a tall maiden).

(xiv) TG31, early nineteenth-century Cretan love-song, whose import is 'who will be the lucky man to marry you?'.[232]

(xv) TG30.

(xvi) Cypriot song of praise (*painema*),[233] addressed to a maiden: TG32.

The cypress motif clearly belongs to the larger underlying system of vegetal imagery which has been postulated in the previous sub-section; but is this motif ultimately a popular, or a purely literary one? Perhaps a decent argument for the priority of folk usage in a limited number of cases is the internal coherence of the imagery as evidenced in such diverse sub-literary material as *Geoponica* and folk-song. In the specific case of the cypress motif, we may draw attention to its function in traditional song. The term *kuparissi*, though grammatically neuter, has two connotations in popular Greek wedding-song: it may be used of a young man, i.e. symbolising a pert, phallic body (cf. Artemidorus, p. 250.23-4 [Pack]), or it may be applied to a nubile woman (never a married woman) presumably because, as M. Coulton[234] argues, its slenderness, in contrast to the fan shape of fruit trees, which symbolise fertility, implies that the girl is still unmarried. The motif of the cypress, then, is conceivably a morphological constituent of popular tradition.

2c. Natural objects or phenomena

Either party may be compared to a natural object or seasonal phenomenon e.g. the sun, moon, a star, etc. This motif represents a well-established compliment which is not confined to nuptial song: cf. the allusive (endearing) addresses at *Odyssey* 16.23, etc. and *astêr* ('star'), referring to a pretty child or handsome person from Homer onwards;[235] also cf. the moon metaphors in Sappho frr. 34 (LP) (in conjunction with Julian *Orationes* 3.109c [Bidez-Cumont]) and TA1.6f.[236] As instances of nature motifs in wedding-songs we may adduce the following testimonia:

TA10.1709f.
TB2.26f.
TF8a.17f.; TF8b.24f.[237]
TG8

2d. Bird motifs

The comparison of a human being to a bird, though attested in ancient Greek tradition,[238] is hardly a culture-specific motif. Cf., for instance, Song of Songs 1.15, 2.13f., 4.1, 5.2, 6.9, where the bride is likened indirectly to a pigeon or a dove (*peristera*).[239] In later Greek tradition, presumably from the time of Prodromos at the latest, the associations attaching to certain species of birds show signs of discontinuity with ancient usage. A most striking example here is the motif of the partridge. In Aristotle's day the *perdix* was regarded as proverbially salacious and mischievous[240] and would be unlikely to be featured in a compliment to a woman. As Artemidorus demonstrates, these associations were in force until late antiquity.[241] The positive connotations of the partridge are evidenced from the Middle or Late period onwards;[242] and the polite comparison of a bride or a marriageable woman to a bird generally can be traced from the same period (see TF1.8)[243] and has persisted in modern folk-songs, particularly love-songs and wedding-songs; see e.g. TG26-7.

3. Gold and silver imagery

Gold imagery does not occur in any testimonia relating to wedding praise earlier than TB4.30-1, and TB2.28. In Theocritus the epithet *khrusea*, used of Helen, is to be expected in the encomium of a semi-divine figure and, moreover, in an explicit comparison to Dawn.[244] At *Aetia* loc. cit. Apollo's oracle, addressed to Cydippe's father, turns into an endorsement of Acontius (fated to marry the maiden) and his family. Although the collocation of gold and electrum is a direct borrowing from pseudo-Hesiod,[245] the god's quasi-nuptial compliment as a whole is not based on any known literary model and is noteworthy for figuratively equating a mortal with gold. Now the formal structure of the utterance itself is attested in modern Greek wedding-songs;[246] so it may appear plausible that Apollo's compliment is not atypical from the perspective of thematic treatment either. This might suggest that gold imagery was in fact applied to mortals in erotic praise generally and in wedding praise in particular before the Hellenistic period and that, consequently, the distribution of our evidence may be accidental.[247] Two other considerations, if taken together, may indicate that gold imagery would have been apt to occur in ancient wedding-songs. (i) The ancient Greeks associated anything a supernatural being had or did with gold, a fact which is reflected in the continous use of this metal both as substance and decoration in cult-images of gods and votive offerings.[248] Hence, also, at Aristophanes *Clouds* 272 the Clouds use golden buckets to draw water from the Nile, and at 598-9 Ephesian Artemis lives in a *pankhrusos oikos*; see Ph. Kakrides' note on *Birds* 572-4 (pp. 117f.); also *Frogs* 483 (Xanthias' exclamation 'O golden gods!'). In the sixth to fourth centuries BC a taboo on the use of gold and conspicuous luxury by (non-barbarian) mortals can be diagnosed in metropolitan Greece; the literary and archaeological evidence suggesting that gold was destined normally for religious purposes at this period is discussed by B.B. Shefton.[249] (ii) Besides being a quintessentially divine status symbol, the archaic *topos* of 'golden hair' etc. *may* refer particularly to the sphere of Aphrodite and Eros and so ultimately raises various erotic implications: see Calame (1983), 329 ad TA2.54; *Birds* 697 (with Ph. Kakrides' note, p. 140), 1738 ('the golden wings' of Eros); n. 247 above. See also Alcman fr. 3.68 (Davies) 'golden shoot', employed in a comparison to convey Astymeloisa's charm and sex appeal; the erotic implications of *ernos* ('shoot') when used of a young ephebe will be examined in Chapter IV below; further, see Sappho fr. 132. 1-2 (LP). In his poem of honour of Polycrates, Ibycus S 151.41-5 (*SLG* [Page]) stresses that two youths, Troilus and probably the Sicyonian Zeuxippus, are as indistinguishable in beauty as gold is from brass.[250] It has already been shown that a comparison to a god or hero, whether direct or indirect, was standard procedure in the context of the popular wedding;[251] the epithet 'golden', with both *makaristic*[252] and conceivably even erotic connotations, may therefore have been applied to the bridal pair as an auspicious politeness.

In three of Dioscuros' poems, TD4.6, TD5.9, and TD6.24, the epithets 'golden' and 'silver'[253] refer to the newlyweds; whether this usage stems directly from Callimachus or some other source is an open question. Formally speaking at least, these passages, stressing as they do the parity of the couple by means of a special type of parallel structure, have close analogues in modern Greek wedding-songs: see B.7.iii above. If the resort to a modern 'control' is at all valid, it may be arguable that Dioscuros probably drew his gold and silver motifs from popular usage. By contrast, the gold motifs in Leo Magister (TE3.7, TE5.1, etc.) are direct borrowings from ancient lyric.

We may now turn to the song preserved in Constantine Porphyrogenitus' *De Caeremoniis* (TE1). It is worth observing that within the chromatic hierarchy which governed Byzantine literary portraiture and iconography alike, gold was the supreme colour.[254] The gold imagery in Porphyrogenitus' song is therefore likely to be highly conventional: *khrusentimos* (of the nuptial couch), a literary-sounding coinage, and *khruson* (of the couple) fittingly amplify the official occasion and its participants. At the same time, it is perhaps significant that the epithets in question occur in a wedding composition with recognisable 'folk' elements.[255] Lastly, as regards the modern Greek evidence, the physical commodity itself and its imagery fulfil a sympathetic function not only in many social rituals, including the wedding, but also in the accompanying songs and utterances.[256] See TG12.3; TG13.7-8;[257] TG15.1; TG18.2.

II. Nuptial Praise

4. Mythic exemplum

It has been noted that both ancient and modern wedding-songs articulate praise through a mythic parallel.[258] In the ancient specimens the superhuman comparison, whether direct or not, offers extravagant erotic or other praise and, as shall be argued shortly, so does duty as a kind of *amplificatio*. Mythic comparisons occur as compliments in Homer, where they are not necessarily restricted to the context of weddings. In Sappho's circle, as well, they appear to be a routine compliment of physical beauty: see esp. frr. 31.1 (LP) (examined below), TA1.4.,[259] 21-3.[260] The comparison of the bride to a mythic figure has already been remarked: cf. TA15. The fragment features erotic praise of the bride by means of an indirect comparison with Helen and Hermione, both mythological *exempla*. It should be observed that Hermione's beauty, like her mother's, was proverbial.[261] TA14 directly compares the bridegroom's stature[262] and impetuous stride with those of Ares, deemed a general prototype of manly virtues.[263] TA8a probably drew a comparison of the bridegroom to Achilles, both in physical appearance and deeds.[264]

The patent object of a generic *eikôn* which sets up a parallel between a divine or heroic figure and a mortal is to praise the latter with respect to (a) external appearance, stature[265] and bearing, (b) conduct and moral qualities in general and (c) good fortune and material happiness (*olbos*). On (a) cf. *Odyssey* 6.5-16 (Nausicäa is compared to a goddess in point of natural beauty, *phuên kai eidos*;[266] loc. cit. 19 (her two attendants are likened to the Graces), 102f. (Nausicäa, who is playing with her peers, is compared directly with Artemis[267] hunting and overtowering her nymphs), 149f. (= TA11: Odysseus compares Nausicäa to Artemis with reference to *eidos te megethos phuên te*), 243-5 (= TA12), where Odysseus, cast as a potential husband, is likened explicitly to a god.[268] Also cf. the complimentary adjective *theoeidês* in the sense of 'of godlike appearance' (LSJ, s.v., I); *isotheos*, *antitheos* and lastly *theoeikelos*, in Homer, Sappho fr. 44.34 (LP), etc.,[269] often meant as compliments of external beauty; also the standard conceit, datable from the Hellenistic period onwards, of assimilating a comely woman to a goddess: e.g. Callimachus, *AP* 5.146 (= xv [*HE*]); Rufin. op. cit. 5.15.5-6, 36.3, 48.4, 62.5, 73.1f., 94.2-3; *adespoton* op. cit. 5.95, etc.[270] Mainly as a moral exemplification the paradigmatic pairs of Odysseus and Penelope and Peleus and Thetis would be ready to hand and therefore likely to be employed in ancient wedding-song.[271] Peleus and Thetis are cited as (at least in part) a moral or 'moralising' *paradeigma* in Alcman fr. 42 (LP) and Pindar *Pythian Ode* 3.86f. (S.-M.). In one of the preponderant versions of the myth – the Olympian one used by Homer – the couple sometimes embodies the norms of reverence for the gods and probity: Thetis figures as a modest virgin nymph and Peleus as an uncommonly virtuous man who was honoured with a worthy wife.[272] Yet this marriage might also furnish a *paradeigma* which is not exclusively or necessarily moral: e.g. in TC7b this couple serves as a prototype for sexual congress. Despite its eventual flaws, some of which were conditioned by literary

39

objectives,[273] the wedding of Peleus and Thetis was especially auspicious and attractive to the popular mind, not least because it was attended by all the gods and was therefore perceived as the grandest wedding ever.[274] In general, the inferences to be drawn from this *exemplum* (or any wedding *exemplum*, for that matter) would depend on the performer's particular objectives and other circumstances. It is conceivable that TA16, which treats of the wedding of Peleus,[275] was intended for an actual wedding. The gods' best wishes (v. 6) would, by extension, bode favourably for the couple, particularly the bridegroom. Third, and just as important, a divine *eikôn* will invariably carry the association of good fortune and happiness, at least to some degree; cf. TA30 (the *exemplum* of Callisto's union with Zeus).[276]

Sappho fr. 31 (LP), though unlikely to be a wedding-song *per se*, is worth remarking for its explicit equation of the man (Sappho's sexual foil) with a god: he is termed *isos theoisin* (v. 1).[277] The ego-narrator seems to be jealous at the sight and sound of a couple; and the catalogue of symptoms of her intense emotional state, if read in a psychoanalytical fashion, may reveal her as implicitly both identifying and competing with the man.[278] He is therefore not simply a rival but a positive foil against which Sappho evaluates herself as well as her chance of winning (or winning back) the other woman. Devereux[279] detects in this flattering comparison an element of 'overvaluation' of the phallos and hence secret envy and admiration; 'equal to gods', then, is applied to the man first and foremost because of his physical attributes,[280] notably his endowment with a penis. But that does not rule out the possibility that, given the particular psychodynamics of the poetess's reaction, the expression simultaneously refers to the man's extraordinary good luck in having elicited some sexual or other positive response in Sappho's female beloved.[281] As has been noted, it is quite possible that an *exemplum* or a series of *exempla* may subsume more than one associative strand in varying degrees, depending on the context. For instance, in TA11.149f. Odysseus likens the nubile Nausicäa to Artemis *prima facie* on physical grounds. At the same time the embarrassing and rather precarious situation in which he finds himself must imply that the paragon used will also be particularly appropriate to a modest virgin,[282] for as Homer informs us, the hero is speaking 'cunningly and with kind words' (v. 148) and would be unlikely to make an indecorous diplomatic pitch.[283] Rufinus *AP* 5.70 (= xxvi Page [1978])[284] illustrates two groups of characteristics – straightforward physical beauty on the one hand, and mental and/or less tangible traits such as wisdom and manual dexterity on the other – through a succession of divine *paradeigmata* which refer to a woman.[285] Perhaps the sophistication which we may assume for Sappho should allow us to gather that the divine comparison in fr. 31 (LP) is dictated by her allusiveness. It appears in any event highly likely, considering the sexual orientation traditionally attached to the poetess, that the comparison is a compliment with erotic overtones, connoting 'fear of loss and despair at the impossibility of competing with the man'.[286]

To return to the wedding: the *exemplum* does not only extol the bride or bridegroom but it also significantly elevates the occasion and, by corollary, explicit or implicit, the guests themselves.[287] The device's inherent function of *amplificatio* can be deduced from instances where it serves to cast in a negative light and so deflate the occasion and the participants: e.g. in Euripides *Iphigeneia at Aulis* 1080f. the exemplary wedding of Peleus and Thetis contrasts with the mock wedding of Achilles and Iphigeneia, thereby deflating it.[288] Cf. TA18.1731f., the realistic wedding-song,[289] whose central albeit implied *exemplum* is the *hieros gamos* of Zeus and Hera.[290] Not only does the poet parallel the wedding procession of the actors with the archetypal *hieros gamos*; the divine comparison is made unambiguous by the end of the song where Peitheterus' 'apotheosis' is celebrated by himself (1755f.) and by the chorus in its final address (1764-5). The hymenaeal *exemplum* pointedly frames and so serves to amplify the two-fold occasion, namely the personal triumph of Peitheterus and the military victory of the birds.

The wedding-song's magnification of the events also correlates with the couple's ambiguous position astride divinity and humanity during the ritual; this liminality appears in fact to be brought out in many vase scenes, perhaps most fittingly in the visual pun of marine Nymphs (Nereids) striking the poses of ordinary brides on a fifth-century BC Attic *pyxis*.[291] An arguably 'popular' vestige of the nuptial *exemplum* lies in its very function of *amplificatio*. If our contemporary field data are at all applicable here, the ancient *exemplum* probably corresponded to the *amplificatio* enacted at the ritual level in the popular wedding. In the modern Greek wedding the elevated manner in which the *drômena* are carried out suggests that the couple is in fact sublimated into 'sacred' personages. We may cite the following data that bear on this amplification of the event and its two protagonists. (i) The bridal couple wears crowns, in themselves considered as 'holy' objects which confer fertility and generally serve an apotropaic function.[292] By virtue of the crowns, the couple itself becomes 'holy'.[293] (ii) The couple are clad in garments the colour of porphyry, their crowns (which they sometimes wear for two or three days) resemble royal ones; moreover, they adhere to stylised behaviour (e.g. total silence) and are addressed in song as *basilias – basilissa* ('king – queen'), *soultanos – soultanna* ('sultan – sultana'), *rigas – rigissa* ('king – queen' < Latin *rex, regina*). The ceremony thus becomes comparable to an imperial enthronement or investiture.[294] A religious/secular model, grounded at least partly in church doctrine and imperial practice, may be posited at first: the couple is styled as king and queen of creation and as an imperial couple.[295] But even this model, assuming that it is entirely valid, would hardly have been applied at the popular level if it did not rest on a substratum of analogous doctrines and practices.[296] It is obvious that the occasion of the wedding has consistently been felt to be sacred and worthy of ritual elevation; possibly the details just examined are simply accretions to the pre-existing paradigm of the *hieros gamos*.[297]

If indeed the *exemplum* correlates with certain of the customary actions which presumably characterised the ancient wedding, what are the implications for the *Birds*? It may be the case that here the popular device of the *exemplum* is being exploited along grandiose hymnic lines in a way that suits the play's *dénouement*.[298] In the more specialised context of the wedding-song later known as the *kateunastikon* a mythic paradigm may also serve as a decorous sexual allusion: cf. Sappho fr. 27 (LP), esp. vv. 8-11 and 12, conceivably a discreet 'code' for marital coitus; Menander Rhetor 406.8f. (RW) (the encouragement to coitus will focus on mythic *exempla* among other items).[299] Last but not least, it should be noted that the *exemplum* later became a fixed component of rhetorical epithalamia;[300] cf. TC6, TC7a-b. Menander's prescription that an analogy with a god should be direct can be explained from characteristically Greek ideas such as *theios anêr* ('godly man')[301]. The Greeks seem to have combined (although they did not mentally confuse) the secular and sacred spheres, and in particular worship (*Kultus*) and homage (*Ehrung*), with great ease; they were thus apt to resort to a divine analogy or identification under many circumstances, e.g. daily conversation (cf. *Odyssey* 6.151f.),[302] tomb inscriptions and memorials (from the early fourth century BC) and later public oratory and ruler cults.[303]

In the early Christian period the celestial marriage of Christ (= bridegroom) and the Church (= bride) was already a theoretical *topos*, one of its sources probably being Ephesians 5:22-5.[304] This ideal for human marriage was incorporated in both Church practice and Patristic writing. At the end of his *Symposium* Methodius, Bishop of Olympus (c. 311), inserted a *sui generis* composition[305] (a *psalmos*, as it is designated), which praises chastity (*hagneia*) as a spiritual marriage. Written in alphabetic acrostic, it is delivered by the virgin saint Thecla on behalf of a chorus of virgins waiting outside the bridal chamber; at the end of each strophe they repeat the same refrain. Though technically not an epithalamium, the work is heavily dependent on clichés and devices characteristic of the rhetorical epithalamian speech and derives its arguments from the marriage of Christ and the Church (e.g. vv. 35f., 104f.; cf. Thaleia's speech in Musurillo-Débidour, pp. 90f.). It is significant that several exemplars, male and female, of chastity (e.g. St Thecla, Joseph, Susannah, the Virgin Mary) are used.

At roughly the same period nuptial paradigms occur in St John Chrysostom's sermons. In his homily on Genesis (TD8) Chrysostom explicitly contrasts the union of Isaac and Rebecca with contemporary weddings. Moreover, by virtue of Ephesians 5:32, early Christians were enjoined to transfigure their union in marriage by enacting the mystical marriage of Christ to the Church; among the examples drawn from the New Testament, this marriage is perhaps the archetype *par excellence* and receives its fullest treatment from St John at *PG* 62.135f. (*hom.* 20 in *Eph.* 5 = Field iv. 299f.). Chrysostom gives a list of archetypes at TD9a, the chief one being the wedding at Cana; from his catalogue of exemplars in TD9b (Jacob and Rachel, Mary and Joseph, Adam and Eve, etc.) we can infer the 'supernatural' (or 'metaphysical') significance of marriage, although it need not follow that the Church invested marriage with a sacramental character from the outset. Indeed, the contrary is probably the case: the civil forms and responsibilities of matrimony appear never to have been challenged or played down in Byzantine history. It may be as well here to outline briefly the evolution of the wedding ceremony in the Orthodox Church.[306]

Despite Tertullian's dogged objections,[307] the pagan custom of crowning the bridal pair continued; it was later interpreted in a more positive light and overtly recognised by the Church.[308] Marriage was an affair which directly concerned the civil authorities and was carried out by means of the traditional *coniunctio dextrarum* by the bride's father and through the imposition of special wreaths. Alongside the coronation the couple had the option of making their union public by communicating and receiving the blessing of the local priest or bishop at the end of the Liturgy. Under Justinian the priest was empowered to act as a notary public and could thus seal the union from a civil point of view as well. Until the sixth century, if not later, therefore, the wedding ceremony, which involved a large number of popular practices, must have taken place outside the Church, mainly at the bride's house. This supposition derives from the following facts, which corroborate further the underground status, as it were, of the popular wedding: (i) the early Church Fathers give no account of a strictly religious wedding rite; (ii) none of the canons dating from the Early and Middle periods refer to a religious rite; (iii) until the eleventh century the Church (e.g. St Basil the Great) opposed the marriage of slaves, effectively allowing more than half of the population to follow their own customs.

The silence of our sources reflects in varying degrees the Church's bias towards monasticism, which was deemed a superior alternative to marriage, and whose sacramental character had never been in question.[309] By contrast, doctrinal uncertainty as to the nature of marriage can be detected until the late thirteenth century and in fact persists today. In the early tenth century Leo VI's Novella 89 established a distinct religious rite which included the custom of crowning and, until the fifteenth century, the Eucharist. Here again it is possible to detect the hand of the civil authorities, rather than that of the Church, at work. All marriages between *free* citizens which were not sanctified by the Church by the ritual prescribed were henceforth considered invalid; in the eleventh century the wedding ritual was made obligatory for slaves as well.[310] It does however seem only too likely that the legislation in question did not suppress wedding practices outside the Church; a citizen (or subsequently slave) was now required merely to make a stop at the local church for the marriage service.

The main part of the service, the Office of Crowning (*stephanôma*), from which TE4 and TE6-8 are taken, features a series of 'extraordinary' figures which through sermonising tradition (see notably St John Chrysostom above) had quite early become the key paradigms in the (popular) wedding: see, in particular, the supernatural unions of Christ and the Church (TE7), which is one of the readings used in the Office. Choricius' *exempla* generally comply with Menander's recipe. Let us examine *Oratio* V (*In Zachariam*). As an incitement to coitus[311] the writer rehearses the examples of Peleus and Thetis and Cyrus and Aspasia (pp. 84f., ll. 16f. = TD11a). Demophon (pp. 85f., ll. 21f. = TD11b), interestingly, constitutes a less exalted and somewhat flawed model (although it is not a negative example) which the bridegroom betters in respect of self-control and probity (cf. *enkratês semnotês*.)[312] In *Oratio* VI (*In Procopium et alios*, p. 90, ll. 7f. = TD12a) the writer demonstrates the power of Eros by inserting a *hypomnêsis* consisting of well-known *exempla*; these precedents, of course, are supposed to apply loosely to the nuptial pair, thereby complimenting it.[313] Further, the marriage of Peleus and Thetis is singled out as anomalous and unequal (pp. 96f., ll. 20f. = TD12b), whilst Zeus and Hera figure as paragons of conjugal *isotês* ('equality'). With the exceptions of Demophon and Peleus and Thetis, Choricius uses ancient myth principally to set a standard of positive comparison and emulation for the benefit of the couple.[314]

Prodromos draws on mythological comparisons in one wedding composition only, his prose epithalamium written for the sons of Anna Comnena and Nicephoros Bryennios (*PG* 133.1397-1406): cf. TF9). His remaining epithalamian works, all in political verse, are wholly innocent of the type of mythic allusions prescribed by Menander Rhetor. By contrast, Nicetas Choniates, roughly contemporary with Prodromos, integrates in *Oratio* 5 a variety of stereotypical comparisons, including that of Alexander the Great (p. 41, ll. 4f. = TF8e) and, furthermore, adds biblical exemplars (e.g. Joseph, p. 37, l. 9 = TF8c) for good measure. Choniates' adherence to rhetorical dictates in this regard proves, however, to be rather superficial; his fundamental divergence from accepted practice perhaps betrays an irreverent attitude to the ancient archetypes, which is more than offset by his exaggerated admiration of Isaac II Angelos and his bride, Margaret of Hungary. In keeping with epithalamian convention, the couple are compared directly to Odysseus and Penelope (pp. 38f., ll. 26f. = TF8d); the analogy is probably intended here not merely as a physical and moral compliment but additionally as a fulsome allusion to political events.[315] Set directly beside Alexander the Great and his foreign bride, the couple are shown to surpass the historical model in numerous respects. On p. 42, ll. 1f. the conventional version of the marriage of Peleus and Thetis is related, only to be summarily depreciated point by point. The writer caps his mythological account with the antithetical observation 'Such were the mythical events of which the descendants of Peleus and Thetis boasted in former times; the present thrice-fortunate nuptials are grander and more glorious than the mythical ones' and then proceeds to highlight the superiority of the imperial wedding and its principals even vis-à-vis Peleus and Thetis, the near perfect match: the palace is more splendid than Chiron's cave and the environs of Pelion; there is no apple of discord, because the bride's beauty, indisputable *per se*, attracts everyone's attention, the bride in fact outshining Aphrodite in point of beauty and Hera and Athena with reference to wisdom and so forth. Yet Choniates' originality is not limited to his selective and at the same time editorialising deployment of ancient allusion;[316] the author also uses the biblical figure of David as an implicit parallel. In the manner set forth by Menander Rhetor, David is invoked as a divine witness of the proceedings. It is worthwhile noting that King David is doubly apposite, both in his capacity as extraordinary bridegroom ('the gentle King, promoted by God ... being himself a bridegroom ... he will exult at having run his course like a giant' p. 42, ll. 24f. = TF8f.) and musician *sans pareil* ('the lover of song and psalms'). Here, Choniates' originality lies in the telling conflation of the respective roles of Peleus and Apollo as divine (or semi-divine) bridegroom and divine master musician.[317]

Let us now examine the modern specimens of the mythic *exemplum*. The song from Epiros (TG13) is performed on the morning of the wedding, after the bride is ushered by her female friends into the room where she will be dressed. Some of her friends remain outside the room, praising the bride's beauty and in fact anticipating two particular stages in her ritual adornment: the combing of her hair by her friends and the 'finishing touch' of adding her head-dress, with dangling gold coins (*phlôria*). Notably, by means of biblical allusion (Absalom, Joseph, angels) the protagonists – the bride and her friends – are compared with 'mythic' figures; the comparison of the bride is direct whereas that of the girls is indirect.[318] Another common nuptial *exemplum* is Digenis. This 'mythic' paradigm is applied implicitly but nonetheless unquestionably to the bridegroom. As recent field data from Cyprus show,[319] the opening ten or so verses of the Cypriot Akritic song *o rias tis Anatolis kai o vasilias tis Disis*[320] are often performed either when the bridegroom and his party fetch the bride from her house to conduct her to the church or during the wedding feast. The song describes Digenis' intrepid abduction of an unspecified princesss who has been betrothed to somebody else; Digenis is portrayed as a bridegroom and much attention is devoted to his well-known virility and the fabulously lavish preparations for the wedding. Now we may note three more songs featuring divine *exempla*. TG17 appears to be an appropriation – or Christianisation – of the wedding of Peleus and Thetis, with Apollo/David playing the lyre and the gods/angels taking part in the festivities. The people of Aegina c. 1912 probably imagined (*pace* Luke 20:34f.) that there are weddings in Heaven; the point here being that the exemplary (celestial) wedding feast had a considerable analogue in the earthly proceedings. In TG14 the couple are compared to the twin saints Cosmas and Damian, the patrons of physicians, in respect of beauty and general compatibility (cf. 'How beautifully you're matched like the Holy Anargyroi'). Lastly, the investment of the Panaghia with sexuality is rather striking in TG16.

By way of conclusion, two observations may be offered as to the marriage *exemplum*. First, modern *exempla*, like their ancient counterparts, fulfil the general function of *amplificatio*, as well as the specific one of attributing physical and even erotic praise to the bridal couple.[321] The currency of modern 'mythic' *exempla* in wedding-song and even arguably (in some cases) the annexation of ancient paradigms must suggest an autonomous development proceeding in parallel with the conventions of written discourse; such a parallel life would have virtually been assured by this device's intrinsic popular appeal and its appropriateness to a ritual context.

5. Makarismos

As a rule congratulations are addressed to A (usually the bridegroom) or B (usually the bride) or both on the following grounds: (i) A is lucky in general; (ii) A or B is handsome; (iii) A is extraordinarily lucky in marrying B, who is beautiful or well-born; (iv) A and B are both well-born. Felicitations are normal in a wedding in a great many cultures; there is however in Greek tradition one distinctive type of congratulation which can be documented from antiquity on. The thematic content of the *makarismos* in question can be paraphrased in this way: A is *makar* (here = 'mainly fortunate') on the strength of his association with B, who is exceptionally attractive or in some cases well-born, gifted, etc.[322] At a second remove, then, the *makarismos* reflects favourably on the bride. By the same token, a *makarismos* addressed to the bride implicitly commends the bridegroom for certain extraordinary qualities: e.g. TA31. The syllogism 'B is praiseworthy for her beauty, etc.; A is married or somehow closely associated with B, ergo A is also praiseworthy' is typical of a traditional mentality which sets store by external appearance, or 'face': cf., for easy instance, Hesiod *Works and Days* 702f. (on the importance of a 'good' wife to one's reputation and standing) and Plato *Lysis* 205d-206a (an encomium of an eligible *erômenos*, written by his successful lover, amounts to praise of the lover).[323]

Let us consider this second type of *makarismos*:

TA11.154-7 (Nausicäa's parents and brothers are congratulated because of her almost supernatural beauty: cf. the implications of loc. cit. 151-2 in conjunction with the force of *toinde thalos* ['a flower so fair']); loc. cit. 158-9 (Nausicäa's future husband is congratulated for the same reason)

TA18.1721-2 (the bridegroom is *makar* owing to the bride's *kallos* ['beauty']); ibid. 1725-8 (the Birds are *makares* because of the bridegroom's extraordinary *tukhê* ['good luck']); TA21.7 (Peleus is deemed *olbios* on the grounds of his bride's divine status); TA22, examined immediately below; TA26 (the bridegoom is congratulated because of the bride's semi-divine status as one of the Heliades)[324]

TA29; TA29x (the bride is to be congratulated because of the bridegroom's attractiveness); also cf. TA27a.313f. (where *gamoumena* ['wedded'] has a causal force)

TB1.16[325]

TC1.4-5

TE3.67-8 (the bride's parents are *makares* presumably owing to her outstanding *kallos*)[326]

TG18, TG20

The ingredients of TA22, though not in themselves unique, may repay attention for the particular manner in which they are arranged.[327] The fragment conceivably formed part of a choral song performed during the *consummatio matrimonii*.[328] The song's three main ingredients are inevitable in *any* wedding encomium (even nowadays) and clearly are stylised features, not necesarily referring to the actual identities of the couple: (i) the introductory *makarismos* of the bridegroom (vv. 1-2); (ii) praise of the bridegroom's physical aspect (v. 3, possibly vv. 3-4); (iii) erotic (physical) praise of the bride in vv. 3-4. Page (1955), 122 n. 3 suggests that *oppata* ('eyes') (v. 3) and *prosôpôi* ('face') (v. 4) may be those of the bride, who would have been mentioned in the lacuna in v. 3. This hypothesis seems likelier if we compare the *makarismos* of the bridegroom in this fragment with the identical formula in TB16, which motivates the praise of Helen. The erotic praise of the bride in Sappho thus constitutes in effect an *epexegesis* of the *makarismos* of the bridegroom. If this reconstruction is tenable, TA22 may be taken as an example of the type of felicitation which appears to be particular to Greek tradition.

D. Conclusions

The wedding-encomium is essentially functional and must be viewed as an integral part of the process of sexual initiation and acculturation inherent in the wedding. The functional basis of nuptial praise not only accounts for its continuous existence since antiquity but also makes it likely that the overriding content has always been profoundly erotic.[329] A great number of motifs and formal devices have been employed consistently in wedding-song in Greek culture, at least from the time of Sappho, our first direct source of the epithalamium. In particular, the considerable scale and frequency with which certain motifs and their associated imagery have been featured over time must suggest a body of traditional material. Yet at the modern end of the continuum it may be asked: which aspects of this tradition are archetypally 'popular'? The consideration of the external evidence bearing on the transmission of putatively popular motifs is at once bedevilled by two related problems: (i) the appreciable likelihood of 'contamination' of popular material by literate culture and, secondarily, the multiple 'contamination' of both sub-literary and literary material; (ii) the literary nature of the overwhelming number of ancient and medieval testimonia, and consequently the virtual absence of internal (qualitative) controls.

Under these circumstances, it is clearly difficult to document in full detail the intricate regress of 'intertextual' relationships which have come into play in our material as a whole, and thereby to extrapolate popular features from this corpus. Nonetheless, on the basis of what can be known or reliably surmised about literary practice from antiquity onwards, we can delimit approximately the likeliest 'intertextual' relationships by constructing a 'stemma'. In so doing, we must reckon with two countervailing probabilities: (i) in the event of interaction (and hence 'contamination') between a literary and a sub-literary medium, influence is likelier to filter through from the higher medium to the lower one than the reverse; and (ii) the sub-literary epithalamium, which can be shown to have always existed in the Greek language, *probably* enjoyed a parallel and, in many points, autonomous career. These facts, if borne in mind together, argue for the 'diachronicity' of our material.

Here we may return to our original query: which motifs and devices employed so consistently in nuptial praise are likeliest to be 'popular' in origin *and* particular to Greek culture? *Faute de mieux*, an indirect if highly suggestive indication of popular lineage may be sought by investigating the specialised *context* within which a given element is bound to figure; and, accordingly, a motif's or device's function and significance must be weighed alongside its attestation. Sub-literary pedigree may be inferred largely on functional ritual grounds in at least five out of a total of seven or maybe eight cases of continuity: (i) the simile conveying pre-eminence (B.2a); (ii) the mythological *exemplum* (B.5; cf. C.4); (iii) parallel construction entailing *parêchêsis* (B.7); (iv) antiphonal question and answer (B.10); (v) the exaggerated exclamation 'nowadays there is no other bride as eligible as our bride' (C.1); (vi) various aspects of nature symbolism, notably the encomiastic motif of the cypress (C.2b); (vii) gold and silver imagery (C.3); (viii) the special type of *makarismos* discussed above (C.5).

III

Nuptial Blame

Nuptial blame, and especially blame (*psogos, psogoi*) by way of ridicule, is a mirror image, a systematic reversal, of nuptial praise as I have reconstructed it.[1] This low genre was featured in ancient Greco-Roman culture[2] and is a constant in modern Greek and, one suspects, a high number of existing cultures.[3] Three questions, therefore, will concern me in the this chapter. In the first place, what are the probable reasons for the general phenomenon of mockery and obscenity at *any* traditional wedding? Second, throughout the ancient, medieval and modern periods, what is the evidence, internal and external, of this phenomenon in sources in the Greek language? Third, within the relevant compass of the Greek testimonia, which, if indeed any, humorous motifs connected with nuptial blame at least *appear* to have persisted and why?

1. The synchronic (anthropological) view

A necessarily cursory examination of a cross-section of data drawn from East Africa, Morocco and modern Greece allows several generalisations which may be of analogical value for the present investigation. Because it involves a partial rupture of the relations between the bride and her immediate kin, marriage creates a sociological transition which may have emotionally painful and disturbing repercussions within a community.[4] Westermarck (1914), 345f. described the temporary disturbance of social order, noting, for instance, that during the fetching of the bride by the bridegroom's party, bachelors and unmarried women often fought, cursed or robbed one another. John Campbell remarks that among the Sarakatsani of Epirus the marriage contract is in the nature of a peace treaty between two previously opposed social groups, and describes the colourful and humorous byplay between the two bodies of kin.[5] As these parallel observations seem to suggest, the possibilities of conflict arising out of the novel situation, and especially the psychological inhibitions of the bride and her family, can be expressed and concomitantly defused through real or simulated fights or highly conventionalised ridicule.

Furthermore, if it is true that the removal by marriage of a daughter from the patriline is a formalised 'rape', then wedding-songs of a vituperative or even obscene character may be a survival or, one might say, a re-enactment, at a much later stage, of the recriminations which were exchanged between two clans in the wake of rape. Mock or actual recriminations, often entailing violence, are apt to mark a wedding, especially its aftermath. As Evans-Pritchard observed in connection with the Kyo wedding, after the bridegroom has deflowered the bride before witnesses in his home, the bride's female peers beat him and shout 'you have killed our sister'. This animosity is reciprocated by the bridegroom's family, who refuse even to offer refreshments to the bride's representatives on the grounds that 'they are enemies'.[6] Nuptial blame ranging from jokes and comic songs to regulated obscenity is thus the verbal equivalent of the physical or pretended aggression of the bridegroom and his clan on the one hand, and the physical or pretended resistance of the bride and her clan on the other.[7]

The various forms and degrees of aggression and resistance in reality belong to a much larger combination of antagonistic social forces which are unleashed during the highly public performance of the wedding. To cite Winkler, 'The transition from the protected inner sanctum of one house to that of another along public thoroughfares exposes the symbolically vulnerable family members, bride and groom, to malignancy which is both inevitable and invisible.'[8] Prescribed enmity and envy are only to be expected particularly in a face-to-face society propelled by 'perpetual jockeying for position'.[9]

In relation to the ancient evidence of violence and resistance, real or sham, out of which *iocatio* probably emerged, Seaford[10] should be consulted. He details the circumstantial evidence, literary and iconographic, which clearly suggests that fear on the part of the bride was actually expressed at the ceremony and that certain aspects of marriage ritual resembled an abduction, e.g. the lifting of the bride, denoted by the expression *kheir epi karpôi*.[11] In this connection it is perhaps worth pointing out two items of anthropologial interest which have been overlooked.

(i) In both poetry and prose from the classical period onwards the expression *ou memptos* is conventionally used to describe a good match or marriage partner, male or female: Euripides *Phoenissae* 425, *Ion* 1519, *Helen* 1424, esp. *Iphigenia at Aulis* 712; Phoenix 2.10f. (Powell, p. 233), Plutarch *Cato* 24.3, etc.[12] The expression corroborates, it would appear, the ritual or real antagonism documented by Seaford and others.

(ii) Catullus 62.36 'at libet innuptis ficto te carpere questu': the chorus of the boys addressing Hesperus, dismisses the complaints of brides to the evening star as fictitious, namely *simulated*, carping. More to the point, the jocular and/or bawdy elements which may be discerned in Sappho fr. 110 (LP)[13] (= TA49) and *possibly* fr. 111 (LP)[14] (= TA14) can be paralleled from the wedding-song at the end of Aristophanes *Peace*,[15] from Theocritus 18, and from Catullus 61 and 62.[16] Apart from Catullus, the formal *Fescennina iocatio* which presumably occurred in the popular wedding in late antiquity can be deduced mainly from St John Chrysostom. According to Chrysostom, during the torch-lit *domum deductio* the bridal couple's slaves, overcome with drink, split into groups attached to the bride and bridegroom respectively, and competed in improvising jocular and obscene utterances – *oneidê kai aiskhra* (TD16a), *skômmata* (TD16b), *borboron*

1. A procession, which includes a young male flute-player, conveys water in a beribboned *loutrophoros* for the bride's bath. Attic red-figure *loutrophoros* by the Washing Painter, 430-420 BC. Athens, National Museum 1453. From Dar Sag III. 1649, fig. 4861.

2. The sea-nymph Thaleia (seated) being adorned for her wedding by two other nymphs. Attic red-figure *pyxis* by the Eretria Painter, 435-430 BC. London, British Museum E 774.

3. Raising the torches, the bride's mother guides the bridal pair towards an altar. Above these figures note Eros and the girl flute-player. Attic red-figure *calyx-krater* by the Painter of the Athens Wedding, *c.* 410 BC. Athens, National Museum 1388. Courtesy of National Museum.

4. Attic black-figure volute-*krater* (the 'François Vase') by Ergotimos and Kleitias, 570-560 BC. Third frieze from the top: The marriage of Peleus and Thetis. The bride sits indoors; Peleus stands outside, ready to welcome the divine guests, some of whom arrive by chariot. Florence, National Archaeological Museum 4209. Courtesy of American School of Classical Studies, Athens.

5. Older *hetaira* (with double chin) grasps a youth's erect penis. Attic red-figure vase, *c.* 500 BC. J. Paul Getty Museum, Malibu 80. AE 31.

6. Eros plucking a flower. Attic red-figure *aryballos*, late fifth century BC. Copenhagen, National Museum. Courtesy of American School of Classical Studies, Athens.

7. The bride, supporting her veil with her right hand, leads a line dance accompanied by a lyre. Attic red-figure *lebes gamikos* from Rheneia by the Syriskos Painter, *c.* 470 BC. Mykonos Museum 970. From C. Dugas, *Exploration archéologique de Délos*, XXII: *Les vases attiques à figures rouges* (Paris, 1952), pl. 57.

8. Rugged good looks, even in a mummy portrait, excited the poet Strato's imagination. Mummy portrait of an (?) athlete from Arsinoë, Egypt, *c.* early second century AD. London, British Museum EA 74711.

9. Harvesting barley: Reaper and binder each wear a narrow loincloth. Roman mosaic, early third century AD. Archaeological Museum, Vienne, France. Courtesy of American School of Classical Studies, Athens.

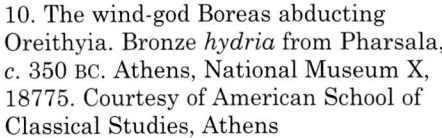

10. The wind-god Boreas abducting Oreithyia. Bronze *hydria* from Pharsala, *c.* 350 BC. Athens, National Museum X, 18775. Courtesy of American School of Classical Studies, Athens

11. Attic red-figure *lebes gamikos* by the Painter of Athens 1370, second half of the fourth century BC. On the bowl, the bare-breasted bride is receiving gifts after the wedding. The columns allude to her prestigious new abode. Below, the two winged figures may both be the goddess Persuasion, who induced the bride to give in to the bridegroom. Athens, National Museum 1371. Courtesy of DAI Athens.

12. Zeus as a Byzantine emperor with the infant Dionysus on his knee. From a twelfth-century MS. Courtesy of Ekdotiki Athinon & Hagios Panteleimon Monastery, Mt. Athos.

13. Eros (left) and a young male leading a winged horse: a Byzantine parody of Greco-Roman artistic and literary models. Detail of the Veroli Casket, Constantinople, mid to late tenth century. Ivory and bone on wood core. London, Victoria and Albert Museum 216-1865.

skômmatôn, rhêta kai arrhêta oneidê pêri tôn gêmantôn (TD16c) – which referred to the couple.

We are entirely deprived of direct evidence for the period extending from late antiquity to the modern period. On anthropological grounds, however, it is legitimate to suppose that conventionalised 'joking' was bound to occur during the period for which we lack documentation.[17] St Nicodemos of the Holy Mountain (TG37), who wrote in the late eighteenth century, warned laymen to desist from uttering jokes and low language at weddings; cf. TG38. Finally, it may be instructive to note how little a wedding procession in Chrysostom's day differed from its modern Greek analogue; as John Campbell records: '... whenever the procession passes through or close to a village both Sarakatsani and villagers line the path ... The watchers laugh excitedly and try to draw the riders into an exchange of bawdy quips and jokes ....'[18] Further modern testimonia will be considered below.

2. The diachronic view

Largely literary until the modern period, the testimonia for nuptial *iocatio* may now be considered: see pp. 113-16.

2a. The bumbling bridegroom

In the second part of this chapter I examine from a diachronic point of view two motifs connected with ribald wedding-songs, the first being the motif of the bridegroom who is unresponsive on his wedding night. I begin with Sappho.

From Demetrius' comments (TA49) on Sappho fr. 110a (LP) we may infer that the female singer(s) mocked the bridegroom and the doorkeeper (*thurôros*), exposing them both as boorish (*agroikos*).[19] The *thurôros*, being the bridegroom's friend (as Pollux tells us)[20] and presumed accomplice in the traditional struggle preceding the *consummatio matrimonii*, easily became the target of Sappho's sophisticated wit.[21] But if the doorkeeper's feet were said to be laughably large,[22] what characteristic did the poet impute to the bridegroom?

Sappho probably did not allege a physical defect; rather, as Russell and Wilson propose,[23] the bridegroom was ridiculed for being reluctant at the prospect of deflowering the bride. The accusation that the bridegroom is cold is arguably a popular cliché, highly apt for a wedding-song. Perhaps the earliest attested (and hitherto unremarked) exemplar of the laggard bridegroom is Margites – the hero, if one can call him that, of a curious parody of the epic genre which probably dates to the seventh or sixth century BC (West prints three fragments from the eponymous poem.) 'An archetypcal village-idiot', as Kirk describes him,[24] Margites could barely dig or plough or count beyond five, and he did not even know whether he was born from his mother or father. Nor was he any more adept at discharging his conjugal responsibilities. On the night of his wedding, he either did not know what to do or he was afraid to sleep with his bride lest she complain to her mother about his incompetence: cf. TA50. (She at length duped him into applying 'therapy' to her 'wound'.)

The bridegroom is the specific object of sexual *iocatio* in Theocritus' epithalamium for Helen: cf. TB10. In the four initial questions (vv. 9-11) the chorus pretends that Menelaos is incapably drunk;[25] as Dover notes in his commentary ad loc.: '... the chorus has no actual grounds for supposing any such thing.' Again, this particular aspersion may point in the direction of popular and/or literary stereotypes. This supposition gains support from two considerations. (i) The drunk bridegroom has a precedent in Cyclops in Euripides *Cyclops* 511f., and Plutarch *Lycurgus* 15 subsequently acknowledges the problem of the intoxicated bridegroom.[26] (ii) It may be possible to reconstruct the humorous proverb, the imperative *endoi pantes* (cf. 'all aboard!'), according to which the bridegroom prefers convivial fun to the bride and acts *para prosdokian* as a doorkeeper, locking himself and his friends inside (or maybe outside) the *thalamos*: see Dover's note on Theocritus 15.77. In the ensuing declarative sentence (vv. 12-15) the chorus reproves the bridegroom for being inconsiderate. From their female perspective, the painful, emotionally and physically, surrender of virginity on the first night is indeed inescapable, but Menelaos, had he planned to get drunk, could have given Helen an extra evening to play at home with her peers. A mock reproach like the one in vv. 12-15 has a basis in social reality and can best be understood as symptomatic of the distrust or possessiveness which each clan or gender group feels towards the bride and bridegroom respectively.

From the mid-third century AD at the latest, the reproach of the laggard bridegroom, whatever its ultimate provenance, was enshrined in rhetorical theory. In a total of six passages in his *kateunastikos logos* or 'bedroom speech', Menander Rhetor humorously warns the bridegroom not to be sluggish: see TC12.[27] At TD17 (cited in Russell and Wilson at Menander Rhetor 406.13 [p. 319]), a talking crow reproaches Cadmus for shambling along to his bride Harmonia. Finally, the sixth-century scholar Choricius (not in Russell and Wilson) also illustrates the *topos* in question in his epithalamian speech to Zacharias (TD18): because the bridegroom is thought to be shy, Choricius encourages him by means of mythical *exempla*.

That then is the sum of evidence from ancient and Byzantine literature for this motif; a comparable version will be noted in a modern Greek folk-song shortly. In the meantime it may be opportune to turn to a wedding composition by Theodore Prodromos (dating from the early or middle twelfth century). This *sui generis* epithalamium (TF11) is worth examining because it represents probably the only instance of a *Fescennina iocatio* in Byzantine literature.

As we saw in Chapter II, Prodromos' satirical epithalamium is formally a *diegertikon* in high poetic style. The second wedding composition featured in the Lucianic *Amarantos or an old man's loves*,[28] it is sung by a comic poet, Chaerephon (not to be confused with the Socratic enthusiast in

Clouds), in honour of the aged philosopher and doctor Stratocles and his young bride.[29] The song derives its humorous impact from the fact that (i) Chaerephon performs it in broad daylight and even before the nuptial pair has entered the *thalamos*, i.e. he unnecessarily urges the bridegroom to wake up and be vigilant (v. 8); and (ii) he calls the bleary-eyed octogenarian bridegroom a *kouros* ('lad') (v. 7). All along, Stratocles has been quite keen to bed his young bride (who is repelled by him) and the singer knows this; now Chaerephon's song inflames him so much that he immediately retires with the girl to the bridal chamber. Prodromos' debt to ancient paradigms and especially rhetorical precept is unmistakable:

(i) vv. 1-6 follow Menander Rhetor's prescription that Aphrodite and mythical figures connected with marriage should be extolled in the proemium of the wedding speech (Menander Rhetor 399.20f. [RW]).

(ii) v. 8 *egreo mê se phugêi perdikos agra*, consisting of an imperative combined with a dependent clause of caution, recalls distantly, if no less tellingly, Aeschylus *Eumenides* 140-8.[30]

(iii) The plant metaphors *komaei* and *tethêle* in (v. 12) conform to the routine comparison of the bride to a blooming (if vulnerable) flower or plant e.g. Sappho fr. 105c (LP); also cf. Archilochus fr. 188. 1 (*IE*, i [W]), who reminisces about the blooming skin of a maiden.[31] Moreover, according to Menander Rhetor 407.4f. (RW), in his exhortation to coitus the speaker must refer to the fact that the bride is tantalisingly ripe for a husband (*protrepsêi ... kai apo tês hôras tês korês*).[32]

(iv) vv. 13-14 'the rose reigns among flowers/Myrilla is a rose among maidens': the implied comparison to a rose is more than probably a rhetorical item inherited from Greek erotic writings; cf. Gow's note on Theocritus 10.34; esp. Philostratus *Epistles* 51: 'the rose is the favourite flower of Sappho and she compared her more beautiful virgins to it in an encomium';[33] Menander Rhetor 404.8 (RW) suggests that the bridegroom might be likened directly to a rose. Furthermore the formal structure of the comparison in vv. 13-14 recalls the distinctive type of simile used in ancient encomia; cf. Chapter II section B.2a above.[34]

(v) The reference to the sun (v. 15) is only normal in a song which is supposed to be performed at dawn; additionally, cf. Menander Rhetor 406.25f. (RW), who notes that the bedroom speech must as a matter of course mention the evening and especially the stars.

(vi) True to Menander Rhetor's epithalamian recipe (404.26f., 411.18f. [RW]), Chaerephon concluded with the wish, clearly understood in v. 16, for offspring. The collocation of *kuparittos* and *kêpos* ('garden') of course, is a distinct reminiscence of Theocritus 18.30, but in Theocritus *kuparittos* refers to the bride, Helen.

So far we have supplied Prodromos' epithalamium with a highly learned pedigree. On closer inspection it may be possible to distinguish several traits which are not necessarily or exclusively literary. At the *formal* level, we notice: the *anaphoras* of *derkeo* (in v. 7), parallelism in vv. 9-10, and especially the uncouth form of the comparison in vv. 13-14. Were the poet strictly adhering to ancient precedent he should have written: 'As the rose is pre-eminent among flowers, so is Myrilla pre-eminent among maidens.' Instead he varies the conventional structure in this way: 'A is pre-eminent among X, B is equal to A and (therefore) pre-eminent among Y' (i.e. the poet not only retains the first term, A, of the initial analogy, but he also turns the second analogy into a metaphor). It is noteworthy that none of the comparisons in Prodromos' ceremonial epithalamia admits of unusual variation. The loose construction in these verses may be a stylistic lapse; or perhaps it is a deliberate attempt to impart a popular flavour to the song. As regards content, we may note the following:

(i) The hyperbolic sentiment that Myrilla is queen among her peers can be paralleled from the exaggerated compliments which are formulaic in modern Greek wedding-songs: cf. TG39, a wedding-song from Crete.

(ii) The image of the partridge (v. 8), used of the bride, is indisputably a vernacular feature, as has been shown in Chapter II (section C.2d).

(iii) The motif of the cypress in v. 16: the figurative use here probably also refers us to the popular domain; cf. Chapter II section C.2b.

The cumulation of various arguably vernacular features or, at least, of features which are common to both learned and popular tradition, rather strengthens the case that Prodromos' amusing wedding-song is not a typical product of mimesis.[35] It is especially suggestive that the partridge motif is standard in modern Greek wedding-songs, as are the sentiments expressed by means of the traditional type of simile in vv. 13-14. What is more, a comparative glance at two modern *diegertika* (TG40, TG41)[36] may confirm the closeness of Prodromos' epithalamium to vernacular song.

Now we may return to our main enquiry by looking at the particular humorous motif which concerns us. In modern Greek wedding-songs, the laggard bridegroom is a frequently attested motif, as witness the wedding-song TG42, recorded in 1903. Here the singer(s) jokingly warn the bridegroom not to eat and drink overmuch, lest he lose his sexual interest and forfeit his bride.

2b. Negative ecphrasis and the motif of the randy hag

Before documenting a second motif connected with wedding jests in the Greek language, it may be appropriate to remain a little longer at the modern end of the time-scale and to examine certain popular comparanda. Generally, as has already been noted (see Chapter II section B.8), nuptial compliments are stylised and therefore rarely refer objectively to the identity of the couple. By the same token, nuptial *iocatio* will invariably misrepresent the couple, and it will do so by undermining and reversing normal encomiastic practice. Such subversion permitted and instituted by convention can be readily detected in the pejorative *ecphrasis*, moral and/or physical, of either party, which essentially gives a negative, or reverse, impression of the complimentary *ecphrasis* sung at a wedding.

TG43, a morphologically and metrically extraordinary specimen,[37] at least in comparison with mainstream demotic song, reverses the formal *ecphrasis*; it exemplifies the ways in which a singer might playfully disturb or even overturn the expectations and rules of the marriage encomium. That the allegations of the song are flippant and consesquently not strictly true can be substantiated from the chorus' disclaimer 'We've told lies, bridal farts' (vv. 19-20), namely 'low and preposterous exaggeration'. Parenthetically, it is worthwhile in this connection to remember that stylised negative *ecphraseis* or descriptions apparently characterised certain of Archilochus' invective poems;[38] the regular occurrence of this device in modern Greek folk-tales and folk-songs[39] may further confirm the affinities of iambic poetry with sub-literate song.[40]

TG44 is another example of *iocatio* which is formulated against the backdrop of wedding compliments. The editor of the song labels it a *satiriko niphkato*, i.e. a comic wedding-song; it must be noted at the outset that its precise context is not known. The song falls into two roughly parallel parts, the humorous abuse of the bride, which is explicitly announced in vv. 4-8 (see especially v. 7 *ti niphi ti psigadiasti*, 'the blameworthy bride') and developed in vv. 9-16, and the similar abuse of the bridegroom in vv. 20-8. This parallelism recalls the conventional structure designated in Menander Rhetor as *kata sumplokên antexetastikôs*; see Chapter II section B.7(ii). We may now distinguish the following motifs:

(i) 'A rusty lock / has lost its key', vv. 9-10 appropriately refer to the bride, who in v. 11 is termed outright an 'old hag' (*grigia*), q.v. immediately below. Presumably a cross-cultural motif, 'lock' signifies the *pudendum muliebre* and is employed here metonymically of the bride.[41]

(ii) In vv. 13-20 the bride is depicted as lacking the barest minimum requirement of a trousseau (not to mention a proper dowry). It is obvious that this particular criticism correlates to, and subverts, the encomiastic topic of the bride's wealth.

(iii) vv. 11-12 'an old hag is getting married / and marries her son', i.e. someone young enough to be her son: the laughable disparity between bride and bridegroom is hardly a realistic detail but must instead be referred to the quintessentially popular cliché of the hag who pursues younger men.[42] For instance, cf. the proverbs 'an old hag with a single tooth / searched for a man (or husband), the old fart' (Politis, *Paroimiai*, iv.148.82; cf. ibid. 140f.49-52; 145.62), and 'God save you from the love of an old hag / because she'll stick to the nape of your neck like a fly on a piece of meat' (Naxos).[43] The motif of the licentious hag can also be documented well enough in song tradition. Thus, consider this humorous song from Thessaly:

> Down by the Steps of the Franks [toponym]
> a pasha runs,
> a God-awful cuckold.

His commands ordain,
5   as do his orders.
     Yesterday, or the day before yesterday, on Sunday,
     I read an order
     that old hags must marry –
     all [of them] wrinkled sheep's skins;
10 they must take *two* men,
     an old man and a young one.
     And the old hags, when they heard this,
     set to bathing, to combing their hair,
     to polishing themselves [i.e. primping] before the looking-glass!
15 One said to another:
     – Babo dear, where are your teeth,
     and [esp.] your teeth which sprouted when you were twelve?
     – Last autumn
     I had some sour milk
20 and my teeth fell out,
     including my twelve-year teeth.
     A hag, an ugly hag
     pressed against an old man
     – Old man, marry me!
25 – Devil, spare me this burden!

(Tsetsos [1981], 113, no. 215)

The scenario here (esp. vv. 10-11) rather resembles the episode in Aristophanes *Ecclesiazusae* (to be discussed shortly), in which old women are granted the right to a young lover.[44] Assuming that the folk-song just quoted does not reflect literary influence,[45] the coincidence in outline and even detail between this comparandum and *Ecclesiazusae* may suggest that Aristophanes relied upon a popular paradigm for this particular episode. Further, this Thracian song attests the *topos* under consideration:

Old lady Zambetoula
with her white braid,
an old hag of one hundred years,
is looking for a husband (lit. a match)
and the bridegroom out of sorrow –
5   blood is running out of his nose:
     [imagine] an old hag of one hundred years
     looking for a husband!

(*Thrakika* 11 [1939], 213f., no. 364)

The humorous modern cliché in fact bears comparison with the ancient comic and, subsequently, satirical *topos* of the *vetula repuerescens* (cf. Plate 5). In Aristophanes sexual intercourse between young men and older women is ridiculed, the man being represented either as an unwilling victim (in *Ecclesiazusae*)[46] or a kind of gigolo (in *Plutus*)[47] and the woman

56

as sexually desperate and/or experienced enough to grant extraordinary favours.[48] Machon vi (Gow) (fl. *c.* 260-250 BC) mentions a *parasiton hupo graos trephomenon plousias* who is said to enjoy a sexual rapport with her. But the motif of the hag here serves rather as a pretext for a witty barb against parasites (the pun on *trephomenon*) than as a slander of old women.[49] Nicarchus' first century AD satirical epigram (*AP* 11.71), however, reproduces the *topos* unambiguously:[50]

> Nikonoê enjoyed her prime, I too admit – but this was when Deukalión looked across the boundless waters [i.e. of the Great Deluge]. Now of these events we have no knowledge, but we do know that she should be on the look out for a grave, not a husband.

Other late antique sources bear out the currency of this motif, suggesting that it was a humorous cliché. Thus, Lucian's rhetor contrasts Rhetoric, depicted as an attractive bride, with a comic *graus*: *kai gamein ou graun tina tôn kômikôn* (*Rhetorum praeceptor* 26). Zenobius, who in the second century AD compiled an epitome of earlier collections of *paroimiai*, included the proverb *graus bakheuei* ('the old woman is dancing in Bacchic frenzy') and glossed it in this manner: 'Of those who perform acts out of season, for it is appropriate for *young* women to dance' (*CPG*, i.57.96 [Leutsch-Schneidewin]).[51] A variation of the proverb is found in the collection of popular proverbs ascribed to Diogenianus (also second century AD); see *CPG* i.234.10. (Macarius in the fourteenth century and Apostolius a century later repeat Zenobius' version verbatim: ii.154.4; 352.60.) The *Philogelos* (third to fifth century AD), a low-level handbook of jokes intended mainly for conversationalists, preserves a joke about two lecherous hags:

> A young man invited two lewd hags and told his household servants: 'Offer wine to one and screw the other since she wants it.' The women cried in unison: 'We're not thirsty.' *Philogelos* 245 (Thierfelder, p. 120)

The strong implication that old women are also apt to enjoy drink derives from Aristophanes.[52]

The next instance of the crone-motif dates to the twelfth century. Prodromos' archaising poem *kata philopornou graos*[53] is formally an extended apostrophe of a hag: it consists of a series of insults, nearly all of them calqued on ancient precedents. Naturally enough, one of the main allegations against the old woman is that she is extraordinarily lustful and therefore capable of all sorts of sexual antics (cf. esp. vv. 4-15, 37-8, 55-8, 76-9). The vernacular romance *Callimachos and Chrysorrhoë* (early fourteenth century) features reminiscences of the motif in question. At v. 1320 a wicked old witch (*kakomagos graia*) dances lustily (*erôtikôs na orkhêtai*) after magically putting the hero to sleep. And in v. 1788 she is described as *hê polutropos hê moikhalis hê graia*.[54] Finally, a fourteenth-century codex containing a collection of humorous popular proverbs (*Aisôpou kosmikai kômôdiai kat' alphabêton*)[55] includes the proverb: 'An old woman, on hearing a tumult, said: "Give me a man".'[56]

In the light of the preceding discussion, we might conclude that the stylised representation of the bride as a (libidinous) hag in the modern wedding-song TG44 has a firm 'historical' basis. The randy hag clearly has been a recurrent figure of fun throughout the various stages of Greek culture and is therefore only too likely to inform a bawdy joke, especially at a wedding.

(iv) In yet another formulaic slur the singer(s) assimilates the bridegroom to a shepherd (vv. 25-8), proverbially one of the lowliest occupations for a man. The phrase *de (m)pas na voskês provata* ('Why don't you go pasture sheep', v. 25) sounds, in fact, rather like a proverb,[57] and it often occurs in medieval Greek folk-song as a maiden's rebuff to a would-be seducer. Calling someone a shepherd is probably as bad as taxing him (or her) with being a swineherd. As for precedents of the latter, see (a) Machon xvi.330-2 (Gow): the prostitute Gnathaena draws an uncharacteristically clever parallel between turning out swine at dawn to feed and breaking off her services at the same time. The comic impact of her words of course derives from the double sense of *hus* and from the pragmatic consideration that pigs were fed at dawn,[58] but it is also possible that Gnathaena is ridiculing her own profession by comparing it indirectly to swineherding:

> ... Wretched chap,
> are you now asking me for my arse when
> it's time to turn out the sows to feed?

(b) At Luke 15:15f. the prodigal son undergoes a complete (and highly dramatic) reversal by being reduced to working as a swineherd. (c) Constantine the Rhodian (*c.* 950), in his abusive epigram addressed to the eunuch Theodore Paphlagon, makes three rather inane allusions to pigs and swineherding;[59] his last comment may be based on the formula 'go pasture your pigs':

> Being from the very homeland of pig-and-acorn-breeders, listen carefully, young Porky the Paphlagonian, and tend pigs, for you come from a family of pigs.[60]

It is important to remember here that swineherding is bound to have low associations in most cultures; see Luke (cited above) and n. 57. At any rate, given that 'go pasture your pigs' is formulaic abuse, the related phrase 'go pasture your sheep' vel sim. is probably no less formulaic.

3. Conclusion

By way of conclusion, it is time to set out the implications of the survey carried out in this chapter, which like the preceding one, has been conceived as a case study of the enrichment and variation of a specific repertory of traditional motifs and formal devices.

III. Nuptial Blame

From a synchronic (or rather 'long synchronic') point of view, the wed-ding-encomium is essentially functional and must be examined as an integral part of the process of sexual initiation and acculturation inherent in the wedding.[61] The functional basis of nuptial praise not only accounts for its continuous existence since antiquity but also makes it exceedingly likely that its overriding content has always been profoundly erotic. If we look at the converse genus of nuptial blame and especially ridicule we notice that this, too, has a socially constructive function: the channelling of residual hostility into a prescribed form. Praise delivered at a wedding will be sympathetic, attracting good luck and protecting the couple against ill fortune. At a secondary level, jocular behaviour and language are apo-tropaic in function, and are intended to chase away spirits or visitors who are perceived as intrinsically unwelcome.

Working within this bipartite functional/ritual context, I have under-taken both in this and the previous chapter a retrospective analysis of certain features common to wedding compositions, literary and popular, and other related specimens attested in the three main phases of the Greek language. In so doing, I have not so much hoped to prove the common origins and diffusion of certain motifs and formal devices connected with wedding songs, as to indicate that a finite corpus of traditional material has been regularly deployed, albeit with significant permutations, over a long period.

Of course, much of the conventional material under review in this chapter in particular must descend ultimately from sub-literary and espe-cially ritual tradition; and although sub-literary (oral) tradition is not susceptible of diachronic scrutiny, it is difficult to deny that unsophisti-cated song exists now and must have always existed in the different phases of the Greek language, as in all other cultures. Indeed, the investigation of the motif of the bumbling bridegroom has, it is hoped, illustrated the debt of ancient literary culture to unsophisticated media. The motif in question is first adumbrated in the *Margites* and attested in Theocritus 18, in the context of a *Fescennina iocatio*; and Sappho may also have depicted her *agroikos* bridegroom as disinclined or unable to perform his duties behind the guarded doors of his bedroom. Any attempt at reconstructing the 'history' of this motif beyond the early sixth century AD, when it last occurs in a full-dress epithalamian speech, is at best conjectural. The minimum inference however remains that the motif had popular affinities in antiq-uity, as our modern comparisons seem to suggest.

We may next consider the humorous motif – or cliché – of the *vetula repuerescens*. The motif has recurred in both literary and sub-literary sources since Aristophanes. As an object of derision the crone who pursues and even marries a young man has evidently held attraction in popular Greek tradition, as probably in other cultures. In the Greek setting, the explanation for the persistence of the motif cannot be divorced from a historical consideration, namely the demonstrable interrelationship between archaising and popular influences. A sure sign of the joint and mutually reinforcing roles of literary and popular media in preserving this motif is the fact that the randy crone appears with her Aristophanic trappings in an early Byzantine jestbook addressed chiefly to conversationalists.

Although none of the few ancient specimens of the *Fescennina iocatio* features this low figure, its occurrence in a modern Greek wedding-song may imply that the hag in hot pursuit of a young match may have been a suitable nuptial joke in antiquity. Equally, it is conceivable, though not provable, that the bride herself was either styled as an old hag or implicitly compared to one, notably by means of a song about the marriage of an old hag to a younger man; here, again, our modern Greek evidence *may* possess an analogical force. As a type of formalised blame delivered within a small community by a singer, a negative *ecphrasis* of physical and/or mental traits need not be taken at its literal value, but may be composed largely or even exclusively of clichés and other standard elements.[62] This may bolster the case that (i) a tendentious and at the same time highly stylised physical and/or moral *ecphrasis* of the bridal couple was possible if not probable in the ancient wedding, and (ii) the bride could more specifically have been portrayed as a lustful crone.

Lastly, it is opportune to ask: what does the foregoing survey of two humorous motifs imply with regard to the general question of 'continuity'? Because the generic features of modern Greek wedding-songs – and folk-songs generally – are a composite of various stages and precedents, it must usually remain a matter for conjecture whether a given motif or image owes its existence to learned or vernacular tradition, or to a vernacular tradition enhanced by a long literary past – or most probably, a literary tradition that has borrowed from and in turn influenced popular culture. Whatever the ultimate affiliations of the greater part of this traditional material, the persistent occurrence of a number of differentiated motifs and formal structures in folk-songs must be put down to the continuous if uneven dialogue between, or the reciprocal interleaving of, literate and illiterate media throughout the ancient, medieval and modern periods. Even rhetorical theory, which may at first sight strike one as an implausible or remote variable, has coloured popular media: in the particular cases of vulgar humour and invective, were we to attempt to frame a 'stemma' with a view to describing the various directions in which literary, sub-literary and popular influence has travelled, rhetorical theory would surely constitute a prominent 'branch'.[63] Furthermore, Prodromos' *diegertikon*, partly reliant on rhetorical theory and mimesis, has considerable confirmatory value: the second half of the song closely resembles subsequent popular song in theme and structure and may actually fit the much-discussed evidence for an experimental phase of *haute vulgarisation* in Byzantine letters in the twelfth century.

If nothing else, Prodromos' song bears out the common territory between medieval literary and modern sub-literary or popular compositions within the same genre. To be sure, then, the conventions of form, content and symbolism informing modern Greek wedding-songs as well as other types of song are ineradicably cultural; that is, they partake of the rich and complex inheritance of Greek culture as a whole.

60

IV

Harvest Imagery and the Motif
of the Apple

In her epithalamia, most of which are metrically heterogeneous and may therefore have been assigned by Alexandrian scholars to a separate book (Book 9), Sappho emerges more colloquial than elsewhere in tone, style and subject-matter.[1] In language too, it is possible that she adheres to the colloquial register, allowing her 'vernacular' to intrude even in her wedding-poems in dactylic metre, e.g. frr. 44 (LP), 105a, c (LP), 142 (LP);[2] we must however remind ourselves that we possess no evidence at all for the spoken language of the poet's time.[3] Sappho's naive style is a conspicuous feature in a number of these compositions and can only be derived from popular song.[4] An obvious popular mannerism is repetition: in the anaphora of *pherêis* in fr. 104 (LP), in the expansion of *akrôi* to *akron ep'akrotatôi* in fr. 105a (LP) (henceforth TA51a) and, finally, in the repeated *ôs arao* (following Bowra's reading)[5] in fr. 112 (LP) (= TA22), we might detect a 'touch of the colloquial manner'.[6] Furthermore, the self-conscious correction of thought, or *epanorthôsis*, in TA51a.3f. *ou man eklelathont', all' ouk edunant' epikesthai* ('no, they have not forgotten it entirely, but they could not reach it'), is equally a mark of sub-literary or popular influence.[7]

The point of departure for this chapter is in fact the latter fragment.[8] The poem as it has survived is a simile followed by an *epanorthôsis*; its context and point are supplied by Himerius (TA51b, below): the bride is likened to a reddening sweet apple which, being still not fully ripe (*pro hôras*), remains beyond the reach of competing apple-pickers; but when at length the apple is ripe (*kath' hôran*),[9] the bridegroom, who is eligible enough to bear comparison with Achilles,[10] may pluck it (*trugân to mêlon*) and enjoy its bloom (*kharin akmasdousan*).[11] Himerius' comments beg a broader question that cannot but interest both classicists and anthropologists: what sort of imagery was employed in antiquity to portray a young person, and more particularly a maiden destined to undergo sexual initiation at marriage? Can any of these motifs be categorised with some degree of confidence as popular? The pertinent testimonia are on pp. 116-20.

1. Vegetal motifs in general

The comparison, implicit or otherwise, of a young person, or of his or her physical characteristics (or sometimes of the evanescent attractiveness of virginity or youth)[12] to a plant, flower or fruit is a persistent one in ancient Greek sources. Generally, the image of human life as a tree, plant or flower and the assimilation of a young (and hence attractive) person to an item drawn from the botanical realm are predictable from most cultures, ancient and modern.[13] Moreover, the high probability that this chiefly aesthetic identification stems from the popular mind must imply that a great many literary instances of the vegetal motif, from Homer onwards, are likely to reflect everyday usage. The sensual affinities particularly between flowers and youthful beauty, coupled with the observation that the fragrance of flowers is sexually stimulating, prompted the traditional Greek view that flowers are the favourite abode of Eros, who is *kallistos* ('most beautiful') himself because of his youth, tenderness and good looks;[14] cf. Plate 6. Given the universal character of nature analogies, it is essential to survey in synoptic fashion the expression of the relevant imagery in ancient Greek sources and to point out which formulation(s) appear(s) to be conspicuously Greek. The identification of a person with a plant, flower, etc. can be deduced from three groups of testimonia, each of which will be listed in a separate section.

1a. A youth as a flower, fruit or plant

In the first group a youth, presumably in his or her prime, is compared to a flower bursting its bud, to a ripe fruit, or to a tender (cf. *terên*) plant;[15] often the imagery will have sexual implications. Here follows a tentative *index locorum* (arranged chronologically) which may also serve as a supplement to Alexiou's and Seaford's documentation:[16]

**Iliad 18.56-7; loc. cit. 437; 22.87 *philon thalos* (Hecabe's address to Hector); *Odyssey* 6.157, **162f. (see TA11, discussed in Chapter II sections B.2, 3, C.2a); 14.175; Alcman fr. 3.68 (Davies), with his note (p. 40) and Calame (1983), 410 ad loc.; Sappho frr. **105a (LP) (= TA51a); **105c (LP), examined below; **115 (LP) (= TA9, on which see Chapter II sections B.2, C.2a); 132 (LP); further in Chapter II n. 212; Ibycus fr. 288.1 (*PMG* [Page]) *Kharitôn thalos*;[17]

Aeschylus *Agamemnon* 1525 *ernos* (of Iphigeneia as an offspring);[18] TA52; **TA53 (the young generation is viewed collectively as the 'blossom' of the country: FJW iii.31f. ad loc.); **ibid. 998; *Tragica adespota* 403 (Nauck) (in both cases the protection of young persons is compared implicitly with the guarding of fruit: FJW iii.291f. on *Suppliants* 998); Pindar *Pythian Ode* 9.36-7 (S.-M.) (= TA56: the plant metaphor underlines Apollo's admiration of Cyrene); **Sophocles *Trachiniae* 144-9 (Lloyd-Jones) (= TA11a) [the text is insecure] (a *parthenos* is compared indirectly to a flowering plant protected against the elements: see Easterling [1982], 93-5 and now Davies [1991]a, 89-92 on this paratactic comparison); Euripides *Iphigenia in Tauris* 171 (Iphigeneia addresses Orestes, presumed dead, as *thalos*), cf. 232 (neither in Gow);

IV. Harvest Imagery and the Motif of the Apple

Theophrastus *Characters* 21.9 (cited in Gow's note on Theocritus, op. cit. immediately below); Clearchus of Soli, *Erôtikos logos* fr. 25 (Wehrli iii.18): 'The solicitation through [gifts of] flowers and fruit ... invites those who accept them to give in exchange the prime (*hôra*) of their body. Or perhaps keeping to themselves the beauty (*hôra*) of these [sc. flowers and fruit] as a consolation and relief from their loved ones' beauty (*hôra*), they gratify their desires. That is, the yearning for their loved ones is driven away by the presence of these [sc. flowers, etc.].' (This testimonium is indirect evidence.) Further on, Clearchus notes (loc. cit.) that beautiful and ripe individuals are attracted naturally i.e. almost instinctively by reason of a hidden affinity, to flowers: 'For it is natural that those who consider themselves beautiful and in their prime (*hôraios*) should gather flowers. It is for this reason that Persephone's female companions are said to gather flowers, and Sappho says she saw "a tender girl picking flowers"' (fr. 111[D.]);[19]

Asclepiades xxiv.919 (*HE*) *peithous anthea kai philiês* (of two well-matched boys or youths); id., xxxiv.970 (*HE*) *hieron thalos* (of a beautiful woman); Theocritus 7.44 (*ernos* is used of a young man); cf. 24.103f.; 28.7 *phuton*; 11.39 (= TB11, discussed below); **18.30 (see TB2, discussed in Chapter II sections B.2a, C.2b); TB12; Herodas 2.76 (cf. Chapter II n. 201);[20] Meleager xxxi.4158f. (*HE*) ... *en anthesin hôrimon anthos, / Zênophila Peithous hêdu tethêle rhodon* (for translation see n. 33 below); id., xxxvi.4186 (*HE*) *trupheron thalos* (of Zênophila); lvi.4288-9 (*HE*); Peek 1541.3 (Cos, second/first century BC) *kluton ernos* (of a youth who is *artikhnous*, v.7); *SEG* XVIII 594.1-2 (Cyprus, second/first century BC) *ernos elaias* (of a virgin; cf. Menander Rhetor immediately below);

Oppian *Halieutica* 2.683 *orpêx* (cited in Gow, 142 on Theocritus 7.44); Strato *AP* 12.205.3-4 (a boy of twelve, unripe for love, is compared indirectly to *omphakes*: cf. Chapter II n. 207 and discussion below); *Peek 988.1-2 (Thessaly, second/third century AD) *hôs neon anthos* (of a fifteen-year-old virgin);[21] Menander Rhetor 404.5f (RW) (= TC13; discussion in Chapter II section B and section 2 below).

Further late antique testimonia up to the fourth century inclusive are examined in Chapter II section C.2a-b, to which may be added Gregory of Nazianzus *AP* 8.32.1 *hieron thalos*.

1b. Withering

The equation of a young person specifically with a flower or fruit may also be confirmed indirectly by closely parallel literary and epigraphical evidence of two motifs: first, the motif of the withered flower, which is a very general metaphor in Greek poetry, and second, the comparison of untimely death to a flower or fruit plucked before its prime. In its associations and its application to human beings the theme of withering is universal;[22]

63

certain instances drawn from serious literature and funerary inscriptions in Greek may nonetheless deserve notice:

Aeschylus *Agamemnon* 197 *katexainon anthos Argei-|ôn* (of the attrition of the Argives' patience);[23]

Isocrates 1.6 *kallos ... nosos emarane* (cited by Gow-Page immediately below, who note that *marainein* is the equivalent of *têkein*);

Asclepiades iii.822 (*HE*);

Peek 1541.2 (Cos, second/first century BC) *harpaxas s'Aidas san emaranen akman* (epitaph of a youth);

Longus I.18.25f. (Reeve, p. 10) *Daphnis de marainetai* (withering is used figuratively here, as in Aeschylus loc. cit. and Asclepiades above, of the physical ill-effects of a psychological state);[24]

*MAMA I 102.9f. (Laodicea, before AD 212) (a dead child is compared to a withered rose).[25]

1c. Plucking

The third identification – a youth is likened to a flower or fruit plucked just before full maturity – comes from funerary and nuptial contexts alike, that is, from poetic descriptions of death in battle, from poetic (especially tragic) descriptions of marital defloration and evocations of marriage-song in general, as well as from subsequent funerary inscriptions. The negative associations of harvest imagery in tragedy can be paralleled by the use of the same terms to denote death in the funerary inscriptions. On the basis of these parallels, moreover, it may be possible to diagnose 'bridal anxiety' or resistance in the ancient wedding and, more particularly, the conceptual correspondence between the sexual initiation of a female at marriage and the transition associated with death.[26]

The martial instances of plucking denote violent and frequently premature death in battle. We may distinguish:

(i) TA52. As FJW note ad loc. (iii.16f.), the image of killing in battle as 'reaping' (*therisdein*) is conventional; in this usage human beings are commonly the subject and the human victims are compared, sometimes explicitly, to a *stakhus*: testimonia in FJW, loc. cit.; cf. *Suppliants* 664-6 (= TA55, discussed below) and the related usage in *Agamemnon* 563 (sc. Paris) *ethrisen* (= 'destroyed') *domon* (not in FJW).[27]

(ii) TA53. The editors ad loc. (iii.31 663-6n.) draw attention to *makhlos* in the earlier passage (TA52). This epithet and certainly the surprising description of Ares as 'bedfellow of Aphrodite' (TA55 below) in the present context forge the connection between rape and slaughter (which was mentioned at TA52).[28] Cf. TA54 (discussed below).

(iii) TA55. *Keirein* and its compounds, when used figuratively of killing men (= 'cut down'), is synonymous with *therisdein* (cf. discussion of TA52 above) and, like the latter, implies a more thorough procedure than *drepein*. In its transferred sense *keirein* may be construed with a human object e.g. *andras*, or more frequently a periphrasis e.g. *aôton* (sc. *hêbas*) as here, or *anthos poleos*, etc.: testimonia in FJW iii.33 666n.; to which add *IG* XIV 2040.3-4 (funerary inscription, outside Rome, pre-Christian) *hoia gar arkhomenon rhodon eupnoon eiaros hôrei / exetemes* (= 'cut away') *rheisdês prin khronon ektelesêi* ('like a fragrant rose budding in springtime, / you cut [sc. her] away from her root before she lived her time to the end').

(iv) TA55a (not in FJW's note on *Suppliants* 637-8). *apolôtisdô* = 'cull' is a *hapax* in *IA* and occurs in the figurative sense of 'to cut down, destroy'.

That then is the sum of evidence for harvest imagery as conventionally employed to denote death, especially (violent) death in battle. In at least one instance we noticed that Ares' activity as a metaphorical harvester of the blossoms of youth might sustain in hindsight a sexual nuance. It may be instructive now to look at the instances in which the imagery of culling flowers or fruit is intended to convey sexual consummation:[29] Mimnermus fr. 1.4 (*IE*, ii [W]); TA54; Pindar *Pythian Ode* 9.37 (= TA56), 109-110 (S.-M.); frr. 122.7-8 (M.) (= no. 1.7-8 [van Groningen]); 123.1 (M.) (= no. 2.1 [van Groningen]); TA57; Asclepiades xli.1004-5 (*HE*); Nonnus *Dionysiaca* 1.351, etc. The verb employed most often is (*apo*)*drepein* or (*apo*)*drepesthai*, construed in all cases but one (i.e. TA54) with an inanimate or abstract object, e.g. *hêbas* or *hôras karpon*,[30] *hêbês anthos*, *erôtôn*, etc. Of the foregoing testimonia four should be singled out in particular:

(i) TA54. Here the young women of Thebes fear that the young girls among their number will undergo a type of capture. The scholia attach a straightforward sexual meaning to *ômodropôn* (-*ous* Hutchinson): *hupo tôn ômôs autôn drepomenôn tên hêbên pro tôn nomimôn gamôn*.[31] As Hutchinson notes ad loc., *ômo*- points rather to the prematurity of their departure (cf. 334 *nomimôn proparoithen*; also cf. the implications of *omphax* or *omphakes* used of a young boy or girl);[32] -*dropous* (= 'plucked') connotes not only abrupt separation or, one might say, physical abduction, but very probably also sexual violence, only too likely to follow on the enforced departure of young girls from their home. On this reading the chorus is contrasting explicitly illegitimate capture and unseasonable defloration with the legitimate and seasonable phenomenon of *agôgê* and defloration at marriage.[33]

(ii) TA54a. This is an exact parallel (not in Hutchinson) to the Aeschylean passage (*apolôtiei* is the only word which does not appear to be corrupt here).

(iii) TA56. Apollo forthrightly declares his sexual designs on Cyrene in terms of cutting grass. Compare:

(iv) TA57.

There is a further set of ancient testimonia which is highly pertinent to the present discussion and which should now be reviewed. We may begin with the harvest imagery found in the slightly *risqué* wedding-song at the end of *Peace*: TA58 (= TA43). It is important that the lines in question, obelised by Platnauer in his edition of the comedy, were not preserved in some ancient texts of *Peace*, as a scholion contained in a manuscript (Marcianus gr. 474) of the play informs us. If, following Dover's largely formal arguments,[34] we admit the strong possibility that these 'four crude, childish lines' – or at least the first (1340) and third (1342) – are genuine, then it is obvious that the euphemism *trugêsomen autên* represents a sexual metaphor comparable to the one adumbrated in TA54 and TA54a. Now the latter examples contain only an innuendo and so hardly qualify as direct parallels. For more direct comparisons we must turn to the evidence afforded by funerary inscriptions of a later date than *Peace*: and, as will be seen in due course, modern Greek folk-songs provide unequivocal parallels to the Aristophanic usage.

First, then, the epigraphical evidence. In four funerary inscriptions referring to premature death, the dead person, usually a female, portrays the process of separation[35] figuratively as Hades plucking a flower or fruit: see TC14, TC15, Peek 1997.3, *IGSK* XXXIX 58.1. These last examples find a neat parallel in the harvest imagery implicit in the metaphorical *therisdein* discussed above (= 'to kill in general, especially prematurely') and notably in the usage attested in Theodoridas vii.3532-3 *(HE)*[36] *houtô dê Pulion ton Agênoros, akrite Moira, prôion ex hêbês ethrisas Aioleôn …*; ('Undiscerning Fate, did you thus prematurely cut off from the Aeolians Pylios, son of Agenor still in his prime …?') We may also note in passing that the inscriptions (especially TC15) are probably the first unambiguous witnesses of the image of *Hades* as a *harvester*, a motif not clearly represented in the art and literature of the previous periods.[37]

The Egyptian inscription, TC15, is remarkable in that it associates the image of a virgin's abduction by Death (read: marriage to Death) with the image of the culling of a rose. Here the girl addresses a passer-by and, buried in her bridal outfit (v. 3),[38] she relates the circumstances of her death: she was ready to leave her father's house to wed (vv. 5-6) when she was seized by Hades like a rose[39] snatched before its prime (v. 3 *aôros* in conjunction with vv. 7-8) and, by explicit corollary, became *his* bride instead. Plainly, Hades is visualised first and foremost as a rapist; moreover, his assumption of the role of bridegroom here, as in e.g. Peek 658.7f., 683.5, 1249.5-7, 1553.3-4, is a natural consequence of the fact that he intervened at a time when marital coitus seemed most appropriate if not likely. In tragedy the death of an unmarried virgin is described in terms more applicable to her impending wedding;[40] in TC15, as in a large number of epitaphs, it as if premature death, epitomised rather dramatically in real life by death before marriage and often rendered even more tragic in the inscriptions by the fiction that death occurred during the marriage rite,[41] is transformed by the popular imagination to abduction by and marriage to Hades himself.[42] The motif of abduction by Death is cross-cultural;[43] but, as we have just observed, what appears to be unique – and this is particularly obvious in TC15, where the interchangeability of nuptial and death imagery (especially in vv. 3-4) suggests a macabre marriage rite – is that ravishment by Hades ia aligned with the snatching of fruit.

IV. Harvest Imagery and the Motif of the Apple

Viewed in the light of later inscriptions (which may serve as a sub-literary control) Aristophanes' putative *trugêsomen autên* makes perfect sense. Within the context of a wedding-song, *trugân* is obviously a rustic usage, or at least a colloquial euphemism for *binein*. Like the figurative *therisdein* and the synonymous expressions previously noted, *trugân* retains the association of violent physical action, although the action threatened in *Peace* borders on 'gang-rape'; at a dramatic level *trugêsomen autên* corresponds to the manhandling of the bridegroom by the chorus.[44] Furthermore, as in the harvest imagery used of premature death, Aristophanes' agricultural euphemism rests on the implied analogy between a nubile female who is susceptible to male aggression and a fruit or plant that is ready to be plucked (cf. Plate 9). At the same time this nature analogy necessarily implicates the agent of aggression, Hades in the case of death/abduction, and the dominant male in the case of sexual aggression, in a second metaphorical equation. In both cases the male aggressor is a vintager, that is, a cultural agent of a natural process. It is this network of abstract relationships that informs the use of harvest imagery in the inscriptions and in Aristophanes.

A related instance of *trugaô* as a sexual euphemism occurs much later, in an epigram (TD19.5) by Macedonius Consul (sixth century AD).[45] The poem is noteworthy for the allusive elaboration of imagery taken from the vintage; on the antecedents of this erotic imagery in Song of Songs and the sophistic novels, see n. 49 below. The poet's beloved is compared indirectly to an *ampelos*[46] which has long, trailing arms (i.e. clusters) of reddish grapes: such certainly is the import of her epithet *rhodopêkhus*, which, like its synonym *rhododaktulos*, is normally attached to Dawn and also other immortals.[47] Just like a real *ampelos*, she is an object of great care (v. 3), and Macedonius supposes that one day she might have a wrinkle like a crooked tendril (v. 8). Further, from vv. 5-6 it is understood that the poet has waited until the autumn (the season of the vintage) to enjoy his beloved's ripeness, and, accordingly, he wishes that her autumnal prime will last forever. In keeping with the metaphor of the vineyard, the poet employs the verb *trugaô*, but combines it with an abstract object to convey sexual consummation; cf. the specialised use of (*apo*)*drepein* or (*apo*)*drepesthai*, discussed earlier.

It is interesting to note that the harvest metaphor, expressed by the verb *trugân*, preserved its sexual meaning in the Middle and Late Byzantine periods.[48] Leo Magister (tenth century) features the image in an epithalamium in anacreontics addressed to the Emperor Leo. The poet's concluding *protropê pros tên sumplokên* (see Menander Rhetor 405.23f. [RW]) is discreet but unmistakable: see TE9. The harvest metaphor is put to highly provocative use in the archaising Comnenian romances by Eustathius Makrembolites and Nicetas Eugeneianos. In Makrembolites' work the heroine Hysmine, reminding the hero of their hitherto chaste relationship, implicitly likens herself to a garden cultivated and protected by him: see TF12,[49] probably either an ironical (and very witty) use of the ancient nuptial motif of the protected garden (on which see n. 39 above) or a

67

sacrilegious rendition of the motif of the *kêpos kekleismenos* found in Song of Songs 4.12.[50] Eugeneianos also resorts to polite harvest terms when he quotes remarks whose sexual import is only too plain. Thus in a fictitious account to his captor, Charicles cites his beloved's immodest response to his advances: see TF13, for which TA51a is a likely model.[51] And subsequently a man woos the heroine with the remark that her beauty tempts him to *trugân* her: see TF14.

Two centuries later, in *Callimachus and Chrysorrhoë* (TF15) we notice an instance where the term *trugêtês* appears to be a clever sexual *double entendre*: the hero, disguised as a gardener, meets his beloved and, calling himself a *trugêtês tôn rhodôn sou*, arranges a further assignation.[52] (We must remember that they have rendezvoused on other occasions and have made love.) But here, as in two love-songs (*katalogia*) quoted in the slightly later *Achilleïs* (976f., 1223f.),[53] *trugân* used in connection with luxuriant vegetal imagery suggests a different area of sexual metaphor, namely the invasion of a *locus amoenus* by a male as entry into the *female pudendum*.[54] *trugân*, be it noted, appears as a euphemism for *binein*[55] in the *ecphrasis* of the young heroine's beauty in the *Achilleïs*: see TF16.

We may next consider the post-Byzantine and early demotic testimonia where *trugân* may admit of sexual interpretation. Here is a popular love-song dating to the fifteenth and sixteenth centuries: TG45. *Phili*, repeated four times in six lines, is erotic. It appears here (vv. 5-6) to be a synecdoche referring to the speaker's beloved: the 'harvesting' of the 'kiss' by an unspecified party implies that the maiden is extending sexual intimacy to a man (or men) other than the singer. In later folk-song *phili* and the verb *philaô*, *philô* are employed allusively of courtship, suggesting a man's sexual advances, while *trugaô phili* is a well-attested agricultural euphemism.[56]

As a sexual *double entendere* in modern Greek folk-song *trugaô*, *trugô*, appears to be construed absolutely (e.g. *ela na trugêsoume*) or *c. acc. rei*. The profuse plant imagery in the relevant song tradition probably symbolises the female *pudendum*, as noted already; here, again, the verb is not a strict synonym for *binein*.[57] We may however adduce two instances in which the construction suggests a personal object. In the first song, TG46, from a traditional love-alphabet dating to the seventeenth century, the beloved is apostrophised as a 'luxuriant climbing vine' which the love-struck singer wishes to pluck. Second, TG3 may be examined. *Matia*, *mavra matia* (v. 4) is a conventional synecdoche for the beloved, especially a maiden, in folk-song and colloquial speech.[58] *Na trugêsoun* (v. 4) here refers to attempted 'gang-rape'.[59] The song's scenario may in fact be compared to John Campbell's vivid account of the 'honourable' institution of bridal abduction among the Sarakatsan shepherds in Epirus: 'The man, together with one or two trusted kinsmen, mounted on fast horses, waylay the girl when she is collecting wood or water at some distance from her home ... One wife, who is now happily devoted to her abductor, ... was beaten about the head and body and dragged fifty yards by the hair' (J. Campbell [1964], 129-30; 308-9).

IV. Harvest Imagery and the Motif of the Apple

The evidence reviewed points to the harvest metaphor (*trugân*) as a recurrent usage in Greek tradition. The metaphor can be traced to an inherent system of imagery that establishes an analogy between a human being and the plant world. At the same time the dominant (sexual) figure of the *trugêtês* appears to be a salient feature of popular tradition. *Trugân* as a euphemism is arguably a colloquial expression as suggested by its occurrence in the popular-style *humenaios* in *Peace*; this conclusion is justified by its use also in the sense of *binein* in the vernacular *Achilleïs*, as well as by associative erotic imagery (e.g. *trugaô phili*, *trugaô karpon*) which can be documented in folk-song from the late Byzantine period onwards.

2. The motif of the apple

It has been demonstrated that in antiquity, as in later periods, a young person and especially a marriageable girl was regularly compared to a handsome plant or fruit, and that, conversely, premature death (among other states) was likened to a flower or fruit withered or plucked before its prime. The sexual associations of plucking fruit, in particular, have been shown to be constant throughout the history of the Greek language. In this concluding section, we shall return to the erotic symbolism of the apple (and of the apple-gatherer) as analysed by Himerius. There is good reason for looking at the motif of the apple: like the cypress,[60] this motif affords one of the best documented cases of continuity. Littlewood's treatment of the ancient and medieval evidence is irreplaceable in this connection;[61] the remainder of this chapter will be concerned with supplementing his evidence where necessary in order to argue that both types of comparison, direct and indirect, of a nubile girl to this fruit share an unbroken pedigree.[62]

Himerius' remarks (TA51b) regarding TA51a, if correct and if read in the manner to be suggested, expose the erotic symbolism that arguably was familiar to Sappho's circle from popular song. It appears likely that in wedding-songs from seventh-century Lesbos the bride could easily be compared to an exquisite apple which was, in a real sense, an *akron aôton*[63] and that, equally, the bridegroom might be compared to someone who in effect *lôtisdetai* this fruit.[64] As well, the sexual connotations of a 'harvester' and 'culling fruit' were probably well-known to Sappho's audience. Where, then, does her originality lie?

Conceivably the image of the apple-gatherers striving but failing to grasp a still-unripe apple represents a divergence from popular tradition. The *malodropêes* may symbolise all the other young men of the community who competed unsuccessfully for the beautiful girl whom the bridegroom has secured; cf. the competing suitors in TE10 (discussed below). If such an interpretation is valid, these other men serve indirectly as a butt of the communal mockery and denigration normally reserved for the bridegroom and his party[65] and more directly as a foil to the bridegroom.

Parenthetically, it may be noticed that Sappho fr. 105c (LP), which

69

stems more clearly from a context of bridal anxiety and antagonism, also features a corporate image of men, yet it differs crucially from the first fragment. The antagonism underlying fr. 105c (LP) seems to be directed against men in the abstract – note the emphatic *andres*[66] and the blanket portrayal of men, presumably including the bridegroom on his wedding night, as brusque and brutal rustics.[67] In contrast, TA51a plays down the threatening potential of men in general.

To return to the poet's originality in TA51a: by means of her symbolic apple-gatherers, Sappho may have displaced her residual hostility to a party other than the bridegroom; however that may be, it seems at any event a reasonable hypothesis that through this image she gave herself latitude to deal sympathetically with the bridegroom. She in fact likened the bridegroom auspiciously to Achilles in conduct (cf. TA51b '[sc. she] put the young man on a par with the hero in his achievements')[68] and contrasted him, perhaps directly, to the unsuccessful, unheroic men. If the poet intended a particular psychological effect in TA51a, it may have been this: to appease the bridegroom through high compliment, and at the same time to reassure the bride and her clan that his intervention was non-hostile and (relatively) free from pain, physical and emotional, if only because it was seasonable and legitimate.[69]

In the fragment just discussed, the 'sweet apple' represents the desirable bride. The positive connotations of a *glukumalon*[70] apparently also account for the occurrence of the term in TB11. Here the identification of a nubile woman – actually, a Nereid – with a type of apple is manifest. *Philon glukumalon*, pointedly embedded in a *paraclausithyron* which is undisguisably rustic in tone, is employed as a term of endearment with flattering associations. Because *mêlo(n)* occurs in medieval and modern Greek popular sources as a formulaic address (see below), it should not be ruled out that Theocritus' usage is colloquial.

From Theocritus to the tenth century we possess some evidence for the association of a girl with an apple. In Euphorion's (?) poem *Geranos* (see B12, not in Littlewood) a nubile girl *may* have been likened to an apple. Although the context is unknown, it may nonetheless be tempting (and partly justifiable in view of Sappho and Theocritus) to construe *hôrion* as an attributive adjective and to conjecture that the subject of the simile is a girl ripe for marriage. Menander Rhetor's obligatory apple simile (TC13, not in Littlewood) may of course be part of an archaising recipe; yet it may also reflect popular encomiastic practice. Here we should recall that the first half of the relevant prescription, namely that the bride may be compared to the olive, the fairest of plants, can be paralleled by a funerary inscription from the late first century BC in which a dead virgin is compared explicitly to an *ernos elaias*.[71] The importance, moreover, of TC13 can scarcely be overestimated, given the pervasive influence of Menandrian precept until the end of the Byzantine period.[72]

The next attestation of the girl-as-an-apple-motif is found in aetiological myth recorded by the tenth-century polymath Ioannes Geometres in the first of his three classroom encomia of the apple; see TE10. The myth is unmatched in ancient and Byzantine literature. Conon's version of the Narcissus myth[73] somewhat resembles Geometres' myth in its plot; the myth preserved in Servius Auctus (in Vergil *Eclogues* 8.37), the only ostensible literary precedent for a metamorphosis of a human being into an apple-tree, is an etymological tale unconnected with erotic symbolism.[74] It may be the case, as Littlewood argues,[75] that Geometres invented the myth in order to illustrate the fruit's erotic significance. At the same time, however, the assimilation of the girl's physical traits – her beauty and her complexion – to those of an apple is specific enough to suggest that Geometres may have integrated his exercise with a known *aition*, possibly a popular one, or a more diffuse (sub-literary?) source associating a maiden with an apple. (The motif of competing suitors may also be popular or sub-literary in origin.) The rhetor's recourse to popular tradition[76] gives us an alternative explanation for this unique myth: and this supposition derives independent support from a funerary epigram by Nicolaos Callicles (fl. late eleventh century), in which a young woman is equated with an apple.

The testimonium TF17, which is not noted either by M. Alexiou or Littlewood, antedates Prodromos' 'startling' comparison, as Alexiou calls it,[77] of a dead heroine to a withering apple (*Rhodanthê and Dosicles* VI.299 [Conca]), and is possibly the earliest Byzantine (secular) example of the apple metaphor referring to a young woman. Callicles' epigram is a husband's lament over his bride, who died in full flower, supposedly shortly after her wedding. In addressing her, the speaker represents himself as a sapling supporting a golden apple (i.e. the bride as a prize possession); the fruit, on falling, 'wronged' the tree, presumably emblematic of the promise of their life together. The *orpêx* harks back to Sappho fr. 115 (LP) (= TA9) and the detail of the golden apple is undoubtedly taken from mythology;[78] but the allusive (and of course highly complimentary) use of the apple will recall the flattering address which is standard in later folk-poetry (q.v. immediately below). Callicles' metaphor of the fallen apple should also be correlated to the assimilation of a person who grieves or dies prematurely to a shrivelled apple. This image can be traced at least to the twelfth century;[79] in post-Byzantine demotic tradition the expression *sa marameno mêlo* is a formulaic simile in ritual laments and love-songs.[80]

The suggestive address *mêlo(n)* (*mou*) has just been mentioned. Needless to say, this term of affection will have encomiastic overtones, reflecting the admiring comparison, in the popular mind, of the beauty of an eligible maiden to that of a blushing apple.[81] We can document this allusive usage as follows:

(i) TF18 (not in Littlewood), stemming from a Cretan milieu of the first half of the fourteenth century.

(ii) TG48, from the sixteenth-century Trebizond redaction of the *Digeneïd*, is ultimately based on the Escorial version; the testimonium is part of a love-song sung by the heroine to Digenis.

(iii) TG49: in this mock billet-doux the poet compares his addressee to an apple, among other fruit and plants that have sensuous associations.

(iv) In a lament (TG50, not in Littlewood), recorded in the mid-seventeenth century, over Paros, the island is apostrophised first as an apple tree,[82] then as an apple from the Garden of Eden. (Note the word-play arising from *Paro*, the vocative of the island and *Paradeisou*, the genetive of Paradise, in the original.) The popular erotic and religious strands of the apple are combined here; the identical term, *mêlon tou Paradeisou*, is used of a maiden in the late Byzantine *Achilleïs*.[83] It is relevant that the 'official' negative associations attaching to Eve's apple seem to be absent from all medieval and modern examples.

The more recent attestations of the apple motif should not escape notice. The first example (TG51) is a typical allusive address to the bride. In the second example (TG52) the apple is a symbol of the future bride; we shall turn to the final example after giving a brief summary of our survey of the apple motif.

The apple's erotic significance can be documented in a variety of sources from Sappho onwards. Sappho employs the apple in a simile referring to the bride, and the metaphorical use of the fruit is reflected in Theocritus and, subsequently, from the period of the Byzantine writer Callicles at the latest. Although it is hazardous to extrapolate too confidently for the Byzantine and early post-Byzantine periods, it is perhaps more implausible, and somewhat legalistic, to raise the objection that the equation of a girl with an apple arises independently of the classical tradition. There are at least two simple reasons for reckoning Theocritus' usage and that found in Callicles as aspects of a larger tradition. First, Menander Rhetor, who is a key paradigm during most of the Byzantine period, 'enshrined' the comparison to an apple and, second, a transferred identification, especially by way of an encomiastic address, cannot realistically be thought to have become extinct in popular media or even literate discourse, and not least because this type of address was prevalent in the formal lament and wedding compositions[84] in late antiquity and throughout the Byzantine period. Aristotle had registered the common currency of metaphors in daily speech and their interchangeability with similes in prose and poetry alike.[85] One further fact may corroborate the pagan pedigree of the apple motif. Even when it figures in the Christian guise of the 'apple of Paradise' in folk-song, the apple motif is innocent of the pejorative associations with which Christian theology invested it. Had the motif not been classical this particular usage would have been uncomplimentary in modern folk-song.

The continuity or otherwise of the identification of a girl or attractive young woman with an apple thus becomes a question of probabilities. *Prima facie* it seems highly probable that Sappho's simile in TA51a owes its existence to popular style. If this is so, we might legitimately approach Himerius' relevant comments as in effect a 'synchronic' account of the poem: his commentary furnishes the underlying associations that were readily comprehensible in his day. That these associations, especially that of the apple with the bride, were 'internalised' in the popular sphere in antiquity may perhaps be confirmed by the extent and nature of the controlling evidence from Byzantine and especially post-Byzantine vernacular sources. We may conclude by considering a modern Greek wedding-song, TG53, which almost replicates the imagery in Sappho's fragment.[86]

V

The Wings of Desire: Popular
Amatory Wishes

> ... her mistress, having made no headway by ordinary means in her
> affair with the Boeotian, intended that night to become a bird and fly
> in at his bedroom window ...
>
> Apuleius, *The golden ass*, tr. Robert Graves.
> (Penguin Books, 1950), p. 88

1. Type A fantastic wish

(a) *Class 1*: 'Would that I were X [usually an object or animal] and
   would that Y [access to beloved] occurred.'

Two popular *scolia* dating from some time between the period of Pisistratus
and the fifth or even fourth century may serve as a convenient close for our
enquiry of 'continuity'. Because the case for continuity will necessarily
entail a historical review and discussion of literary and sub-literary material, it is as well once again to tabulate the testimonia chronologically: see
Testimonia, pp. 120-4.

In the ancient songs TA59 and TA60, printed in Page's *Poetae Melici
Graeci* as *carmina convivialia* 900 and 901 respectively, the singer expresses the fanciful wish to be changed into an object and anticipates that
the consequences of this 'metamorphosis' will be distinctly pleasurable.[1]
Dio Chrysostom in *de regno* 2.63 (von Arnim) quotes the songs as specimens of Attic *scolia* which rather befit festivals of fellow-demesmen
(*dêmotai*) and fellow-members of a phratry (*phratores*) i.e. local festivals
celebrated by people who knew each other well ('[sc. wishes] not suitable
for kings but for members of demes or phratries in a jovial or extremely
relaxed mood'). By Dio's day these two old favourites had been committed
to a song-book.[2] The songs are also quoted in Athenaeus 15.694c f.[3] Bowra
may have been right in situating the purported context of TA59 within the
setting of the City Dionysia.[4] His particular date of Elaphebolion 8, however, is uncertain, as the question of the relative dates of the events
connected with this festival is highly problematic. At any event, the
dithyrambic contest between choruses of boys which TA59 may take for
granted probably occurred in the two days before the dramas.[5] Bowra's
alternative conjectures as to the ceremonial underlying TA60 are worth

quoting: 'It is just possible that the *khrusion* is the golden basket carried by a maiden of noble birth in the same festival of Dionysus,[6] but we should expect it to be more precisely characterised, and it seems more likely that it refers to the sacred vessels of gold and silver, *pompeia khrusa kai argura*, which were carried by virgins of noble origin and unblemished reputation in the Panathenaic procession. Perhaps the words *katharon noon* support this view.'[7]

Solemn though the purported occasion was – and it is crucial to remember that in early Greek song, which was largely of the sympotic variety, the singer might reconstruct or entirely fictionalise a familiar but non-present situation[8] – the implications of the wish in either song are frankly amatory and unserious. It is no wonder that Dio characterised them as unfit for a king and likelier to occur in an atmosphere of levity. As will be established shortly, these wishes characterise a certain genre, conceivably linked to the symposium or its aftermath, the *kômos*:[9] the fantastic wish for access to a favourite may thus also be a complement to the love-toast delivered at a symposium.[10] Significantly, this type of amatory wish is also a very ancient Near Eastern conceit.[11]

The wishes in TA59 and TA60, incidentally, are closely related to the escapist wish for wings which is common in Greek tragedy;[12] the tragic genre will be dealt with in section 2 below. It is appropriate also to compare here the more general erotic wishes attested chiefly in four poets who are roughly contemporary. The idle (homoerotic) wishes at Alcman fr. 1.74-5 (Davies) are part of a priamel which culminates in the affirmation of Hagesichora's irresistible attractiveness (cf. v. 77). In vv. 74-5 the girls wish that the beautiful (but absent?) Astaphis were their own and that Philylla and two other maidens were looking at them:[13] *Astaphis [t]e moi genoito / kai potiglepoi Phillula*, etc. ('If only Astaphis were mine, if only Philylla were to look my way and Damareta and lovely Ianthemis' [tr. Campbell ii.367]).

An identical formulation is found in Hipponax fr. 119 (*IE*, i [W])[14] *ei moi genoito parthenos kalê te kai tereina* ('If only a girl both beautiful and tender were mine') and the locution *ei moi genoito* ('if only … were mine', i.e. 'if only I could get') also appears at the base of a fifth-century BC Attic cup, ostensibly a gift from an *erastês* to his *erômenos*.[15] Third, Archilochus fr. 118 (*IE*, i [W]), couched as a wish, is clearly a plea for access to an *erômenê* or fiancée:[16] *ei gar hôs emoi genoito kheiri Neoboulês thigein* ('If only I might thus touch Neoboulê on her hand').[17] Finally, Pindar's seventh *scolion*[18] features a wish which is clearly homoerotic. The *scolion* itself consists of a wish (vv. 1-2) followed without any connective by an exhortation (vv. 3-4):

May you love and indulge in love (*erôs*) at the right time. My soul, don't pursue actions [sc. characteristic of a man] older than the number [i.e. of your years].

The wish has the force of a generalising proposition whose implication may run: 'May one be an active partner (cf. *erân* in the original) and generally do that which Eros demands (cf. *erôti* / *kharisdesthai*) at the proper time of life, sc. in one's youth.'[19] In the exhortation of the next two lines the singer applies the proposition to himself in particular, in effect urging *carpe diem*: 'don't act like an old man'.[20]

Now with respect to TA59 and TA60, further *conferenda* show that we are indeed dealing with a special type, which yields the paradigm of two or more co-ordinated wishes envisaging proximity or contact with the beloved (who is absent or otherwise unavailable) by way of a metamorphosis, direct or implied. The first wish expresses the desired change of shape; the ensuing co-ordinate wishes in reality spell out the pleasant consequences of the fancied change.[21] Thus, consider TB13 ('Would that I might become yon buzzing bee, and come into thy cave'), uttered by an unnamed goatherd in the course of his serenade to Amaryllis. The context of this wish has no little importance: these verses are part of the *paraclausithyron* proper, since the goatherd imagines the component of the *kômos*.[22] Homer supports the high probability (if he does not imply the actual genre) of a fanciful wish delivered at a symposium. Having drunk copiously, Odysseus remarks to Eumaeus before forming a wish himself (*Odyssey* 14.463-6, 468-9; cf. ibid. 503-5):

'Hear me now, Eumaeus, and all the rest of you, his men, while I tell a boasting tale; for the wine bids me, befooling wine, which sets one, even though he be very wise, to singing and soft laughter, and makes him stand up and dance, and sometimes brings forth a word which were better left unspoken ... *Would that I were young and my strength firm as when we made ready our ambush, and led it beneath the walls of Troy*' (tr. Murray-Dimock ii.71).

Indeed, it is likely that wishes of the general type 'Would that I were X ...' were originally sung as improvised distichs during courtship.[23] In due time, symposiasts or komasts competed with one another in the improvisation of such ditties, and probably even later these compositions were elaborated into songs of varying length and complexity which became part of the fixed song repertory of a symposium or *kômos*. It may be recalled that, from the archaic period down to the fourth century AD, the symposium and its aftermath, during which the *paraclausithyron* was sung, were the occasions *par excellence* in which exclamations and wishes of an erotic nature might normally occur; and all such utterances would be formulated *meta parrhêsias*.[24] Barrett's remark on the force of *genoiman* in *Hippolytus* 732 (= TA61) is relevant: '*genoiman* rather than *eiên* is normal in these wishes, where the speaker is thinking rather of the immediate (and perhaps temporary) change from his present state than of any continuance in the new one.'

TB13a (q.v. immediately below) resembles the passage from Theocritus with respect to content; but formally speaking *AP* 5.83 *adespoton* (= anon. ix [Page 1981], p. 319), preserving as it does co-ordinated wishes, offers a closer parallel.[25] TC16, finally, deserves comment. According to the editors, the writer, a *paidiskê*, forms an audacious wish to fly to her master, who is abroad (probably on military duty). The tenor of the letter suggests a considerable degree of intimacy; the wish may therefore be taken as a quasi-amatory wish which implies a 'metamorphosis'. The expression *ôphelon ei* appears to be unexampled and may be a solecism, although *ophelon* (or *ôphelon*) in the sense of *eithe* + indicative imperfect or aorist is commonly used in the New Testament to express a contrary-to-fact wish (Blass-Debrunner-Rehkopf, par. 359.1).

Lastly, we may consider anon. ix, addressed by a man to a woman. Here the series of three wishes recalls the well-known mythic scenario of abduction by a wild, impregnating wind; cf., for instance, the abduction of Oreithyia by Boreas (see Plate 10).[26] In Greek myth winds generally move at irresistible, destructive velocities, much like Eros.[27] According to Hippocratic medicine, winds easily penetrate the porous skin of men and women alike, thus importing disease into the body.[28] The anonymous wish gives vent, as it were, to the same egocentric aggressiveness which apparently underlies the exceptionally high number of rapes in Greek myth.[29]

    (b) *Class 2*: 'Would that I were X [usu. an object or animal]
              in order that Y [access to beloved] might occur.'

It is possible to sub-divide Type A wishes according to syntactical criteria into a second class: a wish for a change + a final clause spelling out the object of the wish. Class 2 is a more abundantly attested than class 1 and is formally identical with the wish for wings (in this case to get to where one is not) in TA62;[30] see also the structure of TB14, Callimachus' 'escapist' wish for youth. We may list class 2 wishes in this manner:

    (i) TB13a. The poet envies a bird caught by Dexionicus, whom he loves, and in the concluding verses wishes he were a thrush or a blackbird so that he might pour out his voice and tears into the hands of his beloved.

    (ii) TB15.[31]

    (iii) anon. x. 1986-7 (Page [1981], p. 320) (= *AP* 5.84 *adespoton*).[32]

    (iv) TB16. These are the concluding two lines of a 'farewell epigram'.[33] Andragathus, Meleager's boy-love, has departed for Rhodes. The poet bewails this fact, then checks his sorrow by reverting to an improbable, almost childish reverie, in effect: 'Would that I could turn into a dolphin and speed you to Rhodes myself!' Cf. TB17, Cyclops' regret (bordering on a class 2 amatory wish) that he had not been born with gills.[34]

    (v) TB16a. Of the epigram itself Gow and Page note: 'An original motif, neatly phrased.' The motif of an agent of sleep who replaces Hypnos is certainly a clever invention; but the desire to undergo a 'metamorphosis' in the name of love is nothing novel and, moreover, the grammatical structure involved is a variation on what emerges as a typical structure: a wish (albeit unattained in the present [Goodwin, par. 731-2]) + a consecutive clause which is also final in its implications (ibid., par. 587.3) + a co-ordinate final clause connoting an unfulfilled condition (ibid., par. 333).

(vi) TC16a. This is part of a pederastic epigram by Strato. A veritable Pygmalion, he so much admires the wooden panel-picture of a handsome youth that he wishes he could change into a wood-worm to devour it. Rugged good looks, even in a portrait painted in encaustic, were enough to excite the imagination of a poet like Strato (see Plate 8).

(vii) TC17. A man supposedly is speaking to a woman, perhaps a *hetaira* at a symposium. Here, again, fanciful shape-changing affords direct contact. The mirror, the first item in the catalogue of transformations, was a woman's characteristic accessory in antiquity,[35] while the tunic (*khitôn*) mentioned was a woven undergarment covering a man or woman's body. The speaker imagines that by becoming a mirror he will forever be able to gaze at her in her moments of self-admiration.[36] Moreover, once changed into her tunic he will of necessity be joined to her on a daily basis,[37] since she will invariably either wear or carry this article of clothing.[38] The expectation of everlasting contact (e.g. 'so that you might *always* see me') is a universal conceit; Greek tragedy and middle comedy as well as a number of funeral inscriptions and magical papyrus spells look forward to a life-long bond or even one which is fancied as enduring beyond the grave.[39] The culminating command (v. 16) is quite possibly a flippant exaggeration, that underscores the symposiast's exclusive claim to proximity to the woman he desires.[40] The symmetrical repetition which is evident in vv. 5-12 as a whole *may* be a sub-literary trait; cf. the similar structure in Longus (TC18), which is probably a concession to popular style. In v. 9 *thelô genesthai* (in effect, 'I would like to become') is dictated by the need for variation, as is the interjection *gunai* ('lady') that occurs in the wish formulation in v. 11. The poet then introduces a different parallel structure, a triad of wishes dependent on a single optative (vv. 13-16), but even within this new format creates a further *variatio* by omitting from v. 15 the expected *dat. loci* and by substituting a command for a final clause in v. 16.

(viii) TC18 (not in Page). Chloë utters this wish in the course of her soliloquy. The parallelism is a sure sign of Longus' rustic affectations. Unlike most of the foregoing examples, which look forward to a future event, this wish refers to a past object which was not attained:[41] cf. the regret expressed by Cyclops in TB17 above.

Byzantine testimonia

It is time to review the Byzantine evidence for wishes for a metamorphosis. The two salient testimonia of this period are indubitably products of mimesis. Theophanes' (eighth-century) epigram, TE11, closely resembles, in both phraseology and syntax, anon. x above. Nicetas Eugeneianos, author of the twelfth-century verse romance *Drosilla and Charicles*,[42] includes a series of Type A class 2 wishes which, though generally based on antique paradigms, are probably also intended to bring to mind the subject-mattter and tone of the *Strassenpoesie* current in his day.[43] At TF19 the reminiscing Cleandros directly quotes his own serenade ('lovely songs'), complete with a refrain ('Bright moon, guide the wayfarer with your light'),[44] which he once addressed to his beloved Calligone. We note the following correspondences between Eugeneianos and the late-antique *Anacreontea* (TC17 above):[45]

TF19, vv. 332-3 ~ TC17, vv. 5-6
ibid., vv. 334-5 ~ ibid., vv. 7-8
ibid., vv. 337-8 ~ ibid., vv. 9-10
ibid., vv. 339-40 ~ ibid., vv. 11-12.

Eugeneianos follows his Anacreontic prototype in subject-matter, though not in metre.[46] In the medieval romance the refrain ('Bright moon, guide the wayfarer with your light')[47] serves to mark off each series of wishes. Eugeneianos preserves the first four items of his source (mirror – tunic – water – perfume), but omits the fifth and sixth (the breastband and pearl); like TC17.15-16, though, he finishes off his catalogue of imaginary transformations with the melodramatic (masochistic?) wish to be trodden by his beloved's sandals. As might be expected of a resourceful imitator, Eugeneianos diverges from his model in syntactical structure. In TF19.337f., attraction to the preceding (pure) optative explains the optative in the final clause *hôs ... skhoiên* in vv. 337f. Moreover, *variatio* is achieved obviously by using *heuretheiên* (v. 332), *phaneiên* (v. 337), and the final conjunction *hôs* in vv. 337-40, and by resorting to the impersonal construction *êrkei genesthai* (vv. 343f.) instead of the optative. Cleandros' implied wish at vv. 343-5 is actually an expansion of the succinct *asyndeton* at TC17.15-16. These adjustments notwithstanding, the Byzantine romancier reproduces throughout the typical construction underlying his model: 'Would that I were X in order that Y might occur,' where Y amounts to unhindered, constant contact with one's beloved.

In a later episode Charicles (the hero) proposes marriage to Drosilla (the heroine), suitably enough, in a small garden (*kêpion*),[48] and nothing deterred he plainly suggests that Drosilla might now surrender her virginity: TF20. Both verbally and syntactically the passage is modelled on an anonymous epigram, anon. ix.[49] Eugeneianos has, however, varied his composition mainly by substituting *Zephuros* for the more general *anemos* (a key term) and *sterna* for *stêthea*, which is less frequent in poetry after Homer.[50] *Zephuros*, owing especially to its obvious amatory associations in Greek poetry, is even a superior choice.[51] No less negligible is this wind's traditionally mild character;[52] cf. *eukraes* in TF20, v. 110 above.

Before looking at the late Byzantine and modern testimonia we might comment briefly on the evolution of the optative and other means of formulating wishes in the Greek language. By late antiquity the potential and wishing optative disappeared as a separate category in the vernacular, except in a few fossilised usages (*ho mê genoito*).[53] The pure optative (especially in the aorist tense) is not however rare in the New Testament, although there already is a strong tendency to adopt the imperative (e.g. *anathema estô*) in requests and curses alike; the particles *ei gar* and *eithe* (which introduce wishes) are defunct in New Testament Greek.[54] Generally, from the Hellenistic period onwards the hortative subjunctive was extended to accommodate the function of the pure optative[55] (e.g. Septuagint Book of Ruth I.9 *dôê Kurios humîn kai heurête anapausin*; Athanasius Alexandrinus 1.740A *all' eithe kan akousês hina su peisthês*); in modern Greek the subjunctive, preceded by *eithe* (archaising), *ampotes* or more usually *makari*, similarly serves to express a wish (*na se kharô! na zêsê!*).[56] The wishing optative was nonetheless preserved, often imprecisely, in the literary Greek of the Hellenistic and Roman periods.

From the time of Prodromos at least, wishes incapable of fulfilment in the present or past are formulated by the particles *as* or *na* or by the elliptical phrases or interjections *makari na, ô na, (ô) pou na, Khriste mou (Panaghia mou, mana mou) na, akh na*, combined with the aorist indicative or, in modern Greek, the imperfect (referring to present) or the pluperfect (referring to the past): e.g. 'Ptocho-Prodromos' IV.220 (Eideneier) *Khriste na tên epepesa*.[57]

Post-Byzantine/modern testimonia

The purely modern specimens are found in popular sources and clearly bear resemblance to the ancient wishes in structure and sentiment. It should however be noticed at the outset that owing to the complicated (and potentially ambiguous) character of *na*-clauses in modern Greek, a precise distinction between class 1 and class 2 wishes is very often problematic. Roughly speaking, modern amatory wishes for a 'metamorphosis' are formally analogous to class 1 wishes.

TG54, possibly from the southern Aegean, is undatable although the MS. (Brit. Mus. add. 8241) dates from *c.* 1450.[58] *Na elthô hopou koimasai* ('so that I may come to where you are sleeping'), following on the express wish *Peristeraki na genô* ('May I become a little pigeon'), can be loosely termed a volitive use (see Mackridge [1985] 9.4.2.2.1b), even though its relationship to the main clause is difficult to pin down. *Sphikta na se periplakô* ('so that I may embrace you tightly'), because it is more closely related to a verb of motion (*na elthô*), may well be a volitive use indicating destination (Mackridge, ibid.); yet even if it is taken as dependent on the opening it is still volitive. The fourth *na*-clause, *panta na me thumasai* ('so that you may always remember me'), however, stands notionally as a final clause (on which see Mackridge 9.4.2.2.5a), although it is not introduced by *dia na* (or *hopôs na*), which would have been available as a final conjunction.[59] TG54 may thus tentatively be categorised as a class 2 wish, and its popular provenance can be verified by noting that the distich has a variant in current-day Rhodian love-songs (*pelisteraki(n) tha genô na katsô sto(n) laimo(n) sou, / na sou philisô tin elia(n) pouheis to maoulo(n) sou*) and moreover that its components are formulaic (*peristeraki na genô nartô opou koimasai, sphikta na se angaliastô, panta na se thimoumai, na se sphiktangaliastô*).[60] TG55, from a slightly later period, is similar to TG54 in theme.

In *Erotocritos* (= TG56), dating presumably to *c.* 1610,[61] the hero ardently wishes he could somehow reach his beloved in gaol; the wish he utters (TG56) is clearly popular. Here, again, the syntax is rather involved. *Na petaxa* ('if only I could fly') is a strict wish parallel to the opening one (*as êmoune pouli*, 'if only I were a bird'). On the other hand, *na perasô ta teikhia* ('to cross over the walls') and *na mpô mesa stê khôra* ('to get into the town') suggest destination and are volitive, since both clearly depend on a verb of motion, *petaxa* (Mackridge 9.4.2.2.1b). Consider now the quasi-amatory wish TG57, which occurs in a lament sung by an Epirot woman over her husband, who was killed in combat against the Turks. The successive *na*-clauses after the main wish in the imperfect are volitive and hence are in the same tense as the head verb (see Mackridge, loc. cit.). (*Eithe* is very likely to be an emendation made by the editor.)

TG58, consisting as it does of two co-ordinated wishes (*êthela na'moune nero*, etc. + [sc. *êthela*] *na'nai kapsa dunatê*, etc.),[62] and similarly TG59 approximate most to the formal structure of the ancient class 1 wishes. Lastly, in TG60 and TG61 the womenfolk in eastern Thrace (now part of Turkey) bemoan the absence of the men at the harvest and wish to be changed into a feature of the seasonal landscape.[63] (*na me therizês, na me kratês, na me lakhtarizês* [TG60] and *na pinê* [TG61] are all governed by nouns and should therefore be construed as equivalent to relative clauses or clauses of result; see Mackridge 9.4.2.2.4.) *Therizô* ('harvest') in TG60, like *trugaô, trugô* ('harvest, reap') in other folk-songs, may well admit of a sexual interpretation;[64] and the image of drinking from a cool spring in TG61 is endowed with positive associations which are quite understandable in the eastern Mediterranean and familiar from other modern Greek folk-songs. The image here may suggest a wish for a kiss; cf. the sensual significance of drinking from a river in the summer heat in TG58.[65]

2. Type B fantastic wish

In the second part of this chapter I shall attempt to reconstruct another category of popular wishes with erotic or hedonistic overtones. The wishes in question are in the form 'I wish I *had* X, Y and Z', where X, Y and Z are desirable objects and/or persons (sometimes viewed as objects). The wishes, moreover, may involve some degree of fantasy, as will readily be seen. The relevant testimonia, drawn from various periods, are listed on pp. 121-4. Let us consider these specimens.

TA63.esp.1-2 and TB18 may be provisionally assigned to the genus under examination; sadly, the context of both is unknown. Johannes Kakrides[66] pointed out the formal affinities between a strophe from a post-Hellenistic *scolion*, TC19,[67] and certain modern Greek popular wishes, arguing on the basis of such coincidence that the ancient passage depended on sub-literary or even popular tradition. Following Kakrides' lead, we shall examine the *scolion* and then assess at greater length the modern evidence touched on in his brief discussion.

The *scolion* itself is a fragment, consisting of seven strophes of four lines, and edited most recently by N. Hopkinson. The strophes are so arranged that the initial letters of each are an alphabetic acrostic, possibly as an aid to memory.[68] As the connection between the strophes is tenuous and, furthermore, each strophe is set apart by the phrase *aulei moi*, 'play your pipe for me', which is either a singer's command to the piper or an abbreviation for the refrain,[69] it seems rather likely that the strophes were performed by turns by individual guests at symposia. The metre is the miuric, a highly anomalous and innately erudite trait. The fragment as a whole treats of the archetypally popular *carpe diem* theme,[70] while certain sentiments and phrases are taken from the Theognidean corpus (esp. Theognis 1039-70b *IE*, i [W])[71] and Solon,[72] both obvious sources for sympotic *thumosophia*. At the same time the numerous concessions to *koinê* vocabulary[73] and syntax,[74] coupled with the relative end-stopping and certain sub-literary echoes,[75] confirm the admixture of high and low elements in this composition.

The third strophe, which consists of two wishes with a love interest (vv. 11-13 and 14) may repay closer inspection. The wishes are linked loosely to the preceding strophe; Kakrides suggests that they are prompted by the exhortation 'strive rather to find out where you might buy perfume and crowns' in v. 9.[76] From the start the singer sets out his desiderata in ascending numerical order: *three* fountains of honey, *five* fountains of milk,[77] *ten* fountains of wine,[78] and *twelve* of perfume; and all are imagined to be *autorhutoi*, i.e. inexhaustible.[79] The singer's major preferences so far are perfume and wine (in that order). The *klimakôton* however is suddenly suspended. As though deliberately setting himself right (or perhaps he is tacking on an afterthought), the singer inserts two lower-number items, namely, *two* fountains of spring water and *three* fountains of water cool as snow (the latter, which was used to chill drinks at symposia, was a luxury item).[80]

In the foregoing verses the singer has not only multiplied his perennially flowing fountains, achieving a total of thirty-five, but he has also differentiated them more or less according to his *goûts de luxe*. The fact that he has faltered momentarily in his arithmetic progression can matter very little, since his intention in composing the *scolion* was to entertain. Finally, the topic of wine (v. 12) leads naturally to the related theme of love. (The link between the interests of Dionysus and those of Aphrodite are attested particularly in popular thought and literature: see Dodds [1960], 123 on Euripides *Bacchae* 402-16.) Taking up the last theme, the singer now caps his fantastic catalogue by wishing for a *pais* and a *parthenos* at each spring: *paida kata krênên kai parthenon êthelon ekhein* (v. 14). His sexual tastes are remarkably ambidextrous, although indifference to the gender of a sexual partner can hardly have been remarkable in itself.[81] This second wish brings the strophe to its climax and serves almost as a punchline, for it is a striking and unexpected supplement to an already extravagant wish.

In vv. 11-13, then, the singer has drawn up an extraordinary sympotic menu and includes perfume for good measure. Having looked forward to refreshment, he then proceeds in v. 14 to his chief desideratum: the company of young ones, thirty-five boys and thirty-five girls in all. Lastly, a grammatical point may be raised. The construction *êthelon ekhein* ('I wish I had'), repeated prominently at the end of vv. 11 and 14, has direct bearing on the popular associations of both wishes. The desiderative imperfect *êthelon* + infinitive is employed in New Testament *koinê* to express wishes, whether realistic or ones whose fulfilment in the present or future is open to doubt.[82] The periphrasis in question probably reflects the colloquial equivalent of the optative. (By contrast, *eboulomên* + *an* + infinitive which Hopkinson [n. ad v. 11] adduces as a parallel, is more clearly a learned construction.) See also the indecent wish in anon. *AP* 5.99 (not in Blass-Debrunner-Rehkopf). The colloquial tone of *êthelon ekhein* (= 'I wish I had') in TC19 can be further realised by comparing the later demotic usage *êthela* + *na* + past indicative, where the imperfect *êthela* arguably has a modal force and *na* + past indicative has replaced the infinitive;[83] compare TG62, dating to the fifteenth or sixteenth century, and TG58 (cited in Kakrides op. cit., 231), which similarly consists of two co-ordinated wishes, the first being introduced by *êthela* + *na* + past indicative.

Compared with other types of ancient wishes, TC19 may well constitute a unique, unmatched case. The analysis of the strophe will hopefully have demonstrated, however, that its components are largely sub-literary and, moreover, that the form of the two wishes involved may in fact be popular. To the internal evidence elicited from the ancient record we may now add comparable modern Greek examples, which may fortify the supposition that TC19 is based on a popular stereotype. The subsequent instances which we shall examine shortly may stand in direct line of descent from ancient sub-literary or popular tradition, or they may be an entirely coincidentally engendered category or genus. Be that as it may, the modern wishes are valuable *at least* as morphological parallels. On closer inspection certain features shared by the ancient and later material may even seem so striking as to suggest that the *scolion* and the modern Greek wishes in fact derive from a common non-literary tradition, albeit one that has undergone significant morphological transformations over time.

TG63 is the earliest modern example available of a Type B wish. Actually the wish itself is rather short (a contrary-to-fact wish referring to the present), while the subordinate *na-* clauses which follow (vv. 263-4) serve to elaborate the consequences of the wish. The object of the singer's desire or metaphorical appetite (v. 262) is an apple, a motif with an indisputable amatory pedigree.[84] As frequently happens in modern Greek folk-song, the chain of associations emanating from the given image leads in more than one direction. Here the colour and sweet taste of twenty apples are deliberately compared to a woman's (two) lips (v. 261).[85] In the ensuing verses the image of the single apple may signify her body (v. 265) or conceivably her breasts or cheeks.[86]

TG64, a rhyming jocular song with anti-clerical undertones, belongs to the popular tradition of the *Krasopateras*. The theme of the bibulous monk who utters slightly irrreligious wishes can be traced directly to the *Krasopateras*, a sub-literary poem which has enjoyed continuous oral transmission possibly since the thirteenth or fourteenth century.[87] TG64 not only exemplifies clearly the pattern 'I wish I had X, Y and Z', but it also reproduces a humorous *klimakôton*, since the final desideratum is both the most incongruous and the most important item; see the 'punchline' in TC19.[88] The discreet manner in which the wish is couched cannot obscure its deeper erotic interest. It goes without saying that monks who have strayed from the fast – and consuming eggs fried in butter is an egregious ascetic lapse – are only too liable to indulge their sexual appetite as well.[89]

The song from Lesbos, TG65, replicates the pattern just mentioned. By the time the singer reaches his final item, which here also happens to be a human agent, he has shifted his appetite for food to the sexual sphere. Because the last desideratum comes as a surpise (and an obscene one at that), it is plain that vv. 3-4 operate as a 'punchline' or climax. TG66, an exquisite distich recorded in the last century, puts one in mind of the pseudo-Anacreontic (popular) wish 'Would that I could become your tunic / so that you might always wear me' (TC17.7-8). Furthermore, as in the anonymous epigrams ix and x, the modern singer imagines that his transformation will enable him to touch the woman's breasts.

3. Conclusions

If I could only change my sex, face and age and take on the looks of a young and pretty woman so that I could kiss you with all of my heart.

Marcel Proust to a young man

Two recognisable genera of amatory wishes have concerned us in this chapter; accordingly, my conclusions may be offered in two sections, each devoted to a particular genus.

Type A

The *carmina convivialia* (TA59, TA60) attributable to the period from roughly the late sixth to the fourth century, are the earliest witness of a popular genre which may be described as a wish for access to a beloved by way of a 'metamorphosis' into an object or animal: the speaker or singer normally imagines a temporary change of shape with a view to overcoming a physical or psychological barrier to the beloved. The likeliest context for such a fanciful formulation is the symposium or its aftermath. The uninhibited, ludic atmosphere of a symposium must have encouraged individual or group exercise in libidinal wish-fulfilment. (What possibly underlay a great many of these wishes was the phantasy, which is especially common among children, of becoming omnipotent and changing shape at will.)[90] From a syntactical point of view this genre can be sub-divided into two classes. It is interesting to note that class 2, which is more abundantly attested, consists of a final clause (in the subjunctive or optative) and is formally identical with the tragic wish TA62.

The ancient genus recurs over a long period in serious and sub-literary sources alike. What is more, the context of a rustic *kômos* to which two of the literary testimonia (TB13 and TB17) may be assigned greatly strengthens the supposition prompted by a comparison of the unambiguously sub-literary evidence (TA59 and TA60 in conjunction with TC16): the Type A amatory wish ('Would that I were …') is a *colloquial* device. Hence its recurrence in a range of epigrams spanning the Hellenistic and Roman periods probably reflects adherence to a popular stereotype. It appears in fact more than likely that the popular wish in question became a *literary* conceit in the Hellenistic period. As such it conceivably would have well suited the Alexandrian penchant for low realism and psychological plausibility: at least in Theocritus the form of the wish as uttered by two importunate lovers (who are profoundly rustics) carries conviction.[91]

Type A wishes also appear in a serenade quoted in Nicetas Eugeneianos' verse romance (see TF19). Eugeneianos' particular choice of the low-grade *Anacreontea* as the model for his serenade is arguably dictated by mimesis; yet given the Comnenian vogue for realism and the interest in vernacular tradition, we may legitimately ask whether the content of the serenade did not intentionally also recall certain popular formulations of the writer's day. Two arguments in favour of the 'continuity' of this distinctive type of wish are that (i) the late medieval vernacular *Krasopateras*,[92] which appeared about two centuries after Eugeneianos' romance, features an elaborate series of wishes for a transformation of nature and (ii) subsequent folk-songs contain wishes closely analogous in structure and theme to those featured in the twelfth-century serenade.[93] Perhaps the most secure inference to be drawn from the preceding typological study is that the ancient convivial wishes have parallels in Greek oral folk-poetry datable from the late fifteenth century at latest. This fact points to a startling 'continuity': the Type A wish has remained intact despite radical changes in the morphology of the language.

Type B

Although a few of its traits are learned, the Roman *scolion* (TC19) can be categorised more plausibly as a sub-literary composition. The wish exemplified here is in the form 'I wish I *had* X, Y and Z', where X, Y and Z have pleasurable or even erotic connotations. A juxtaposition of similar wishes which occur regularly in modern Greek folk-song may lead us to suspect that the wish found in the *scolion* typified a second genus and that the postulated genus was in fact popular. More tentatively, the affinities in respect of structure as well as significant detail between the ancient and modern wishes may warrant the conclusion that Type B wishes have been a consistent feature of popular song in the Greek language.

Epilogue

His mother was a Christian and his father a pagan.
from a Cretan folk-song quoted in
J. Kakrides (1979), 14

A civilisation, then, is neither a given economy nor a given society, but something which can persist through a series of economies or societies .... A civilisation can be approached, therefore, only in the long term ...
Braudel ([1963] 1994), 35

It is time to sum up and evaluate the implications of this enquiry. By means of four 'case studies', of which the first three touch mainly the social context and traits of popular wedding-songs, I have sought to bring into sharper focus the very considerable repertory of popular erotic motifs and stylistic devices available to literary or, at any rate, literate poets in Greek antiquity: the debt of Sappho's lyric in particular, but also of other genres such as epic poetry, tragedy and the epigram to oral tradition may by now be clearer. Second, an attempt has been made to reconstruct the long and rather complicated process by which certain genera of song evolved within the Greek cultural setting. Many of the songs' details have in fact been shown to follow such a coherent pattern and to recur so consistently and in a variety of sources that it is sometimes hard to dismiss these correspondences as inevitable coincidences. Without some knowledge of the various stages in the songs' long growth, it is impossible to appreciate them fully, either from the social-anthropological or the historical perspective. Indeed, the point can perhaps be put more strongly: it is a misconception, at least in my view, to suppose that the descriptive study of medieval and modern Greek folk-songs, especially wedding-songs, can be kept separate from the study of critical, historical and linguistic questions to which they give rise.

Why, it may be asked, have numerous elements associated with popular love poetry apparently persisted, often with significant permutations, from antiquity into later periods and even until quite recently? One good reason may be that the everyday expression of concerns of the first order such as courtship, copulation, marriage and death can have changed only very gradually and inequably. What is more, popular song, from late antiquity on, must have been affected in varying degrees by higher, especially archaising tradition, which, perhaps, had itself picked up archetypally popular elements (we cannot prove this), enhanced them and passed them on more vividly to those who read or heard them. Accessibility to literate culture is indeed a ponderable datum, recognised by social anthropology, and we must reckon that throughout the ancient and Byzantine periods contact between the high sphere and the low was usually somewhat *de haut en bas*.

To expect that *homo Byzantinus* of the early and middle periods drew a firm practical distinction between the sophisticated trappings of late antique culture and the more mundane and, in particular, ritual and customary formulations of that culture is perhaps unrealistic; only a Church Father was capable of such distinctions. A merging and agglomeration of popular pagan and Christian forms and practices can be documented well enough in the early period, and throughout the later periods the constant, if uneven interleaving of literate and illiterate media must in its turn have also facilitated a 'syncretism', in respect of both popular mental constructs and popular practices, which Church Fathers from St John Chrysostom to Nicodemos Hagioreites frequently acknowledged and decried. An instance of 'syncretism' may be cited in connection with wedding practices: the mythic *exemplum*, which had *a priori* a sympathetic function in ancient wedding-songs, could be accommodated in early Christian and subsequent Byzantine popular practices; the historical evidence examined shows that this device was regularly deployed in Greek tradition, in erudite writings and popular nuptial songs alike.

In the ancient and Byzantine periods influence, we have noted, usually 'filtered through' from high poetic tradition to low. Popular poetic tradition might even so evolve more or less autonomously in certain cases, so that the relationship between the motifs and devices in literary texts and inscriptions and those in hypothetical contemporary folk-songs might be more subtle than a direct borrowing. The pervasive gold and silver imagery attested in wedding-songs, the *makarismos*, the combination of parallelism with *parêchêsis* which also typifies wedding-songs, the motifs of the cypress and the apple, and the sexual metaphor of *trugân* may have existed independently of literary influence. Here it may be instructive to recall that the latter metaphor, as evidenced in a modern Greek folk-song about a 'gang-rape', appears to preserve the 'stemmatic relationships' to the ancient usage as well as, if not better than, most of the literary testimonia from antiquity and the medieval period, and shows conclusively that a disputed passage in *Peace* is defensible as a popular euphemism for *binein*.

By itself the question of 'continuity' – or rather, the cumulative enrichment – of popular poetic tradition over time is comparatively unimportant unless approached in a historical manner. Nothing more can be profitably said here about 'continuity', except perhaps with regard to the four cases reviewed in this book: and these particular instances have two wider philological implications which together may serve as the signal findings of this enquiry. First, numerous formal features and erotic motifs common to certain types of modern Greek folk-song are clearly datable to the tenth or, at the very latest, the twelfth century. (This is a fact sometimes disregarded or played down by scholars.) And second, many of the generic aspects of medieval folk-poetry evolved out of a variegated song tradition whose main influential stages and precedents can be traced, ultimately, to ancient Greek culture.

Testimonia

Unless otherwise indicated, the testimonia have been translated by the author.

Chapter II

Archaic and classical

TA1 Sapph. fr. 96.6-9 (LP). Tr. Campbell i.121

Now she stands out among Lydian women like the the rosy-fingered moon after sunset, surpassing all the stars …

TA2 Alcm. fr. 1.43-56 (Davies). Tr. Campbell ii.365

… but our illustrious choir-leader [sc. Hagesichora] by no means allows me either to praise or to fault her [i.e. Agido]; for she herself seems pre-eminent, just as if one were to put a horse among grazing herds, a sturdy, thunderous-hoofed prize-winner, one of those seen in rock-sheltered dreams. Why, don't you see? The race-horse is Venetic; but the hair of my cousin Hagesichora has the bloom of undefiled gold, and her silver face – why do I tell you openly?

TA3 *Il*. 1.113-15. Tr. Murray-Wyatt i.21

'For in fact I prefer her to Clytemnestra, my wedded wife, since she is in no way inferior to her, either in form or in stature, or in mind, or in handiwork.'

TA4 Sapph. fr. 114 (LP). Tr. Campbell i.139

Demetrius, *On Style*

The graces arising from the use of figures of speech are clear and numerous in Sappho; for example, her use of repetition where a bride addresses her virginity, and her virginity replies to her using the same figure: 'Virginity, virginity, where have you gone, deserting me?' 'Never again shall I come to you: never again shall I come.'*

*Text and metre of v. 2 uncertain [tr.'s note].

TA5 Sapph. fr. 56 (LP). Tr. Campbell i.99

I do not imagine that any girl who has looked on the light of the sun will have such skill at any time in the future.

TA6 Sapph. fr. 108 (LP). Tr. Campbell i.135

O beautiful one, o graceful one …

TA7 Sapph. fr. 113 (LP). Tr. Campbell i.137

For, bridegroom, there [was?] never another girl like this one*

*Text uncertain [tr.'s note].

TA8 (a) Sapph. fr. 105a,b (LP) (= 105a [V]). Tr. Campbell i.131

As the sweet-apple reddens on the bough-top, on the top of the topmost bough; the apple-gatherers have forgotten it – no, they have not forgotten it entirely, but they could not reach it.

TA8 (b) Himerius, *Orations* 9.16 (Colonna, p. 82). Tr. Campbell i.133

It was Sappho who compared the girl to an apple ... and likened the bridegroom to Achilles and put the young man on a par with the hero in his achievements.

TA9 Sapph. fr. 115 (LP). Tr. Campbell i.139

To what may I well compare you, dear bridegroom? I compare you above all to a slender sapling.

TA10 Ar. *Av.* 1706-14 (Dunbar). Tr. Sommerstein (1987), 193f., with modifications

Second Herald: O you whose fortune is entirely good, with blessings too great to express, O thrice-happy winged race of birds, welcome your monarch to his opulent halls! For he approaches, shining as no brilliant star in gold-gleaming course has ever shone to behold, nor has the far-gleaming splendour of the sun's rays ever so shone out as does he who comes, bringing with him a wife of beauty unspeakable to describe, and wielding the thunderbolt, the winged weapon of Zeus.

TA11 *Od.* 6.149-69. Tr. Murray-Dimock i.231f.

'I clasp your knees, my queen – are you a goddess, or are you mortal? If you are a goddess, one of those who hold broad heaven, to Artemis, the daughter of great Zeus, I liken you most nearly in looks and in stature and in form. But if you are one of mortals who dwell upon the earth, thrice-blessed then are your father and your honoured mother, and thrice-blessed your brothers. Great must be the joy with which their hearts are always warmed because of you, as they see you entering the dance, a flower so fair. But that man in his turn is blessed in heart above all others, who shall prevail with his gifts of wooing and lead you to his home. For never yet have my eyes looked upon a mortal such as you, whether man or woman. Now in Delos once I saw such a thing, a young shoot of a palm springing up beside the altar of Apollo – ... – in the same way, when I saw that, I marveled long at heart, for never yet did such a tree spring up from earth. In like manner, lady, I marvel at you, and am amazed, and fear greatly to touch your knees ...'

TA11a S. *Trach.* 144-9 (Lloyd-Jones). Tr. Lloyd-Jones (1994), 145

For such are the places of its own where youth is nourished, and it is afflicted neither by the sun god's heat, nor by rain, nor any winds, but uplifts its life in pleasures, untroubled, till the time when one is called a woman rather than a maiden, and gets during the night one's share of worries ...

TA12 *Od.* 6.100-9. Tr. Murray-Dimock i.227f.

... they threw off their headgear and fell to playing at ball, and white-armed Nausicaa was leader in the song. And even as Artemis, the archer, roves over the mountains, along the ridges of lofty Taygetus or Erymanthus, joying in the pursuit of boars and swift deer, and the wood nymphs, daughters of Zeus who bears the aegis, share her sport, and Leto is glad at heart – high above them all Artemis holds her head and brows, and easily may she be known, though all are beautiful – so amid her handmaids shone the unwed maiden.

TA13 *Od.* 6.243-5. Tr. Murray-Dimock i.239

'... but now he is like the gods, who hold broad heaven. Would that such a man as he might be called my husband, dwelling here, and that it might please him to remain here.'

TA14 Sapph. fr. 111 (LP). Tr. Campbell i.137

On high the roof – Hymenaeus! – raise up, you carpenters – Hymenaeus*! The bridegroom is coming, the equal of Ares, much larger than a large man.

*The position of this refrain is uncertain [tr.'s note].

TA15 Sapph. fr. 23 (LP). Tr. Campbell i.73f.

... [hoped?] ... of love ... [for when] I look at you face to face, [not even] Hermione [seems to be] like you, and to compare you to golden-haired Helen [is not unseemly] ... mortal women; and be assured, by your ... [you] would [free?] me from all my cares ... (dewy) banks ... to stay awake all night ...

TA16 Sapph. fr. 141 (LP). Tr. Campbell i.155f.

There a bowl of ambrosia had been mixed, and Hermes took the jug and poured wine for the gods. They* all held drinking-cups, and they offered libations and prayed for all manner of blessings on the bridegroom.

*This sentence does not necessarily follow without a break [tr.'s note].

TA17 E. *IA* 1036-79 (Günther). Tr. Morwood (1997), 115-16

Chorus (*sings*): What joyous sounds did the god
of marriage song ring out
to the strains of the Libyan lotus pipe
and the lyre that loves the dance
and the pipes of reed,
when the fair-tressed Muses of Pieria
who stamp their golden sandals on the ground
at the feasts of the gods
came along the ridge of Mount Pelion
to the wedding of Peleus,
celebrating in their melodious songs
Thetis and the grandson of Aeacus
on the centaurs' mountains throughout Pelion's woods?
And the descendant of Dardanus,
the beloved plaything of Zeus' bed,
was drawing off wine
mixed in the depths of golden bowls,
Ganymede the Phrygian.
And along the bright white sands
the fifty daughters of Nereus
celebrated the wedding as they twirled
in the circles of the dance.
And with their staffs of silver fir, with their garlands
of fresh foliage, the revelling company
of human horses, the centaurs, came
to the feast of the gods and the wine-bowl of Bacchus
and loudly they cried: 'O daughter of Nereus,
the son you bear
will be a great light to Thessaly –

so Chiron, instructed in the art of Phoebus,
has declared.
He will come at the head of his Myrmidons
with their spears and shields
to burn the famous land of Priam to ashes,
his body clad in his suit of golden armour,
the work of Hephaestus' forge,
which he will receive as a gift
from his divine mother,
from Thetis who bore him.'
Then it was that the gods poured blessings
on the wedding of the first of the Nereids,
and daughter of a noble father,
and her marriage with Peleus.

TA18 Ar. *Av.* 1720-42[b], 1748-54 (Dunbar). Tr. Sommerstein (1987), 195f., with modifications

> *Chorus*: Arise, stand aside, form a front, make way!
> fly round him who is blest with blest fortune!
> Oh, oh! her charm, her beauty!
> How enviable for this city the marriage you have made!
> *Chorus-Leader*: Great, great is the good fortune that surrounds the race of birds
> thanks to this man: so now welcome
> with marriage-procession songs and bridal chants
> our lord and his Princess.
> *Chorus*: Once upon a time Olympian Hera
> and the Great One who ruled over the gods
> from his lofty throne
> were united by the Fates
> with such a wedding-song as this.
>
> Hymen O, Hymenaeus Oh!
> Hymen O, Hymenaeus Oh!
>
> And all-flourishing young Eros
> of the golden wings guided
> the tautened reins
> as groomsman at the wedding of Zeus
> and the blessed Hera.
>
> Hymen O, Hymenaeus Oh!
> Hymen O, Hymenaeus Oh! ...
>
> O mighty golden blaze of the lightning!
> O immortal fiery bolt of Zeus!
> O thunders that rumble beneath the earth
> and at the same time bring down the rain!
> With you this man now shakes the earth;
> he has gained power over all that Zeus possessed
> and Princess too, who sat by Zeus's throne, is his.
>
> Hymen O, Hymenaeus Oh!

TA19 (a) Ar. *Av.* 1755-62 (Dunbar). Tr. Sommerstein (1987), 197f., with modifications

> *Peisetaeros*: Now follow the marriage-festivity,

all you winged tribes
of my fellow-singers, to the sacred ground of Zeus
and to the bridal bed.
[*to Princess*]: Stretch out your hand,
blest one, take hold
of my wings, and dance with me;
I'll lift and bear you up.
[*Peisetaerus and Princess lead the way out, dancing; the chorus follow, singing
as they go.*]

TA19 (b) Ar. *Av.* 1763-5 (Dunbar). Tr. Sommerstein (1987), 199

Chorus: Alalalai! Hail Paean!
Hurrah for your triumph,
O most exalted of gods!

TA20 E. *Hel.* 638-40 (Kannicht)

Menelaos: I hold [my wife, the daughter of Zeus and Leda] ...
<*Helen*>: whom my brothers, those young men on white horses,
pronounced happy, happy [*ôlbisan, ôlbisan*] [in my wedding procession] ...

TA21 Hes. fr. 211.7-14 (MW)

[lacuna] he reached Phthia, mother of flocks,
bringing many possessions from spacious Iolkos,
Peleus Aiakidês, beloved to the immortal gods.
When the people saw him, all marvelled in their hearts,
how he sacked a well-built city and how he achieved
a delightful marriage and all spoke these words:
'Thrice-blessed [*makar*] Aiakidês and four times prosperous Peleus,
[lacuna] a great gift Olympian Zeus whose voice resounds afar
[lacuna] the blessed gods brought to fulfilment;
who, mounting the holy marriage-bed in these halls
[lacuna] father Zeus, son of Kronos made ...'

TA22 Sapph. fr. 112 (LP). Tr. Campbell i.137

Happy bridegroom, your marriage has been fulfilled as you prayed, you have the
girl for whom you prayed ... Your* form is graceful, your eyes ... gentle, and love
streams over your beautiful face ... Aphrodite has honoured you outstandingly.

*These words are addressed to the bride [see tr.'s note].

TA22x E. *Cycl.* 511-12 (Seaford)

Chorus: With a lovely look in his eyes,
he goes forth in beauty from the halls

TA23 Pi. *P.* 3.88-93 (S.-M.). Tr. Race i.255

... yet they are said to have attained
the highest happiness of any men, for they even heard
the golden-crowned Muses singing on the mountain and
in seven-gated Thebes, when one married ox-eyed Harmonia,
the other Thetis, wise-counseling Nereus' famous daughter;

the gods feasted with both of them,
and they beheld the regal children of Kronos on their golden thrones and
received
their wedding gifts.

TA24 E. *Andr.* 1218

> *Chorus*: It was in vain that the gods pronounced you happy [*ôlbisan*] at your wedding.

TA25 E. *Alc.* 918-21

> *Admetos*:... a noisy band of revellers followed, pronouncing my dead wife and me happy [*olbisdôn*] because, being of noble family, the offspring, both of us, of *aristoi*, we were a married couple.

TA26 E. *Phaëth.* 227, 240-4 (Diggle)

> *Maidens*: Humên, humên!
>   O blessed one [*makar*], O king greater even in prosperity [*olbos*] [sc. than other kings], because you will marry a goddess and throughout the boundless earth you will be celebrated in song as the only mortal son-in-law of the gods.

TA27 (a) E. *Tr.* 308-14 (Biehl). Tr. Kovacs iv. 47, slightly modified

> *Cassandra*: Raise it, bring it on, bring a light! I honour, I make gleam <for you> (see, see!)
> with torch fire this holy place, Lord Hymenaeus!
> <Hurray!> Blessed is the bridegroom,
> blessed too am I, to a king's bed
> in Argos wedded!
> Hymen, Oh Hymenaeus, Hymen!*

> *The marriage cry addressed to Hymen, the god of marriage (see tr.'s note).

TA27 (b) E. *Tr.* 331-41 (Biehl)

> *Cassandra*: Humên, Oh Humenaios, Humên. Dance, mother, laugh loud; whirl here and there, joining your loving step with the measure of my feet. Shout the refrain *Humên O* together with the blessed songs [*makariais aoidais*] and joyous shouts of brides! Come, O daughters of Phrygia, with your lovely clothes, sing of the man destined for my wedding bed, my husband!

TA28 Ar. *Pax* 1334-53 (Olson); cf. TA33x, Ar. *Pax* 1363-4 (Olson). Tr. Sommerstein (1985), 131f., with modifications

> *Chorus*: Hymen, Hymenaeus, Oh!
> Hymen, Hymenaeus, Oh!
> Thrice-happy one, how deservedly
> you now enjoy these blessings!
> Hymen, Hymenaeus, Oh!
> Hymen, Hymenaeus, Oh!
> [*Fullfruit is brought to the chorus, and raised on the shoulders of two of them.*]
> *First Semichorus*: What shall we do with her?
> *Second Semichorus*: What shall we do with her?
> *First Semichorus*: We'll 'harvest' her!
> *Second Semichorus*: We'll 'harvest' her!
> *First Semichorus*: Now, let's us in the front rank
> lift up the bridegroom
> and carry him, men!
> *Chorus*: Hymen, Hymenaeus, Oh!
> Hymen, Hymenaeus, Oh!
> Hymen, Hymenaeus, Oh!
> Hymen, Hymenaeus, Oh!

Testimonia to Chapter II

TA29 E. *IA* 1404-11 (Günther). Tr. Morwood (1997), 126

Achilles: Child of Agamemnon, a god meant to make me happy – if I could only win you as a wife. I envy Greece because she is blessed in you and you because you are blessed in Greece. Your words were noble and worthy of your fatherland. … and you have pondered on what is good and what is inevitable. Now that I have seen your character, I long still more to marry you.

TA29x Eub. fr. 102.1-5 (*PCG*, v. 249 [K.-A.])

O blessed [*makar*] for having in her bedroom / soapwort that is wafted through the air, / it clings close to a body* most delicate / [?]** round a bridegroom with beautiful hair, / as ivy grows round a reed, / [?]** having melted away through love / of a tree-frog[?]

*Presumably the bride.
**Text uncertain.

TA30 E. *Hel.* 375-7 (Kannicht). Tr. Morwood (1997), 130

Helen: O happy [*makar*] Callisto, once a maiden in Arcadia,
who climbed from Zeus' bed on four paws

TA31 E. *HF* 492-3

Megaira: I too am destroyed, I who once was called blessed [*makaria*] by mortals on account of you [sc. Heracles].

TA32 E. *Hel.* 1433-5 (Kannicht). Tr. Morwood (1997), 161

Theoclymenos: My whole land must ring with joyous [*makariais*] songs so that men may envy my wedding with Helen.

TA33 Sapph. fr. 103 (LP). Tr. Campbell i.129

(1) … for … speak …
(2) [Sing of] the bride with her beautiful feet …
(3) … the violet-robed daughter of Zeus …
(4) … putting aside anger … violet-robed …
(5) [Hither,] holy Graces and Pierian Muses
(6) … when … song(s) … the mind …
(7) … hearing a clear song …
(8) … bridegroom, for annoying [to?] companions …
(9) … her hair, putting down the lyre …
(10) … golden-sandalled Dawn …

TA33x Ar. *Pax* 1357-60 (Olson). Tr. Sommerstein (1985), 133, with modifications

Chorus: Hymen, Hymenaeus, Oh!
Hymen, Hymenaeus, Oh!
His is long and thick -
And *her* fig is sweet.

TA34 *inc. auct.* fr. 26 (LP) (= Sapph. fr. 103 b [V]). Tr. Campbell i.129

… chamber … the bride with her beautiful feet …

TA35 (a) *Il.* 6.376-86. Tr. Murray-Wyatt i.303

'Come now, serving women, tell me true; where went white-armed Andromache from the hall? Is she gone to the house of any of my sisters or my brothers' fair-robed wives, or to the shrine of Athene, where the other fair-tressed women of Troy are seeking to propitiate the dread goddess?'

Then a willing housekeeper spoke to him, saying: 'Hector, since you urgently command us to tell you true, neither is she gone to any of your sisters or your brothers' fair-robed wives, nor to the shrine of Athene, where the other fair-tressed Trojen women are seeking to propitiate the dread goddess; but she went to the great wall of Ilios ...'

TA35 (b) *Od.* 2.28-46 (a composite question followed by a composite answer)

TA36 Sapph. fr. 140a (LP) (= 140 [V]). Tr. Campbell i.155

'Delicate Adonis is dying, Cytherea; what are we to do?'
'Beat your breasts, girls, and tear your clothes.'

TA37 (a) *CEG* I 459 (Rhodes, *c.* 600-575 BC)

[*Side A*] This memorial [sc. of an athletic victory?] I, Idameneus, made so that I might enjoy eternal fame [*kleos*].
[*Side B*] May Zeus annihilate whoever should harm it!

TA37 (b) *CEG* I 456 (Thera, sixth century BC?)

Eumastas, son of Kritoboulos, lifted me [sc. a heavy stone] off the ground.

TA38 *CEG* I 120 (Thessaly [Demetrias], *c.* 450 BC?)

Sphinx, Hades' hound, what vengeance [do you bear] that you [always] watch over me, / sitting [sc. you] ... in my death? / Stranger, ...

TA39 Simon. epigr. XXXI (Campbell iii.548). Tr. Campbell iii.549

– Give your name, father's name, native city and victory.

– Casmylus, Euagoras, Rhodes, Pythian boxing.

TA40 Testimonia in M. Alexiou (1974), 232 n. 16

TA41 *carm. pop.* 852 (*PMG*)

Athenaeus, *Scholars at Dinner* (on dances). Tr. Campbell v.239, slightly modified

In private life there was also the one [sc. dance] called *Flowers*, which they danced putting actions to the following words:

Where are my roses, where are my violets, where are my beautiful celery-flowers?
– Here are your roses, here are your violets, here are your beautiful celery-flowers.

TA42 *carm. pop.* 876c (*PMG*). Tr. Campbell v.261

Torti-tortoise, a girls' game, is rather like The Pot (see fr. 875): one girl sits and is called 'tortoise', and the others run round her asking

Torti-tortoise, what are you doing in the middle?

and she answers

I'm weaving a web of Milesian wool.

Then they shout back

And how did your son die?

and she answers

He jumped from white horses* into the sea.

*I.e. from a horse-drawn chariot [tr.'s note].

TA43 Ar. *Pax* 1340-3 (Olson)

> *First Semichorus*: What shall we do with her?
> *Second Semichorus*: What shall we do with her?
> *First Semichorus*: We'll 'harvest' her!
> *Second Semichorus*: We'll 'harvest' her!

TA44 Sapph. fr. 30 (LP); also cf. Sapph. fr. 43 (LP). Tr. Campbell i.79

... night ... maidens ... all night long ... might sing of the love between you and the violet-robed bride. Come, wake up: go [and fetch] the young bachelors of your own age, so that we may see [less] sleep than the clear-voiced [bird].*

*The nightingale [tr.'s note].

TA45 *inc. auct.* fr. 24 (LP) (= Sapph. fr. 117b [V])

[Text uncertain] *Humênaion!*

TA46 Sapph. fr. 116 (LP) Tr. Campbell i.139

Farewell, bride, farewell, worthy bridegroom

TA47 Sapph. fr. 117 (LP). Tr. Campbell i.139

Farewell, bride, and farewell the bridegroom.

TA48 Pi. fr. 128 c. 6-8 (Race ii.362). Tr. Race ii.363

The one* sang *ailinon* for long-haired Linos;
another sang of Hymenaios, whom the last of hymns** took
when at night his skin was first touched in marriage

*Presumably 'song' is the subject. [ed.'s note].
**I.e. a dirge, when he died on his wedding night [ed.'s note].

Hellenistic

TB1 Theoc. 18.9-21. Tr. Gow (1952), 141f.

'So early hast thou fallen asleep, dear bridegroom? art thou then so heavy-limbed, so fond of slumber? or hadst thou been drinking overmuch when thou castest thyself down on thy bed? If thou wast eager to sleep so early thou should'st have slept alone, and should'st have left the maid with other maids at her loving mother's side to play till late toward the dawn, for to-morrow's morrow and its morrow, and all the years to be, Menelaus, she is thy bride.'

'Happy groom, some good man sneezed for thy success, when with the other princes thou camest to Sparta, and of all the heroes thou alone shalt have Zeus, son of Cronos, as father of thy bride. His daughter has come beneath the one coverlet with thee, an Achaean maiden such as who none other walks the earth, and wondrous shall be the child she bears if it be like its mother.'

TB2 Theoc. 18.26-31. Tr. Gow (1952), 143

'Fair, Lady Night, is the face that rising Dawn discloses, or radiant spring when winter ends; and so amongst us did golden Helen shine. As some tall cypress adorns the fertile field or garden wherein it springs, or Thessalian steed the chariot it draws, so rosy Helen adorns Lacedaemon.'

TB3 Theoc. 18.38 Tr. Gow (1952), 143

'Fair, gracious maiden, a housewife now art thou.'

TB4 Call. *Aet.* iii, fr. 75.30-4 (Pfeiffer)

'For I say that you will be conjoining Acontius [to Cydippe] as one mixing not lead with silver but electrum with gleaming gold. You the father-in-law go way back to [King] Codrus, whilst the Cean bridegroom is descended from the priests of Zeus Aristaios ...'

TB5 Theoc. 18.32-7. Tr. Gow (1952), 143

'None from her basket winds off such yarn as she, nor at her patterned loom weaves with her shuttle and cuts from the tall loom-beams a closer weft. Nor yet is any so skilled as Helen to strike the lyre and hymn Artemis and broad-bosomed Athene – as Helen, in whose eyes is all desire.'

TB6 Peek 1214.1 (Folegandros, third/second century BC?)

Stranger, you said 'goodbye [*khairein*]' to me, Diogenes, who am under the earth
...

TB7 Theoc. 18.56-7. Tr. Gow (1952), 145

'Ere day we too will come again when the first songster raises his gaily-feathered neck from sleep to crow.'

TB8 Theoc. 18.58

'*Humên Oh Humenaios*, may you rejoice in this wedding!'

TB9 Theoc. 18.49

'Farewell, O bride; farewell, bridegroom having an excellent father-in-law.'

Pre-Christian Roman

TC1 Rufin. *AP* 5.94 = xxxv Page (1978)

You have the eyes, Melitê, of Hera, the hands of Athena,
the breasts of the Paphian goddess [sc. Aphrodite], the ankles of Thetis.
Fortunate the man who beholds you, three times prosperous whoever hears
    you,
a demigod he who kisses you, an immortal he who has intercourse with [lit.
    'marries'] you.

TC2 Men. Rh. 408.12-16 (RW) ('bedroom speech'). Tr. RW, 151f.

'Now the earth is adorned with flowers and made beautiful with plants, as you are now in the bloom and height of beauty; trees mingle with trees, so that this becomes their initiation and marriage.'

TC3 Men. Rh. 403.26-404.10 (RW) ('wedding speech'). Tr. RW, 143f.

The third general topic is that of the bridal pair. This is most elegantly handled if it proceeds by complex counter-examination: e.g. 'marvellous is the youth, marvellous too the maiden; skilled is he in educational accomplishments and [?] with the lyre; famous is he for the arts of the Muses, she for the dignity of her character'. If you are not in a position to say this, you can say that he is outstanding in letters, she in weaving and in the works of Athena and the Graces. Alternatively, in complex form but without counter-examination: 'Who would not praise the virtues of both, the temperance in them, the moderation inherent in them?' One can also praise the couple by separating the praises of the two and keeping them distinct, though beauty must always be treated as regards both of them, in the form of a comparison: 'Is not she like the olive, most beautiful of plants, and he like the palm?' 'He is like a rose, and she is like an apple.' You should also describe what the young man's glance is like and what he is like to see, how graceful and fair of face, how shaded with youthful beard, how newly come to manhood. As for the girl, be cautious in describing her beauty because of the scandal that may be caused, unless you are a relation and can speak as one who cannot help knowing, or unless you can remove the objection by saying 'I have heard ...'

TC4 Methodius *Banquet* (Musurillo-Débidour, pp. 310-21). Tr. Musurillo (1958), 152f.

[vv. 12-13] I desire to be sheltered in Thy life-giving arms and to gaze forever on Thy beauty, Blessed One.

[vv. 20-1] I have escaped the Dragon's countless bewitching wiles, O Blessed One. Awaiting Thy coming from heaven, I have braved fire and flame.

[vv. 31-3] ... the choir of virgins calls upon Thee, perfect Flower, Love, Joy, Prudence, Wisdom, Word!

[vv. 36-9] Queen arrayed in beauty, receive us too with open doors within the bridal bower, O Bride of unsullied body, gloriously triumphant, breathing loveliness! At Christ's side we stand in robes like thine, singing, O youthful maiden of thy blessed nuptials.

[vv. 56-7] Clearly did Abel foreshadow Thy death, O Blessed One, as bleeding he looked to heaven and said: O Word, I beseech Thee, receive me cruelly slain by my brother.

[vv. 61-3] Thy valiant servant Joseph, O Word, did carry off the greatest prize of chastity, when a woman burning with desire sought to draw him by force to an unlawful bed.

[vv. 78-80] The two judges were inflamed with desire when they saw the texture of Susanna's fair form. Said they: 'We have come, dear lady, desirous of secret intercourse with you.'

[vv. 103-6] Unsullied maid, God's blessed Bride, we thy bridesmaids hymn thy praise, O Church of body snow-white, dark-tressed, chaste, spotless, lovely!

TC5 Luc. *Symp.* 41

Or such indeed a young lady as the divine princess Cleanthis was tenderly raised in the palace of Aristainetos, surpassing all other maidens, superior to Cytherê [sc. Aphrodite] and also Helen herself. Rejoice, you too, bridegroom, mightiest of mighty ephebes, superior to Nireus and the son of Thetis [sc. Achilles]. And we in turn will sing many times for you [pl.] this epithalamian hymn, common to both of you.

TC6 Men. Rh. 400.7-28 (RW) ('wedding speech'). Tr. RW, 137

Such are the prooemia of the formal speech. In the relaxed or non-oratorical style, they have less artifice but are without expansive ornament; the presentation is more explicit, as in a treatise, though with the same ideas. In this more relaxed manner, one may begin with a narrative, using it to express one of the ideas we have mentioned: e.g. 'When Dionysus married Ariadne, the young Apollo was there and played his lyre', or: 'At the marriage of Peleus, all the gods were present, and the Muses too, and each of them was concerned to give a wedding present appropriate to himself; so one gave gifts, another played the lyre, some of the Muses played the flute, some sang, and Hermes made the announcement of the marriage. And I see the same kind of thing here with us now: some are leaping around, some shouting for joy, and I am speaking and singing of the marriage.' Or alternatively: 'When Megacles married Agariste, and the noblest of the Greeks met together, no poet, no prose-writer was late; the orator spoke, the historian read his books aloud to the company, and everyone sang the praises of the marriage. Our lady here is no whit inferior to her of Sicyon, so that the same thing has happened a second time [?]'

TC7 (a) Men. Rh. 405.24-8 (RW) ('bedroom speech'). Tr. RW, 147

So let us take up Heracles or some other figure who has shown courage in marriage, not indeed treating all Heracles' heroic deeds, but only his achievements in his unions with women or nymphs ...

TC7 (b) Men. Rh. 408.32-409.5 (RW) ('bedroom speech'). Tr. RW, 153

You should say something also about Dionysus – how 'he is a fine god for weddings, filling the heart with courage, filling it with confidence, giving boldness; for he was no laggard himself, but a brave performer in wedlock. Thus also Aeacus made Aegina the daughter of Asopus his bride, Peleus Thetis, Zeus Leda, ...'

TC8 Peek 1871 ([=*SEG* XXX 1063], Paros, second century AD)

A. 'Explain, of which parent, utter your name and [that of] your husband and tell your age, woman, and the city you're from.'

B. 'My father [was] Neikandros, my homeland Paros, my name was Sôkratea, and when I died Parmeniôn my bedmate laid me in this grave ... I was near the age of six years removed from 30 [viz. 24] ...'

TC9 Bion *Epitaph on Adonis* 88-9 (Reed). Tr. Reed, 131

... He [sc. Hymenaeus] was no longer singing 'hymên, hymên!', no longer his own song ...

TC10 'Oppian' *Cynegetica* I.341 (Mair)

singing 'humên, humenaion', he [sc. the bridegroom] strides into the nuptial chamber

TC11 Men. Rh. 411.18-20 (RW) ('bedroom speech'). Tr. RW, 157f.

Finally, you should add a prayer, asking the gods, on the couple's behalf, for a happy union, felicity, a lovely life, the birth of children, and the other blessings we have already mentioned.

Early Byzantine

TD1 Jo. Chrys. *hom.* 12 in Col., *PG* 62.386 (= Field v. 306D f.)

I commend the fact that virgins are present, honouring their contemporary [fem.], that women are present, honouring the maiden brought to them; this has been rightly ordained. For there are two choruses, that of virgins and that of married women. The former deliver [sc. the bride], the latter receive her. The bride is between these, being neither virgin nor woman, for she is departing from the former sphere and entering into the latter group.

TD2 Him. *Or.* 9, 11.263-6 (Colonna, p. 86)

But if one also needed a song, I would have given one like this:

'Bride, full of rosy Cupids, bride, most beauteous statue of the Paphian goddess [sc. Aphrodite], come to the bed, come to the marriage-bed, gently playing, sweet to the bridegroom. You follow the evening star willingly while admiring silver-throned Hera, goddess of marriage.'

TD3 George the Grammarian [early sixth century] no. 8, vv. 32-7 (an epith. in Anacreontics: Bergk iii.375)

Lovely bride, described as belonging to a handsome bed-partner who loves moderation, you pass to a worthy spouse. Therefore, O blessed one [*makaira*], may you rejoice in having been yoked to an honourable marriage-bed.

TD4 Dioscuros of Aphrodito [*c.* 520 – *c.* 85] no. 21 (Heitsch XLII, pp. 146-7). Tr. MacCoull (1988), 89, with modifications

[v.3] You are marrying a bride who is an enviable Ariadne

[vv. 6-10] Gold has embraced gold, and silver has found silver. You raise up the honey-sweet grape cluster, in its bloom of youth; Dionysus meticulously tends the fruit of your wedding, wine, love's adornment, ...

[vv. 13-14] Like splendid Menelaus, but more tawny coloured, you cherish your Helen, a wife who will not leave you.

[vv. 18-23] I desire to weave accurately your extremely lovely image ... whose bright beams flash with joy like the moon. Your body has surpassed prize-winning Bellerophon, and your beauty is that of measureless excellence. To judge impartially, you have outdone Achilles and Diomedes, and easily out-stripped Ares and brave Herakles.

TD5 Dioscuros of Aphrodito no. 22 (Heitsch XLII, pp. 147-8). Tr. MacCoull, 108, with modifications

[vv. 1-3] Bridegroom, your wedding is filled with the dancing of the Graces; bridegroom, your wedding [sc. is filled] with gently nurtured roses; bridegroom, your wedding [sc. is filled] with honey-sweet grape clusters.

[vv. 9-14]... like gold you have found a golden bride, both of you [like] heroes, she ripe as a honey-comb ... [lacuna]. Bridegroom, bend your mind to love; Zeus himself in heaven, because of Europa's beauty, is still known to have become a bull; for love of Leda he is still known to have become a swan. You carry your Europa over the threshold, not over the sea ...

TD6 Dioscuros of Aphrodito no. 23 (Heitsch XLII, pp. 148-9). Tr. MacCoull, 111-12, slightly modified

[vv. 7-8] ... look how the bridegroom and the bride are coming; truly they have surpassed Bellerophon in likeness

[v. 21] Go away, evil eye, away from this marriage graced by God

[vv. 23-4] Isakios, strong of spirit, you have found your noble bride, as gold has gained gold and silver has found silver.

TD7 Greg. Nyss. *Cons. in Pulcheriam*, p. 463. 2f. (Spira)

... the lofty palm-tree [i.e. Theodosius] ... the well-born vine-tendril [i.e. Flacilla] which, entwined by the palm, gave birth to this blossom ...

101

TD8 Jo. Chrys. *hom.* 49 in Genes., *PG* 54.443

Did you see what kind of bride the patriarch took to marriage? A woman drawing water and carrying a pitcher on her shoulders ... Regard the bride's nobility: when she saw Isaac she asked who he was. Here consider ... that nowhere were there these excessive and senseless things [i.e. of today], nowhere the Devil's pomp, nowhere cymbals and flutes and dances ... but rather every seriousness, every wisdom, every virtuousness ... Let women imitate this woman [sc. Rebecca], let men emulate this man [sc. Isaac]. Let them attend to taking a bride in this manner.

TD8x Dioscuros no. 24 (Heitsch XLII, pp. 149-50)

[vv. 6-11] I call you by your name, 'Aphrodite celebrated in song by all'; you are easily most lovely, having the beauty of the Paphian goddess, who stands at Cupid's side; Desire has forged your form ... Look ahead to your handsome, well-beloved husband Paul, god-like, charming, utterly like Bellerophon ...

TD9 (a) Jo. Chrys. *In illud: 'Propter fornicationes uxorem'*, *PG* 51.210

As to the fact that ... current practices are a new departure, remember how Isaac took Rebecca to wife, how Jacob wed Rachel ... Indeed, whilst they had a *sumposion* and a meal more splendid than usual, ... flutes, pipes and cymbals ... and all other obscenity were banished.

TD9 (b) Jo. Chrys. *hom.* 12 in Col., *PG* 62.387-8 (= Field v.306f.)

A wedding is not a mere spectacle, is it? It is a great mystery and a visible sign of a great thing ... In what sense is it a mystery? Two come together and make one ... When coming together, they constitute neither an image without a soul nor an earthly image, but [sc. they] constituting an image of God himself, do you [sc. for all that] introduce so much noise? ... For a woman and a man are not two human beings, but one; and it is easy to prove this on numerous grounds, as from [sc. the example of] Jacob, from [sc. the example of] Mary the mother of Christ, and from the words 'Male and female created he them' (= Gen. 1:27).

TD10 Jo. Gaz. [early sixth century] no. 3, vv. 5-6 (*epithalamios logos* in Anacreontics: Bergk iii.344)

... the young Cythera a young Phaëthon conducts.

TD11 (a) Chor. *Zach.* 13-14 (FR, pp. 84-5)

Why, dear chap, do you hang your head towards the ground and change the colour of your skin [i.e. become red] as proof of your shame? The desire for a comely virgin once drove even Theseus out of Attica, and Love did not in the least shrink from the contest ... Indeed, Aspasia ... utterly overcame even Cyrus, son of Darius and Parysatis ...

TD11 (b) Chor. *Zach.* 17 (FR, pp. 85-6)

Demophon was an Attic youth, one of the well-born. He lived, moreover, an idle life and was a profligate ... If therefore matrimony takes a dissolute young man and tends to teach him continence, what might Aphrodite legitimately accomplish in uniting with innate dignity? ...

TD12 (a) Chor. *Proc.* 11-12 (FR, p. 90)

On account of him [sc. Eros] Zeus assumed all guises, on his account the sea was bereft of Poseidon ... it would take too long to tell how Apollo fell in love with Daphne, Dionysus with Ariadne ...

102

TD12 (b) Chor. *Proc.* ibid. 42-3 (FR, pp. 96-7)

Now Peleus' marriage is seemly. But it does have a blameworthy aspect in that the relative value of each of the married couple is out of tune [i.e. unequal]. Thus, even in the epic poems Achilles reflects his mother in respect of deeds, but taking his father to task for his [sc. mortal] nature, he blames him for the anomaly of his marriage in relation to his mother. Equality, then, in a marriage is an agreeable thing, and this conceivably is the point of the myth which has Zeus wedded to his sister ...

TD13 Him. *Or.* 9 (*protheôria*, i.e. 'preface') (Colonna, p. 75)

... The [sc. epithalamian] speech ends in an *ecphrasis* of the bride, which describes her poetic beauty, the length [sc. of this section] of the speech depending on its particular subject.

TD14 Chor. *Zach.* 19-20 (FR, pp. 86-7)

Now the poet [sc. Homer], not having, it seems, a large store of terribly comely women, strives to deck out, in part, nature's unadorned state with words, calling one woman 'fair-cheeked', the other 'fair-ankled'. I, on the other hand, shall adorn the bride – see how she's been charmed by the adjectives, how intently she looks, how she lends a more attentive ear! – well, so as to oblige you, I shall adorn the bride with Sapphic song: 'Your form is graceful and your eyes honey-sweet, love is spread round your beautiful face and Aphrodite has honoured you outstandingly' [cf. TA22]. But since you have not yet heard Sappho's lyre, let us yet again beg the poet to cheer the maiden: 'In build and in stature, in mind and in handiwork [cf. *Il.* 1.115] did she most marvellously and closely resemble the immortal goddesses.'

TD15 Chor. *Proc.* 10f. (FR, p. 94)

I praise the brides for having been delivered to such true lovers, such temperate youths. Not unreasonably do they tend to their good character ...

Middle Byzantine

TE1 Constant. Porphyr. *De Caerem.* ii.90 [81] (Vogt, p. 181)

'I gathered flowers of the field, and entered the bridal chamber in haste;
I saw a sun [i.e. a day] joining the couple on a bed as precious as gold;
they were embracing one another with desire and longing;
joy to their handsomeness, sweet to behold and roses as beautiful as roses;
joy to the golden couple.'

TE2 (a) Ps. 128.3f. = *Officium coronationis nuptiarum*, in *Euchologion sive rituale Graecorum*, ed. Jacobus Goar (corr. repr., Graz, 1960), p. 314 (OSB version)

Your wife shall be like a fruitful vine
in the very heart of your house,
your children like olive plants
all around your table.

TE2 (b) Ps. 37.37, Hos. 10.1 (Rahlfs) = Goar, op. cit., 317

Raise them like the cedars of Lebanon,
like a luxuriant vine.

TE3 Leo Magister [late ninth – early tenth century] no. 2 (Anacreontic poem, 'On the occasion of the wedding of Emperor Leo': Bergk iii.356-7) [vv. 17-18] Lovely-voiced maiden, golden sapling, accept these cymbal-voiced songs.

[v. 23] Sun, you have found a luminous spouse
[vv. 29-30] Splendour with a beautiful complexion, blossom of colour, radiance of a body possessing the blossom of a pearl

[vv. 35-6] Rose-coloured, handsome, lily-white, the bride-groom, in the bloom of youth, is a wonder to behold.

[vv. 53-4] Lovely Penelope ... I scatter violets fragrant as nectar in your bridal alcove.

[vv. 67-8] Princess, child of blessed parents [*makarôn*], you possess the beauty of the Graces

TE4 Goar op. cit., 319

Bridegroom, be exalted [imper.] like Abraham and be blessed [imper.] like Isaac and increase [imper.] in number like Jacob, etc. And you, bride, be exalted [imper.] like Sarah and rejoice [imper.] like Rebecca and increase [imper.] in number like Rachel, etc.

TE5 Leo Magister no. 5 (Anacreontic poem, 'In honour of Augusta Helen, wife of Constantine the Younger': Bergk iii.361f.)

[vv. 1-2; cf. v. 49] Sweet-haired, roseate, golden blossom, accept these virgin-voiced songs.

[v. 43] Sun, you have found a luminous spouse ...

[vv. 61-8] You appeared, a fair-haired girl with the breath of blossoms, indeed, you surpassed those with eyes like the Graces! Child of blessed [*makarôn*] parents, you possess the beauty of the Graces ... Rose-coloured, handsome, lily-white, the bridegroom Constantine, in the bloom of youth, is radiant.

TE6 Goar op. cit., 315-17

Oh God, who through your love of mankind transformed the rib of our forefather Adam into a woman ... having said, 'Be fruitful, and multiply [= Gen. 1.28] and have dominion over the earth [cf. ibid.]' ... who blessed your servant Abraham and opened Sarah's womb and made him a father of a multitude of nations, who granted Isaac to Rebecca ... who united Jacob with Rachel ... who received Zacharias and Elizabeth ... who came to Cana in Galilee and blessed the wedding there ... so bless this marriage ... grant that they might live to see their children's children.
...Bless them as you blessed Abraham and Sarah ... Isaac and Rebecca ... Jacob and all the patriarchs ... Moses and Sapphira, etc.

TE7 Goar op. cit., 318 = Eph. 5: 22-33 (OSB version)

Wives, submit to your own husbands, as to the Lord. For the husband is head of the wife, as also Christ is head of the church; and He is the Saviour of the body. Therefore, just as the church is subject to Christ, so let the wives be to their own husbands in everything ...

TE8 Goar ibid. = Jo. 2:1-11

(On the third day there was a wedding in Cana of Galilee, and the mother of Jesus was there. Now both Jesus and His disciples were invited to the wedding. And when they ran out of wine ...)

followed by the prayer:

... You who in the divine economy of salvation deemed it worthy at Cana of Galilee to render matrimony honourable through your presence, preserve now these your servants, so-and-so [masc.] and so-and-so [fem.], etc.

Late Byzantine

TF1 Theodore Prodromos op. cit. in n. 221 below

Queen of goddesses, Cypris,
Desire, master of mortals,
Marriage, guardian of life,
I sing of you in prose,
I glorify you with verse,
Desire, Marriage, the Paphian [i.e. Aphrodite].
Young man, behold the maiden, behold her.
Arise lest your quarry of a partridge escape you.
Stratocles, beloved to Cythêrê,
Stratocles, Myrilla's man,
look at your beloved wife,
she has long hair, she is abloom, she is radiant;
the rose reigns over flowers,
Myrilla is a rose among maidens.
Helios [i.e. the sun god] reveals your bed;
may a cypress spring forth in your garden.

TF2 Theodore Prodromos XIII (Hörandner)

[vv. 2-4] Convene the demes, summon the Senate,
make ready, in turn, the royal wedding alcove,
celebrate, in turn, the new Comnenian marriage.

[vv. 13-19] Rejoice / Hail, I say, bride far-shining and most regal,
bearing an august lineage going back three generations,
notable in soul, conspicuous in bodily beauty,
fair, exquisite branch of an exquisitely beautiful garden-olive,
indeed, you have joined yourself to a bridegroom supreme among all others,
a young, exquisite, well-born, magnanimous soldier,
good in every respect and handsome and attuned to you.

[vv. 25-7] You've gained a most radiant partner in life,
unrivalled by anyone, the dwelling of all graces
of soul and body and good fortune.

TF3 Theodore Prodromos XIV, vv. 29-41 (Hörandner)

Rejoice / Hail, I say, bride far-shining, bride supreme amongst brides,
regal in soul, regal in body.
Indeed, you've found a bridegroom worthy in all respects,
a beautiful woman [sc. has found] a handsome man, an august woman an
    august man, an exquisite woman an exquisite man,
one conspicuous among his peers, the wonder of his peers ...

It was not appropriate for you, O extraordinary and most handsome
    bridegroom, ...
not to be joined in wedlock with the most beautiful of women.

For this reason you have won her as no other [sc. has won] another,
and you are marvellously prominent through your union with her,

as ivy round a plane tree and a vine-branch round a laurel, etc.

TF4 Theodore Prodromos XX, vv. 56-9 (Hörandner)

Salute, though he is not here, the ruler most mighty,
who raised up an exquisite grape-vine from the west
and planted it in royal gardens,
so that you might be entwined with his vine-tendril and grow
together with it.

TF5 (a) Theodore Prodromos XLIII, vv. 11-20 (Hörandner)

Your qualities and the greatness of your grace [are]:
valour, vigour, considerable stature,
gratifying speech, a character serious and gentle,
and a first-rate appearance, as they say, worthy of a monarch.
These then are the things concerning you, bridegroom.
The nuptial chamber, the bridal alcove, the bridal procession,
has a double beauty for you, is twice as great for you;
for you have taken such a bride, a bride so young,
unrivalled in appearance, incomparable in character,
more nobly born than many, etc.

TF5 (d) Theodore Prodromos XLIII, vv. 11-13 (Hörandner)

Bride, you've found a bridegroom; bridegroom, you've found a bride,
a handsome man [has found] a beautiful woman, an august man an
august woman, an attractive man an extremely attractive woman,
a youth a young maiden, a young maiden a youth, etc.

TF6 Nicolaos Eirenicos op. cit. in n. 231 below

(1st chorus, vv. 1-2 [= 7-8, 10-11, etc.])
Ivy runs up alongside a shapely cypress,
my queen is a cypress, my king is ivy

(2nd chorus, vv. 29-30 [= 34-5, 37-8, etc.])
Iron loves a magnet, the bridegroom
loves the bride, etc.
(2nd chorus, cont'd, vv. 46-9)
Iron loves a magnet, the bridegroom loves the bride,
the mighty Doukas loves the well-born woman, the choice bride.

Rejoice / Hail, laurel and ivy, hail, cedar, vine-branch,
rejoice / hail, emerald, gold, etc.

TF7 Manuel Philes (or Th. Prodromos?) IX, in *Carmina* ii (Miller, pp. 269-70)

[To a ring with a seal showing two lovers, out of whose breasts two trees have
grown and have linked their topmost clusters into one]

The trees that have grown together into a single tree, [sc. to these] may you give
the fruit of lovers, marriage.

TF8 (a) Nicetas Choniates *Or.* 5, in *NCOE* (van Dieten), p. 36, 11.7f.

He leaps and hastens to celebrate and as though divinely possessed by the rites,
he wishes to dance ... and after gathering the flowers of praise from the
undefiled meadows cultivated by rhetoric, he prepares this royal bridal alcove,
strewing it with some such things as the following: The bridegroom king is
exceedingly attractive among young men, the bride queen is a maiden altogether

beautiful, radiant in the glow of spiritual beauty, excellent in respect of her outward shapeliness, and having nothing blameworthy, etc.

O sweet day, this on which the young king is marrying a young woman, an attractive man an attractive woman, a blossoming man a blossoming woman, a man boasting of a royal lineage of three generations [sc. is marrying] a woman descended from Julius Caesar. And being himself the sun, he is in conjunction, and jointly rises, with the far-seen moon ...

TF8 (b) Nicetas Choniates *Or.* 5, in *NCOE* (van Dieten), p. 43, ll. 21-5.

For you have brought her out like a vine, though not out of Egypt [cf. Ps. 79:9], but from the place whence God through his prophet commands the north to bring his daughters [cf. Is. 43:6]. Let him say: 'Who is she that looketh forth as the morning, fair as the moon, clear as the sun?' [= Song of Songs 6:10].

TF8 (c) Nicetas Choniates *Or.* 5, in *NCOE* (van Dieten), p. 37, 11.8-20

But if in his dream prudent Joseph saw stars making obeisance to him as if to another sun [cf. Gen. 37:9], to you in your waking state, a Joseph younger and more prudent to be sure, will these stars in their changing courses make obeisance too. Now, so that this speech might shed more brilliant illumination in its treatment of the bridal couple, if it is to set matters forth in a manner more lucid even than the sun, as they say: the bridegroom is young, prudent, of good memory, courageous, magnificent, eminently educable [cf. Pl. *R.* 487a], whom long ago the son of Ariston [i.e. Plato] described and sought as one destined to lead a life most fortunate amongst men; but never found, stopping just short of his shadow. To us, however, God has granted that we should see him and, as the same person [sc. Plato] says, he is of fair complexion like the children of the gods [cf. *R*. 474e] and 'ruddy and withal of a beautiful countenance' [= I Samuel 16:12] like courageous and gentle King David; in accordance with his [sc. good] heart he has been 'found by God' [cf. Ps. 88:21], a king wise and at the same time courageous, a brave and mighty spearman, ... charming all things wild through his power of persuasion and violence, the attendant of Hermes and Ares ....

TF8 (d) Nicetas Choniates *Or.* 5, in *NCOE* (van Dieten), pp. 38-9, 11.26f.

Yes, after your divinely-favoured betrothal to her, you, being of handsome stock yourself, have offered wedding-gifts most handsome so as to avert every cause of prolonged vexation and to see, suddenly, a 'bright day' instead of a most sorrowful and gloomy one; in the manner of that much-suffering Ithacan hero of many wiles, you sailed away from the place that gave you birth, and accumulated for yourself a larger 'way of thinking' [cf. *Od.* 1.3] and sufficient experiences, for you intermingled with many peoples. Then, after so long you were espied in your homeland ... which you found badly tyrannised and oppressed rampantly by a large number of utterly insane lovers, just as he [sc. Odysseus] found Penelope overpowered by unseemly suitors.

TF8 (e) Nicetas Choniates *Or.* 5, in *NCOE* (van Dieten), pp. 40, 11.12f.; 41, 11.4f.

... Once king Alexander, after his defeat of Darius the Persian, celebrated a wedding-feast both for himself and his companions and held the nuptial meal in the men's quarters, which had one hundred couches ... His bride was a barbarian ... But whatever things concern *your* bridal chamber, bridegroom and king, are splendid and, in the eyes of prudent men, more desirable by far than Alexander's preparations ... and things concerning your queen bride are more splendid and unlike the case of Alexander ...

TF8 (f) Nicetas Choniates *Or.* 5, in *NCOE* (van Dieten), p. 42, 11.24f.

In order to increase the merriment, let David with his lyre be present and let him sing the nuptial song – the gentle King, promoted by God, [sc. singing] to you, most gentle and God-ordained emperor; for being himself a bridegroom who goes forth from his nuptial chamber, he will exult at having run his course like a giant. We might command David the lover of song and psalms to sing, calling you a handsome bridegroom, one travelling from his chamber full of splendour and brilliance, a giant on account of your speed and manliness ...

TF9 Theodore Prodromos 'Epithalamium for the sons of the most fortunate Caesar (i.e. 'junior emperor')' in *T. Prodromi scripta miscellanea, PG* 133.1404B

Mythology, even if we accept as true the tales of weddings which you relate, I surpass these. Whereas you unite Thetis, the daughter of the old man of the sea, with Peleus, I unite the daughters of the most illustrious ministers with the sons of the junior emperor. Whereas you attend a wedding in a rocky cave, I do so in the palace itself. Whereas you feast with Aphrodite, Hera and Athena, I do so with the entire company of Ladies, all of them more regal than Hera, wiser than Athena, and more beautiful than Aphrodite. Whereas you bring in Eris [i.e. Strife/Competition], though she pretends to be self-invited, and toss her apple into the middle – the infamous apple that sparked off the entire war of the *Iliad* – and thereby disrupt the feast ... I for my part welcome Eris to the nuptial dinner, not 'the reprehensible kind nor the kind that rejoices in misfortune, but the one that is commendable when perceived [cf. Hes. *WD* 12-13, 28]'. Thus more seemly by far and more glorious than mythic accounts – though such events never occurred – are the present proceedings.

TF10 Nicetas Choniates, 'Verses declaimed by the demes on the occasion of the wedding of Isaac I Angelos and Margaret of Hungary', *NCOE* vv. 9-22 (van Dieten, pp. 44-5)

Hail, <yes> hail, awe-inspiring King, killer of the barbarians,
image of the heavens' beaming morning star,
with as many beams of light as it shoots forth at us, with so many rays
do you yourself shine as bringer of light and cheer everyone thoroughly;
lo! the other disc, the other scattering of light also
flashes forth from your present union of marriage;
if light shines from within the imperial porphyry
[sc. imagine] from the ceremonies of the regal wedding just celebrated,
what kind of foreign-tongued chorus will break forth in your honour.

Hail, you with eyes of the Graces, noblest of women,
offshoot of great, hoary-crowned, courageous kings,
you, like a glowing, completely round moon,
Isaac Angelos is taking to wife on a wedding-bed thrice-glorious ...

Post-Byzantine / Modern

TG1 *Laogr.* 19 (1960-1), 98, no. 78. 7-10 (Trianda, Rhodes), performed during the bathing of the bride

Beautifully bathe her beautiful shoulders,
for they are Pasha's courtyards and Vizier's streets.
Who can comb her curly hair
and who can pour water on her without going mad?

TG2 Papadopoullos (1975), 91, no. 83, presumably performed as the bride was adorned (Cyprus, nineteenth century)

We're changing the attire of the pearl-like young bride,
whom her mother steeps in golden things,
for tonight she [i.e. the bride] will be putting the beautiful bird [i.e. husband]
    to sleep beside her.

TG2a Wedding encomium (*painema*), sung in Constantinople in the sixteenth century; published by Knös (1970), 245

She had much gracefulness
like the brilliant moon,
and she shone in the dark
bright like the day.

TG2b Politis (1932), 181, no. 145.1-2

Bride, limpid water and all-brilliant moon,
your match is enviable and a handsome young warrior [see TG21 on *pallikari*].

TG3 Poulianos (1964), 198 (Ikaria)

My bride most fair, today is your joy [fig. wedding],
nightingales have come from Frankland [i.e. the west] to see your beauty.

TG4 Politis (1932), 181, no. 145

Like ivy which clings to a tree and spreads out,
[so] may the bride come together with the bridegroom and put down roots.

TG5 L.A. MS. 2474, p. 24 (unpubl., Kariotes, Leucas, 1958), performed by the bride's friends, male and female

Bridegroom, bridegroom, don't scold our bride,
cherish [pamper] her like a white rose.
Bridegroom, I ask a favour of you, grant me a favour,
don't cause the blossom we're giving to you to wilt.

TG6 L.A. MS. 2455, p. 65 (unpubl., Simi, 1962)

As ivy winds round the branch [?],
so also has our bride wound round a pearl.

TG7 Politis (1931), 270 (Rhodes), performed antiphonally as the bride was escorted to the church

A. As a red flower 'shines' in the green meadows,
    so also does the bridegroom 'shine' among brave young men [see TG21 on
    pallikari].
B. As a red flower 'shines' in the green meadows,
    so also does the bride 'shine' among brides.

TG8 Poulianos (1964), 198 (Ikaria)

As a white horse 'shines' in a green pasture,
so also does the bride 'shine' beside the bride-groom.

TG9 Hyphantes (1972), 162 (Epirus)

Fortunate is the mother who escorts the sun,
who escorts the sun to accept the moon, etc.

TG10 L.A. MS. 2455, p. 53 (unpubl., Simi, 1962)

The sun is the bridegroom and the bride is the moon,
and all the in-laws are roses and lilies.

TG11 L.A. MS. 2455, p. 54 (unpubl., Simi, 1962)

> The bridegroom, who is doubly handsome, is dressed
> and the sun is off to marry the moon.

TG12 Tarsouli ii.324 (Astypalea), sung during the wedding feast

> Bride, when they set you in the middle of the church,
> young and old [alike] said: 'Joy to him [i.e. congratulations to him] who has
>   her [as wife].'
> My bride, bar of gold, my bride, bar of silver,
> bride, a new [i.e. a second] All Holy Virgin, with her humility.

TG13 Hyphantes (1972), 117-18 (Epirus)

> You have the hair of Absalom,
> the beauty of Joseph, the beauty of Joseph.
> Fortunate, of lucky days
> is the young man who will take you, is the young man who will take you.
> You have hair that is thoroughly blonde
> flowing over your shoulders, flowing over your shoulders.
> Angels combed it
> with golden combs, with golden combs.
> Today is worth
> gold coins by the bushel, gold coins by the bushel,
> on which [sc. day] such a young woman
> will join such a brave young man, such a brave young man.

TG14 *Laogr.* 19 (1960-1), 110, no. 93.1 (Rhodes)

> How beautifully you're matched like the Holy Anargyroi,
> like Venetian gold coins [lit. florins] with large rims.

TG15 L.A. MS. 2186, p. 21, no. 1 (unpubl., Ano Viannos, Nomos Heracleiou, Crete, 1956)

> Your hair, my bridegroom, casts golden rays,
> your cheeks have the beauty of St George.

TG16 *Laogr.* 2 (1910-11), 57, vv. 20-1 (Thrace), performed as the bride was being adorned

> How beautiful is our bride, like a drawn Panaghia,
> like the Panaghia-with-Christ who is painted.

TG17 *Laogr.* 4 (1913-14), 139-40, no. 117 (Aegina), sung during the wedding feast

> In the heavens above
> the angels are attending a wedding,
> they make merry and take their leisure
> and the Apostles are holding a feast;
> David is playing the harp,
> Jacob is playing the psaltery.
> Over there if a dance happens to be struck up,
> the monks also join in,
> and whoever should criticise them,
> may he be full of miserable pain.

TG18 Baud-Bovy i.185-6, no. 74a (Rhodes)

> Rejoice, bridegroom, in your lot, rejoice in your destiny,

for you've put a piece of gold by your side.

TG19 L.A. MS. 2455, p. 427 (unpubl., Simi)

My beautiful little bride, my beautiful little bride, joy to, joy to [i.e. congratulations on] your destiny (repeated twice)

TG20 L.A. MS. 2455, p. 60 (unpubl., Simi, 1962)

My bride, how auspiciously you've chosen and taken a cross with diamonds, the sun with its rays.

TG21 Politis (1932), 178, no. 138

Joy [i.e. congratulations] to the red apple-tree,* joy to the brave young man
  [*pallikari*],**
who will reach out to pluck the golden apple.

* The symbolism of the apple, used here of the bride, is discussed at length in Chapter IV. The 'Red Apple' is also a Byzantine motif representing imperial power over the world: Littlewood (1978), 52 (Appendix).

** The 'diminutive' form *pallikari* = 'young, strong warrior', with specific associations of active sexual prowess and youth; the non-dimunitive form is unattested in modern Greek. See Shipp s.v. *pallêx* ['a youth below the age of *ephêbos*', LSJ]: > *pallêkari*, 'already *P. Oxy.* 1862 (VII) *ta pallêkaria sou* and 1863.4, with parallels cited by the editors; see also Sophocles under both nouns'.

TG22 L.A. MS. 2455, p. 430 (unpubl., Simi, 1962)

The bridegroom is [series of melismatic turns], the bridegroom is [series of melismatic turns] gold and the bride, and the bride is a sprig of jasmine.

TG23 L.A. MS. 2186, p. 22a (unpubl., Ano Viannos, Heracleion, Crete, 1956)

Handsome is the bridegroom and handsome is the bride,
for he/she has beautiful eyes – may he/she live long!

TG24 *Laogr.* 13 (1950-1), 330, no. 21 (Cos)

A good/handsome man has chosen a good/handsome woman and they've become a match, etc.

TG25 Vavoules (1950), 210-11, sung during the wedding feast (Crete)

Let us praise the bride,
who is the adornment of the world.
Her hair is like a crown
and her body like a column.
She has a small forehead,
round as a little bitter orange.
She has eyebrows like a braid,
which a painter cannot make.
She has eyes of sapphire,
beautiful and sugar-sweet.
She has a comely face,
which drives every young man mad.
She has a nose like a finger joint,
a mouth like a ring, etc.

TG26 *Makedonika* 1 (1940), 161-2; cf. ibid., 163

My maiden/daughter, what mother made you

and you're as white as milk?
And the breast you've sucked
was a pearl
and the cradle that rocked you
was golden?

– My mother was a partridge
and my father a pigeon;
where are you, my family
and my large clan?
Come near me,
gather my hair,
lest strangers should take it
and work spells on us
and I should fall dead
and they should separate us.

TG27 D. Petropoulos (1959), 19

Wake up, young man and bridegroom,
wake up, for dawn has broken,
wake your partridge too,
who's asleep beside you.

TG28 Karapatakis (1960), 156 (Grevena)

Wake up, my master, wake up, my good master,
wake up, embrace a cypress-like body
and a white neck, breasts like a lemon,
like cool water that comes from a fountain
and from the mountain.

TG29 L.A. MS. 2892, p. 634 (unpubl., island of Chalki), designated as 'dawn-song'

Hey! Wake up, for E[-ros] ... wake up, for E- ...
Hey! Wake up, for Eros is passing ...
Hey! Wake up, for E[-ros] ... wake up, for E[-ros] ... wake up, for Eros is
    passing ...
Hey! Wake up, for Eros is passing by your neighbourhood, etc.

TG30 Pachtikos i.70 (Bithynia), performed by a chorus of maidens as the bride was
dressed; cf. ibid. 81 and Tarsouli ii.182 for a similar choral wedding-song

Seated, you appear as a tower,
standing, as a cypress [*aman* i.e. refrain].

TG31 Pashley i.253 n. 31 (Crete)

My slender little cypress
    with your red cap,
who will sleep
    under your shade?

TG32 *Laogr.* 19 (1960-1), 537, no. 7 (Cypriot *painema*)

Oh! my slender cypress, my twined poplar,
I was looking for you for a long while
and now I've found you alone.

TG33 L.A. MS. 2186, p. 21 (unpubl., Ano Viannos, Nomos Heracleiou)

My eyes have never seen such a bride
who has [so] many dotal objects, who also has a house.

TG34 Op. cit. above (unpubl.)

I've searched the world over, East and West.
I've never seen such a face shining like a diamond.

TG35 L.A. MS. 1508, p. 163 (unpubl., Messenia, 1944)

However many weddings I've been to, I've never seen such a couple,
the bride being marjoram and the bridegroom a golden bell, etc.

TG36 L.A. MS. 1800, p. 29 (unpubl., Naupaktia, 1952), sung at the wedding feast

However many weddings I've been to,
I've never seen such newlyweds;
the bride being a little turtle-dove
and the bridegroom a little pigeon.

Chapter III

Archaic and classical

TA49 Sapph. fr. 110b (LP) = Demetr. *Eloc.* 167. Tr. Campbell i.135. Cf. Sapph. fr. 110a (LP); Ar. *Pax* 1340-3, 1359-60 (Olson), on which see Chapter IV below

In different vein Sappho makes very cheap fun of the rustic bridegroom and the door-keeper at the wedding, using prosaic rather than poetic language.

TA50 Margites fr. 4 (*IE*, ii [W])

(1) Eust. in Hom.
In this vein we have also understood foolish Margites [from the verb *margainein*, i.e. 'to be foolish'] ... supposedly he was of extremely well-to-do parents, but when he married he did not bed down his bride; at length swayed [by her mother], she pretended that her lower parts had been injured and claimed that no other drug would avail unless the male genitals were applied to them; and thus it was that he approached her for therapeutic reasons.

(2) Dio Chrys. 67.4 (von Arnim ii. 170.12)
... he certainly would not be much more intelligent than Margites, who was unaware that after marriage one has to have intercourse with one's wife.

(3) Hesych. s.v. *Marge<i>tês*
This was some simpleton who knew nothing about intercourse with a woman. And so his wife exhorted him, telling him that a scorpion had stung her and that she had to be cured through impregnation.

(Further testimonia in West, *IE*)

Hellenistic

TB10 = TB1.9-15

Pre-Christian Roman

TC12 Men. Rh. 410.9-18, 26-30 (RW); cf. TC7(b). Tr. RW, 155f.

After the prooemium, you will come to the exhortation to the young man: 'I knew you as second to none in times past, I knew your prowess, in hunting and wrestling. Show me this strength and prowess in the present juncture. Do not fear that any of the present company will reproach you. We are all children of marriage, and some of us have been initiated, some are about to be, and some pray to be.' You should then call on the audience to join in the exhortation, and escort him, willy-nilly, to the bedroom ... You should continue with an exhortation based on the past. 'Remember your courtship, how long it took, how many years it was before you just managed to succeed, how the girl's parents gave consent only very late – and now that you have her, do you take things easy, as if you'd forgotten?'

Early Byzantine

TD16 (a) Jo. Chrys. *PG* 61.104, *In Epist. I ad Cor. hom. 12* (= Field ii.144C)

... but they even conduct her ostentatiously through the marketplace, escorting her with torches in late evening so that she is exhibited to everyone ... And they do not stop here but accompany her with ugly expressions; and this is customary among 'the many'. Fugitive slaves, then, and countless worthless rogues forthrightly utter whatever they may like both to her and her future husband ... What is more, there is even a kind of diabolical rivalry among those encouraging such behaviour, i.e. to surpass one another in competing in insults and ugly expressions, through which they shame those who have gathered; the winners [sc. of this sordid competition] depart, i.e. whoever hurled the most insults and the most hideous words.

TD16 (b) Jo. Chrys. *PG* 54.488B, *In Gen 29 hom. 51*

What then could be more laughable than this habit, i.e. when husband and wife become the butt of jokes and infinite abuse from household slaves and worthless persons? ... Indeed, is it permitted to anyone who so wishes to utter everything without hesitation in the evening, and to smite both the bridegroom and bride with jokes?

TD16 (c) Jo. Chrys. *PG* 51.212C, *In illud, propter fornicationes uxorem, etc. I*

Besotted with drink and food, they pour down every kind of filthy joke upon the heads of the bridal pair, engaging in a kind of diabolical rivalry with one another; and as if those who have come along are enemies, each respective group competes against the other in addressing insults, speakable and unspeakable, to the couple and in imitating those ranged against them; and this mutual emulation, conducted with every manner of excess, causes the bridegroom and the bride to become ashamed.

TD17 Nonn. *D.* 103f.

Why, bridegroom, are you travelling sluggishly?

TD18 = TD11

Late Byzantine

TF11 = TF1

Post-Byzantine / modern

TG37 St Nicodemos of the Holy Mountain (fl. late eighteenth century), *Pêdalion* (Venice, 1804; rp. Thessalonica, 1974)

... and they listen to those lewd and erotic songs ..., and I won't mention the other sins that take place at weddings ...; that is, the improper words, the unabashed jokes, the foul language, ...

TG38 Karayiannis (1983), 71: *niphkato* ('wedding-song') from Lesbos

In the tall house,
the bridegroom is fucking the bride,
and because of a sweetness so great,
he's licking his fingers.

For other instances of crude wedding-song see: Aravantinos (1880), no. 353 (the bride is a preposterously corpulent *gourmande* who urinates after a meal and floods the village); op. cit., no. 360 (the bride is so ugly that the guests at the wedding feast lose their appetite); *Laogr.* 32 (1982), 53f., no. 40 preserves a more recent song about a 'big-shouldered' (*platôna*) bride.

TG39 L.A. MS. 2186, p. 22 (unpubl., Ano Viannos, Heracleion, Crete, 1956)

Queen of queens, empress of empresses,
you're the most beautiful among all other brides.

TG40 = TG27

TG41 = TG28

TG42 D. Petropoulos ibid., 17-18: wedding-song, recorded in Thrace in 1903

Do you hear, do you hear, Mr Bridegroom,
what your mother tells you?
Don't eat, don't drink too much wine,
lest you fall asleep
and the 'brigands' cross over,
[and] take your handkerchief,
your first engagement token.

TG43 *Archeion Pontou* 1 (1928), 161: processional song performed (in Argyroupolis, a Christian town) as the bride left her house to be led to the church; as the party approached the church they immediately took up a religious hymn

We have a bride and we're off,
but if they don't take her what will we do?
Her teats (vulg.) [are] squash,
they bang, take the [?].
Her head [is] a bronze cauldron,
[imperative] eat up lots of property and sell it.
Her legs [vulg.] [are] shapely,
groom, she needs cheap shoes.
Her height [is] short,
oh, I'll say it straight.
Her hair [is] like thin wire,
her heart doesn't want you.
Her little mouth [is] small,
a bitter wine glass.
Her hands [are] white [as] snow,
they'll hold the needles.
Groom, groom, dance,
caress the bride.
We've told lies,
bridal farts.

TG44 Wedding-song from Lesbos, published in *Trivolos*, ii (1937), 1001

> If I sing of the bridegroom
> the bride will grow furious,
> let me sing of them both
> and never mind the best man.

> Come, friends and enemies,
> gather round,
> the blameworthy bride
> come now see.

> A rusty lock
> has lost its key;
> and an old hag is getting married
> and marries her son.

> If you only had woollen cloth and a wool coat,
> if you only had underpants as well,
> if you only had pap to eat
> and never mind love.

> If you only had a door also,
> even if it were old,
> made from a cypress plank,
> and a door made from purslane.

> And the bridegroom [son-in-law] who is now our kin,
> he's not from Yera,
> rather he's from Nio Chorio
> for the sake of stench and filth.

> Why don't you go pasture sheep
> and five or ten geese,
> for you're not worthy,
> my son, of a wife [woman].

Chapter IV

TA51a = TA8a

TA51b = TA8b

TA52 A. *Supp.* 636-8 (FJW). Tr. FJW i.107

Chorus: Wanton Ares, he that harvests mortals in fields ploughed by others!

TA53 A. *Supp.* 663-4 (FJW). Tr. FJW i.107.

Chorus: But let the blossom of its [sc. the city's] youth be unculled ...

TA54 A. *Th.* 333-5 (Hutchinson). Tr. Hutchinson, 97.

Chorus: It is a lamentable thing that young girls
should be plucked unripe and should travel
to the end a hateful journey from their homes
before the customary rites of marriage.

TA54a E. *IA* 790-2 (Günther). Tr. Morwood (1999), 107-8 (slightly modified)

Chorus: †'What man, tightening his grasp on my luxuriant locks
as I weep,

will pluck me as a flower is plucked,
from my country as it dies?'†

TA55 A. *Supp.* 664-6 (FJW). Tr. FJW i.107f.

Chorus: ... and may Aphrodite's bed-fellow, man-slaying Ares, not shear off its [sc. the city's] tenderest bloom!

TA55a E. *Supp.* 448-9 (Collard)

Theseus: ... when one cuts away and culls the [sc. choicest] young men like one cutting away with strokes a wheat stalk in a springtime meadow

TA56 Pi. *P.* 9.36-7 (S.-M.). Tr. Race i.345

'Is it right to lay my famous hand upon her
and indeed to reap [*keirai*] the honey-sweet flower from the bed of love?'

Cf. ibid. 109-11 (Tr. Race i.353):

... they were eager to cull [*apodrepsai*]
the blooming fruit of golden-crowned Hêbê [i.e. youth]

TA57 Archipp. fr. 50.3 (*PCG* ii.555 [K.-A.])

O blessed one [*makar*], you who pluck Aphrodite's garden on girls clad in wool

TA58 = TA43

TB11 Theoc. 11.39

singing of you, my dear sweet-apple ...

TB12 Euphorion (?) fr. 11 (de Cuenca, p. 49) = fr. 188 (van Groningen, p. 234)

Seasonable like an apple which grows red on the loamy banks of tiny Sidus [a village near Corinth]

TC13 Men. Rh. 404.5f. (RW) (= TC3)

'Is not she like the olive, most beautiful of plants, and he like the palm?' 'He is like a rose, and she is like an apple.'

TC14 *SEG* XVIII 594.1-2 (Cyprus, second/first century BC)

[like] a tender olive sapling cut down by gusts of wind, I, Sôs[tratê], was cut away from my father's house

TC15 Peek 1238 (listed in *SEG* XLII 1501), (Leontopolis, Egypt, first century AD). Cf. Peek 1997.3 (listed in *SEG* XLIV 1724); *IGSK* XXXIX 58.1

Stranger, weep for me, once a virgin in my prime, who delighted in my great halls; for, well before my time, dressed in lovely bridal garments I received as my lot this hateful wedding chamber of a grave. For at the very moment when the crashing commotion of revellers in front of my folding doors was bringing word to leave my father's house, Hades suddenly took me, like a rose that had blossomed in a garden under fresh moisture, and made off. Stranger, I was [twenty] years old.

TD19 Macedonius Consul *AP* 5.227

Every year men harvest grapes, and no-one, when cutting a cluster, ignores the tendrils. But having entwined a gentle bond in the knot [sc. of my embrace], I hold you, rosy-armed lady, delight of my devotion, and harvest passionate love. And I cannot wait for another summer or spring, because you are all charm and

117

grace. So, may you be in your prime forever – yet [even] if a crooked tendril of a wrinkle comes, I will bear it because I love you.

TE9 Leo Magister no. 3, vv. 27-8 (Anacreontics for the wedding of the Emperor Leo: Bergk iii.358)

Therefore, having been overcome by the shafts of Desire, gather the apples!

TE10 Ioannes Geometres, 'An encomium of the apple' (IV), in Littlewood (1972), 17-18

They say that there once was a beautiful virgin, with many passionate admirers of her beauty. But being chaste and not giving up her prime [i.e. virginity], she made her admirers even more unhappy in their love. Until then they had been in love like admirers and competed with one another; [but] afterwards they became drunk and killed each other in their rivalry in love. The maiden stood near them and pitied them, she felt shame before the survivors and wept for herself; and through a wish she became an apple-tree, as beautiful as she was beautiful, as white as she was white, and as red as she was modest.

TF12 Eustathius Makrembolites, *Hysminê and Hysminias* VI.8.3 (Conca)

'Hysminias, you lovingly cultivated me like a garden [*katekêpeusas*], whom you called "my Hysminê"; put [imper.] a fence round the garden for my sake, lest the hand of a passer-by harvest me.'

TF13 Nicetas Eugeneianos, *Drosilla and Charicles* IV.274f., 283f. (Conca)

'From my rose-bed gather my roses;
lie down and I shall join you.
What will you eat, poor chap? There's no fruit here.
And if there's no ripe apple in this small garden,
accept my bosom instead of an apple ...
Instead of the interlacing of a tree and its branches
which one causes when wishing to gather in its fruit,
I am the tree: here, cling to me ...
Pick fruit sweeter than honey.'

TF14 Nicetas Eugeneianos, *Drosilla and Charicles* VI.568-71 (Conca)

'Only you have appeared as a meadow teeming with charm ...
And now you seem to me lovely to be harvested, maiden,
like the ripe fuit of the topmost branches of a tree.
So, open the doors of your small garden
and only let me eat and be sated.'

TF15 (anon.) *Callimachos and Chrysorrhoë* 2082-7 (Kriaras). (Cf. id., 927 and Chapter IV n. 48 below.)

He says:

'It is written by Fate that you should be the Lady,
whereas to me it has been granted to *pluck* roses [*trugô ta rhoda*].
You are Lord of the plants, I guardian of the garden.
If you lie regally on your couch,
you will find your valet [sc. himself] to be a guardian and protector
and a gatherer of your roses [*trugêtên tôn rhodôn sou*] and a keeper of your
    plants.'

TF16 (anon.) *Achilleïs* 821f. (Hesseling)

Her breasts were aflame with a high beauty,
her bosom is an amorous paradise;
I envy whoever harvested her and thoroughly had his fill of her.

TF17 Nicolaos Callicles no. XXII, vv. 16-17, 20-2 (Sternbach)

TF18 Stephanos Sachlikis, v. 353 (Wagner). Cf. TG48-9 below.

And she [sc. a whore] calls you 'rose' and calls another 'apple'.

TG45 Pernot (1931), 22, no. 4 (fifteenth/sixteenth century)

I sowed wheat in the earth and rice in the sand,
a kiss on the river bank and an olive tree in the garden,
and now they've come and told me, they're reaping the wheat
and they're pruning the olive and harvesting the kiss.
Go to the devil, kiss, and love, [go] wherever you came from,
and may my youth live on, I'll find a kiss again.

TG46 Papadopoullos (1977), 201, vv. 66-7 (Cyprus, sixteenth century?)

[letter N] May I come in to harvest you, my luxuriant climbing vine,
and [= for] you've struck [sc. dazzled] me in my eyes like a gust of the north
    wind.

TG47 *Laogr.* 20 (1962), 224, no. 28 (Roumeli)

Down there in the Villages of the Vlachs,
where the Vlachs sleep separately,
klephts went out to tread [grapes] and plunder,
to harvest black eyes.
They took a Vlach maiden,
a young shepherdess.
They take her down to the seashore
and in private they question her.
'Why are your lips painted,
your hair dishevelled?'

TG48 Trebizond MS. *Dig. Akr.* 7.1991 = Z.2878 (Trapp)

'My blooming rose, my fragrant apple'

Cf. TF18; *Dig. Akr.* Esc. 181 (E. Jeffreys): 'the slender girl sat there like a shrivelled apple'; TG49.

TG49 Pernot (above), 30, no. 11.146f. (fifteenth/sixteenth century, love-alpha-bet).Cf. TF18, TG48.

Again, noble maiden, I write to you, again I greet you,
again, you're receiving a love letter from grieving lips.
'A rose, an apple and a quince
and basil [is] the maiden.'

TG50 Bouvier (1960), 12, no. 7.5 (seventeenth century)

O Paros, fragrant apple tree, apple of Paradise.

TG51 Politis (1931), 269 (first printed in 1869; from a wedding-song performed on the day after the ceremony)

Walk on, red apple, fragrant quince.

TG52 Karapatakis (1960), 67 (Grevena; from a wedding-song performed by the bridegroom and his entourage several days before the ceremony)

I did well to fall in love with an apple from my neighbourhood, –
   ah, red apple,
apple from my neighbourhood, apple from Ioannina!

TG53 Politis (1932), no. 138

Fortunate [and worthy of congratulation] is the red apple tree, fortunate [and worthy of congratulation] is the brave young man, who will reach out to pick the golden apple.

Chapter V

TA59 *Carm. conviv.* 900 (*PMG* [Page]). Tr. West (1993), 178

I wish I were a lovely lyre of ivory,
and lovely boys would take me to
their dithyrambic dance.

TA60 *Carm. conviv.* 901 (*PMG* [Page]). Tr. West (1993), 178

I wish I were a lovely pendant, big, fine gold,
and a lovely lady would wear me
with purity in her heart.

TA61 E. *Hipp.* 732-4 (Barrett). Tr. Barrett, 299

Chorus [*sings*]: Oh that I might be in the secret hollows of the mountain-steeps, and that there a god might make me a winged bird among the flying flocks.

TA62 S. *Oenomaos* fr. 476 (Lloyd-Jones [1996]). Tr. Lloyd-Jones, 247

Would that I could become a high-flying eagle, so that I could fly beyond the barren ether over the waves of the gray sea!

TA63 Anacr. fr. 361 (*PMG* [Page])

Myself, I would not wish for Amalthea's horn [i.e. horn of plenty] nor to reign over Tartessus for a hundred and fifty years.

TB13 Theoc. 3.12-13. Tr. Gow (1950), 3

Would I might become yon buzzing bee, and come into thy cave ...

TB13a Rhian. x.3254-5 (*HE*) (= *AP* 12.142.5-6)

Would that I were a thrush or a blackbird so that I might emit my cry and my sweet tears in his hand.

TB14 Call. *Aet.* I, fr. 1.32-5 (Pf.). Tr. Trypanis (1958), 9

... but let me be the dainty, the winged one [i.e. the cicada]. Oh, yes indeed! that I may sing living on dew-drops, free sustenance from the divine air; that I may then shed old age ...

TB15 'Plato' i.584-5 (Page [1981], p. 162) (= *AP* 7.669)

You are gazing at the stars, my star; would that I could become the sky so that I might look at you with many eyes.

TB16 Meleager lxxxi.4436-7 (*HE*) (= *AP* 12.52.5-6)

Would that I were a dolphin so that,

carried upon my shoulder
and having been ferried across, he might see Rhodes,
full of sweet boys.

TB16a Meleager xxxvi.4186-9 (*HE*) (= *AP* 5.174). Cf. id., *AP* 5.171.

... if only I now alighted upon your eyelids, in the guise of Hypnos [Sleep] without wings, so that not even he who charms the eyes of Zeus [Hypnos] might visit you, but [in order that] I alone might possess you.

TB17 Theoc. 11.54-5. Tr. Gow (1950), 89, slightly modified

Alack that my mother bore me not with gills, so that I might have dived down to thee and kissed thy hand.

undatable anon. ix (Page [1981], p. 319)

If only I had become the wind, and if only going out of doors, you bared your breasts and received me as I blew.

undatable anon. x (Page [1981], p. 320)

If only I had become a purplish rose so that, after plucking me with your hands, you might make a gracious gift of me to your snow-white breasts.

TB18 Call. fr. *incert. sedis* 549 (Pf.)

I wish I had something to entice a boy

TC16 Mitteis-Wilcken (1912), i.566f., no. 481 (*c.* Hadrian's reign)

If only we could fly and come to greet you!

TC16a Strat. *AP* 12.190.3-4. Cf. id., *AP* 12.208

Would that I could become a long, trailing wood-worm, so that I might leap up and devour these pieces of wood.

TC17 *Anacreont.* 22 (West) (second-fourth century AD). Tr. Campbell ii.193

Once Tantalus' daughter* became a stone standing among the Phrygian hills; once Pandion's daughter** became a bird and flew, a swallow. If only I could be a mirror, so that you would always look at me; a robe, so that you would always wear me; water, that I might wash your skin; perfume, lady, that I might anoint you; a band for your breast, a pearl for your neck, a sandal – only you must trample me underfoot!

*Niobe [tr.'s note]. **Philomela [tr.'s note].

TC18 Longus I.14.7-8 (Reeve, p. 8)

'If only I had become his herdsman's pipe so that he might blow upon me, if only [sc. I had become] a goat so that I might be pastured by him.'

TC19 Drinking-song (XXVII) (Hopkinson, pp. 80-1)

Seek not to do wrong nor strive against anyone if he does wrong.
Avoid killing and combat, forebear from quarreling,
and you will scarcely suffer and not regret this later.
Play your pipe for me (refrain?).
You've seen the spring, winter, summer; they are the same forever;
the sun itself has set and night is away [sc. from day] in due order.
Don't trouble to enquire where the sun is from or where water is from,
but rather where you might buy perfume and garlands.

121

Play your pipe for me (refrain?).
I wish I had inexhaustible fountains: three of honey,
five flowing with milk, ten of wine, twelve of perfume,
two of spring water and three of water cool as snow;
I wish I had a youth and a maiden at each spring!
Play your pipe for me (refrain?).

undatable anon. *AP* 5.99

Standing beside you, citharode, as you play your lyre, I should like to strike your highest string – and loosen your 'middle string'.

TE11 Theophanes *AP* 15.35

If only I had become a white lily, so that after plucking me with your hands, you might satiate me the more with your flesh.

TF19 Nicet. Eugen. *DC* II.331-45 (Conca)

Bright moon, guide the wayfarer with your light!
Would that I were present as a mirror, Lord Zeus,
so that you would always see me, Kalligonê;
would that I could become a parti-coloured tunic of gold fabric,
so that I would be able to touch your dainty flesh.
Bright moon, guide the wayfarer with your light!
Would that I came to be water, so that I might be able,
in my good luck, to anoint every part of your face every day;
would that I could become perfume, so that I might be able to anoint
your lips, cheeks, hands, eyes, mouth.
Bright moon, guide the wayfarer with your light!
It would be enough for me to become a small golden slipper
and to bear only to be stepped upon
by the flat of your foot.

TF20 Nicet. Eugen. *DC* VIII.110-13 (Conca)

Virgin, would that I could now become Zephuros [i.e. the West Wind] and would that, after baring your breasts, you took me in as you saw me gently blowing your way.

TG54 *Erôtopaignia*, 125-6 (H.-P.)

May I become a little pigeon so that I may come to you where you are sleeping, so that I may embrace you tightly, so that you may always remember me.

TG55 Pernot (1931), 38, no. 24

May I become a little swallow,
    so that I may come to your bedside,
so that I may build my little nest on your pillow,
so that I may chirp, so that I may wake you,
    so that you may always remember me,
so that you may remember me, my slender one,
    for as long as you live.

TG56 *Erotocritos* IV.919-20 (S. Alexiou)

'If only I were a bird, if only I could fly straightaway, to cross over the walls and to get into the town!'

TG57 Gazis (1828), 32

Oh! ... if only I might become a bird,
    if only I might fly high,
if only I might find the eagle, so that I could ask him
    where you were killed, my colourful hawk!

TG58 Vavoules (1950), 124 (Crete)

I wish I were water in the river, where you do your washing,
and [I wish] the heat were intense, and you bent down to drink me.

TG59 Karayiannis (1983), 87 (Lesbos)

If only I were – what might I be? ...
The hem of your dress,
and if only I could bend to see
the hole of your cunt.

Further obscene wishes from modern Greece are noted in the Addenda below.

TG60 *Thrakika* 12 (1939), 361

If only I could become wheat stalks for you to harvest, a handful to hold and to
yearn for.

TG61 *Thrakika* 12 (1939), 360

If only I could become a cold spring at harvest so that my love could drink until
he finished harvesting.

TG62 Pernot (1931), 36, no. 21; cf. ibid., 38, no. 26.

I wish I could kiss you when the trees bloom, and [I wish] birds chirped on the
branches.

TG63 *Erôtopaignia* 260-5 (H.-P.)

Twenty apples lie in a gold dish,
red and sweet [dimin.] like your two lips,
and I stand, I yearn for them and declare:
    If only I had an apple,
so that I might smell it at night and sleep sweetly,
and so that I might kiss it at night and be consoled,
so that I might have consolation as though you were at my side.

TG64 Regas (1958), 34 (Skiathos) (The editor himself was a priest; the verses are
set to a known religious melody.)

On Mount Athos
and at the Monastery of Pantocratôr
three abbots were saying:
'If only we had – if only we had *what*?
A gurnet boiled in water
and fried eggs,
sizzling in butter,
and freshly baked bread
and muscat wine
and a nun [*gerontissa*, lit. 'a female elder']
of up to eighteen years
to offer us drink
while we tippled
and great be His mercy [liturgical phrase].'

TG65 Karayiannis (1983), 87 (Lesbos)

If only I had a soft cake
and a skinned mackerel
and the teacher's cunt
[freshly] taken out of the bath.

TG66 Oikonomides (1881), 150 (Olympus)

If only I were a gold button on your inner garment,
if only I kissed your pearl-like breast.

Addenda

Chapter I

n. 25: On the *Ptochoprodromica* and the increasing likelihood that Theodore Prodromos is their author, see now M. Alexiou (1999), 91-109.

Objection 4: For a linguistic analogy, cf. Horrocks (1997), 166-8 on convergence phenomena, datable to the Middle Ages, in the syntax of Balkan languages. We might also compare 'cultural convergence' set in motion among 'Hellenised' Anatolian populations by the gradual and uneven Turkification from the eleventh to the fifteenth century: see Vryonis (1971), especially chs I and VII. On Arabic and generally Islamic influence on learned and popular literature in the Greek language from the seventh to the eighteenth century, consult Garland (1990), 81 n. 74, 84 n. 82; on the influence of the ancient Greek novel on Arab poetry, ibid., 64 n. 8.

Chapter II

Testimonia: I omitted the epithalamium composed of six hexameter lines and printed as *P. Ryl.* 17; it dates to the Hellenistic or even Roman period.

Testimonia: For Himerius see Kennedy (1983), 141-9; on the rhetorical school of fifth- and sixth-century Gaza, particularly John the Grammarian and Choricius, see ibid., 169-77.

Section B.8 ('Physical description and *ecphrasis*'): On TA 1713 see Dunbar (1995), 747; on TA 1723, ibid., 754-5 ad 1723-4.

Section B.11 ('Refrain'): On the *Humên*-refrain at the end of *Birds*, now see Dunbar, 756-7 ad 1731-42 & 759 ad 1736. On the refrain in TC9 see Reed (1997), 246 and cf. Chapter II n. 164.

Section C.2a ('Fruits, flowers and plants'): According to Artem. 4.2 (Pack, p. 247) an *ampelos* is an auspicious dream image because its tendrils are associated with the union of marriage.

Section C.2c ('Natural objects or phenomena'): On TA 10.1709f. see Dunbar, 746-7.

Section C.5 ('*Makarismos*'): On TA 18.1721-2 see Dunbar, 754.

For certain nuptial *topoi*, including the customary beatitude (see C.5 immed. above) and the praise of the bridegroom's hair (see B.8 above), also consult Hunter (1983), 195-6 ad Eub. fr. 104 (= fr. 102 [K.-A.]).

Chapter III

On the alternative possibility of Fescennine obscenity in Sapph. fr. 111(LP), see Kopidakis (1989), 45-54.

Chapter V

A wish referring to homosexual love-making occurs at Call. fr. 571 (Pf.). Tr. Trypanis (1958), 267:

... would that you, who cast lewd eyes upon boys, might make love to the young in the manner ordained by Erchios*. You would have a city of noble men.

*Otherwise unknown [tr.'s note].

Meleager xxxv.4184-5 (*HE*) represents a sympotic amatory wish:

... would that, having placed her lips to mine,
she could now, in a single draught, drink in the soul within me.

In the following song from Lesbos (Karayiannis, 90) the singer articulates a Type A, class 2 wish which reflects a genuine sexual phenomenon:

If only I were a brick in your garden
so that your cunt
would piss on me.

Also cf. ibid., 92:

If only I were a step on a stair,
if only I grabbed a piece of it (sc. cunt).

Appendix V

On *phlyakes* and their iconography, now see Taplin (1993), 48-54.

Appendixes

I. Ancient wedding rituals: the visual and literary evidence re-examined

For a bibliography of AG (largely Athenian) marriage ceremonials see: Diggle (1970), 149 n. 1 on E. *Phaeth.* 227; Hague (1983), 140 nn. 1 & 3; Oakley (1982), 113 n. 3; Redfield (1982), 199-201; Oakley & Sinos (1993), *passim*; Perentidis (1997), 179-204. For fresh epigraphic evidence esp. of post-nuptial sacrifices in Cos: Dillon (1999), 63-80.

A systematic examination and correlation of the iconographic and literary evidence of the nexus of rituals comprising the ancient wedding is undertaken by Fraser (1985), Oakley & Sinos (above), and, with crucial corrections and supplements, by Perentidis (above), who convincingly assigns the *epaulia* to day 2 and the controversial *anakaluptêria* to day 3.[1]

(1) *Day 1: apaulia hêmera*

(i) Preliminaries

(a) *proteleia* (sc. *hiera*) i.e. outdoor pre-nuptial sacrifices (and libations) performed separately by the bride and bridegroom to Artemis, Aphrodite, Zeus and Hera, etc.: Oakley & Sinos, 11-12; Perentidis (1997), 185-6;[2]

(b) bride's offer of a symbolic object e.g. her veil, belt, toys, hair clippings: Oakley & Sinos, 14-15; Perentidis, 186;

(c) ritual cleansing (bath) of the bride and bridegroom in water collected from a particular spring or river (*loutrophoreia*): Fraser (above), 19-30; Oakley & Sinos, 15-16; Perentidis, 185 (cf. Plate 1);

(d) the bride's toilette (adornment, see Plate 2) and the dressing of the bridegroom: Fraser, 31-44; Oakley & Sinos, 16-21, 134 n. 45 (further bibl.);

(ii) *ta apaulia*: the bridegroom slept beside a girl who was *amphithalês*[3] at his future father-in-law's house: see esp. Perentidis, 185-9 on this rite, which rather signalled a phase of asexual/bisexual liminality than of separation.

Stages 1 (a)-(d) above are clearly 'rites of separation'.

(2) *Day 2: epaulia hêmera*

(a) a feast, usually in the bride's house: Fraser, 51-8; Oakley & Sinos, esp. 22-4;

(b) *pompê* (or *agôgê*), the torch-lit nocturnal procession (preferably under a full moon) by chariot,[4] mule-cart or on foot to the bridegroom's house; the bride, who was veiled, was now transferred to her new abode: Fraser, 74f., 86f., 119f.: Oakley & Sinos, 26-34; Perentidis, 189-92 (see Plate 3, which features, unrealistically, an unveiled bride);[5]

(c) *katakhusmata* i.e. dates, coins, dried fruits, figs and nuts were tossed at night over the couple as they entered the bridegroom's house or over the bride as she sat by the hearth in his house: Oakley & Sinos, 34-5; Perentidis, 192;

127

(d) *ta epaulia*: under the protection of *Artemis epauliê*[6] the bride slept beside a *pais amphithalês* at the bridegroom's house: Perentidis, below.

Stages 2(b) & (d) mark rites of liminality; 2(c) is a rite of incorporation.

(3) *Day 3: anakaluptêria hêmera*

(a) in the morning the bride received gifts (*epaulia dôra* or simply [*ta*] *epaulia*) of a symbolic and/or practical character, which were brought to the bride-groom's house by a procession of children: Fraser, 175-210; Oakley & Sinos, 38-40; and esp. Perentidis, 193-6;

(b) *ta anakaluptêria*: at a special feast (*hestiasis tôn gamôn*) held at the bride-groom's house, he ceremoniously unveiled the bride before the guests and offered her a gift: Oakley & Sinos, 25-6, 30, 32; cf. esp. Perentidis, 196-210;[7]

(c) the bride accepted and ate an apple or quince (obvious love-symbols)[8] given to her by the bridegroom; after the preparation of the nuptial bed (*klinê*), the couple were escorted to the bridal chamber (*thalamos*) and the wedding night, featuring the *copula carnalis*, ensued: Fraser, 155-9; Oakley & Sinos, 35-7; esp. Perentidis, 197-8.

3(a), a continuation of 2(d), is a rite of liminality; 3(b), the unveiling of the bride, marks her incorporation into her new household. Contrary to what one might expect (on the basis of comparative, e.g. Germanic evidence), among the Greeks the culminating *prima nox*, 3(c), did not signify any change in the bride's biological, social or legal status; it was rather her preceding unveiling, 3(b), that marked this wide-ranging change.[9]

To Fraser's and Oakley's and Sinos' documentation add: epithalamian (?) in elegiac metre, possibly by Posidippus, *SH*, no. 961 (Ll.-Jones-Parsons, p. 464), vv. 5 ?, 7, 18, which refer to Arsinoë's bath. Additionally, in a papyrus fragment, P. Oxy. lix.3966, vv. 8-10, attributed to Menander (*Karchêdonios, Phasma*?) a character remarks that '[it is customary] / to bring [the lustral water (*loutra*)] for those marrying from the fountain / and [to sing] to the accompaniment of a flute'.

II: Song and dance in the ancient and Byzantine wedding

The visual evidence of the vases, which supplements much of the literary evidence, clearly confirms that music and in particular song and/or dance accompanied the following events or ceremonial actions of the wedding:

(i)

(1) The *loutrophoreia* i.e. the procession bearing the high-necked water-jar (*loutrophoros*): e.g. Attic red-figure *loutrophoros* by the Washing Painter (= Plate 1, discussed by Oakley & Sinos, 15-16): a young boy playing double flutes sets the pace for a procession (which includes the future bride) going to or returning from the fountain house. See also Oakley & Sinos, figs 16-19; discussion, ibid., 16.

(2) The pre-nuptial toilette of the bride: e.g. Attic red-figure *lebês gamikos* by the Washing Painter. New York, MMA 16.73 (= Oakley & Sinos, fig. 37; discussion, ibid., 20): the bride, seated and about to be adorned with a ribbon, plucks the strings of a harp while gazing dreamily up at Eros (is she playing a love-song?). See also Oakley & Sinos, figs 24-7 (discussion, ibid., 17-18); figs 36, 38 (discussion, ibid., 20, 45).

(3) *Pompê / agôgê* i.e. the procession to the bridegroom's house: e.g. (a) Attic black-figure *amphora* by the Painter of Berlin. London, British Museum B 197 (= Oakley & Sinos, fig. 66; discussion, ibid., 29): Holding his lyre, Apollo, among other divinities, escorts the couple; a Siren, seated beside Apollo and beneath his lyre, perhaps personifies his song. (b) Attic red-figure cup by the Amphitrite Painter.

Berlin, Staatliche Museen F 2530 (= Oakley & Sinos, fig. 91; discussion, ibid., 33): a young man (or is it Apollo?) with a lyre stands between the advancing couple and the bridegroom's house. See further Oakley & Sinos, figs 62-3, 64 (discussion, ibid., 28); 74 (discussion, ibid., 31); 87-9 (discussion, ibid., 33).

(4) Ceremonial entrance into the bridegroom's house and/or procession to the bedroom: e.g. (a) Attic red-figure *loutrophoros-hydria* by the Sabouroff Painter. Copenhagen, National Museum 9080 (= Oakley & Sinos, figs 92-5; discussion, ibid., 33-4): a youth is playing flutes as the couple enter their new home and proceed to the bedroom. (b) Attic white-ground *pyxis* by the Splanchnopt Painter. London, British Museum D 11 (= Oakley & Sinos, figs 96-8; discussion, ibid., 34-5, w. 138 n. 92): the bridegroom leads a hesitant bride toward a flaming altar (or hearth) in his house; in front of him steps a boy playing flutes. See also Oakley & Sinos, figs 108-11 (discussion, ibid., 36).

(5) *Epaulia* i.e. ritual gift-giving on the third day: e.g. Attic red-figure *pyxis*. Berlin, Staatliche Museen 3373 (= Oakley & Sinos, figs 115-19; discussion, ibid., 38): a girl plays flutes, setting the rhythm for those carrying sundry gifts to the seated bride.

(ii) On wedding-dances in general: as the literary and visual evidence shows (see Oakley & Sinos, figs 54-8, 59; discussion, ibid., 24-5), both sexes, including the bride and bridegroom, danced at various stages of the wedding, but they did so separately; musicians were also present (see Plate 7).

(iii) The varied literary evidence of popular wedding practices (including the bath) and songs in Byzantium is to be found mainly in Koukoules iv. 73-119. (Much of K.'s information should be re-classified and interpreted accordingly.) The *pastos* referred to in many sources was an 'arrangement of curtains, a sort of (ornate or dyed) bed-canopy for the nuptial pair' and was introduced to Greece from Egypt during the Roman period: see Lane (1988), 100-23; also Oakley & Sinos, 35, 138 n. 98. The term is still used in the environs of Paphos in Cyprus, but refers to the embroidered cloth on which the bridal couple sit to receive their wedding guests. However, as Lane ibid., 119 notes, in Rhodes the *sperveri* is the nuptial bed-canopy apparently denoted by the ancient *pastos*.

III. Sexual initiation in the modern wedding

The sexual and especially the initiatory interests of modern wedding-songs can be documented from such songs as the following, which was recorded over a century ago on the island of Kastellorizo. It purports to be an exchange between the bride (and her *pudendum*) and the bridegroom on their first night. It was sung however by the older women probably either during the bride's bath or towards the end of the wedding feast (when people became more relaxed). The bride was pressed to repeat the main song, and she probably obliged:

L.A. MS. 434.70 (unpubl., Kastellorizo)

Say it, my daughter/maiden, and don't be ashamed,
for your mother also said it, and your aunt said it too:
'For your sake I was hiding my large cunt (*pouttaros*),
my hefty cunt (*mounnaros*), big as a plate [or trough],
which has eighteen crypts and eighteen arches;
within each arch nine Janissaries are hiding:
– Where are you going, Janissary, where are you going, dear Janissary?
– O my cunt (*mounni*), I'm going to hide myself over there, in the shavings,
where they weigh cocks and big balls.'

129

For a similar but less *risqué* song cf. Aravantinos (1880), no. 373 (cited in Chapter III n. 41). *Pouttaron<pouttaros*, the augmentative form of *pouttos*, on which cf. Eideneier (1977), 318, svv. *poutti(n)* and *pouttos*. On antiphonal question and answer in modern Greek folk-song see Chapter II section B.10. The term 'Janissary' in vv. 6-7 evokes violence; in v. 7 it refers to the bridegroom and in hindsight is probably also a euphemism for the *membrum virile*.

IV. Sappho fr. 104a (LP) and a modern nuptial lament

The following lament was recorded at the turn of the last century in Cappadocia; it was sung by the bride as she rode horseback from her village to that of the bridegroom, presumably at dawn:

Pachtikos i.15, no. 12[1]

> The East [i.e. dawn] has broken and the West has lit up [i.e. dawn has broken];
> the birds have gone to their pasturage and desolate persons have gone to the West;
> and so also do I, in my desolation, go towards the Bridge of Adana.

v. 1, a *hendiadys* (see below), is actually a well-known formula, that lends the flavour of a ballad to the bride's complaint; cf. Passow (1860), 326; Spyridakis-Petropoulos (1962), 137. v. 3, the punchline as it were, requires explanation. The destination of this mythical bridge is almost a cliché for an exceedingly lengthy task, difficulties or danger and, moreover, may even evoke the notion of crossing into the world of the dead: Beaton (1980)[a], 120f. (In the latter case the lugubrious overtones may well support the diagnosis that marriage, from the bride's perspective, was perceived as a death; see Chapters III and IV *passim*.) *erêmoi* ('desolate, lonely persons') (v. 2) is curious: very probably it refers here to wayfarers or even exiles. 'To the West' (or 'westward') in the same line doubtless implies 'away from home'. The parallelism in vv. 1-3 is a mark of oral technique; see Chapter II section B.7. The formal structure and its relation to the song's content may be analysed thus:

(v. 1) A ~ A ', where the corresponding hemistichs make up a *hendiadys* for dawn, a natural and inevitable event;

(v. 2) B ~ B', where the second pair of hemistichs expresses (i) a natural or inevitable event (the movement of birds) following closely on dawn, and (ii) another but different kind of event (the movement of persons away from home), also following on dawn;

(v. 3) C (the bride's journey), a largely cultural event which is viewed as inevitable as, and thus parallel to, the movement of birds and as similar in implication to the movement of persons away from home.

It may be of interest to apply the foregoing popular paradigm to a reading of Sapph. fr. 104a (LP). Needless to say, the interpretation which ensues is purely conjectural. Here is Sappho's song (tr. Campbell i.131):

Hesperus, bringing everything that shining Dawn scattered, you bring the sheep, you bring the goat, you bring back the child to its mother.

v. 1 states directly the popular *topos* (?) that dawn despatches certain creatures and individuals to their respective daytime activities;[2] cf. vv. 1-2 of the modern song. More importantly, the Cappadocian lament might prompt two inferences: (i) *contra* Burnett (1983), 223 n. 33, Sappho's poem is *not* playful but was indeed a serious complaint or lament sung by the bride or another party speaking on her behalf; (ii) *contra* Page (1955), 121 n. 1, the point of Sappho's song was not so much a direct contrast between the natural course of events heralded by daybreak i.e. the 'homeward' return of sheep, goats and children, and the bride's absence from home, as it was the *inevitability* of her removal to the bridegroom's home in the evening (sc. 'just as inevitably, Hesperus, you convey me to my new home'). This second line of interpretation differs from Page's tentative reconstruction merely in nuance, and assumes that, if a popular source underlay the composition, the poetess was deliberately conforming to, not diverging from it. In the light of the modern comparandum, it seems at any event likelier that Sappho drew a parallel between the natural course of certain events and the *domum deductio* or its aftermath.

V. Carmina 'Locrica'

According to Athen. 14.639A the Peripatetic philosopher Clearchus of Soli mentioned in his *Erotica* a genus of love-songs known in his time as *Lokrikai ôidai*, which he characterised as scarcely any more decent in subject-matter than the poems of Sappho and Anacreon. Erotic songs of a non-literary nature may be meant by the term *pornôidiai* at Ar. *Ran.* 1301,[1] and the prevalence of such songs was probably a sub-literary phenomenon connected with the mime and particularly the imitation of dramatic arias from tragedy.[2] Athen. 15.697B preserves one of the three surviving samples of the 'Locrica' and gives us some additional information about them. Frivolous in tone (ibid. *tas kapurôteras ôidas aspasdetai mâllon tôn espoudasmenôn*), the songs dealt with the themes of love and infidelity (ibid. *moikhikai tines tên phusin*). Moreover, if he is to be trusted, Locrian songs were widely diffused in the region loosely known in antiquity as 'Phoenicia'[3], and they may have been played on the *cithara* (cf. Athen. 14.368B *kitharisai tas erôtikas ôidas*). In all our specimens a woman addresses her lover.[4] Here is the song found in Athenaeus and printed by Page as *carm. pop.* 853 (*PMG*):

ô ti paskheis; mê prodôis amm', hiketeuô·
prin kai molein keinon, anistô,
mê kakon <se> mega poiêsêi
kame tan deilakran.

hamera kai êdê· to phôs
dia tas thuridos ouk eisorêis;

Athenaeus, *Scholars at Dinner*

For Ulpian here welcomes the more frivolous songs rather than the serious ones, the so-called Locrian songs for example, randy like this one:

Oh, what's the matter with you? Don't give us away, I beg you. Get up before he* comes, in case he does great harm to you and to me, poor wretch! Look, it's day! Don't you see the light through the window?

Ulpian's country Phoenicia is full of this sort of song.

*The singer's husband [tr.'s note].
Tr. Campbell v.241

The woman, awakened by the light of dawn streaming through her window, begs her lover to leave immediately, lest her husband return. On the whole, the diction of the song is hardly ordinary. The question *ô ti paskheis*; though, is a colloquial expression used to attract attention; it has virtually an active sense i.e. 'What's the matter with you? What *are* you doing?', and is addressed to someone who seems to be acting ineptly or recklessly: cf. Stevens (1976), 41, with parallels from tragedy and comedy. The parenthetic construction of *hiketeuô*, itself probably a colloquial word,[5] in v. 1 also has parallels in tragedy; see esp. Soph. *Ph.* 1181 (Lloyd-Jones) *mê, ... el- |theîs, hiketeuô*, which similarly conveys a desperate plea to an intimate. *molein* (v. 2) is highly poetic, as is probably *deilakra* ('pitiable', see Ar. *Pl.* 973). There is nothing consistently 'Locrian' i.e. south Italian here from a dialectal point of view. The song exhibits rather an erratic admixture of dialects such as we find in pseudo-literary inscriptions from the middle Hellenistic period onwards (although the song may be much earlier in date).[6] Cf. Ionic and poetic *keinon*, almost contemptuously of the cuckold; Aeolic *amm', kame*; Doric and Aeolic *hamera*; Doric contraction *eisorêis*. The first two lines are probably Ionic, if we accept West's scansion.[7] *kai* in v. 2 is a surplus syllable and may be deleted;[8] perhaps the line is corrupt. vv. 3-6, on the other hand, are clearly iambic-trochaic.[9] The diversification of the opening metre is not surprising, as purely Ionic songs are rare except in certain cults.

The subject of Athenaeus' song is distinctively popular: ancient storytelling (e.g. Aesop) and the popular comic stage, notably the *phlyakes*, Aristophanes and the mime, abounded with unfaithful wives and secret rendezvous in general. See, for instance, Ar. *Thesm.* 392, 470f., 493 (in the latter passage the husband returns unexpectedly at dawn); Athen. 14.621C (*ho de magôidos ... hupokrinomenos pote men gunaikas kai moikhous kai mastropous*, etc.); further on these motifs (with iconographic evidence) in Trenkner (1958), 80f., esp. 83-4, 155f. The reference to daylight in v. 4 is natural, since dawn spelt the end of a nocturnal tryst; in literature a lover conventionally regretted daybreak as premature,[10] and that is also the case here.[11]

Now we may consider this dialogue song,[12] inscribed *c.* 150 BC in the necropolis of Marisa (Marêshah) (*lyricum adesp.* 5 [Powell, p. 184]):[13]

<Gunê:> Ouk ekhô ti soi pathô ê ti kharisômai·
kâita keimai meth' heterou, se mega philousa;
Alla nai tên Aphroditên mega ti khairô
hot<t>i <toi> sou thoimation enekhura keitai.

<Anêr:> All' egô men apotrekhô, soi de katalipô
eurukhôriên pollên. <Gu.> Prâsse hot<t>i boulêi.
Mê kroue ton toikhon, psophos engignetai,
alla dia tôn thurôn neuma s' hik<n>eitai.

<Woman:> I don't know what to undergo for your sake or what favour to
    grant.
Goodness, am I in bed with another man, though I love you much?
Yet by Aphrodite, I'm very glad
that your cloak lies [here] as a pledge [sc. of your return].

<Man:> Well, as for me, I'm running off and leave you
ample room for manoeuvre. <?Woman:>Do what you will.

[The final two verses are translated on p. 133 below.]

These eight lines are not a grave superscription and have no explicit connection with the loculus; they are attributable to someone of culture.[14] vv. 1-6 are straightforward trochaic trimeters, but with two (or possibly even three) faults which betray an amateurish versifier: *pathô ê* (v. 1) and *Prâsse hot<t>i* (v. 6) are two instances of inadmissible hiatus;[15] *pollên* in v. 6 should be ∪ – but is – –. The metre changes wholly unexpectedly at vv. 7-8; v. 8 is composed of three cretics[15] and a spondee. The fact that the song ends in a different, and more complicated, metre may suggest that the final two lines belong to another song. As will be seen shortly, these two lines may seem inappropriate also on grounds of sense.

The man arrives at a bad moment and finds his *erômenê* in bed with another man; she addresses him excitedly and he (the original lover) responds noncha-lantly. *pathô* and *kharisômai* (v. 1) are both used as sexual euphemisms; see Dover (1978), 140 n. 7; 44f., 83, 157. *kâita* (v. 2) introduces, often in mid-speech as here, a surprised, indignant or sarcastic question: Denniston (1954), 311; further, Stevens ibid., 47. The woman may be feigning surprise at her predicament, or she may be genuinely annoyed by it. The *himation* (v. 4) professedly treasured by her is a guarantee that the man will return: for a personal article as a pledge of fidelity cf. Delphis' pledge of a small jar to Simaetha at Theoc. 2.156.[17] The man's reaction in vv. 5-6 may be complacent; if so, it may be the case that his beloved is a *hetaira*. But perhaps more likely, his reaction is at bottom sarcastic and contemptuous, tantamount to '*I* don't care what you do. By all means, go ahead, have as many men as you like!'. Such angry pseudo-politeness would well suit a lovers' quarrel. There is no reason why *Prâsse hot<t>i boulêi* should not be an expansion of the man's earlier statement *soi de katale<i>pô / eurukhôriên pollên*[18] (i.e. 'I leave you room for manoeuvre'); a redistribution of speakers here would make better sense. vv. 7-8, already suspect on metrical grounds, do not fit what has preceded. In the last distich someone is knocking on (or against) a wall, whereas the man in v. 6 has declared his readiness to leave. It seems possible either that the last two lines have been interpolated from another song or that they are the beginning of a new song.[19] Either way, the lines in question belong to another 'Locrian' song. Here, again, a woman in distress seems to be addressing her lover. They are in bed, and she warns him:

'Don't bump[20] against the wall. It makes a noise.[21]
But <apart from that, even> through the doors <even the sound of> a nod reaches you' (where 'you' = 'one').

Supplemented in this way, v. 8 is a hyperbole that has the air of a common expression or a cliché; cf. the English (referring to a building with poor sound-proofing) 'You can hear the man in the next room turn the pages of a book!'

VI. *Carm. conviv.* 889 (*PMG*)

A song couched as a fantastic amatory wish was probably a staple of the sympo-sium, as we have seen in Chapter V. In this section we shall consider another convivial song in the form of a wish (no. 6 in Athenaeus' collection). It was current in the early fourth century BC[1] and almost certainly emanated from the popular domain (tr. Campbell v.283):

eith' exên hopoios tis ên hekastos
to stêthos dielont', epeita ton noun
esidonta, kleisanta palin,
andra philon nomisdein adolôi phreni.

If only it were possible to see what everyone is
like by opening his breast and, having looked at
his mind, to close it up again and regard the man
as one's friend for his guileless heart.

The first two verses are phalaecean and the third verse is the normal third verse of a *carmen conviviale*. Grammatically, the *scolion* is an unreal wish referring to an object unattained in the present (Goodwin, par. 731). As such it may be compared with the wishes TB21a, TB22, TC16, and TC18 examined in Chapter V. *estin* in v. 1 has been attracted into the imperfect by *exên*.[2] *epeita* in v. 2 serves as a loose connective, the equivalent of *epeita de* in prose; the overall construction of the song is casual and rather reflects colloquial syntax. *stêthos* in the singular, as used of the seat of feeling and thought, is non-poetic (see LSJ II, s.v.). *adolôi phreni* should be taken as 'by reason of his guileless heart'.[3]

Nous here means 'purpose, attitude' as often in e.g. Aristophanes.[4] But the procedure of dividing up (*dielont*) a man's chest in order to discover the *nous* and hence the *phrên* must imply that these nouns are used synonymously in the song as locations or containers of a person's true (especially bad) attitudes and sentiments.[5] Rather unsurprisingly, *nous* and *phrenes* are treated here as synonymous with *splankhna*, or 'innards':[6] like innards, both are imagined as containing and therefore *concealing* true emotions. Moreover, the combination of *adolos* with *phrên*, though attested here for the first time,[7] is natural: the capacity of the *phrên* to motivate outwardly friendly behaviour when in fact contrary emotions are felt underlies *Il.* 9.313,[8] Achilles' oblique barb at Odysseus, 'who hides one thing in his *phrenes* but speaks another'.[9]

For the need to guard against hidden *dolos*, cf. *carm. conviv.* 903 (*PMG*) and Praxill. fr. 750 (ibid.). The *scolion* which concerns us doubtless coloured E. *Hipp.* 925-7[10] 'Alas, men should have some clear test of their friends established, a way of judging their hearts [*phrenes*], to show who is a true friend and who is not' [tr. Morwood (1993), 65] (cf. *Hipp.* 616-17), and the need for reliable external *tekmêria* of men's character is actually a *topos*: Thgn. 119f. (*IE*, i [W]), E. *Med.* 516f., Hyperides fr. 229 (198),[11] etc. The contrast Alcibiades draws between Socrates' physical resemblance to Silenus and his *sôphrosunê* (Pl. *Smp.* 216d.5f.) is also relevant: '[sc. Socrates] is invested with this appearance on the outside, exactly like a sculpted Silenus; but if opened from the inside, you just can't imagine ... the extent of his self-control' (not in Page or Barrett).

The imaginary process of probing a man's inner organs recalls ritual divination through inspection of animal entrails, as Padel notes.[12] The *scolion* is derived from the Aesopic aetiological fable about the judgement by Momus of Prometheus' creation, man:[13] Momus criticised Prometheus 'because he did not hang man's *phrenes* on the outside so as to prevent malicious persons from escaping notice, and so that what each had in mind might be obvious' (*CFA* no. 102 [Hausrath & Hunger i.1.128-9]). Because of Prometheus' miscalculation, mortals cannot divine their fellows' feelings. The Titan may (according to the well-known Aeschylean tradition) have invented extispicy,[14] but, alas, he devised nothing comparable in connection with forecasting or at least gauging the purposes and sentiments of one's drinking-companions and people in general.

VII. *Carm. conviv.* 904 (*PMG*)

ha hûs tan balanon tan men ekhei, tan d'eratai labein
kagô paida kalên tên men ekhô, tên d'eramai labein.

The old sow's got a nice acorn,
    but has her heart set on another;
and I've got one pretty girl,
    but have my heart set on another.
(Tr. West [1993][a], 178)

The *scolion* is in the Asclepiad metre; *de* in both lines is antithetical. The Doric of v. 1 (possibly from a proverb) changes to Attic vernacular in v. 2. The admixtures of dialects is intended to make the composition sound more literary and can be paralleled from other popular and sub-literary specimens e.g. *carm. pop.* 853 (*PMG*)[1] and epitaphs from the middle Hellenistic period onwards. The four opening words of the song announce the theme, which is the lower and more irrational aspects of erotic desire. (Here, as in *carm. conviv.* 905 [*PMG*], the singer takes his audience into the sphere of *pandêmos erôs*.) The singer's preferences are as irrational as the sow's – or so he claims. The parallel drawn between the animal world and human affairs is a popular trait;[2] Sapph. fr. 104a (LP) probably featured such a comparison (Appendix III). What is more, the form of the indirect comparison involving *kai* is identical with that found in the Cappadocian lament discussed in Appendix III. The topic of this *scolion* is related to the conceits of *l'embarras du choix* and inconstancy familiar from later epigrams: e.g. Polystr. i.3040f. *(HE)* (= *AP* 12.91); Meleager xxiv.4124f. *(HE)* (= *AP* 5.198), a catalogue of named favourites and of their respective alluring features;[3] id. xviii.4088f. *(HE)* (= *AP* 12.86) (wavers between a woman and her son); anon. i.3646f. *(HE)* (= anon. *AP* 12.90); anon. ii.3654f. *(HE)* (= anon *AP* 12.89); anon. xix.3722f. *(HE)* (= anon. *AP* 12.88) (torn between two named males); Paul. Silent. *AP* 5.232.

The conceit of inconstancy in love also informs various modern Greek folk-songs. The following may be a case of male braggadocio (Tsetsos [1981], 117, no. 223; humorous song from Thessaly):

I ask you, girls,
put me in the middle
so that I may kiss whomever I like.
May I kiss Eleni –
she's burnt my heart.
May I kiss Agoro,
who's as red as a pomegranate.
May I kiss Vasilo,
who's as red as an apple.
May I kiss Argyro,
[she] brings the dance round.
May I kiss Angelo,
somehow I don't want her overmuch.
May I kiss Stamato,
who has a plump cheek.
May I kiss Savvoula,
somehow I feel nauseated.

The catalogue of the singer's favourites entails syntactical parallelism. Imagining himself to be in the midst of an all-female 'chorus', he first gives the name of the desired girl ('May I kiss …'), then he states her attractive quality by means of either a relative causal clause or a grammatically unconnected causal sentence. The song's symmetry is spoilt however at vv. 12f. and 16f. by the singer's capricious (or actual) revulsion; cf. the sow's irrational tastes in the *scolion*.[4] The catalogue of named favourites, incidentally, also occurs in Meleager: cf. xxiv.4124f. *(HE)*, just cited.

VIII. *Carm. conviv.* 905 *(PMG)*

pornê kai balaneus tôuton ekhous' empedeôs ethos·
en tautâi puelôi ton t'agathon ton te kakon loei.

The whore and the bathman always have the same habit:
they wash the good man and the bad man in the same tub.
(Tr. Campbell v. 291)

The sentiment expressed here, as at *carm. conviv.* 904 *(PMG)* above, is less dignified than anything we find in the rest of the collection. The *scolion* may be an example of the denigration of prostitutes which was practically *de rigueur* in the symposium: cf. Arch. fr. 302 *(IE,* i [W]), Alc. fr. 117b.28f. (LP), Thgn. 1367-8 *(IE,* i

[W]).[1] v. 1 has the air of a proverb or cliché,[2] and v. 2 is a witty expansion thereof. *puelos* (= 'bathing-tub', as in Ar. *Eq.* 1060, *Pax* 843, *Th.* 562, etc.) is used figuratively of the prostitute's *pudendum*, wherein she 'bathes' all sorts of men indiscriminately; the term does not occur elsewhere in the same sense. The following popular riddle, or *ainigma*[3] (Settas [1976], 23 [Euboea]), exemplifies material very similar to that found in the ancient song:

> This is why I've bought you
> and spent my money:
> so that I may lay you on your back,
> so that I may do my work.

The customary answer is *skaphi* (= 'washing trough') at the literal level and prostitute at the figurative one.

IX. Ar. *Ran.* 621-2

At Ar. *Ran.* 621-2 Xanthias' reservations about the treatment to be accorded to his 'slave' have been taken by Stanford (1963), 125 as a 'parody of the reservations which a merciful master would make'. Stanford speculates that these exceptions may be completely fanciful and notes that others have seen a reference to symbolic, cathartic rites.[1] But a jocular and, to all appearances, formulaic curse that occurs in a modern Rhodian folk-song features imaginary tortures clearly parallel to those in *Ran.* This suggests that Xanthias' ridiculous proviso reflects a genuinely colloquial usage. Here is the song (Baud-Bovy i.244):

> Last evening I went by the Church of the Saviour,
> and an ill-fated widow was washing her dress,
> she laid it out on branches and *that* they snatched from her.
> If by any chance *I* snatched it, may I die an unjust death,
> may they stone me with eggs in a frying pan,
> may I hang from cabbage, may I fall into the lettuce patch,
> may they smash my head with peeled eggs,
> may they smash my teeth with fresh mitzithra-cheese.

The cheese in question is the softest of cheeses, made from sheep's milk. The long, flippant curse (occupying more than half of the song) suggests that something prurient or improper has taken place and that the narrator is self-consciously guilty.

136

Notes

I. Problems, Sources and Strategies

1. Earlier attempts at dealing comparatively with ancient Greek and later tradition are detailed by Kyriakidou-Nestoros (1978). For some of the most recent and fruitful uses of comparative methodology in approaching literature, consult (in alphabetical order):

M. Alexiou (1974); (1986), 1-40
Contiades-Tsitsoni (1990), 110-32
Dover (1987), 26f.; (1988), 219-20; (1997), 67-70
Herzfeld (1972); (1973), 1-19
J. Kakrides (1949), esp. ch. 5; (1971)[a]; (1979); (1983); cf. (1971)[b], 244 n. 1 for a list
    of interpretations of ancient Greek poetry advanced by Kakrides on the basis of
    modern Greek folk material
Ph. Kakrides (1974), *passim*
Krikos (1976) [a historical-comparative study]
Littlewood (1974), 33-59; (forthcoming)
Papadakis (1979-81), 227-86
D.A. Petropoulos (1958), 3-26; (1959), 5-93
Richardson (1986), 61-77
Shipp (1979)
Sifakis (1988); (1992), 139-54; (1996), 95-110; (1997), 136-53
Tuffin (1975) [a historical-comparative study]
Walcot (1970)
Whitman (1964), 281-93

2. It was for this very reason that Lesky supported the resort to modern Greek field data, particularly popular tales, in analysing Homer. See A. Lesky, in *RE* Supplbd., xi, col. 778, s.v. 'Homeros'. By drawing from modern vernacular, Shipp (1979) was able to recover the meanings of rare or obscure words, as well as their dialectal and chronological distribution in antiquity. As he remarked (p. 1): '... modern evidence will often contribute to the correction or sharpening of our traditional interpretations of words by offering new suggestions.'

3. Griffiths (1995), 85-103, esp. 88. See Scobie (1983), 1-4, 11-30 on the rich variety of oral genres, from work-songs and bogey-tales to aretalogy, among the masses in the Greco-Roman world. A further bibliography of ancient folk-songs and tales is available in J. Kakrides (1971)[b], 180f., 242 n. 18. In addition, cf. J. Petropoulos (1989), 159-64.

4. Cf. Finnegan (1977), 17: 'An oral poem is oral in terms of (1) its composition, (2) its mode of transmission, and (3) (related to (2)) its performance. Some oral poetry is oral in all these respects, some in only one or two.'

5. See Dover (1987), 1-15, 107-15 on preliterate features in archaic Greek poetry, esp. Archilochus.

6. On the debt of ancient Greek prose genres, tragedy, comedy and the mime to popular story-telling in particular, see Trenkner (1958), esp. 189-91 (motif index); on *Märchen* elements in satyr plays, see Sutton (1980), esp. 130f., 162, 174f., 182f., 185-7; Dover (1997), 67-70 (a stylistic analysis).

7. See Chapter V below.
8. Vryonis in Vryonis (1978), 237-56; Browning (1983)[b], 111-28.
9. Vryonis (1978), 246-8, 253f. n. 22; Browning (1983)[b], 119-21.
10. On the conservative role of the Byzantine educational system, see n. 12 below; for the similar role of rhetorical education in the medieval West, see Curtius (1953).
11. See Constantelos in Vryonis (1978), 135-51; for a review of the archaeological evidence for the survival of popular religious paganism up to the fifth century, see Gregory (1986), 229-41; on Christianisation right through the sixth century, now see Bowersock (1990) and Mitchell (1993). Consult Stewart (1991), esp. 6-7, 149-50, 244 on the 'synthesis' (as opposed to mere syncretism) of ancient Greek and Hebrew traditions informing Orthodox beliefs in the Devil and evil spirits.
12. On the Byzantines' ever-evolving dialectal relationship to their classical and post-classical heritage, now see Browning (1995), 17-28.
13. As for the enduring impact of the Second Sophistic, Horrocks (1997), 80 puts it nicely: '... Christianity notwithstanding, the long-term influence of these guardians of the Hellenic heritage ... was so profound that they effectively determined the linguistic and literary mind-set of the Greek élite for the next 1,800 years.' The written and spoken language of, among other agencies, the Church, the imperial bureaucracy and not least the upper echelons of the military exerted a 'passive' if steady influence upon the speech of the illiterate majority throughout the Byzantine period: ibid., esp. 252-3; on the role of ecclesiastical Greek post 1453: 294, 325f. Also cf. the mutual influence of the *great* (i.e. text-based, official) tradition and the *little* (i.e. popular or local, orally transmitted) tradition in the evolution of Orthodox beliefs regarding the supernatural: Stewart (1991), 10-12, 147f., 222f., 243f. See further Chapter II.A on the interaction of high and low media.
14. *De Caerem.* ii.82 [73] (Vogt, p. 165). Neophytos' testimonium is discussed by Beaton (1980), 77-8.
15. On the Church Fathers' resistance to secular entertainment see Rydén (1974), 251; also J. Petropoulos (1989).
16. For eroticism in Byzantine society and literature consult Beck (1984); see also Garland (1985) (a good source-book); Beaton (1996), esp. 216-17. On the differing degrees of erotic innuendo and action in the Comnenian and Paleologue romances, see Garland (1990), 62-120.
17. Namely, the *Epitaphios thrênos* (c. ninth century) and the *Stavrotheotokia* (ninth century), discussed in M. Alexiou (1974), 63; (1975), 116-21, and now in Tsironi (forthcoming); and N. Callicles (late eleventh century), *Nicolai Calliclis carmina*, xxii (Sternbach, pp. 334f.), examined in Chapter IV below.
18. Preserved at *De Caerem.* loc. cit. in n. 14 above.
19. See Chapter II below.
20. So Beck (1971), 26.
21. See M.J. Jeffreys (1981), 313-14.
22. For the twelfth-century romances, see Beaton (1996), esp. 70-88, 210-14.
23. *Eustathii ... opuscula* (Tafel, pp. 328-32).
24. On 'realism' in the Comnenian romances see Chapter V n. 43; on the trend towards colloquialism in largely classicising works of the twelfth century, see Chapter II n. 219 and Chapter III n. 35.
25. On linguistic experimentation and the rise of the literary vernacular, see Chapter II n. 219; Beaton (1996), esp. 11-13, 18-21, 210f. On the four 'Poems of Poor Prodromos': Beaton op. cit., esp. 95-6, 224 n. 17 (bibl.). S. Alexiou in *Dig. Akr.*, 108f., 127f. suggests that the twelfth(?)-century original of the *Digenis* borrowed many

aspects of its plot, as well as themes and verbal formulae from folk-ballads in existence since the tenth century, and in turn inspired the folk-songs which later resulted in the so-called Akritic cycle. Further on the 'proto-romance' *Digenis Akrites* in Beaton (above), 30-51, 214-16, 222-4 (with n. 111); for a new edn (with a translation and full discussion) of the Grottaferrata and Escorial versions of *Digenis*, now see *Dig. Akr.* (E. Jeffreys).

26. On these verse romances consult E. Jeffreys (1981), 116-27; Beaton (1996), esp. 101-34, 217-22.

27. On *Krasopateras* see Eideneier (1988).

28. Further on this work: cf. Chapter V below.

29. This was a predominantly literary *Kunstsprache* which over time assimilated an ever-increasing proportion of colloquial (oral) elements: Beaton (1996), esp. 185-6.

30. Owing to such factors as dogmatic and linguistic differentiation, Byzantine society and literature remained largely impervious to alien and especially western elements: Browning (1983)[b], 114-17; Kazhdan & Epstein (1985), esp. 170f.; Geanakoplos (1976); but eastern elements had a direct impact on Byzantine *literati*: see Kehayioglou (1988), 156-66. The features of the Paleologue romances which are apparently borrowed from western prototypes are either superficial, decorative elements (so Beck [1971], 128) or in reality due to a joint heritage stemming from identical classical and scriptural sources but developed independently along similar lines: cf. E.M. Jeffreys (1968), esp. 149 n. 1, 201. Jeffreys concludes that literary influences, by and large, seem to have flowed from east to west rather than vice versa. Most recently, Beaton has allowed that though the impetus for using the vernacular in the Paleologue verse romances probably came from western-ruled regions, Byzantine awareness of western *topoi* and narrative devices *appears* to have been vestigial at this time; the question of western (particularly Crusade) influence at any rate still remains unresolved: Beaton (1996), esp. 18-21, 97, 224, 154-63, 219-29.

31. On the 'oral background' of the Paleologue romances and their subsequent oral performance: Beaton (1996), esp. 177-88, 222-4.

32. See Chapter IV, esp. n. 53. Even so, *Callimachos* has a higher degree of learned traits, particularly stylistic and metrical, than the other vernacular romances: Beaton (1996), 118.

33. See Chapter V nn. 58 and 87.

34. See now Beaton (1996), esp. 178-80, with nn. 48 and 50 on formulaic and thematic resemblances between vernacular poetry of the twelfth and fourteenth centuries on the one hand, and folk-songs from the fifteenth to the twentieth century, on the other. Cf. Browning (1983)[a], 92: '... they [sc. the generation of Dionysios Solomos] found in the Ionian islands of which Solomos and others were natives, a living tradition of literature in vernacular Greek, which, though it survived on the lips of humble peasants, went back through Venetian Crete and the vernacular literature of the late Byzantine world to the first creative breakthrough of the spoken tongue in the twelfth century.' At many points the *Ptochoprodromica* appear directly to reflect verbal and structural traits of medieval folk-poetry which are preserved in modern Greek folk-song: see Chapter II n. 103. It is also suggestive that, as with the *Krasopateras*, the *Erôtopaignia* and other late medieval compositions, portions of a fourteenth-century verse bestiary survived in oral versions (in Cyprus): cf. Papacharalambous (1945-6), 262-3; also Chapter V n. 87.

35. Browning (1983), 90. Also see Beaton (1996), 189, with n. 2.

36. On Cretan Renaissance literature: Holton (1991); Beaton (1996), 199-206.

37. On which see Mastrodemetres (1983), 94.

38. Id., 95-6. Bancroft-Marcus (forthcoming) dates this work to 1573-87.

39. Holton (1988), 144-55, with n. 1 (bibl.); id. (1991); Beaton (1996), 204-6.

40. See Bakker (1978) and now Bakker & van Gemert (1996).

41. For this chronology see Beaton (1996), 263 n. 84 (bibl.); on the controversy over the date of *Erotocritos*: ibid., 264 n. 115.

42. Browning (1983), 91; *Dig. Akr.* (S. Alexiou). On the language of *Erotocritos*, see Beaton (1996), 186-7, with n. 77.

43. Holton (1988); Bakker (1978), esp. 107, 115. See also Chapter III n. 45.

44. On the translation and adaptation of six medieval romances of chivalry in the late Byzantine period and their diffusion from the early or mid-sixteenth century onwards, see Beaton (1996), 135-45, with n. 33. On translations of Italian Renaissance authors see Morgan (1960), 256f.; Kehayioglou (1988), 162.

45. On chap-books cf. Morgan op. cit., 224-5; Kehayioglou (1984), 233-50. On the rhymed Alexander 'romance' and *Apollonios of Tyre*, see Beaton (1996), 140-1.

46. Thus also S. Alexiou (1992), 36-7; Beaton (1980)a, 160. On the interaction of *Erôphili* with song tradition see Puchner (1983), 173-235. That written sources may not merely have influenced popular song but entirely engendered certain types of song is a distinct (if somewhat unusual) possibility: Mango (1954), esp. 46-7 argues that the oral tradition of Daskaloyannis and Aledakis emerged from written accounts. The generative impact of a high form can also be illustrated by the case of story-telling. Manusakas and Puchner have extrapolated a seventeenth-century literary original from the oral variants to which it gave rise: see Manusakas & Puchner (1984). See also Chapter III n. 45.

47. See Chapter III n. 45.

48. Finnegan (1977), 29 (emphasis mine).

49. Baud-Bovy (1936), i; id. (1935-8), i-ii.

50. Bausinger (1961).

51. See esp. Röhrich in Bausinger and Brückner (1969), 117-33.

52. See esp. Baud-Bovy (1979-85), 549-59; (1988), 218-27.

53. Haslam (1981), 35-45. The other specimens are listed in West (1982), 165 and discussed in Baud-Bovy (1979-85) and (1988).

54. Haslam (1981), 37. Further on the oral origins of the political metre, see Chapter II n. 188. Maximus Planudes (late thirteenth century) also derived the 'political' verse from the catalectic tetrameter. Beaton (1996), 245, n. 34 rules out such an origin. Perhaps the structural considerations that follow will prompt non-classicists to reconsider this matter.

55. For the prosodical changes from the Hellenistic age onwards, see West (1982), 162-4.

56. The frequency of these violations can be easily deduced from the fact that a literary poet dating from the period of the fourth to the seventh century offended richly against the quantitative scheme in his attempts to write a supplement (mostly in tragic trimeters) to the end of E. *IA*: West (1981), 73-8 (cited in E. *IA* [Günther], *IA* 1578-1629 n.).

57. On melodic forms see Beaton (1980)[b], 1-11; Baud-Bovy (1979-85) and (1988); Horrocks (1997), esp. 318.

58. On rhythmical constraints as a conservative factor in the *politicos stichos* consult Sifakis (1988), esp. 39-40, 77-9 (S.'s book is an excellent morphological guide to modern Greek folk-song; in particular see ch. 4, of much interest to the Homerist, and ch. 5). It is convenient to note here that a high number of modern songs which will be discussed throughout this book consist of one or more rhyming distichs. This form first occurs consistently in the fourteenth-century Cretan poet Sachlikis but systematically in learned and popular modern Greek poetry from about 1500 or slightly earlier, and was probably adopted through the agency of Italian or French literary works circulating in the Aegean islands; cf. Beaton

(1980)ᵃ, 148-50. Common structural features of the rhyming distich are the absence of enjambment and the antithetical or complementary relationships between each line and between the two hemistichs in each line: see Sifakis (1988), 137-46, who draws upon the often-neglected findings of Baud-Bovy and Kyriakides.

59. See Dover (1987), 109-10. Allusiveness, often approaching the enigmatic and elliptical, typifies modern Greek folk-song; cf. n. 61 below and Chapter II nn. 70 and 234 (bibl.); section C.2 (discussion). See also n. 64 below.

60. The corruption of the songs' texts is another methodological problem. Many compilers either avowedly (cf. Politis in his canonical *Eclogai*, 7) or tacitly 'emended' their texts; see Kyriakidou-Nestoros (1978), 96.

61. For analyses, esp. along semiotic lines, of motifs and imagery in modern Greek folk-song see in particular Beaton (1980)ᵃ, 58-64, 126-8; Sifakis (1988), 44-9, 57-60 (S. shows the correspondence between content, i.e. motifs and images, and formal features in certain crucial verses of Klephtic songs), 50-1; further attempts at defining discrete 'signs' in the songs: 70-2, 95f., 111, 118-19, 123-4, 128-9.

62. *Laogr.* 20 (1962), 230, no. 51.

63. See Chapter IV below.

64. See conveniently: Baud-Bovy (1935-8), i.248, ii.263, vv. 10-12; Ioannou (1966), 207; Merlier (1931), 29. Cf. the similarly complex system of sexual and emotional allusion in Santal love-songs: Archer (1974), 66, 223.

II. Nuptial Praise

1. For examples of the straightforward, non-hymenaeal erotic encomium cf. Sapph. frr. 34 (LP)?, 82a, b (LP), TA1. Further exx.: Alcm. fr. 3.66f. (Davies); Ibyc. fr. 288 (Davies), classified by Athen. 13.564f. as a (homoerotic) *epainos*. On the *topos* of surpassing all rivals see n. 236 and also section C.2 ('Nature imagery') below. Erotic praise of two maidens (who may be *choragoi*) occurs in the context of a ritual (possibly a puberty initiation rite) described in TA2, on which see Calame (1977), i; but cf. Griffiths (1972), 7-30, who argues that this context is precisely hymenaeal. For a bibliography of archaic wedding-songs and customs see C. Brown (1992), 201; also n. 2 below.

2. Recent study of the ancient wedding along symbolic, ideological and histori-cal lines includes Oakley & Sinos (1993) as well as the essays by Redfield, Carsons, Sissa and Brown in Halperin et al. (1990), 115f., 135f., 339f., 479f. respectively; see also Appendixes I-II below. For a comparable treatment of the modern Greek wedding and wedding-songs in particular, see n. 20 below.

3. Hague (1983), 131-43 briefly surveys key literary specimens of ancient Greek wedding-praise.

4. Throughout this study the Byzantine testimonia are subdivided according to the tripartite division of Byzantine chronology proposed by Mango (1980), 1: Early period: AD 324-650; Middle period: 650-1070; Late period: 1070-1453; Post-Byzan-tine/Modern period: 1453-present.

5. Further Comnenian epithalamia, some published, some half-published, some unpublished are listed by Mioni (1973), 116-25; these have been excluded from the Byzantine testimonia.

6. For terms of physical praise, cf. e.g. a southern African bridegroom's song in praise of his bride (in Trask i.70-1) and a Polynesian marriage-song (id. ii.36); also a love-song from Vietnam advertising a list of six qualities (all but one physical) of a girl (a prospective bride?) (id. ii.195).

7. In rejecting Agamemnon's offer of one of his daughters in marriage at *Il.* 9.388-90, Achilles cites physical beauty (*kallos*) and skill in woolwork (*erga*) as though they were canonical qualities of a bride. *Il.* 13.429-33 shows that a talented bride (like Hippodameia) combined not only beauty and skill in fabric-making but also intelligence and good judgment (*phrenes*). Lefkowitz (1986), esp. 40-1, 62-3 notes that a number of (early) Greek myths place a high value on women's mental attributes, particularly their courage and intelligence. For similar popular standards by which prospective spouses might be assessed and praised, compare Aristotle's ideal attributes of young males (*Rh*. I.5.6 '[general] excellence in body, for example, *stature, beauty, vigour, athletic prowess*'; virtues of a young man's mind are '*sôphrosynê* and courage' and of young females '... *beauty and stature, ... sôphrosynê and industry, without servility*'). Also see sections B.8 and B.9 below.

8. As Oakley & Sinos show in their fine study (1993), Athenian pottery dating chiefly from the seventh to the fourth centuries BC illustrates nearly all the discrete stages of wedding ritual and may even reveal technical and emotional details which are either scantily attested or altogether unattested in written sources of roughly the same period. See further Appendix I below.

9. See Appendix II below. Quite possibly songs also accompanied the preparation of the *pastas* or special alcove within the *thalamos* and (from the Hellenistic period on) the *pastos*, on which consult Appendix II. The bath, toilette and *agôgê* were still observed even in St John Chrysostom's day and later.

10. Oakley & Sinos, 15, note: 'Washing is one way to establish divisions, between different activities or from the rest of the world ....' Besides the bath the bride's divestiture of certain articles such as her veil, belt, toys etc. may also have signified a stage of separation from her former existence: see Appendix I below. On rites of passage see Van Gennep (1960 [1909]). Hertz, followed by Van Gennep, noted the similarities between the symbolism of funerary ceremonies, weddings and other initiation rites: Bloch & Parry (1982), 4-5; on further similarities between e.g. circumcision and funerary ritual among the Merina of Madagascar, see Bloch (1982), 214, 219-20, 226-7.

11. The bride's symbolic death is marked not merely by her loss of virginity (see also Chapter III below), but more critically by her transfer from her natal home and her irreversible incorporation into a different social group. The conceptual analogy between a corpse and a new bride is cross-cultural and explains why funeral ceremonies among the Kodi of eastern Indonesia (to cite but one example) replicate marriage ceremonies in treating the corpse (male or female) as a bride: see Hoskins (1987), 176-8, 182, 184-6, 188, 196-8.

12. See Danforth (1982), 39-43 on the bathing of the corpse as a rite of separation/incorporation. It may be the case that seclusion at puberty, i.e. years before marriage, also marks separation.

13. For the ancient Greek iconography of nuptial embellishment, see Oakley & Sinos, esp. 16-17 ('dressing up' of the couple, their families and friends); 21, 34-5 (embellishment of the house and *thalamos*); 33 with n. 78 (decorated cushions in a wedding chariot); 38-9 (general emphasis on adornment). See further Appendix I below.

14. See nn. 26 and 27 below.

15. This canopy serves as a full-length curtain partitioning the bridal bed from the rest of the sitting room. Being embroidered from end to end, it is 'the most splendid type of embroidery in the Aegean': see Zora (1994), 225 and Appendix II (3) below.

16. For an extraordinary *ecphrasis* of the décor of the alcove and the bed-canopy, see the songs in Tarsouli i.117-18.

17. Karapatakis (1960), 65.

18. St John Chrysostom vehemently assailed the public display of the bride amid song and dance, considering it shameless exhibitionism: *PG* 61.104 (= Field ii.143f.).

19. Karapatakis (1960), 86.

20. Laudatory songs are performed at the following stages: (i) the delivery of the dowry; (ii) the preparation of the alcove and the presentation of the bridal couple; (iii) the adornment of the couple; (iv) the dance of the couple at the feast (*tavla*). For detailed ethnographic descriptions of modern wedding practices, cf. Bybilakis (1840), 34f.; Rodd (1892), 90f.; Kambouroglous (1896), 24-61; Abbott (1903), 147-91; Politis (1975), 260-320, id. (1931), 232-322 (both works remain unsurpassed for the wealth of detail and documentation of AG and MG parallels); Vrontis (1932); *Makedonika*, i (1940), 123f. For some of the main anthropological analyses of the modern Greek wedding to date consult: (i) Alexakis (1984), id. (1990); (ii) Hague (1985); (iii) Loukatos (1988), 57-70; (iv) Loutzaki (1983-5), 3-50; (v) Terzopoulou & Psychoyiou (1993), 89-124.

21. Formal congruence may or may not suggest a continuity of significance. For our purposes it is essential that the significance of the rituals of embellishment at either end of the time-scale be determined and compared.

22. Cf. Redfield (1982), 188: 'After the *enguê* (the only legal requirement) is carried out, the remaining ceremonies, often lasting several days, focus on the *gamos* in its primary significance of the sexual act.' Cf. also the connotation of *nympha* in Praxilla fr. 754 (Campbell iv.380): 'You who look so beautifully in through the window, with a virgin's head but a married woman's [*numpha*] body beneath ...' (tr. id., 381). Yet it was the unveiling of the bride and not the subsequent *prima nox* that apparently had greater symbolic ramifications for the ancients: see Appendix I (3).

23. *Implicitly*, coitus in the aftermath of the wedding is regarded as rape; this residual attitude accounts for the ritual hostility, expressed mainly in songs of 'blame', between the respective clans. See Chapter III below.

24. See Oakley & Sinos, 28-9, with nn. 39-40: *likna* or winnowing fans featured in a wedding scene may symbolise the 'refinement' of the couple's primitive sexuality through the wedding ritual; see also cf. ibid. 27-8 on the symbolic value of barley roasting pans or sieves which Pollux, an admittedly late source, says were carried by the bride.

25. This cross-cultural concern is manifest in the ancient *gameô*, 'of mere sexual intercourse' (LSJ) and has even been carried over into colloquial medieval and modern Greek. See LSJ, s.v. *gameô* and *gamos* to which Shipp (1979), 187-8 adds: 'E. *Hipp.* 14 *anainetai de lektra kou psauei gamôn* (euphemistic in tragedy); D. 45.39 *gamoi despoinês*, id. 18.129 *tois methêmerinois gamois* (ironical in D.)'. Cf. the Attic *defixio*, dated to the fourth century BC and published in Wuensch in *IG* III.3 78: ... *mêpote auton gêmai allên gunaika mêde paida* (not in Shipp). Perhaps owing to its sexual connotations the term *gamô* is regularly avoided by the LXX translators, who use synonyms instead (Shipp, 606 n. 124); sch. Theoc. 5.43 glosses *pugisdesthai* as *gamoumai*. Cf. also the force of *gamôn* in TC1.4 and Page's note ad loc. (p. 102). Further, the collocation of *teletê* and *gamos* in TC2 probably means 'initiation through marriage'. *Gamêtiôn* in the sense of *binêtiôn* occurs in the *Vita Aesopi* W 103. As regards the Byzantine period proper, the decorous or euphemistic import of *gamos* is still noticeable in Agathias' (mid-sixth century) moralising epigram at *AP* 10.68.8: *xeinon agousi gamon* = 'to mate', of a homosexual rapport (not in Shipp); cf. ibid. v.7. Additionally, cf. the medical (and philosophical?) euphemism in another epigram by Agathias, *AP* 5.302.19-20: *ton d'humenaion êeidein palamê*, of male masturbation (not in Shipp but in Adams [1982], 161). (For this euphemism see Galen *Loc. affect.* 6.5 [Kühn], etc., cited in McCail [1971], 205-67 [218]. Adams [1982], 159-61 cites further late-antique Greek testimonia and shows that the same euphemism ['marriage' = sexual liaison] occurs independently in Latin.) The *Akathist Hymn* features the euphemisms *klepsigamos*, 'having secretly coupled' (strophe Z), and *apeirogamos passim* (not in Shipp). From the twelfth century, at least, *gamô* appears as a colloquial expression equivalent to the ancient *bineô* although *gamos* preserves its old sense. Thus cf. Tzetzes, not in Shipp but in Hunger (1973), xviii.305, v. 21: *'ouk aiskhunesai, authentria mou, na gamê* *to mounin sou papas;'* ('Are you not ashamed, my lady, that a priest is fucking your cunt?'). In modern Greek *gamaô, gamô* = 'fuck'.

26. From the (late?) archaic period on, the wedding superseded other female puberty rituals and became a girl's main coming-of-age ritual: Bremmer (1994), 71. (On the pre-matrimonial puberty rites of aristocratic girls in the archaic period: ibid. 69f., 81 nn. 4, 7.) See Plate 11 and discussion in Oakley & Sinos, 10, 42: an initiated bride – her bare breasts conspicuously signalling her 'transformation' – receives gifts after the wedding night. Vernant's observation (1974), 37, may be of interest here: '... si les rites de passage signifient pour les garçons l'accès à la condition de guerrier, pour les filles associées à eux dans ces mêmes rites et souvent soumises elles-mêmes à une periode de réclusion, les épreuves initiatiques ont la valeur d'une préparation à l'union conjugale.' Also cf. Redfield (1982), 191: 'We can understand why the bride is the star of the wedding. It is her initiation ... The groom is carried along in the wake of the bride, taking part in a second-hand way. Thus we find that some ceremonies applied to the brides are also extended to grooms ....' As regards the modern wedding, see the unpublished song L.A. MS. 434.70, in Appendix III, performed during the adornment of the bride: she is required to repeat this song, which describes in explicit detail her impending defloration. (By contrast, a young man's rite of initiation is not the wedding but his voluntary or enforced emigration 'abroad': see Terzopoulou & Psychoyiou [1984][a], 119f.)

27. It is quite possible that the ritual proceedings have been consistently supervised and 'directed' by the womenfolk since antiquity: this hypothesis may be made in the light of the iconographic and the modern Greek evidence. The principal agents in the modern wedding are the bride as well as her mother and mother-in-law: e.g. the bridal songs of farewell are addressed to the mother; the mother-in-law welcomes the bride at her new home; even the bridegroom is adorned by women, etc.: cf. Terzopoulou & Psychoyiou (1984)[b], 58-64.

28. As early as the fourth century some Church Fathers held that the state of betrothal (*arrabôn, mnêsteia*), when sealed with the Church's blessing, was almost tantamount to matrimony in practical terms. (The brief rite of engagement is cited but not detailed by Church sources of the Early and Middle periods; but it is certain that until the tenth century the ceremony could be held at the bridegroom's house besides the church.) In 692 Canon Law declared an engaged couple to be properly wed, and Civil Law, namely Leo VI's Novella 74, adopted this view in the early tenth century. Generally speaking, church authorities, influenced in part by popular custom, in part by Old Testament precedent, treated the *arrabôn*-ceremony as more important than the wedding; civil authorities, particularly from the Middle period on, opposed this tendency. See Papadatos (1984), 86-108, esp. 100-8; also part C, below. Further on Byzantine betrothal and marriage in: Laiou (1992 [1985]), 189-201; (1992); Karlin-Hayter (1992), 133-54.

29. Post-marital residence patterns vary. In the north residence is virilocal, whereas in the south it is usually uxorilocal. The bypassing of the Church was not the case only among transhumant communities (e.g. the Sarakatsani) which did not have churches, but elsewhere (e.g. Cephalonia, Crete) as well.

30. The first modern version of a functionally motivated wedding encomium is TG2, dating to the eighteenth century; TE1 seems to be functionally generated as well.

31. This descent may be represented thus:

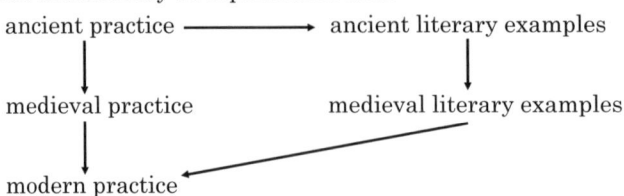

32. Dover (1971) ad TB1.9f.; id. (1980), 11f. on the relation of Pl. *Smp.* to the encomium.

33. These elementary exercise books are first mentioned in the *Rhetorica ad Alexandrum*, dating from the fourth century BC. The first Greek and Latin examples of these textbooks date from the Imperial period; see Russell & Wilson (1981), xxv f. On the *progymnasmata* as a mediating agent in the exchange of motifs from prose and poetic sources see Viljamaa (1968), 13-14; Russell & Wilson, xxxi f.

34. Cf. Gow (1952), ii.348.

35. Russell & Wilson (1981), xxxiii-xxxiv.

36. This distribution of evidence may be accidental: Russell & Wilson, xviii.

37. Ibid., xvii-xviii, xxxiii-xxxiv.

38. The rhetorical schema: (i) proemium with mythological *exempla* introducing the deities present at the wedding; (ii) a description of the power of Eros and a presentation of the history of marriage citing mythic *exempla* and examples from nature; (iii) an encomium of the bridal couple and their families, especially by means of comparison to plants or precious metals; (iv) a discreet exhortation to intercourse (by means of physical praise and mythic *exempla*), which is followed by a wish for harmony, long life and offspring. (This scheme is actually a conflation of Menander's precepts for the epithalamium and the bedroom speech; see Men. Rh. 399.11-412 [RW]; Viljamaa [1968], 125.) Further on rhetorical prescriptions for wedding speeches in late antiquity in Russell (1979), 104-17.

39. Lib. *Or.* 46.49 (Foerster vii.575) mentions the poetic epithalamium: *tois ge poiêtais sunêthes aidein epi thurais numphiôn melê.*

40. The use of the *theatron* by rhetoricians is attested throughout Byzantine history, especially in the Paleologue era: see Hunger in Mullett & Scott (1981), 35-47 (37). But the term may simply mean 'spectacle' or 'audience', as Hunger (1978)[b], i.210-11, himself notes.

41. For Byzantine mimesis see Hunger (1973), xv.17-38.

42. On imitation of Theoc. 18 by Nicetas Eugenianus see Gow (1952), ii.349. Another example of direct imitation may be found in Prodromos' 'wake-up' song (= TF1), discussed under Content. Prodromos' divergence from epideictic precept will be examined below.

43. E.g. hagiography, Romanos' hymns, the speeches in *Callimachus and Chrysorrhoë.*

44. See also Viljamaa (1968), 8-24.

45. See Hunger (1978)[b], i.77-89.; Russell & Wilson (1981), xxxvi: 'The "authority" on epideictic in Byzantine times was known to be Menander.'

46. From numerous sources we can document, though usually without much detail, the co-existence of sub-literary wedding songs from the first century AD onwards:

(1) Plu. *Quaest. conviv.* 667 A

(2) Lib. *Or.* 34.9 (Foerster vii.122)

(3) Gr. Naz. *PG* 37.373

(4) Gr. Nyss. *PG* 46.580

(5) Jo. Chrys. = TD1; cf. ibid. 51.211; 61.104f.; 62.145

(6) Him. *Or.* 9.86 (Colonna) = TD2

(7) Theodoret (*ob.* 458), *PG* 81.252

(8) *Vita Theophanis* (*ob. c.* 817), in Theoph. *Chronographia*, ii.28.14-15 (de Boor, p. 28)

(9) Other hagiographical attestations (a) *Vita S. Xenophontis* by Symeon Metaphrastes, *PG* 114.1021; (b) *Vita Ioannis Damasceni et Cosmae, AIS,* iv.282, 1.24 (Papadopoulos-Kerameus) (indirect evidence); (c) *Vita Eliae Speleotis mon. in Calabria, ActaSS* Sept., iii.880.79

(10) Const. Porphyr. = TE1
(11) Psellos, *M.B.* v. 221, 320, 323 (Sathas)
(12) Prodromos = TF1
(13) Balsamon et al. (twelfth cetury) *Syntagma canonôn*, iii.219f. (Rallis-Potlis), ad 53rd and 54th canons of the Council of Laodicaea
(14) Nicetas Choniates (late twelfth century) *Historia*, 494 (van Dieten)
(15) TG2a
(16) Folk-song (mid-seventeenth century) in Bouvier (1960), 11, no. 4: vv. 4f. treat of the adornment of Evdokia, which is described in terms appropriate to the traditional song motif of 'the wedding-sponsor who becomes the bride'; ibid. 32-3
(17) Eighteenth-century wedding-song = TG2

47. See the discussions of the *exemplum* under Form and Content below.

48. See Dover (1988), 16-30. An ancient writer's portrayal of actual speech depended on his attitude to realism and to the function and status of literature. Prose writers achieved touches of genuine colloquialism but never at the expense of elegance. Even Aristophanes did not faithfully reproduce the speech of slaves or illiterate citizens. On the other hand, early prose in general approached the colloquial register: see esp. id. (1997), 67-70. For the common ground between literary and popular tradition as shown in the inscriptions, see also nn. 119, 271 below and the section on antiphony; and Chapter IV, TC3 (with discussion) *et passim*.

49. Cf. also the awkward syntax of a private letter, cited as TC16 in Chapter V.

50. Meraklis (1985), 59; 61 n. 3 (bibl.).

51. Dover (1987), 107 n. 47.

52. Although mass illiteracy has been the norm for millennia in most parts of the world, we may still assume that literate and non-literate media have continuously co-existed and interacted even within 'primitive' cultures; see Finnegan (1977), 23-4. For a further discussion of the rural-urban and illiterate-literate continuum, see Goody (1968), 1-26, esp. 5-10; but even a highly literate culture can contain oral residues: ibid. 14.

53. I am here overstating the problem, since we do have vernacular texts from the medieval period, although they are not, *pace* Trypanis and Eideneier, oral dictated texts and they do clearly follow a learned 'grapholect' (on which see M. Alexiou [1986], 34). The task of detecting popular motifs is tantamount to extrapolating a spoken *koinê* from the literary specimens to hand; see Chapter I above.

54. On widespread illiteracy in the Byzantine world see Wilson (1983), 1f.

55. See Chapter I above. On homiletic practice and texts see Beck (1959), 398-402; Kourkoulas (1957).

56. See Chapter I above.

57. Kannicht (1969), 189 n. ad TA20 below. On the *Hymenruf* see section B.11 below.

58. For cross-cultural examples of similes, both elaborate and shorter ones, see Finnegan (1977), 112-13.

59. This motif will be examined in section C below.

60. A rhetorical cliché for mutual attraction: cf. below.

61. J. Kakrides (1971)[b], 159f.

62. Cf. *h. Ap.* 194f.: Artemis is pre-eminent among a group of dancing goddesses, which includes Aphrodite; ibid. 200f.: Apollo is pre-eminent vis-à-vis Ares and Hermes (noted in Kakrides [1971][b], 158f.). In the 'face-to-face' society of ancient Greece, visual prominence was a form of 'public recognition' coveted by everyone, from statesmen to athletes: Segal (1995), 187-8. Besides, in wedding-songs, ancient and modern, the prominence motif may signal the ritual separation of the bride or bridegroom from his (or her) peers.

63. Cf. this wedding-song from Crete (L.A. MS. [1956], 22):

Queen of queens, empress of empresses,
you're the most beautiful among all other brides.

64. Calame cites *Il.* 2.480f. ad loc. (Agamemnon is compared to a bull which is distinguished among a herd of cows).

65. See the citation excerpted from a twelfth-century congratulatory speech in Cod. Barocc. gr. 131 fol. 224r. ll.15f. and published by Wirth (1963), 115-17.

66. Cf. Song of Songs 1.9f.

67. M. Alexiou (1974), 186; 239 n. 5. But it appears to be attested less frequently in modern wedding-songs than metaphor (q.v. below). In ancient iambus and monody similes that may echo non-literary sources are found e.g. in: Arch. frr. 42-3, 125 (*IE*, i [W]); Anacr. fr. 413 (*PMG* [Page]). (Arch. frr. 42-3 [W] have the air of a proverb or cliché: Arist. *Rh.* 1413a.1-35 gives instances of such hyperbolic comparisons and notes that they are common in everyday conversation.)

68. The derivative *prepos* is attested in a wedding-song: Kazavis (1940), 135, no. 1, v. 2 (of the bride).

69. Cf. also the southern African song of a bridegroom in praise of his bride: '... even among many women, / she shines like the spring sun rising' (Trask i.71).

70. See Chapter I above. The symbolic mode characterises folk-song across time and place; for easy instance, cf. the imagery in the Song of Songs. On metaphor, sustained or brief, in oral poetry in general, consult Finnegan (1977), 113-14.

71. Silk (1974), 35, 211.

72. See M. Alexiou (1974), esp. 195f., 241 n. 40 for a historical discussion of metaphor in the ritual lament. Cf. Danforth (1982), 96f. for a 'synchronic' view of plant symbolism in Greek folk-songs.

73. At least, this conclusion is prompted by a review of a cross-section of both types of song. Finnegan's cross-cultural evidence (113) bears this out. In oral poetry, as Finnegan notes, 'Metaphor seems to be even more common than explicit simile.'

74. Cited by Russell & Wilson in connection with TC2.7. TD4 is also an implied mythical comparison, on which see B.5 below.

75. See M. Alexiou (1974), esp. 185-7; 239-40 nn. 2-3 and 12 for a comprehensive range of testimonia.

76. This is a hymnographic cliché.

77. The *eikasia* also serves in effect as a laudatory exclamation (q.v.) addressed to the bride or bridegroom. See also B.2 above.

78. Cf. humorous punning comparisons in English such as 'Why is a philosopher like a looking-glass? Because he *reflects*.' According to Silk (1974), 103-4 with n. 3 (test. and bibl.), such stylised comparisons in English throw together, and violently resolve, disparate elements. Further test. and bibl. in n. 79 below. See Halliwell (1991), 291: in ancient Greece this game was an instance of 'festive or celebratory laughter'; through its 'stylised, predictable shape' it controlled the pleasures which it legitimated.

79. On this sympotic genre, consult Fraenkel (1960), 162f., 421-2; and his extensive discussion in his commentary on A. *Ag.* 163, 1244, esp. 1629f. Also Monaco (1963).

80. The *eikasdein-anteikasdein* formula is normally used to convey a superlative comparison; for examples of this formula or equivalent expressions see TA11.149f., Semonides of Amorgos fr. 7.41 f. (*IE*, ii [W]), Ibyc. S151.41f. (Davies), E. *Hel.* 563 (cited by Fraenkel 1960, 422).

81. *Exempla* were also rehearsed through iconography. Numerous Athenian wedding vessels picture nuptial scenes e.g. abductions, adornment scenes, processions, etc. involving divine figures: Oakley & Sinos, figs 32-5, 50-3, 62-3, 100-4, 128-30; see Plates 2, 4.

82. Cf. Faraone (1985), 151 n. 5. The *exemplum* may be particular to Greek tradition; its sympathetic function is discernible in the cletic hymn and in magical incantations. It is noteworthy that *hypomnêseis* featuring the interaction of gods and mortals as also analogies between the gods and mortals are rare in Egyptian hymns: see Riesenfeld (1946), 153-60, esp. 158; Petropoulos (1988), 217. Further on the use of mythic *exempla* in ancient magic: A. Nagy (1999), 34f.

83. With respect to v. 4 cf. a funerary epigram, *Epi. Gr.* 582.1-2 (Rome), which states that the deceased woman was 'sweeter than the Sirens in song, / more golden than Cypris herself'. See also n. 267 below.

84. For mythic comparisons in the twelfth and fourteenth century Byzantine romance, see Beaton (1996), 148.

85. *Olbios, olbos, olbizô* used in the *olbismos* of either party or of the couple, occurs in TA20.640; TA21.7; TA22.1; TA23.89; TA24, TA25.919; TB1.16. (This distinction between *olbismos* and *makarismos* is not made by Diggle in his note on TA26.240.) For attestations of the encomiastic formulae *olbios, hos* and *olbios, hos ... kai olbiê, hê ...,* see Kost (1971), 330 on Musae. *Hero et Leander* 138.

86. Dirichlet (1914), 7f., assumes the former possibility. The *topos* of the *makarismos* was extended to a variety of circumstances and poetic and prose genres: cf. Rossi (1971), 19-20; the formulaic *makar, -ios / olbios* in the context of mystery cults is discussed in Nisbet & Hubbard i.13.17, and in Richardson (1974), 313f. on *h. Cer.* 480. For the *makarismos* in general, also consult Burnett (1983), 237 n. 14 and Calame (1983), 323 on Alcm. fr. 1.37 (Davies).

87. See the preceding section on the *exemplum*. Like this last device, the *makarismos*, by virtue of its implicit analogical function, will attract good fortune. Seaford (1987), 122 cites E. *Supp.* 997 *aoidas eudaimonias* (of Evadne's wedding-song) and Ar. *Ran.* 1182-6 to argue that the *makarismos* bestows *permanent* felicity.

88. For another case of self-congratulation, cf. n. 322 below. For the various instances where the speaker assimilates himself or others to a god, see Headlam (1922), 363 on Herod. 8.111 and Page (1978), 101-2 on TC1.4; such an assimilation appears to be a colloquial cliché.

89. J. Kakrides (1983), 197; see also n. 88 above.

90. Cf. Kannicht (1969), 189 on TA20.639-40. Cf. section B.12 below.

91. The adjective *makar* is uttered in each case as an invocation; see section B.1 above, on exclamation.

92. Cf. *salutatio* and gold imagery, both examined below.

93. Hague (1983), 141 n. 11 wrongly asserts that only once is the bride designated as *makaria* (in TA27a.312) and that this self-applied *makarismos*, delivered by the crazed bride, is an eccentric case.

94. See also encomiastic exclamation above (section B.1) and *salutatio* below (section B.13).

95. The 'life of a bridal pair' mentioned at Ar. *Av.* 161 may have been a byword for uninterrupted bliss: see Sommerstein (1987), 209 and Dunbar (1995), 185 ad loc.

96. Cf. id. TE3.67f.

97. See Finnegan (1977), esp. 98-101, 104-6, 128 on (usually binary) parallelism of structure or meaning and ibid. 63-4 on the related 'adding style', both of which often characterise oral poetry.

98. Cf. Norden (1958), ii.813f., 822f. (For the formal traits of incantatory language mainly in archaic sources, consult Richardson [1974], 229 on *h. Cer.* 228-30; J. Petropoulos [1988], 215f.)

99. In Aristophanes, however, parallelism is generally associated with a 'low' context. See Silk (1980), 99-151 (127-8) for typical instances of unliterary parallelism. Parallelism is the hallmark of demotic song, esp. of the rhyming couplet: Sifakis (1988), 141-3 ('isometric' parallelism), 148-64, 165-76 (*tricolon* with a crescendo effect).

100. On parallelism in ancient Greek literature in general, see Silk (1974), esp. 71-3.

101. v. 19 is a *chiaston*.

102. M. Alexiou (1986), 4, following Kazhdan's chronology of Theodore Prodromos, notes that the datable elements in 'Ptochoprodromos' coincide with what is known about Prodromos' life and historical milieu, and suggests that 'Ptochoprodromos' is actually Theodore Prodromos, the 'begging poems' being genre exercises; see also ibid. 32f. Further, Beaton (1996), esp. 95-6, 244 n. 17 (bibl.).

103. M. Alexiou (1986), 22f. also remarks that Prodromos and 'Ptochoprodromos' both share a penchant for rhetorical devices (e.g. parallelism and antithesis) which are common to the *politicos stichos* of folk-song; her verdict as to 'Ptochoprodromos' is that in many points he 'was consciously exploiting formulaic lines familiar from folk-songs, as would be consistent with his choice of "vulgar" language'.

104. The fragment is discussed in section C.5 on *makarismos* below.

105. Discussed in Dover (1978), esp. 115f.

106. Menander employs the term in an idiosyncratic manner; for the meaning intended see the editors on 403.27f. (RW). See id. on TC3.4f. for the rationale behind this prescription.

107. 404.8f. (RW).

108. 404.6f. (RW) (in conjunction with 403.27f. [RW]). See also section C.3 below on gold imagery.

109. See the section on physical description and *ecphraseis* immediately below.

110. In his epigram TF3.25-8 Prodromos conforms to the method *aneu men antexetaseôs, kata symplokên de* (Men. Rh. 404.1f.[RW]).

111. See *Od*. 17.217. Cf. the (non-nuptial) proverb paraphrased in Pl. *Phdr*. 240c *hêlika terpein ton hêlika* ('one contemporary pleases another contemporary').

112. On alliteration in 'popular' ancient Greek: Silk (1974), 224-7; on ancient Greek assonance and alliteration in general: id. esp. 173-8, 224-8.

113. The text is insecure. MacCoull's philosophical interpretation of this favourite epithalamian line is implausible: MacCoull (1988), 90.

114. Note the catalogue of similes and metaphors which serves as an *ecphrasis* of male or female beauty in op. cit., 4.1f.; 6.5f.; 7.1f. (of the bride); 5.10f. (of the bridegroom). The enumeration of physical and mental qualities is the most common form of *laudatio* in funeral epitaphs in Greek and Latin: see Lattimore (1942), 291f.

115. See section B.3 on metaphor above.

116. J. Kakrides (1971)[b], 160f.

117. E.g. in *h. Ap*. 204f. Artemis' parents react to her beauty; cf. *Od*. 6.106, 157, where Nausicäa's parents likewise react to her appearance.

118. Cf. the Trojan elders' verdict on Helen's beauty, *Il*. 3.146f.

119. In the context of the funerary epigram, the most elaborate *ecphrasis* of female beauty is late (*Epi. Gr*. 169.1-6, Athens) and bears comparison with Ach. Tat. 1.4f. (Garnaud), the most lavish physical *ecphrasis* (in catalogue-form) from this period; also cf. Iamblichos' contemporary *Babyloniaka*, fr. 35.29-40 (S.-W.) for an itemised *ecphrasis* of a young male slave's beauty. The Byzantine set-piece description or *ecphrasis* of a person, esp. a maiden, in turn derived, variously, from the sophistic novels, the *progymnasmata* (Hunger [1978][b], i.188; ii.116f.) and the physiognomical writings of late antiquity (Lambert [1935], 40), on which consult n. 124 below. See e.g. Michael Psellos, *M.B.*, v. 68-74 (Sathas), Christoph. Mityl. no.

81 (Kurtz, p. 52), *Belthandros and Chrysantza* 644-58 (Kriaras, pp. 113f.), the laudatory description of a prize-winning beauty; *Erôtopaignia* (H.-P.), *passim*, etc.; also Beaton (1996), 27-8 (Byzantine *ecphrasis* in general), 110, 147-9 (*ecphrasis* of the physical splendours of the heroine esp. in the vernacular romances); further in Jouanno (1987). The influence on literary *ecphraseis* of painter's manuals and other pictorial sources like history painting, portraits and icons is a little-explored but strong possibility. Finally, on orientalising influences via chap-books in particular see Kehayioglou (1988), 156-66.

120. This item and the following one are also noted in section B.7.ii above.

121. Cf. a similar version in Baud-Bovy i.264.

122. For separate erotic *epainoi* of the bride, with an extensive *ecphrasis* and suggestive compound epithets, see e.g. Kazavis (1940), 138-9, Poulianos (1964), 197-200, etc. For the separate (and mainly erotic) praise of the bridegroom in song, see e.g. Poulianos op. cit., 200-1.

123. J. Kakrides (1971)[b], 29f.

124. On (largely popular) character types in physiognomists and other technical sources, consult esp. Evans (1969) and more recently Gleason (1990), 389-415.

125. Both frr. are also examined under section C, Content, below.

126. See section B.1 above.

127. Kaibel (1892), 249f. (251); Muth (1954), 5f. (38 n. 45).

128. The moral *ecphrasis* (my coinage) was an integral part of at least two of Hermogenes' *progymnasmata*, the *enkômion kai psogos* and the *sunkrisis*: see Hunger (1978)[b], i.104-8.

129. Another departure is his re-formulation of the customary wish for children into an expression of the dynastic ideal of legitimacy of succession.

130. These semi-official eulogies were probably intended for acclamation by the demes, as clearly was Nicetas Choniates' epithalamian speech, TF8. On the unconventional content of Prodromos' *oeuvre*, consult Kazhdan & Franklin (1984), 105-8.

131. Prodromos employs two favourite devices in order to convey the notion of parity: plant metaphors, applied to the couple jointly (q.v. above), and syntactical parallelism combined with *parêchêsis* (see also above).

132. See section B.12 on *anaphora* below. See also Dover (1971), xlviii-l, who also notes that symmetrical repetition ('Type (f)') is exampled in the *Epic of Gilgamesh*.

133. See M. Alexiou (1974), 132, 137-9. The antiphonal dirge is actually eastern in origin: Hall (1989), 83 with n. 123.

134. Alexiou op. cit., 132.

135. On the antiphonal dirge in tragedy, particularly in the *Persae*, Hall (above), 83-4 is excellent.

136. Alexiou op. cit., 138. Alternate exchange was exploited in comedy as well to create the tone of 'low' (popular) lyric: see Silk (1980), 127f.

137. TA35a and TA42 below are cited in Dover (1971).

138. For other Homeric examples and modern Greek analogues cf. J. Kakrides (1949), esp. 109f., 112f.

139. TA37-40, TB6 and TC8 are cited in M. Alexiou (1974), 232 nn. 17-20. On TA37-8 see Hansen ad loc.

140. See Arist. *Po.* 1452b.24.

141. This and TA42 below are undatable, but presumably date from the classical period at latest.

142. On antiphony esp. in children's play songs see Burnett (1983), 69 n. 42. Baud-Bovy (1983), 5-20 (5-7), compares ancient and modern Greek children's songs from the point of view of metrical continuity.

143. See (i) *Il.* 24.723-46, 747-60, 761-76: the musical *thrênos* of the professional female singers is interrupted by a refrain of cries from the women and is subsequently answered by the improvised solo lament (*goos*) of a kinswoman (Andromache, Hecabe and Helen respectively); each *goos* is followed in turn by a refrain of keening uttered by the entire company of women (and men at op. cit. 776) in unison; (ii) *Il.* 19.287-302, 315-39: Briseis' lament for Patroclos is followed by a refrain of cries from the women; this is apparently answered by Achilles' lament, followed by a refrain of cries from the old men; (iii) *Od.* 24.60-2: at Achilles' *prothesis* the Muses sing a lament (*thrênos*) antiphonally. (These passages are discussed in M. Alexiou [1974], 11-12, 131-2; cf. section B.11 immediately below.) Perhaps, however, a distinction (overlooked by Alexiou, ibid.) between antiphony and refrain should be drawn. At *Il.* 24.722, 745, 776 and op. cit. 19.301 and 378 the women's (or men's) refrains simply punctuate, but do not actually *answer*, the *thrênoi* of the *aoidoi* and the *gooi* of the kinswomen.

144. From the sixth century BC the statement by the dead person or his tomb to the passer-by is coupled with a greeting or an address in the vocative.

145. M. Alexiou (1974), 138f., esp. 232 n. 23.

146. See T.K. Abbott (1897), 162, 291; Bruce (1984), 380-1.

147. See also J. Petropoulos (1989), 159-64.

148. See also Wellesz (1961), 35f.

149. *Thriskeftiki kai Ithiki Enkyklopaideia*, i, col. 942-3, s.v. *antiphônia*; also Mitsakis (1971), 53-6.

150. Greg. Nyss. *PG* 46.993, *Vita s. Macrinae* = *Grégoire de Nysse, Vie de sainte Macrine* (Maraval), 248; also 248-9, nn. 3 and 4 ad loc.

151. When, as a counter-measure to the specially composed antiphonal hymns of the Arians, St John Chrysostom instructed the faithful at Constantinople also to stage litanies and sing out of doors, he probably had antiphonal religious songs or hymns in mind: see Pasquato (1976), 273 n. 141.

152. *PG* 61.313 = Field ii.458-9: *Sunêiesan to palaion hapantes, kai hupepsallon koinêi. Touto poioumen kai nûn*, etc. Cf. loc. cit. 315 = Field ii.461: *ho psallôn psallei monos: kan pantes hupêkhôsin, hôs ex henos stomatos hê phônê pheretai.*

153. M. Alexiou (1974), 142f. (For references to antiphony in Bion's literary lament see Reed, 196 ad v. 2; 248 ad v. 92.) See Pasquato (1976), 271 nn. 125-6 and 282 on the prevalent Hellenistic elements which the Church combatted for centuries.

154. Cited and discussed in Chapter I n. 14.

155. Sevcenko (1969-70), 227.

156. The question is addressed by Beaton (1980)[b], 1-11, who makes a distinction possibly relevant to our discussion: although the melodic structure of post-Byzantine secular music has largely remained differentiated, certain *formal* traits may derive directly from Turkish musicians. To a much lesser extent, Church music, from the thirteenth century, was subject to the influences of the Turkish formal system.

157. Burnett (1983), 224 n. 34, remarking that this same pattern of question and answer occurs in children's songs (cf. TA41-2), suggests plausibly, contra West, that TA4 was designed for two voices.

158. J. Kakrides (1983), 90 proposes that two lovers are being reconciled; but see Page (1955), 108-9 for a different interpretation. Further nuptial and in general lyrical examples of antiphony are found in Burnett (1983), 69 n. 43. For intimations of epithalamian antiphony between a male and a female chorus in Sappho and other sources see Seaford (1987), 114 n. 93. (In his interpretation of the exchange in A. *Su.* 1032f., Seaford [1987], 114, does not adduce the ancient testimonia just cited.)

159. See Fraenkel (1955), 1-8 (8).

160. Cf. however the eye-witness report that in Sphakia in the sixteenth century local male dancers 'se respondent [*sic*] les uns aux autres en chantant et dansant à leurs chansons': Belon du Mans (1555), 39.

161. See TG26, examined immediately below. I am grateful to Mrs Helen Psychoyiou for this information. (See also Appendices III and X below.)

162. Limitations of space have made it impossible for me to include a section on erotic magical practices in medieval and modern Greek popular tradition. On certain features of ancient magic see e.g. Gager (1992). On magic in medieval Greek tradition see esp. Psychoyiou (1993); J. Petropoulos (1999)[b], 6-7.

163. See section B.1 above. On the hymenaeal invocation in its various forms in Greek and Latin poetry, see Gow on Theoc. 18.58 and Muth (1954), 8. In Catullus 62 the stanza-refrain is probably borrowed from Hellenistic sources: Fraenkel (1955), 8.

164. See M. Alexiou (1974), 136f. In the ancient lament the refrain consists of either (a) the reiteration of cries or wails (as in Homer) or (b) a metrical statement or invocation (in tragedy); in Hellenistic poetry the refrain is a technical means of marking off stanzas. For Bion's use of funerary 'refrains' see Reed, esp. 196-7, 218. On the use of the refrain in antiphonal responsion see the preceding section. For a possible instance of a refrain in a sub-literary *scolion* see Chapter V.

165. M. Alexiou (1974), 131-7.

166. See the discussion, ibid. 142, of formal elements in Romanos' *Mary at the Cross*. In the Byzantine period the pattern of stanza and refrain was common, stemming from Romanos and, ultimately, from Alexandrian prototypes: cf. ibid. 141-4; on the Byzantine *anaklômenon* in general, cf. the preceding section on antiphonal question and answer.

167. On the Linus-refrain, which is implicitly compared here to the *Humên*-refrain, see Fraenkel (1950), 73f. on A. *Ag.* 121. On the refrain as an index of 'low' style in Aristophanes see Silk (1980), 127f.

168. Also consult Dover (1971), 1 on the refrain in Theoc. 1 and 2.

169. Pellegrino (1958), 137. See also section B.10 on antiphony above, as well as the discussion of the hymn under mythic *exemplum* in section C.4 below.

170. See discussions in M. Alexiou (1974), 146 and Kyriakides (1978), 115-24, 238f.

171. E.g. see Beaton (1996), 118, 149 on rhetorically inspired *anaphora*, sometimes with a series of parallel phrases in the medieval Greek romances of the twelfth and fourteenth century. See Finnegan (1977), 102f. on repetition in general in oral poetry.

172. Both fragments represent a nuptial *salutatio*, q.v. immediately below.

173. See other testimonia listed in Kannicht's note ad loc. Outside the context of wedding-song see also the triple *anaphoras* at Arch. fr. 2 (*IE*, i [W]) and Anacr. fr. 396.1 (*PMG* [Page]), both of which may recall folk-song. For modern instances of triple *anaphora* see n. 175 below.

174. Also a *salutatio*.

175. On the related phenomenon of triple *anaphora* within a verse in folk-songs see Sifakis (1988), 168.

176. M. Alexiou (1974), 138.

177. In polite (colloquial) Greek today *khairete* preserves the double meaning. Additionally, cf. nn. 179-80 below.

178. See *RE*, s.v. 'salutatio'.

179. See LSJ, s.v. *khairô* III.1 a-c. In the wedding-song parodied by Lucian (see TC5) the greeting occurs within the poem but at the beginning of the separate section devoted to the praise of the bridegroom.

180. See LSJ loc. cit., III.2a.

181. *Khairein polla* is frequent in the opening of letters preserved in the papyri (cf. loc. cit. in n. 178 above).

182. The text is insecure.

183. On the demes, see esp. Alan Cameron (1974), 74-91.

184. See Vogt's comments, pp. 185f. ad loc.

185. Reiske on Const. Porphyr. *De Caerem.* loc. cit.

186. Discussed above.

187. Kyriakides (1951), 179-83.

188. The emergence of political verse has been assigned to the early tenth century. Its oral origin still remains a vexed question; see e.g. Beaton (1980)ᵃ, 75f.; (1996), 98-100, 245 n. 32 (bibl.); Kazhdan & Epstein (1985), 85 n. 31. For the use of political verse in court ceremonial, including imperial weddings, possibly by the demes in the Hippodrome, see Hörandner (1974), 75-109; M. Jeffreys (1974), 176-91.

189. More recently M. Jeffreys (1974), 181, has supported this metrical analysis.

190. The first hemistichs in vv. 1, 3 and 4, as well as vv. 5 and 6 are iambic octosyllables.

191. Cf. section B.2a above.

192. Muth (1954), 38 n. 45.

193. Kaibel (1892), 251. In connection with the commonplace 'the prettiest woman under the sun', see Catullus 61.82-6.

194. Cf. TB5.32f.: Helen is praised for her skill at weaving and music. See also section B.9 above (description or *ecphrasis* of moral qualities).

195. See Dover (1971) ad loc.

196. Cf. the force of *essesthai ... eis oudena pô khronon* in TA5.2.

197. See M. Alexiou (1974), 195f., 198f., 241 nn. 52-3, and (1978), 233 n. 46; see further Chapter V n. 65 (cool water or spring). On the other hand, the motif of the cool spring associated with the white cypress is altogether unattested in ancient literature but exampled in inscriptions dating from the fourth century BC and later folk tradition: see M. Alexiou (1974), 202f.

198. Ibid. 188f., 240 n. 15. On the comparison of an individual to the sun in ancient Greek literature see also Calame (1983), 325; cf. section C.2c below.

199. This also holds for comparable symbols featured on late-antique textiles from Egypt: Stauffer (1995), 13 with n. 52. Vegetal motifs in ancient Greek wedding vase scenes bear associations with festivity and fertility in particular: see Oakley & Sinos (1993), 16-18, 21 (garlands, wreaths and plant branches often define wedding scenes); 26-7, 34-5 (the couple or seated bride is ritually showered with flowers or dried fruits in their new home); 35 (the bride eats an apple before entering the bridal chamber); 40 (a bowl of fruit evokes fertility), etc.

200. Men. Rh. 404.5-8 (RW), 407.13-15 (RW) (= TC3, TC2).

201. Cf. the testimonia listed in the sections on simile (B.2) and metaphor (B.3) above; see also Chapter IV. A flower name was borne by a beloved, usually a courtesan in antiquity; applied to a male, such a name would normally connote effeminacy: see Headlam (1922), 98 on Herod. 2.76 and Cunningham (1971), 97 ad loc. Vegetal motifs also occur in love-songs of ancient Egypt, discussed by Dornseiff (1936), 589-601 (cited in Hague [1983], 143 n. 18). See further Song of Songs 1.14, 2.3, of a man; 2.1, 2.2, of a woman. The probable influence of Song of Songs on Greek and religious and secular literature, conceivably including folk-song, will be noted in some detail in this section.

202. Hague (1983), 137; J. Kakrides (1971)ᵇ, 163f. See also n. 232 below. Stigers (1977), 83-102 sets up an exclusive metaphorical equation of flowers with maidens (but not brides) and fruits or fruit-bearing trees with brides and sexually initiated women. Her classification (see particularly ibid. 98 n. 7; 100 n. 15; 102 n. 35) might be challenged as far too rigid, especially in the light of the ancient and other comparable data which we shall be reviewing in this section: for instance, an eligible if inaccessible *korê* can be wooed as *glukumalon* (Theoc. 11.39); see also

Him. *Or.* 9. 16 (Colonna). The vegetal imagery in question actually appears to be used indiscriminately of both males and females, as well as of maidens and brides: e.g. Men. Rh. 404.5-8 (RW), 408.13-15 (RW) (= TC3, TC2), etc.

203. See Easterling (1982) ad loc.: also Seaford (1987) for an excellent discussion of the conventional images of the untroubled (usually grazing) animal and the protected, blooming plant, both used of the bride. As Seaford, 111-12, notes, both images are also employed to express the negative aspect of the loss of maidenhood, whence the motifs of: (i) the deserted or yoked animal, or the animal threatened by animals of prey; and (ii) the flower trodden or plucked.

204. See section C.4 on the mythic *exemplum* below.

205. On the sixth-century notary public and poet, see Maspero (1911), 426-81; Baldwin (1984), 327-31; MacCoull (1988), 59f. (the various literary influences, pagan and Christian, on Dioscuros' *oeuvre*).

206. The comparison to a vine-branch (*klêma*) reportedly occurred in an epithalamium by Eratosthenes. The image of the vine (*vitis*) itself, used of the bridegroom, is more clearly a Roman poetic *topos*. See Fedeli (1983), 72-3.

207. The metaphor of the *omphax* ('sour or unripe grape') is commonly used of a sexually immature girl or boy; cf. Honest. i.2402 (*Garland* [Gow-Page]); Strat. *AP* 12.205.3-4; *IG* XIV.769 (Naples), etc.; Chapter IV n. 46.

208. See Psalm 79.9, possibly the source of TF4.57 and TF8b.21f. (discussed immediately below) as well; also TE2a. On the Hebraic motif of the vine as applied to human beings in the OT and NT see Festugière (1974), 85-6.

209. See Song of Songs 2.2f. (of the bride).

210. The apple motif is discussed in Chapter IV.

211. In general, Romanos' *kontakia* were influenced by a range of scriptural, Patristic, hagiographical and probably sub-literary sources: see Mitsakis (1971), 419-35, 472-82. Tomadakis ii (1965), 129-31 notes that both the language and the narrative technique are addressed to the common man, whence the simplicity and vernacular colouring of the dialogue in Romanos. For slapstick and other popular traits in these dramatic homilies see Averil Cameron (1986), 57 n. 26 (bibl.).

212. See the twelfth-century Byzantine witness of Sappho cited in n. 65 above (= Addenda 117A [LP]): *rhodôn d'habrotêti paraballousa tas numpheuomenas parthenous.* See also Men. Rh. 404.8 (RW) (= TC3); Meleager xxxi.4159 (*HE*); Philostr. *Ep.* 51 (adduced by Russell & Wilson ad Men. Rh. loc. cit.); further testimonia and discussion in Chapter III n. 33 below.

213. The equation of an *ampelos* with a woman is attested in medieval popular tradition as well. According to the dreambook ascribed to Achmet (dating from 813 to the early eleventh century), if a bachelor sees a grapevine in a dream, this symbolises a future wife: 154.20 (Drexl).

214. See also TF6.1-2.

215. See also Horace *Odes* I.36.20 and Catullus 61.33f., 102f., etc. (The foregoing Greek and Latin testimonia are in Nisbet & Hubbard n. ad Horace loc. cit.) Finally, see the marital simile of the ivy bound to the oak in Nicet. Eugen. *DCh* I.324f. (Conca), and the related simile at op. cit., II.298 (Conca) (not in Hörandner ad TF3.41).

216. Cited by Hörandner ad loc.

217. See section A of this chapter.

218. *Achilleïs* 940 (London MS., Hesseling, p. 115).

219. The vernacularisation of literature was one of the radical developments of the twelfth century and was apparently approved by the Comnenian court. The line of demarcation between the 'high' and 'low' linguistic and thematic registers was now more frequently ignored. Thus Prodromos introduced demotic lexical and grammatical elements even in his best archaising verses; and 'Ptocho'– or pseudo-Prodromos employed language that verged on slang: see Kazhdan & Epstein

(1985), 83-6. Even a linguistic snob like Anna Comnena avowedly sought popular oral sources in writing her history. E.g. she seems to have been aware of legends or folk-songs about a mythical rebel called 'Rapsomatis', on whom consult Beaton (1986), 48f.

220. The *diegertikon* exists in modern tradition as well, its perpetuation having been assured by the continuity of the ritual practices of which it forms a part. See TA27-9, examined below.

221. The text is found in a MS. in Vat. graec. 305, one of the main sources of Prodromic material, and published by Mercati (1970), i.162-4. On Prodromos' Lucianic works consult Hörandner (1974), 50-2.

222. Cf. Men. Rh. 399.20f. (RW), discussed briefly in n. 82 above.

223. See section B.12.

224. See section B.7 above.

225. These vernacular features are: (i) the comic motif of the laggard bridegroom (v. 9), to be discussed in Chapter III; (ii) the image of the partridge used of a bride or a marriageable woman (v. 9), q.v. in section C.2d below; (iii) the complimentary image of the cypress (v. 16), discussed immediately below in section C.2b. (Mercati cites ad v. 16 TB2.30 and Christoph. Mityl. no. 75, v. 19 [Kurtz, p. 47] *kuparittos kathaper enthade keisai*, etc. from his lament in Anacreontics for a woman.)

226. On this device see section B.2a above. Prodromos' *diegertikon* will be discussed at length in the next chapter. In the Cretan comedy *Fortunatos*, dating from the mid-seventeenth century, we note the allusive apostrophe (q.v. under sectionB.3a above) *aspri triantaphullia mou* ('my white rose bush'), addressed by the aged doctor to his young fiancée (Act V, scene 6, v. 308 [Vincent, p. 103]).

227. See section B.2a above on the theme and formal structure of this passage.

228. For the date of this testimonium see n. 213 above; see also Artem. below.

229. Dated from 833 to 1400 and published by Drexl (1925)[b], 347-75.

230. The present edition is dated to *c.* 950 AD and was prepared under the auspices of Constantine Porphyrogenitus. The edition is partly based on a corrupt sixth-century compilation of Cassianus Bassus, who incorporated two sources of the fourth century AD. The work is rich in information relating to popular medicine, superstition and magic. See *RE*, s.v. *Geoponica*; Hunger (1978)[b], ii.273f.

231. Full text in Heisenberg (1920), 100-5.

232. So Pashley (1837), i.253 n. 31. Cf. Odysseus' similar compliments in TA11.149f., which also envision the possibility of future marriage.

233. See also TA28.2 and the wedding-song L.A. MS. 102 (unpubl. Mesolonghi, 1914), vv. 7f.: 'How beautifully the two of you are matched in stature, / like young cypress trees in a garden.'

234. Coulton (1983), 28.

235. See Page (1981), 161 on 'Plato' i. See also Call. *Aet.* iii fr. 67.8 (Pf.) *kaloi nêsaôn asteres amphoteroi* (of Acontius and Cydippê); Musae. *Her. et Leandr.* 22f. (Kost). Further on the comparison of a person to a star shining at night in Calame (1983), 334, esp. 408; see following note.

236. The image of the moon in TA1 need not be construed strictly as a nuptial motif; nor need we assume, as does Burnett (1983), 306f., that the poem suggests the homosexual marriage of Atthis and the departed girl. On the commonplace that a person surpasses all rivals as the sun, moon or Lucifer outshines other celestial bodies, see Nisbet & Hubbard i.12.48 (pp. 163f.).

237. All literary and scriptural allusions in Chionates are noted by van Dieten ad loc.

238. The comparisons range from the humorous or denigrating to the decorous. Cf. *korônê* in Arch. fr. 41 (*IE*, i [W]), *possibly* an indecorous metaphor (on which see Dover [1987], 98 n. 6); *korônê* is the nickname of a courtesan at Athen. 13.583a, e and of an old prostitute ibid. 587c; cf. also ibid. 570b, where a high-priced courtesan is a *hierax*. Humorous bird nicknames for men occur at *Birds* 300, 763, 766: see Sommerstein (1987), 217, 246-7, and Dunbar (1995), 248, 471-2, 473 ad loc. The hypocoristics 'duckling' and 'little dove' are terms of endearment at Ar. *Pl.* 1011. On the strictly decorous side cf. the implicit comparison of a poet to a swan at E. *HF* 691, Posidipp. i.3056 (*HE*), etc. Also cf. Alcm. fr. 82 (Davies). Further on ornithological metaphors in ancient Greek poetry in Calame (1977), ii.72f.

239. At Song of Songs, 5.12 the bridegroom's eyes are compared to *peristerai* ('pigeons or doves').

240. Pollard (1977), 60-1. The very derivation of *perdix* from *perdomai*, 'to break wind' (cf. Chantraine, s.v. *perdix*), may confirm this bird's low status in ancient Greek and Indic culture.

241. 180.4-8 (Pack).

242. Achmet, p. 237.15 (Drexl), *hê perdix eis eueidê gunaika krinetai*; ibid. 28f. *hai gar perdikes kath'holou eis gunaikas ê thugateras krinontai*; cf. TF1.8; at *Achilleïs* 935, 1290f. (MS. Nap., Hesseling, pp. 67, 76) the heroine is said to be a partridge in a cage; at *Voscopoula* 266 (S. Alexiou) *perdika* is a hypocoristic for the heroine.

243. *Dig. Akr.* Esc. 320f. (E. Jeffreys): the bride is compared obliquely to a pure-white *peristera* ('dove'), the bridegroom to an eagle; *Erôtopaignia* 292-300 (H.-P.); *Chansons populaires*, no. 95, etc. (Pernot); *Erôphili* (S. Alexiou-Aposkiti); seventeenth-century folk-song, no. 10, vv. 1f. *et passim*, in Bouvier (1960); Pouqueville i.282, nos. 3-4; 283, no. 10. The erotic motif of hunting a bird (viz. a female beloved) is attested from Achmet onwards.

244. See Gow's note ad loc.

245. Cf. *Sc.* 142 '[sc. the shield] shimmered with electrum and gleaming gold' (cited by Pfeiffer ad loc.). Gold and electrum (which was an alloy of gold with silver) were the metals generally enamelled: Higgins (1980), 23-4.

246. See section B.7(ii) above.

247. Cf. *O khrusodaidalton emon melêma*, the emotional address in the youth's serenade at Ar. *Ec.* 973a. It is of course the high-flown language of tragedy and literary lyric in general, but such phraseology would very much suit vernacular love-song. Also cf. 'golden' as a term of amatory endearment in Ar. *Ach.* 1200, *Lys.* 930, *Vesp.* 1341 (all cited by Sommerstein [1983], 237 ad *Vesp.* 1341). To the evidence of gold imagery in the context of erotic nuptial praise add Aristaen. I.10 (Mazal), who stresses the utter parity (and therefore harmony) of Acontius and Cydippe: 'Joining together Cydippe to Acontius, you would not be alloying lead with silver, but rather the marriage will be golden on both sides.'

248. See Lorimer (1936), 14f., who however wrongly notes (p. 21) that apparently with a single and late exception (*khrusostomos*, 'golden-mouthed'), poetic compounds with *khrusos* ('gold') are complimentary and are confined to divinities; but cf. Hall (below). Further on gold and the gods in Shefton (below); G. Nagy (below); Dunbar (1995), 422-3 on *Birds* 670.

249. Shefton (1971), 109-11; id. (1972), 148-9. Perhaps 'taboo' is too severe a diagnosis: according to Plu. *Alc.* 4.5, Anytos (one of Socrates' detractors) had a large number of golden drinking-cups in his house. On gold as a sign of oriental barbarity in tragedy and associated compounds, see Hall (1989), esp. 80-1, 99, 127, 210.

250. See Campbell ([1967] 1982), 309f. ad loc.

251. See the mythic *exemplum* (section B.5 above) and *makarismos* (section B.7 above).

252. See G. Nagy (1990), 278 on the associations of gold with the bliss of immortality in Pindar.

253. The ancient *topos* of 'silver face' denotes extraordinary beauty; see Calame's (1983) note on TA2.5. Adjectival compounds with silver are rare in ancient Greek literature: Lorimer (1936), 29.

254. Gold figures in early Patristic and liturgical texts as a symbol of world beyond: see esp. Averincev (1979), 47-67. (On colour symbolism in eleventh- and twelfth-century Byzantine literature, see Kazhdan & Franklin [1984], 257-63.)

255. See section B.13 above.

256. Papamichaël (1962-3), esp. 69-78.

257. Cf. the ancient belief, mentioned above, that anything a supernatural being has or does may be associated with gold. (In TG2 'immersed [or steeped] in golden things' refers principally to the bride's favoured relation to her mother; she is, in other words, spoilt, or her mother's darling. Secondarily the image may imply that the bride has a valuable dowry.)

258. On ancient Greek mythic parallels, or *paradeigmata*, as broadly 'didactic' and socialising in function, see Buxton (1994), esp. 172-4, 196-8 (with bibl.). For a bibl. of mythic *exempla* in ancient Greek poetry and prose, see J. Kakrides (1949), 41-2 n. 53. Further bibl. of ancient Greek (and Augustan) literary *exempla* in Davisson (1993), 213 n. 2.

259. †*theasikelan ari-*|*gnôta*†: 'like a goddess undisguised', probably Atthis, the addressee. The allocation of characters is problematic; see Page (1955), 92f. and cf. Burnett (1983), 302f., on the textual difficulties in vv. 4-5. Burnett, 302-3 n. 65, following Page, argues quite convincingly that *arignôta* = 'easily recognisable' and moreover that the epithet refers in the first instance to a goddess seen in full, unmistakable epiphany. Cf. TA15.5.

260. For interpretation see Burnett (1983), 312. With respect to external beauty (*morphan*) Atthis (?) is compared with a goddess, whilst the chorus confesses the lesser status of their own appearance. (For the motif of conscious self-denigration cf. Alcm. fr. 1.45f. [Davies], Sapph. fr. 34 [LP] and Theoc. 18.20f.)

261. *Od.* 4.14 *Hermionên hê eidos ekhe khruseês Aphroditês* (Page [1955], 139 n. 1, remarks that *eidos* is not precisely definable). Burnett (1983), 219 n. 23 speculates that the import of the *exemplum* is that 'the bride is now like Helen, no longer like Hermione'. But the two *exempla* may have been chosen because they were both female figures of Spartan myth, and no contrast need be understood. For pubescent Spartan girls as 'little Helens': Bremmer (1994), 70, 81 n. 9 (bibl.); for Helen as a paradeigmatic captured bride in vase scenes: Oakley & Sinos (1993), esp. 8, 12-13, 133 n. 18. On the divine – or in general mythic – parallel with human marriage in epithalamia, see Eisenberger (1956), cited in Ph. Kakrides (1974), 292 n. on TA1.1731-42.

262. Large stature and size were deemed attractive in both sexes in ancient Greece: cf. *Od.* 6. 107-8 (and Stanford [1950] ad loc.); Dover (1971), 233 on Theoc. 18.21; Renehan (1983), 21. Stature was an essential divine attribute: Richardson (1974), 208, 252. For gods as physically imposing 'super-persons': n. 267 below; Bremmer (1994), 12, 23 n. 6 (bibl.).

263. For a broad stride as a normative masculine trait: Polemo (second century AD), in Gleason (1990), 391-3; Aristotle's 'great-souled man' has a slow (i.e. controlled) step. Herakles was also an acknowledged pattern of manhood: cf. Thomson (1966), 135 on A. *Cho.* 163; also E. *HF* 183, Ar. *Nub.* 1048, Men. Rh. 405.24f. (RW). TA14 appears to be modelled technically on an *epiphaneia*, a hymnic description of the approach of a deity: cf. TA10.1709-14 (and Ph. Kakrides ad loc.). Muth (1954), 38 n. 45 regards the reference to a roof, builders and the bridegroom's arrival as indications that this song was performed before the *thalamos* while the chorus anticipated the newlyweds' arrival. (His view however that the reference to building a *thalamos* is an exaggeration warranted by poetic licence may not be entirely correct. The allusion may be a relic of a time when an extra room was added to the *oikos* or 'house' for the son's marriage.) Bowra (1961), 217 considered the poem as a *ktupia*, a type of playful and probably loud badinage meant to be apotropaic; also cf. n. 292 below. Renehan (1983), 20-3 rightly rules out obscenity here.

264. Him. *Or.* 9.16f. (Colonna) (= 218 [V]).

265. See n. 262 above.

266. On Nausicäa's 'divine' beauty, see J. Kakrides (1970), 24f.; further, Zervou (1993), 149f.

267. For Artemis as a model of impressive stature and splendid appearance, see *h. Ap.* 194f.

268. The context of the last two comparisons suggests that epithalamian terms of praise are being used to rich effect; see also n. 280 below. Cf. *Od.* 17.36f. (= 19.53f.), discussed below.

269. See loc. cit., v. 21; fr. 31.1 (LP), to be examined shortly. For further attestations of the high compliments *isotheos*, etc. see Diggle (1970), 154 on E. *Phaeth.* 240.

270. Testimonia in Page (1978), 96 n. ad Rufin. xxvi. (Alan Cameron [1985], viii, 162f., challenging Page's chronology, places Rufinus' floruit nearer to Strato and Martial i.e. *c.* AD 80-100.) See also Lane Fox (1986), 138-40 on this *topos* in the ancient novel. A related *topos* is the comparison in epigrams of an *erômenos* to Ganymede: e.g. Meleager ci, cii (*HE*); Strato *AP* 194, etc.

271. These two marriages are used generally as positive paradigms in Greek and Latin literary tradition: see Burnett (1983), 194 with her n. 29. Odysseus and Penelope are more obviously a moral example. In funerary epigrams women are compared to Penelope: *Epi. Gr.* 471 (Cleonae, second/first century BC), 558 (Rome, *c.* second century AD); further examples with discussion in Peek (1965), 163-4 (cited in Lefkowitz [1986], 140).

272. The exemplification of certain moral virtues is understood in the accounts of the couple and their marriage in *Cypr.* fr. 2 (Davies); *Il.* 24.60; Hes. frr. 209-11 (MW); Pi. *N.* 4 and 5 (S.-M.), esp. 5.33-4 (S.-M.); cf. Ar. *Nub.* 1063 *kai tên Thetin g'egême dia to sôphronein.* (Testimonia and bibl. cited in Burnett, 196 nn. 38 and 42; 197 n. 43.) Of course Thetis will also be a paragon of beauty: cf. *arguropesda,* her epithet in Homer; cf. Rufin. *AP* 5.48.4. But qua virgin nymph who resisted Zeus' advances she may, like Peleus, be used to exemplify moral attributes e.g. chastity, in the first instance.

273. See Bramble (1970), esp. 22. n. 1; 23f.

274. TC6.15f. states this; cf. TA16, discussed immediately below. For depictions of the wedding of Peleus and Thetis ('the greatest social event of Greek mythology') on vases, see Oakley & Sinos (1993), esp. figs. 50-3 (the renowned François vase), discussed, 24; figs. 108-11, discussed, 36-7; figs. 128-30, discussed, 40-2 (the resonances, positive and slightly negative, of this union). The wedding of Cadmus and Harmonia, another archetypally happy couple, was the first mortal wedding ever attended by the Olympians. Each god brought a splendid gift while the Muses and Graces sang to Apollo's accompaniment on the lyre: Roscher ii.1.831f.

275. In this version Hermes is the cupbearer; cf. E. *IA* 1053, where Ganymede is cupbearer. The gods, naturally, drink ambrosia rather than normal wine.

276. Good fortune and happiness are primarily meant in Thgn. 339f. (*IE* i [W]). Cf. A. *Ch.* 59-60 for the observation that 'success' or 'prosperity' (*eutukhein*) characterises a divine (and hence godlike) state; Thomson (1966), 128 ad loc. for further documentation of this *topos.* Additionally, cf. Headlam (1922), 363 ad Herod. 7.111 and Page (1978), 101-2 n. ad Rufin. *AP* 5.94.3-4 (= xxxv.4 [Page]).

277. See n. 269 above.

278. Devereux (1970), 17-31; Dover (1978), 177-9.

279. Op. cit., 22f.

280. A divine comparison couched in general terms may serve as straightforward physical (or erotic) praise: cf. *Od.* 6.15f. (of Nausicäa); op. cit. 243f. refer to

Odysseus, who is said to be *kalos te megas te*, 276-80; finally, cf. Ar. *Thesm.* 1106 (a ship is compared to a virgin of godlike appearance).

281. See Dover (1978), 178. If this (secondary) association is indeed operative, *isos theoisin* closely corresponds to the *makarismos* in TA18.1722-5, where the bridegroom is termed *makar*, i.e. implicitly godlike, because of his extraordinary *tukhê* ('good luck') and *kallos* ('beauty'). (This standard type of nuptial *makarismos* will be discussed below.)

282. Artemis is not only the model of tall stature (cf. n. 262 above) but also the patron goddess of a *korê* ('maiden'). The goddess, as *kourotrophos*, will protect the girl throughout puberty, until her day of marriage; cf. Calame (1977), i.174f., 257f., 281f., esp. 301 n. 254. Because the goddess was such a favourite role-model (thanks in part to the *Od.* passage cited), her name was one of the two divine onomastics given to girls: Bremmer (1994), 75, 82 n. 24 (bibl.).

283. That Odysseus' particular choice of an *exemplum* is wholly honourable can also be inferred from his statements in loc. cit. 161, 166-7.

284.

You have the beauty of Cypris, the mouth of Peithô,
 the physical prime
of the springtime Hours, the voice of Calliope,
the intelligence and wisdom of Themis and the [sc.
 skilful] hands of Athena;
with you, beloved girl, the Graces are four.

285. In *Od.* 17.36f. (= 19.53f.) the poet invokes two paradigms in order to formulate praise that bears on Penelope's chaste behaviour (Artemis) and her external appearance (Aphrodite): … *periphrôn Pênelopeia, / Artemidi ikelê êe khruseê Aphroditê.* At X. *Oecon.* 4.27f. Cyrus is said to be *eudaimôn* because of his exceptional combination of virtue and good luck.

286. Dover (1978).

287. According to Men. Rh. 399.20f. (RW) the object of the proemium in the wedding speech is an *amplificatio* of the couple or the occasion. On the general function of *amplificatio* through mythic or other extraordinary *exempla* in the proemium, see Viljamaa (1968), 104f., 107f., 124, 126. The *makarismos* (discussed below) also functions in effect as an *amplificatio*.

288. For other instances of deflation see Burnett (1983), 194 with her n. 29.

289. Silk (1980), 105-6; also n. 298 below.

290. For that matter, this divine marriage was the implicit paradigm of most Athenian marriages, as weddings normally took place in the month Gamelion (roughly January) during which the 'sacred marriage' of Zeus and Hera was commemorated: Oakley & Sinos (1983), 10; also n. 297 below.

291. Oakley & Sinos (1993), figs 32-5, discussed, 18-19; more on the couple's communion with the gods and quasi-divinisation, ibid. esp. 7-8, 10, 17-18, 28-30, 43-6, 136 n. 41. On *nymphê* as 'bride' and 'goddess' in song, see also G. Nagy (1996) 84, 102-3. On modern Greek nereids as physically idealised (but licentious) brides, see Stewart (1991), 176.

292. Antzoulatou-Retsila (1980), 65f. esp. 82-3, 85f. Further on apotropaic nuptial devices in Pilitsis (1987), 91-114.

293. Ibid., 82f.

294. Ibid., 100f., esp. 107 n. 8.

295. Ibid., 100f.

296. So also id., 110f.

297. For a bibliography of sacred marriage in general cf. Guthrie (1950), 54 n. 1.

298. On the typical hymnic and other traditional elements, including arguably popular features in the last two scenes, consult Ph. Kakrides (1974) nn. ad vv.

1706-45, 1706f., 1706-8, 1709-14, 1728f., 1745-7, 1748-9, 1752; also Dunbar (1995), esp. 744-52 and 757-70. On Aristophanes' 'composite' mode, consisting of high and low elements, cf. Silk (1980).

299. Also cf. Leo Magister no. 2.11-12, 45-6 (Bergk iii.356f.); no. 5.45f. (pp. 361f.). Consult Seaford (1987), 116-17 on Aphrodite's exemplary role of persuading the bride to approach the bridegroom.

300. Cf. Lucian's observation that (hyberbolic) mythic comparisons are best suited to encomiastic poetry and panegyric in general and should not occur in historiography: Lucian. *Hist. Conscr.* 8.

301. Bieler (1935-6).

302. The *exempla* in *Vit. Aesop.* G chs 29.9-10 & 33 (Perry) seem to reflect colloquial usage.

303. On the peculiarly Greek cultural phenomenon of the deification of striking mortals, with particular reference to temple-sharing from the time of the Alexander cults, see Nock (1986 [1972]), 203-51, esp. 241 n. 221.

304. The parallel, however, is not exact in St Paul. Christ is both the head *and* Saviour of the Church, while salvation cannot be predicated of a husband's relation to his wife. The *topos* of Israel as the wife of Yahweh is found in the Old Testament: Is. 54.1-10 esp. v. 5; Jer. 2.2, 32f., 3.1; Hosea 1.2f., 2.1f., 3.1f.; Zech. 1.14, 8.2; cf. Psalm 87.2, 5f. In general, the early Christians described their ideal relationship with God in terms of the imagery of earthly marriage: see Lane Fox (1986), 370-1, 741 n. 74 (bibl.); P. Brown (1988), esp. 259-60, 262, 274-6.

305. On Methodius' hymn and its relation to the *kontakion* and epithalamium see Mitsakis (1971), 127f.; Pellegrino (1958), 43f.

306. I am indebted to the late Dr Benediktos Englezakis of the Holy Archbishopric, Nicosia, Cyprus for discussing with me the rather rarefied history of wedding ritual in the Orthodox Church.

307. Tertull. *de corona.*

308. Jo. Chrys. *hom. 9 in I Tim.*, *PG* 62. 546 (= Field iv.74). On the early Byzantine wedding in general, see Vance (1907), 73-7.

309. On the early Church's dim view of marriage and its ideal of virginity, consult Lane Fox (1986), 355f., esp. 362f.; P. Brown (1988).

310. Meyendorff (1975), 27f.; Politis (1931), 232f.

311. The bridegroom is said to be shy (p. 84, 1.16). Cf. the *topos* of the laggard bridegroom, to be considered in Chapter III.

312. Apparently the Christian concept of *enkrateia* has encroached on Choricius' version of the myth.

313. Also cf. p. 97, 11.21f., for the union of Cadmus and Harmonia, another nuptial cliché, probably drawn from Menander.

314. Photius found the blending of pagan and Christian ingredients in Choricius unappealing: see Wilson (1983), 103.

315. Isaac Angelos' abysmal military and political record, even at the time of his marriage to Margaret, thwarts any comparison with Odysseus' reputation. On Angelos' reign consult *CMH,* iv.i.245.

316. In itself mythological hyperbole (or *hyperochê*) such as Choniates uses is not unattested in ancient Greek and Latin literature. This panegyric *topos* was first used systematically by Isocrates; cf. TD4.20f.; also cf. Verg. *Aen.* 6.801-5, Anchises' *laus Augusti,* according to which Augustus will outdo two mythic *exempla* (Bacchus and Herakles) and a third, mythic-historical one implied by the two (Alexander the Great); cf. Zagagi (1986), 267; other late Latin and western medieval examples in Curtius (1953), 162-5. But Menander Rhetor's instructions do not call specifically for such hyperbolic allusions, which presumably might appear as boastful challenges defeating the purpose of a marriage *exemplum*; we may therefore reckon Choniates' tendentious use of myth as original.

317. Cf. TG14-17, discussed below.

318. The bride herself may be compared to an angel or archangel: see *Laogr.* 13 (1951), 320, no. 33; 330, no. 18.

319. I owe this information to the kindness of Mrs Helen Psychoyiou of the Centre for Folklore at the Academy of Athens.

320. Cf. the version of this song in Spyridakis-Petropoulos (1962), i.10. For similar Cypriot songs, see Mackridge (1993), 153 *et passim*; for the 'Akritic' song-cycle and romance, see Chapter I; Mackridge ibid., esp. 158-9 ascribes the enduring appeal of heroic folk-songs telling of bridal abduction to the fact that these songs have served to uphold the prestigious 'ideal of male aggressiveness' and the expected role of female passivity in medieval and early modern Greek rural society. Further on bride-snatching in Chapter III below.

321. Mythic *exempla* also occur in other types of modern Greek folk-song. Herzfeld (1993), 244, 253 n. 9 cites the importation of recognisable mythic-historical formulae in modern Greek laments: by means of *performative* time, personal grief is 'indexed' against public disasters of the distant, mythicised past, e.g. the capture of a city by the Turks or the Passion of Christ, and thereby rendered more 'intelligible', emotionally speaking, to the performer and audience alike.

322. Cf. *Staphylos* (second century AD?), col. III.1-3 (Stephens & Winkler, p. 434) 'ceaselessly he congratulated himself [lit. called himself *makar*] and called himself blessed on account of the boy'.

323. On the passage see Dover (1978), 154f. Winkler (1990), 74-7 discusses the honour/shame devolving upon men in ancient Greece from the conduct of their wives and kinswomen in general. On the interrelated codes of conscience and shame in ancient Greek and contemporary Mediterranean societies, see Dover (1974), 226-9, 235f., esp. 239 n. 11 (bibl.) and now Cairns (1993), a comprehensive study.

324. On the identification of the bride see Diggle (1970), 158f.

325. Cf. op. cit. 49 *eupenthere* (lit. 'having an excellent father-in-law', 'having excellent relations by marriage').

326. Also cf. id. no. 5.63f. (Bergk iii.362).

327. From a *formal* point of view, the praise of the nuptial pair is here formulated in a manner similar to Menander Rhetor's *kata sumplokên antexetastikôs*, q.v. in section B.7(ii) above.

328. Muth (1954), 38 n. 45.

329. On the extreme conservatism of functional songs in Greek tradition, see J. Petropoulos (1994), 12-17; 44-5.

III. Nuptial Blame

1. See section 3 of this chapter. The countervailing roles of praise and blame, especially in poetic tradition, are common to Indo-European and other societies; on the I-E evidence see G. Nagy (1999 [1979]), 222. See also op. cit., 253f. and Halliwell (1986), 269f. for notable discussions of the implications of Arist. *Po.* 1448a20-1449a38.

2. The perennial concerns of ancient invective (e.g. deformity, parentage, morals, dress, gluttony, etc.) can be traced in e.g. epic poetry and rhetoric. Thus, for a typology of blame and associated motifs see: (i) Süss (1910), 247f.; (ii) Vodoklys (1992). See also nn. 19 and 38 below.

3. See Thompson, *Motif-Index, passim.*

4. See e.g. (co-ed.) Radcliffe-Brown ([1950] 1960), esp. 57f.; id. (n. 7 below); Evans-Pritchard (1965), esp. 76f., 95f.; J. Campbell (1964), 132-5. For the Byzantine and modern Greek evidence, see n. 11 below.

5. J. Campbell (1964), 132-5.

6. Evans-Pritchard (1965), 231f.

7. See Radcliffe-Brown on the South African evidence of long-term obligatory 'joking relationships' between specific relatives and generations; especially prescribed joking and teasing (in some cases reciprocal) serve as a permanent safety valve for the tensions created by a marriage: Radcliffe-Brown ([1924] 1952), 90-116.

8. Winkler (1990), 76.

9. See further ibid., 74-7.

10. Seaford (1987), 107 n. 3; 112.

11. I.e. 'the hand on the wrist', which refers to the bridegroom's forceful and symbolic gesture. It should be remembered that *gamos* may mean both 'wedding' and 'abduction': Oakley & Sinos (1993), 13; Chapter II n. 25 above. For the iconography and ideology of (mostly mythic-paradeigmatic) abductions and resistance, see Oakley & Sinos, ibid., 12-13 (Helen and Theseus), cf. 18; 30-2 (mock abductions of mortal brides); 133 n. 18. Further on the capture and domestication of the bride through marriage in both literature and art in Bremmer (1994), 44f., 73, 82 nn. 17 & 19 (bibl.); Faraone (1990), 238-9 n. 41 for bibl. of bridal theft and feigned resistance. Ephoros (*F Gr Hist* 70 F149.4f. [Jacoby iia.89]) records that in Crete the friends of a boy snatched by an *erastês* customarily put up only superficial resistance, in effect approving this 'rape'. 'Abduction with intent to marry' (*harpagê* under canon law) was an exogamous practice also in Byzantine society: Karlin-Hayter (1992), 133-54; Mackridge (1993), 150-60; cf. Laiou (1993), 123-4, 133f., 156f. For the modern Greek evidence see J. Campbell (1964), esp. 129-30, 308-9 and Chapter IV below.

12. All cited in Richardson (1974), 175 ad *h. Cer.* 83f.

13. Murgatroyd (1987), 224 analyses Sappho's saucy wit in this fragment.

14. Cf. the discussion of TA14 in Chapter II n. 263 above.

15. Discussed in Chapter IV below.

16. In Catullus 61 the elliptic banter addressed to the *concubinus* (vv. 119f.) and the bridegroom (vv. 134-43) and the discreet teasing of the bride (vv. 144-73) correspond to the explicit traditional obscenities of the *versus Fescennini* sung during the wedding procession: thus Fordyce (1961) and also Quinn (1970) ad v. 120.

17. We do know however that bride-snatching was practised in Byzantine society and especially among early twelfth-century Byzantine 'borderers' (Mackridge [1993]); such an occurrence may well have resulted in recrimination that was formalised in nuptial songs.

18. Op. cit., 120. Campbell is actually describing the procession on the morning after the wedding.

19. In Sapph. fr. 57 (LP) an unspecified female is taken to task for being *agroïôtis*, i.e. inelegant, especially in her dress; see Page (1955), 133f. ad loc. (Dress is a common target of ancient invective: see Davies [1984], 172 for bibl.)

20. Pollux 3.42.

21. The *thurôros* was the guardian of the couple's privacy: Oakley & Sinos (1993), 37 with n. 107; doors, partly because they symbolised the bride's passage to a new state, are common in wedding scenes on vases: ibid., 31. It is striking that the doorkeeper-figure has analogues in other cultures e.g. the Kyo of Kenya, as Evans-Pritchard (1965), 230f. observed. The custom of posting a doorkeeper – who was a type of *parakoumparos* i.e. distinct from the 'best man' – before the nuptial chamber was noted in Greece in the late eighteenth century by the diplomat Guys: ' ... lorsque le Compère conduit le Marié au lit nuptial, il le laisse à la parte de l'appartement; il faut qu'il en achète l'entrée par un present au Paranymphe qui la garde' (Guys [1783], 252). The practice has been more recently recorded by folklorists and anthropologists in Greece: G.F. Abbott (1903), 170, 172; Politis (1931), 281; *Laogr.* 23 (1964), s.vv. *gamos-ethima* (*eikonikê palê*); Alexakis (1984), 81.

22. Conceivably, large feet or large shoes were a stock motif in Sappho's day. One is tempted to look forward in time to the slave Demosthenes practically swimming in his enormous shoes in Ar. *Eq.* 319f. (Demosthenes' feet are normal and the joke here is about shoes which are too big because incompetently made.)

23. (1981), 319 ad Men. Rh. 406.13.

24. *CHCL*, i.109. M. Dillon, in an unpublished paper given at the APA Conference in December 1994, noted that Margites is not only a proverbial dunce but also an inept, self-defeating trickster.

25. For the motif of making love until dawn, which is implied at v. 14, see TG40-1 and Appendix IV n. 2.

26. Cited in Seaford (1984), 201 ad E. *Cyc.* 511-18.

27. See also Men. Rh. 408.1f.; 409.1f.; 410.16f.; 410.27f.; 410.29f. (RW).

28. The first epithalamian composition, published in *Notices et extraits des manuscrits de la Bibliothèque Impériale*, viii.2 (Paris, 1810), p. 122 is in elegiac metre and, also like the parody of the rhetorical genre in Luc. *Symp.* 41, it is delivered by a grammarian.

29. Prodromos also wrote sixteen rather racy epigrams on an old man named Machaon who had a much younger wife; these are printed by Miller (1883), 58f. The senile lover is a favourite motif in late antique epigrams and characterises heterosexual and homosexual relationships alike: e.g. Phld. xxvii.3328f. (*Garland* [Gow-Page]); Strato *AP* 12.240.

30. Let us briefly consider the tragic passage: the ghost of Clytemnestra has invoked the sleeping Erinyes with a cry for revenge; at length the latter rouse one another (vv. 140-3) and realise (in vv. 145-8) that their quarry, Orestes, has given them the slip. Prodromos diverges from his 'model' in two main ways: rather than copy the transitive construction *egeir' egeire* of the original, he opts for the middle second aorist imperative *egreo* ('rouse yourself', i.e. 'wake up!') – not a bad alternative, since this particular form is certifiably poetic and occurs, for example, in the same sense in *Od.* 23.5. Second, unlike Aeschylus, Prodromos uses the term *agra* ('quarry') in the literal sense and construes it with *perdix* ('partridge'), which is itself a metaphor for the bride (q.v. immediately below). In keeping with his 'model', however, the Byzantine poet pretends that the old bridegroom will lose his quarry by sleeping (cf. A. *Eum.* 148).

31. *ouketh' homôs thalleis hapalon khroa* ('Your tender skin has lost its former bloom', tr. West [1993]ᵃ, 2).

32. On the complimentary erotic associations of 'ripeness' cf. Henrichs (1980), 7f.; also Chapter IV n. 9 below.

33. For further evidence of Sappho's use of the rose see Chapter II n. 212 above; on the motif in later (sub-literary) inscriptions see Chapter IV n. 25 below. For the connection with love and death add Richardson (1974), 142 ad *h. Cer.* 6. The rose as the fairest of flowers was a literary and probably popular commonplace by late antiquity: cf. the supreme compliment, consisting of the metaphor of the rose at Meleager xxxi.4159f. (*HE*) '... flower of flowers in season, / Zênophila, sweet rose of Peithô, is abloom'; anon. epigr. xxiii.3746f. (*HE*) 'Which is it? Is the garland the rose of Dionysius or is he the garland's rose? I think the garland is less lovely' (tr. Paton, cited by eds ad loc.), where the *laudandus* is understood to be more decorative than even the roses adorning his crown (the original phrasing as a whole recalls informal utterance); *carm. anacreont.* 44.5 (W) 'Rose, finest of flowers'.

34. As an inherently superlative term, the rose is highly suited to comparison of this type.

35. Robinson (1979), 81 correctly states that imitations of Lucian by Byzantine *littérateurs* often strayed from their ancient prototype and could sustain contemporary references and other elements of realism. Furthermore, as Hunger has demonstrated in his comparative stylistic study of Anna Comnena and Michael

Glykas, mimesis (*Umschreibungsmanie*) and colloquialism are by no means mutually exclusive or inversely proportional: Anna Comnena's history, formally a 'high-grade' work, actually contains more colloquial terms than Glykas' 'low-grade' poem; cf. Hunger (1978)[a], 139-70. Two other sets of findings may be cited in support of the thesis that realistic and hence vernacular touches were compatible with literary practice in Prodromos' day. (i) Beck (1984), 122f., detects echoes of *Strassenpoesie* in a *Kabinetstück* in Nicetas Eugeneianos' erudite novel, as well as other indications of realism in the literature and art of the twelfth century; cf. ibid., 138f. (ii) As Kazhdan & Franklin (1984), 112 n. 117 note, Prodromos is often realistic even in his ultra-traditional genre-pieces such as *Rhodanthê and Dosicles* and *Catamyomachia*. Beaton, though acknowledging the 'literary handling of the everyday and the particular' in the innovative twelfth century, nevertheless questions its extent and importance; in his view many alleged instances of 'realism' (including the first cited in [ii] above) have been misjudged: Beaton (1996), 22-3, 28-9 with n. 35; 53, 241 n. 25; 73-4; cf. 81-2, 87 (the psychological plausibility of erotic dreams in Makrembolites' romance).

36. Discussed in Chapter II section C.2a above.

37. Typically the Pontic original preserves the ancient pronunciation of η as *e* (cf. v. 1 νυφεν) rather than *i*. (On the Pontic dialect, see Horrocks [1997], 300 [bibl.], 311-16; cf. Mackridge [1999], 80-1.) The entire song is in tonic trochaics, although from vv. 5 onwards an older quantitative rhythm (trochaic dimeter?) firmly underlies the stress-based rhythm: cf. vv. 8, 18. This *may* however be a coincidence.

38. Cf. Arch. fr. 206 (*IE*, i [W]), *peri sphuron pakheia, misêtê gunê* ('... fat about the ankles, a loathsome lady') *possibly* from a catalogue of ugly bodily parts intended to humiliate a woman (a veteran whore?); fr. 188 (*IE*, i [W]), in conjunction with 478 b *SLG* (Page), describes (whether truthfully or not) the ill-effects of time on the appearance of a woman. (Early lyric also dealt in unflattering descriptions of appearance, including dress and demeanour: e.g. Sapph. frr. 21.6f. [LP], 58. 13-15 [LP]; Anacr. fr. 388 [*PMG* (Page)]; see also n. 19 above.)

39. Cf. Chapter II section B.8-9.

40. See Dover (1987), 107f. on the arguably preliterate conventions inherited by archaic *iamboi*.

41. The image of the 'lock' underlies the ancient *phusikleidion*, a magical spell supposed to cause the female victim's *phusis* to 'open wide', as though unlocked by a key, in readiness for the spell operator: 'I command you, vagina of so-and-so, open wide and receive so-and-so's sperm.' (P. xxxvi.283f. [Preisendanz-Henrichs]). See also (a) this indecent wedding-song, recorded in the last century in Epirus: 'Tonight, [sc. Lady Bride], your lock / will be broken in one go / and the door to your garden / will stand open' (Aravantinos [1880], no. 373, vv. 9-12); (b) the Italian obscene slang *chiavare*, originally meaning 'to nail or to pierce' but nowadays associated with *chiave* ('key') and meaning 'to fuck'; this is reflected in rude gestures of turning a key in a lock.

42. The union of a hag with a young man is not well-represented in Thompson's *Motif-Index*: see Thomson iv.39 (J 445.1 *Foolish youth in love with ugly old mistress*) and 385 (K 1318 *Trickster shifts married couples in bed* [the resulting young couple finds this satisfactory]), the only analogous examples. But cf. n. 44 below.

43. Zevgoli-Glezou (1963), 88.7.

44. Ussher (1973), 216 ad Ar. *Eccl.* 1011-20 cites a Ukrainian folk-tale envisaging an enactment whereby old men must marry young girls and old women must marry young boys. The Thessalian song considered above, though, offers a much closer parallel to the episode in *Eccl.*

45. Reliance on a literary model at countless removes is theoretically possible and in some cases very probable. Fehling (1972), 173-96, for example, has shown that a modern Coan folk-tale resembling the Erysichthon story is a composite of Callimachus and Planudes' translation of Ovid's *Metamorphoses*; yet it may be countered here that a translation of a Latin text by a Byzantine monk (Planudes) is rare enough, and that the conflation of two versions, one in Greek and the other in Latin, of an ancient myth by a schoolteacher in Cos in the last century is equally eccentric. I take the point however that certain episodes in the *Odyssey* and in Apuleius' *Amor and Psyche* have generated similar folktales on a world-wide scale; cf. Fehling (1977) on the *Nachleben* of the latter.

46. *Eccl.* esp. 989f., 1015f., 1037 (*tond'emautês eisagô*; cf. *ton emon autês eisagô* Sommerstein) has nuptial implications, etc.

47. *Pl.* 959f., 975f., 1023f., 1095f.; cf. *Thesm.* 345-50.

48. Oeri (1948), esp. 19-21. Oeri cites Hermipp. fr. 9 (*PCG*, v.567 [K.-A.]), presumably a slanderous remark about Hyperbolos' mother, and Phryn. Com. fr. 34 (*PCG*, vii.410 [K.-A.]) as precedents for the Aristophanic motif. Generally on the negative representation of old women in ancient Greek society, see Bremmer (1987), 191-215.

49. Cf. id. vii (Gow) and the briefer version of the same anecdote, or *khreia*, which Athen. 6.246b attributes to one Pausimachus; also cf. op. cit., 13.584b (a parasite was kept by an old woman and regularly slept with her).

50. Cf. id. *AP* 11.73 (a kinky crone is so eager that she is willing to pay her young partner); op. cit., 328 describes a *ménage à quatre* involving the poet and two other men and a *graus* ('old woman').

51. Zevgoli-Glezou (1963), 88.4 glosses a modern parallel in a similar way.

52. Oeri (1948), 13f., 39f., 72f.; cf. 98. On the ancient Greek *topos* of female dipsomania, see Just (1989), esp. 162-4, 186-7; on the slavish connotations of this proclivity, see id. (1985), 181-2.

53. The poem (in accentual twelve-syllable iambics), wrongly ascribed to Manuel Philes, is printed in Miller ii.306-11.

54. Pichard gives a variant reading: *hê mêkhanis hê graia*. Loukatos (1978), 249 provides a bibliography of witches and warlocks in medieval and modern Greek lore.

55. Codex 525 fol. 28b-29a Bayerisches Staatsbibliothek, discussed in Politis, *Paroimiai*, i.viiif.

56. Ibid., 3.9.

57. Cf. Politis, *Paroimiai*, iv.106, no. 7a, 'You're meant to pasture pigs', etc., of a boorish or incompetent person. Politis also cites a Rumanian parallel.

58. See Gow (1965), 118 ad Machon xvi.332. On dawn as spelling the end of a tryst see Appendix V.

59. Hunger (1978)[b], ii.169 observes that in the Middle period the epigram, like its ancient predecessor, was used as a means of belittling personal enemies. Constantine the Rhodian's *Spottgedichte* (printed in *AG*, ii [Matranga, pp. 624-32]) are full of Aristophanic tags and allusions.

60. *AG*, ii (Matranga, p. 626), vv. 31-3. The compound is, of course, based on *Paphlagôn*, the Aristophanic epithet referring to Cleon: *Eq.* 2, 6; *Nub.* 581, etc.

61. See Chapter II section A above.

62. In a choral wedding-song from North Africa (Trask i.128) the bride describes the bridegroom, supposedly a widower much older than herself, in comic language: '[his] neck-veins stand out like knotted strings. / His beard is like a handful of alfalfa. / His belly is like the bottom of a grain sack.'

63. The influence of rhetoric on the literature (especially the sermons and hymns), the visual arts and even conceivably the character of the Byzantines was pervasive at all periods: see Maguire (1981), 3f. *et passim*. For our present purposes, we may refer to the 'stemma' posited in Chapter II section A. The following considerations may suggest the diffusion of invective motifs via rhetorical practice: (i) the commonplace, *koinos topos*, which took up the demonstration of the accused's vice, the *sunkrisis* and the *enkômion kai psogos* were stock exercises of the *progym-nasmata* of Hermogenes and Aphthonius (*auxêsis* was used to intensify the effect of *epainos* or of its opposite, *psogos*; cf. Tzetzes' commentary on one of his letters which exaggeratedly extolled the ancestry of a government official: *Historiae*, Chilias VII, vv. 295-311 [Leone, p. 267]); (ii) St John Chrysostom and subsequent sermonising tradition reproduced many (non-obscene) invective *topoi*; see e.g. Cataudella (1940), 236-43.

IV. Harvest Imagery and the Motif of the Apple

1. Recently D. Yatromanolakis, among others, has questioned the existence of a ninth book of *epithalamia* in the Alexandrian period; he speculates that Book 8 contained many if not most of Sappho's wedding songs: Yatromanolakis (1999), 179-95. For a colloquial tone cf. e.g. frr. 110 (LP) (= TA49) and 111 (LP) (= TA14), discussed in Chapter III. For real ceremonial and colloquial stylistic elements in the epithalamia see Page (1955), 119f.; Bowra (1961), esp. 214-8, and Chapter II, *passim*.

2. Fr. 44 (LP), assigned to the end of Book 2, is likely to be hymenaeal. Fr. 142 (LP), whose book-source is unknown, may well also be a wedding composition: Burnett (1983), 224.

3. For the view that Sappho's language is generally an artificial literary dialect see Hooker (1977), esp. 47, 49f., 51f.; Bowie (1981). But cf. Dover (1997), 90-5: epigraphic evidence may suggest that many Homeric words derive not from a *Kunstsprache* but from Ionic vernacular.

4. See Bowra (1961). In other isolated poems outside the context of marriage, Sappho also adopts a vernacular tone and manner, similarly characterised by what may be colloquial vocabulary and an aversion from epic formulas and prosodical devices: Bowra, 231-3. Frr. 102 (LP) (a *chanson de toile*) and 137 (LP) (on which see Chapter II n. 158) may be modelled on folk-song.

5. Op. cit., 218.

6. I am quoting Bowra, ibid. On repetition in wedding-songs in the Greek language see Chapter II section B.12.

7. Cf. Meleager lxxi.4366-7 (*HE*) for a more histrionic type of self-correction. J. Kakrides (1983), 93 cites a modern Greek example of *epanorthôsis* in connection with this fragment:

> I fancy that I'm hungry, but I'm thirsty, but I'm not thirsty,
>   I'm sleepy,
> but I'm not sleepy, I keep vigil for you and sigh!

8. We shall consider its thematic content at greater length in section 2 below.

9. On the erotic implications of *ereuthetai* ('turns red') cf. Nisbet & Hubbard ii.5.12 (p. 86), Gow (1952), 161 on Theoc. 7.117 and nn. 45-6 below. 'Ripe' also occurs in the same positive sense of 'nubile' at Plu. *Lyc.* 15.4; discussion of the varied connotations of 'ripeness' in Henrichs (1980), 7f.; further on the particular theme of 'ripe for marriage': Paus. 2.33.2, *AP* 7.600 and the medical writers, discussed in King (1983), 112-13 *et passim*; to which add Men. Rh. 407.4f. (RW), discussed in Chapter III above.

10. On mythical *exempla* in wedding encomia see Chapter II section B.5. Scholars are silent on what seems to me to be a serious implication of Himerius' remarks, namely that the heroic comparison occurred in the same poem in which Sappho likened the bride to an apple.

11. Sappho's extended simile is imitated by Longus III.33.19-24 (Reeve, p. 48); also by Nicetas Eugeneianos (= TF14).

12. For the tragic and comic (colloquial) comparisons of a physical quality of men and women to an obvious characteristic of a fruit cf. e.g. Theopomp. fr. 76 (*PCG*, vii.742 [K.-A.]), cited in Henrichs (above), 21. For cases where *anthos* refers to the beauty of the *pais* see Henrichs (1980), 20-4 (24 n. 44); but cf. the exquisite variation of the *anthos* motif at Pl. *Rep.* 601b.12f. (the bloom of youth *without* beauty). In general for the venerable cliché of the 'blossom of one's youth', frequently in sexual contexts, consult FJW iii.31 on A. *Supp.* 663-6; Silk (1974), 102 n. 16 (test.); on the physical/erotic cliché (?) *anthein* ('to flower, bloom') in the fifth/fourth century BC, ibid., 166 n. 8. (Further, on the symbol of the flower of youth in Pindar and Sappho see Steiner [1986], 28-32.) At Mimn. fr. 2 (*IE*, ii [W]) the brevity of youth is likened to the growth and decay of leaves; cf. n. 13 below.

13. Cf. the Tree of Life: Thompson, *Motif-Index*, ii.413 (E 90); also id., v.51 (M 312.0.4.1). At *Il.* 6.146f. the transience of human life is compared with the seasonal changes of a tree.

14. See Dover (1980) on Pl. *Smp.* 196a 8; also A. *Ag.* 743 (love as a 'stinging', i.e. harmful flower, on which see Padel [1992], 136 with n. 77), and Clearchus of Soli, cited immediately below. See also nn. 23 and especially 52 below.

15. I have left out of account the comparison of a young person to a tree, on which see M. Alexiou (1974), 198f.; 241 nn. 43, 45-6 (testimonia).

16. In both this section and section b below, Alexiou's and Seaford's references are indicated by an asterisk (*) or two asterisks (**) respectively.

17. This testimonium, A. *Ag.* 1525 (immediately below) and all references to Theocritus save 11.38 and 18.30 are taken from Dover (1971), 260 on Theoc. 24.103f.

18. Further attestations of *ernos*, as used of human or divine 'sprigs' in Pindar, Bacchylides and tragedy, are found in Gow (1952), ii.142 on Theoc. 7.44.

19. = Sapph. fr. 122 (LP).

20. To Headlam's testimonia ad loc. may be added Anaxandrides fr. 9 (*PCG*, ii.242 [K.-A.]).

21. Further epigraphs and bibliography in M. Alexiou (1974), 241 nn. 35-6.

22. Conceivably the popular motif of withering is related to the age-old distinction drawn in I-E and Semitic cultures between wet (= life) and dry (= death); this basic distinction underlies the highly ancient, cross-cultural belief in the evil eye: Chryssanthopoulou-Farrington (1999), 23, citing Dundes.

23. For tragic metaphors of plant growth, burgeoning, harvesting and, as here, withering away as applied to agony, madness, sexual passion, etc. see Padel (1992), 134-8.

24. See medieval and modern Greek comparanda in n. 80 below.

25. Roses were proverbially short-lived in antiquity: Nisbet & Hubbard ii.3.13 (p. 61). Further funerary inscriptions in which a young person is likened to a withered rose or a withered olive branch in Wilhelm (1931), 461; Peek 1801.2 (not in Wilhelm). On the varied associations of the rose motif see Chapter III n. 33.

26. See Chapter II section A.2, *passim*; Seaford (1987), 106-7.

27. Cf. Greg. Naz. *PG* 38.2.80-1 (noted in M. Alexiou [1978], 234 n. 5). In modern Greek *therizô* can be construed *c. acc. rei sive pers.* or absolutely to mean 'to destroy, wreak havoc'. Though Greg. Naz. loc. cit. mentions the scythe as Death's accoutrement, the motif probably entered medieval Greek folk poetry via western representational art: Alexiou (1978). Further literary attestations (not in Alexiou) include the (anonymous) moralising poem *Stichoi eis ton Charonta*, Part II, v.27 (seventeenth century?), in Moravcsik (1931), 61 and *Erotocritos* II.361 (S. Alexiou).

28. FJW iii.31: 'Though the context is unequivocally martial and Ares' martial character is unequivocally stressed by the epithet *brotoloigos* in 665 [TA55] ..., his sexual aspect is thus retrospectively seen to be present also right from the beginning of the ephymnion.'

29. The testimonia are listed in FJW iii.31 663-6 n.; further Pindaric testimonia in van Groningen (1960), 53 on *scolion* 2.1 (= fr. 123.1 [M.]).

30. Pindar regularly uses the terms *karpos* and *drepein* to convey non-sexual consummation: e.g. *O.* 6.57-8; cf. Carey (1981), 54 on *P.* 2.73f.

31. Cf. the scholion on *artidropois*: ... *tais de para tên akmên, phêsi, diakoreuomenais, estai klauthmos.*

32. Testimonia in Chapter II n. 207.

33. In the tragic treatment of the fate of Cassandra, Iole and Andromache, their actual captivity, which in the first two cases issues in their death, is associated indirectly with the *deductio* of the bride: Seaford (1987), 112, 127-30.

34. Dover (1988), 218-20. The popular style of the song as a whole can be established by a brief enumeration of certain features in particular: (i) the refrain *Humên Humenai' ô* throughout (see Chapter II section B.11); (ii) the prominent *makarismos* of the bridegroom (vv. 1336-7; see Chapter II section B.6); (iii) the device of question and answer, with assonance and partial repetition (Chapter II section B.10, 11); (iv) the tone of obscene jocularity created by the *double entendre sukologoutes* (v. 1356) and the preoccupation with male and female genitalia (vv. 1359-60; see Chapter III *passim*). In the light of these indisputably popular features the agricultural euphemism *trugêsomen autên* does not seem improbably crude. Further considerations in Dover ibid.

35. In the inscriptions dealing with untimely death the vocabulary of separation is especially prominent. *harpasdein, aponosphisdein, ekkoptesthai*, etc. are used of both male and female victims of Hades or the Moirae: e.g. Peek 658.7, 683.3, 878, 1997, etc. These verbs denote painful and violent separation and have an emotive force.

36. = *AP* 7.439.1-2, cited by FJW 637-8 n.

37. Also cf. FJW ibid. On the *Nachleben* of this motif also see M. Alexiou in n. 42 below. A poignant Byzantine example of Death as a figurative reaper occurs in the lament delivered by Hysmine's mother over the heroine: '[sc. Death] has harvested (*etherise*) my wheat stalk / and plucked (*etrugêse*) my cluster of grapes' (Eust. Makrem. *HH* X.11.4 [Conca]).

38. Cf. Peek 683; further, Seaford (1987), 107 n. 15.

39. For the rose motif in epitaphs see n. 25 above. The rose here is *en kêpôi notisin droseraisi tethêlos* ('abloom in a garden under dewy moisture'): as Seaford (1987), 111-12 shows, the image of the flower sequestered in a garden is familiar from hymenaeal contexts; also cf. Nonn. *D.* I.1.351 (not in Seaford).

40. Cf. Seaford's discussion of Antigone, Iphigeneia, Glauke and the Danaïds: (1987), 107-10, 112f. *et passim*; Rehm (1994) on the perversions and parallels between wedding and funeral rituals with respect to females in Greek tragedy; also n. 42 below.

41. The exaggerated claim that death occurred shortly after preparations for the wedding were under way or even during the wedding ceremony itself is a funerary *topos*: testimonia in Seaford (1987), 107 nn. 19-21.

42. For the bride of Hades motif in the epitaphs see Seaford (1987), 106 n. 11; 112 n. 64 (testimonia); Lefkowitz (1986), 51, 125-6 (marriage to Death as a male *topos*), 129 (its early Christian reflex). The motif has persisted in medieval and modern Greek popular tradition: M. Alexiou (1974), 120-2; eadem (1978), 227, 233 n. 46.

43. But the notion of marriage to death in the case of a virgin is characteristically Greek: M. Alexiou (1974), 230 n. 64.

44. See Henderson (1975), 65-6 on the symbolic aspect of the harvest terminolgy (*trugân, Trugaios, Opôra*) in this wedding-song; also Olson, 317 ad loc.

45. See Aristaenet. II.1.40 (Mazal, p. 67): *didou tois opôrônais tên hôran trugân.*

46. The metaphor of the *ampelos may* have a scriptural pedigree (Chapter II n. 208) or it may be a rhetorical item. The image of the vine also underlies e.g. Phld. x.3218f. (*Garland* [Gow-Page]), where the point however is not the attractive complexion of the *erômenê* but her sexual immaturity (on the related metaphor of the *omphax*, see Chapter II n. 207).

47. See Gow on Theoc. 2.148; 15.128.

48. In another metaphorical usage *trugân c. acc. pers.* occurs in the eleventh-century parainetic *Strategicon* of Cecaumenos in the sense 'to destroy financially, cheat': ch. 55 (Litavrin). This sense is preserved in modern Greek rural dialect: see Minotou (1934), 169. In the verse romance *Callimachus and Chrysorrhoë* (early fourteenth century) the verb occurs with a non-personal object: *hêdonas* (243, 2103; cf. 927), *kharan* (1761), *khôrismon* (2115), *rhoda* (2083), *ampeli* (2465). See also TF4, discussed below.

49. See the sexually charged harvest imagery in op. cit. (i) VII.4.1 (Conca): 'Why should I not pluck (*trugô*) the grape cluster that has ripened ...? Why should I not harvest (*therizô*) the wheat stalk drooping towards the earth?' (the hero's seduction-pitch to the heroine); (ii) IX.19.3 (Conca): '... I shall thoroughly harvest (*katatrugêsô*) the entire vine branch (*ampelon*)' i.e. 'I shall go all the way sexually speaking [sc. with the other woman].' On the erotic implications of the imagery of the vintage in the sophistic and Comnenian novels see Hunger (1980), 23 n. 96; see also TD1, not in Hunger. Evocative harvest imagery also figures in an *êthopoieia* (with more than a few trappings of an *ecphrasis*) composed by Nikephoros Basilakes, an (older?) contemporary of Makrembolites: see *Prog.* VII, 26, examined in Beaton (1996), 26-7; cf. 80-1, 156, 162-3, 212 for a crucial reassessment of supposed 'western elements' in Makrembolites and Basilakes. Finally, for sexual allusion through harvest imagery in modern Greek folk-song, see J. Petropoulos (1994), ch. 4.

50. The motif of the heroine's seclusion in a walled garden also occurs in *Digenis Akrites*, in other twelfth-century romances as well as Paleologue analogues: Beaton, esp. 161-2 (leaves out of account the motif's likely provenance). Littlewood (1979), 105f. notes that in Song of Songs and in three of the Paleologue romances, *kêpos* is equated with the virgin's body and that the detail of the enclosure reinforces the notion of virginity.

51. So Conca ad loc.; see n. 11 above.

52. Beaton (1996), 119-20 briefly discusses this 'playful exchange'; as I hope to have shown, sexual innuendo is here based on highly conventional (i.e. Greek) harvest imagery and is central to the humour. See TF13 for an earlier example of the motif of culling a rose. Additionally, see the image of Eros as a gardener and farmer who harvests a garden in Marcos Angelos' poem (in anacreontics) addressed to this god (fourteenth century): Nissen (1940), 80, vv. 136-40. Eros' connection with flowers and gardens in general is traditional: see n. 14 above and Hunter (1983), 31-6 (in Longus he is also a *poimên*: ibid., 36); at anon. *AP* 9.666, as also at Marianus Scholasticus, loc. cit. 668 and 669, a garden and a park are called Eros; more to the point, in Basilakes' *Prog.* VII, 26 (see n. 49) a group of *Erôtes* pluck apples in a garden; finally, see Littlewood (1979), 98 n. 17.

53. Cod. Neap. (Hesseling). *Callimachos and Chrysorrhoë* and especially the *Achilleïs* (fourteenth century) are distinguished from the other romances by a noticeable connection with simple folk-song; see Beck (1971), 131-2; Megas (1956), 147-72 (on the high incidence of folk-song and fairy-tale motifs in *Callimachos*); Diller (1977), 25-40; Beaton (1996), 248 n. 42. It may be the case that the co-occurrence of harvest imagery in the two romances is due to a common popular source rather than formulaic coincidence: it is highly suggestive that in the *Achilleïs* the imagery occurs twice in songs in popular style (*katalogia*) which are quoted.

54. Featured in both literary and sub-literary sources, the garden – especially branches, fruit, etc. – may symbolise female pubic hair in particular. The equation of the garden with the *pudendum muliebre* was accepted by Freud for psychoanalytical purposes: Littlewood (1979), 106 n. 48; see also Artem., p. 250.20-2 (Pack). What is striking in Greek tradition is the notion of *trugân* and the harvester figure as used of sexual intimacy.

55. Cf. TA58.

56. On the double sense of 'kissing' see P VII.405, 661 (Preisendanz-Henrichs), where *phileô* and *kataphileô* are used of 'petting'; Asclep. xxv.930-1 (*HE*) (= *AP* 5.181.11-12); *Dig. Akr.* Esc., 480-1 (E. Jeffreys) (possibly of intercourse); cf. French 'baiser'. See also Shipp's linguistic note, pp. 126-7.

57. E.g. Lelekos (1888), 90-1; Regas (1958), 15; *Thrakika* 11 (1939), 120.

58. Cf. *Dig. Akr.* Esc. 540, 859, 865, 1580, 1582 (E. Jeffreys); *Erotocritos* II.48 (S. Alexiou); Chortatsis, *Erôphili* (S. Alexiou-Aposkiti).

59. I.e. assuming that the words belong to the Vlachs examining the maiden: her painted lips, suggesting the precocious and provocative use of lipstick, and her dishevelled hair prompt this question. (In the popular mind a woman may keep her hair dishevelled as a sign that she is available: see Ioannou [1966], no. 18.3-4.) On the various meanings of 'Vlach', see Campbell (1964), 1-6.

60. Chapter II section C.2b.

61. Further on the ancient motif in Burnett (1983), 267 n. 102 (who seems to be unaware of Littlewood [1967]), to which add Brazda (1977), 35f.

62. Littlewood (1974), 49 calls the early modern use of the apple as a term of endearment 'a new facet in the erotic symbolism of the fruit'. Yet, on the whole, as Littlewood op. cit., 59 admits, the early demotic poems featuring the apple motif 'show certain affinities not shared by literature in the high language with ... late classical literature' and that 'the nature of the popular evidence suggests an unbroken tradition [sc. of apple imagery] from antiquity to late Byzantium and beyond'. Further, see Littlewood (1993), 83-103.

63. Cf. the metaphorical uses of this expression at Pi. *I.* 7.18 (S.-M.); Call. *Ap.* 112, etc. The poetic word *aôtos/aôton* (= 'the choicest, the finest') had no real connection with flowers and was obsolete by Pindar's time and probably earlier: Silk (1974), 239-40. (*Akron aôton*, fig., persists in modern Greek.)

64. *Lôtisdesthai* = 'cull the best', hence 'choose' presupposes an exquisite flower or fruit: see FJW iii.262f. for examples. For nuptial similes see Chapter II section B.2.

65. See Chapter III, especially section 2.

66. Although the expression *poimenes andres* has Homeric parallels and also occurs at Alcm. fr. 56.4 (Davies) (cf. Calame's testimonia ad loc.), it is not fanciful to argue that this nearly stereotyped phrase acquired a particular emotive impact in Sappho, given its hypothetical context.

67. Sappho's disdain for boorishness in men and (rival?) women is documented in Chapter III n. 19.

68. For mythic *exempla* see Chapter II section B.5.

69. Cf. the particular fear entertained by the chorus at TA54, discussed above, p. 65.

70. Gow-Page, in *HE* 3952 n. (p. 601), following *Geop.* 10.20.1, describe the *glukumalon* as an apple grafted on a quince.

71. *SEG* XVIII 594, cited in section 1a above.

72. See the 'stemma' and discussion in Chapter II section A.

73. Photius, *Bibliotheca*, III.134b.27f. (Henry, p. 20), not noted by Littlewood.

74. Littlewood (1972), 70.

75. Ibid.

76. Littlewood (1974), 59 also raises this possibility.

77. M. Alexiou (1974), 196. The comparison in question is 'the apple is withering' (*marainetai to mêlon*) and it occurs in a lament, which is directly quoted, over the virginal heroine. (Conca notes ad loc. that *mêlon* may also refer to Rhodanthê's bosom; but such ambiguity would ill suit a lament.)

78. Proverbs 25.11 *could* be a source. For the connection of golden apples with love and marriage see Littlewood (1967), 158 n. 24, 163f., 179f.

79. I.e. the putative date of the Escorial *Digenis*. See vv. 181-2 (cited by M. Alexiou [1974]) and vv. 183, 185, 187, 192.

80. Politis (1932), nos. 83.12 (of grief); 209.5 (of the dead) (both cited in Alexiou [1974], 241 n. 39). Additionally, see Bouvier (1960), 12 no. 6.6: *sa marameno mêlo*, referring to the sadness of a young boy who faces execution. *maramenê* is a formulaic adjective in *Erotocritos* and later folk-song meaning 'love-sick, frustrated by love': *Erotocritos* I.1318, 1324, 1743, 1757, 1868; II.207f. (S. Alexiou). This usage may be compared with Daphnis' love-complaint at *Daphnis and Chloe* I.18.25f. (Reeve, p. 10), cited in section 1b above.

81. See Pernot (1931), 34, no. 16.210 (fifteenth/sixteenth century). For a more recent example see Politis (1932), no. 135.5 (cited in M. Alexiou [1974], 241 n. 38).

82. The identification of a woman with an apple tree can be traced to the Byzantine *Achmetis Oneirocritikon* 109.12, 154.21f. (Drexl), which incorporated material from Artemidorus, as well as Christian and Arabic dream-lore. (On Achmet see also Chapter II n. 213.)

83. v. 1586 Neap. Cod. (Hesseling).

84. Chapter II section B.3a.

85. See Arist. *Rh.* 3.1404bf. ('we all use metaphors in our ordinary discourse'), 1406b ('the simile is also metaphor'); Demetr. *Eloc.* 80 ('if a metaphor becomes risky, turn it into a simile'). Arist. *Po.* 1459a.10f. (metaphors are appropriate to tragic dialogue, since it closely reproduces ordinary language).

86. The song is technically a *makarismos* and *salutatio*, q.v. in Chapter II sections B.6, 7, C.5 respectively. 'Golden' apple is an auspicious reference typical of modern Greek wedding-songs: Chapter II section C.3.

V. The Wings of Desire: Popular Amatory Wishes

1. Typically, the rhythm of both is Aeolic.

2. Bowra (1961), 30.

3. Designated as nos. 17 and 18 respectively.

4. Bowra (1961), 380.

5. This dating is suggested by Pickard-Cambridge (1968), 74-9.

6. I.e. during the Proagon: ibid., 61.

7. Bowra (1961), 380-1.

8. E. Bowie (1986), 16f.

9. On the symposium in general see Murray (1982), 47-52; id. (1990) and most recently Davidson (1997). For a bibliography of sympotic song see E. Bowie (1986), 13 n. 1.

10. The love-toast, as other toasts, governs the genetive of the person honoured: cf. Call. *epigr.* 29.1f.; Theoc. 14.19; discussion in Nock (1986 [1972]), 241-2.

11. See West (1969), 132, cited by Dover (1971), 113 on Theoc. 3.12f.; also West (1997), 534. See Fowler (1994), 39f. for translations of seven banquet (?) songs from the 19th or 20th Dynasty ('Cairo love songs'). In one such song (no. 21c) a boy of about fourteen wishes: 'Would that I were | her delicate signet ring ...' As West also notes, this ditty resembles TA60. Comparable love wishes occur in more recent song traditions as well.

12. Testimonia listed in Barrett (1964), 299 on E. *Hipp.* 732-4; see also the escapist wish implied at Psalm 55.6-7 and explicitly stated in Alcm. fr. 26 (Davies) and TB13a (none of these cited in Barrett).

13. Discussed by Calame (1977), ii.89f. If correct, my supposition that these lines are set as a colloquial love wish tells against West's suggestion (West [1965], 199f.) that the verses represent in effect a love spell to be carried out by Aenesimbrota in v. 73. See Alcm. 3.77-9 (Davies), probably a love wish, and ibid., 79-81, possibly a wish-condition (cf. Denniston [1954], 89f.) with strong erotic implications (on which see Calame [1983], 416-18, and Thomson in n. 17 below).

14. Cited by Calame (1983), 338 in his note on Alcm. 3.74.

15. Noticed by Lasserre and cited by Calame (1983).

16. J. Kakrides (1983), 3 interprets this fragment in the light of the tradition that Archilochus was actually engaged to Neoboulê and that his future father-in-law, Lycambes, broke off the engagement.

17. *Thinganein* is the *vox propria* for a man's sexual advance: cf. Thomson (1966), 130 on A. *Cho.* 71-4. Sapph. fr. 16.17-19 (LP) expresses a clear preference (here *bouloimên an = velim*) which amounts to an amatory wish. Aristaenet. I.10.58f. (Mazal, pp. 23-4) features a series of amatory wishes spoken by Acontius.

18. Printed in van Groningen (1960), 125.

19. An alternative and, in my view, less plausible interpretation is that of van Groningen, who notes that *erôti* refers to the eros of *another*. (Presumably one will be active and passive in relation to *different* persons at any given point in his youth: see Dover [1978], 103 *et passim*, and 43f. on the terms *erân* and *kharisdesthai*.)

20. See van Groningen (1960), 127.

21. See Rosenmeyer (1992), 161-6 for an excellent analysis of TC17 in relation to this ancient genre.

22. On which see Gow (1952), ii.64; Dover (1971), 113.

23. See also Rosenmeyer (1992), 161.

24. See n. 9 above.

25. *Par'augas* may simply mean 'out of doors', as Page notes ad loc. On the erotic connotations of the wind see Sappho fr. 47 (LP); Ibyc. fr. 286.9f. (Davies); Horace *Odes* II.9.6. See also n. 51 below.

26. Hdt. 7.189; Pl. *Phdr.* 2.29bc.

27. On Eros as a blustery, blazing northerly, see Ibyc. fr. 286.9f. (Davies).

28. Padel (1992), esp. 52, 55-6, 115-16 on winds.

29. See Devereux (1967), 69-92.

30. The chorus pray to be transported to the site of Pelops' victory; see Pearson ii.130 ad loc.

31. On 'star' used of a handsome child or young person see Chapter II section C.2c.

32. *Aramenê* = in effect 'pluck': see Page ad v. 1087.

33. See the editors' note (p. 652) on v. 4432.

34. A Freudian might say that both speakers have immaturely replaced adaptive thought and behaviour by neurotic daydreaming or phantasy. This applies to a great many of the erotic wishes examined in this chapter.

35. Frontisi-Ducroux & Vernant (1997).

36. Cf. the ancient Egyptian song (21D) in Fowler (1994), 42: 'Would that I had | a morning of looking, | like the bronze that spends | a lifetime with her! | ... Joyous the mirror receiving her gaze!'

37. Cf. the Egyptian song in Fowler, 40: 'Would that I were, | if only for a month, | the launderer of | my sister's linen cloth!'

38. *Phorô* covers both eventualities, as Rosenmeyer (1992), 164 notes.

39. See Lefkowitz (1986), 66-8, 71; Winkler (1990), 97.

40. Rosenmeyer (1992), 165 cites other ancient examples of the poetic (?)

conceit of being trampled by a beloved's sandal; she also detects undertones of 'masochism' in this particular wish. (In a small number of vase paintings and sculptures women wield a sandal as a weapon *and* possibly as a sexual stimulus, but do not tread on their partners: Kilmer [1993], 121-4.)

41. On contrary-to-fact wishes see Goodwin, par. 731.

42. For a complete bibliography of this and other Comnenian romances consult Hägg (1983), 240-1 and now Beaton (1996), 70-88, 210-14.

43. Thus Beck (1984), 122f. ad op. cit. III.135f. Hunger (1980), esp. 11f., 27f., 32 shows how contemporary social ideals and reality are superimposed on the structure of ancient motifs in the romances; such *subsidiärer Realismus* entails a mixed bag including humour and linguistic register. Hägg (1983), 75, apparently following Hunger, diagnoses 'successfully camouflaged anachronisms' in the novels, i.e. realistic elements which are hardly anachronistic at all. See also Chapter III n. 35.

44. The refrain is extraordinarily reminiscent of Theoc. 2.69 *et passim*. See also n. 69 below.

45. A number of scholars, including Conca (1994), 343 n. 19 (cf. id. [1990], 70) and Rosenmeyer (1992), 230, have also noted these correspondences.

46. So also Rosenmeyer (1992), 229.

47. Cf. the refrain in TC19.

48. A conventional and highly symbolic trysting-point: see Littlewood (1979), 95-114; Schisssel (1942), 30-62; further, Chapter IV *passim*.

49. Also noted by Conca (1994), 196 ad loc.

50. See *LSJ*, s.v. *stêthos*.

51. It will be remembered that Zephyros, the spring wind, impregnated the harpy Podargê when she grazed in the guise of a filly near the banks of Oceanos (*Il.* 16.149f.). According to a well-known account, Eros was the result of Zephyros' liaison with Iris (Alc. fr. 327 [LP]; cf. Nonn. *D.* 31.106, 110f.; 39.115f. *et passim*; other testimonia in Voigt, pp. 306f. and in Thomson's note ad *Ag.* 681-98 [p. 60]); see also Mair (1928), 35 n. (d). It comes then as no surprise that this particular wind is invoked in Dioscorides' homoerotic epigram xi.1515f. (*HE*) and that at Rufin. xii.5-6 (Page [1978]) Zephyros is said to 'cut through' Rhodope's *pudendum*. The wind is also closely associated with Aphrodite: *h. Aphr.* 2.3; Call. *Aet.* iv. fr. 110.53f. (Pf.); cf. Burnett (1983), 130 n. 25 for archaeological evidence of this association.

52. Cf. Hes. *WD* 594 (W) and West ad loc. for testimonia.

53. Browning (1983)[a], 30, 35; Blass-Debrunner-Rehkopf, par. 384-5.

54. Blass-Debrunner-Rehkopf, par. 384 with n. 1.

55. Jannaris, par. 1920; cf. ibid., App. v. 19.

56. See also Mackridge (1985), 9.4.2.1.2. (p. 284).

57. Jannaris, par. 1906; Thumb, par. 133; also n. 62 below.

58. N.G. Wilson, *per litteras*; for further particulars consult Beck (1971), 183-4.

59. *Dia na* is found as early as the twelfth century in the 'Ptocho-Prodromic' poems (III.284, 310; IV.191 [H.-P.]), where it is an alternative form. *Hopôs na* is also attested in the Cypriot *Assizes* 221 (thirteenth century), while *gia na* occurs in Chortatsis' *Panoria* II.278 (Kriaras) (*c.* 1590-1600); cf. *ogia na* in the roughly contemporary *Erotocritos*, e.g. I.403; II.282, 1395, etc. (S. Alexiou).

60. Papachristodoulou (1966), 32. The imagery in TG54 is strange, because one does not easily visualise a pigeon embracing a human being.

61. S. Alexiou op. cit., 99.

62. Wishes cast as *êthela* + past indicative will be examined more closely in section 2 below. In modern Greek the construction *êthela* + subjunctive has a modal force: Thumb in n. 57 above. The second wish in TG58 governs the volitive uses *na skiveis, na me pineis.*

63. The seasonal context is discussed in detail in J. Petropoulos (1994), esp. 31-45.

64. Cf. also the song from Roumeli cited in Chapter I and discussion in Chapter IV *passim*.

65. To compare a woman's beauty or more particularly her breasts to cold water (see TG41 in Chapter III) is standard in Greece, though probably unappealing to English sensibility; cf. the traditional encomiastic images at A. *Ag.* 901 *hodoiporôi dipsônti pêgaion rheos* and *AP* 5.168 *hêdu therous dipsônti khiôn poton* (M. Alexiou [1974], 242 n. 52); also anon. x (Page [1981], 320) above. In the twelfth-century (?) *Digenis Akrites* Esc. 585 (E. Jeffreys), a kiss is immediately refreshing to the lips: 'and their lips [i.e. as they were kissing] became cool and wet from sweet desire'. Furthermore, in a love-song dating to the mid-seventeenth century at the latest, the motif of giving cold water to a bird, viz. a (wayward) female beloved, probably signifies a kiss: 'Bird, come, alight on a branch and come into my garden, / so that I may give you cold water, so that I may feed you musk' (Bouvier [1960], 13, no. 10, vv. 5-6; cf. ibid., 48-9 ad loc.).

66. J. Kakrides (1983), 228-34. Kakrides does not cite TA63 or TB18.

67. Cf. West (1969), 132: '... the rare papyrus gives us a glimpse of the kind of thing you might hear in a Greek tavern in Egypt in about the time of Horace.'

68. Hopkinson (1988), 271. Traces of three previous strophes beginning with A, B and Γ suggest that the *scolion* was a series of twenty-four strophes: Powell (1925), 199.

69. Hopkinson ad v. 5. (On the refrain in certain types of poetry see Chapter II section B.11)

70. Cf. Alc. fr. 38 A (LP); Thgn. 973f., 1009f. (*IE*, i [W]); Simon. fr. 20.5-15 (*IE*, ii [W]); Pherecydes Lerius *F Gr Hist* 3 F 119 (Jacoby i.92) (indirect testimonium); Alexis fr. 25.4f. (*PCG*, ii.38 [K.-A.]); Amphis frr. 8, 21 (*PCG*, ii.216, 222 [K.-A.]); Asclep. ii.816f. (*HE*), xvi.886f. (*HE*); Horace *Odes* I.4.18, ibid. 11.8 (with the editors' notes); fr. *adesp.* 1009 (*PMG*) and the Seikilos inscription (*IGSK* XXXVI.1 219, first century AD?), discussed by Baud-Bovy (1979-85), 549-59. For an *index locorum* of this *topos* (with special reference to Greek inscriptions) see Ameling (1985), 35-43.

71. Hopkinson (1988), 271.

72. Ibid. ad vv. 21-2.

73. Ibid. ad vv. 4, 6, 8, 24, 26, 29.

74. See discussion of *êthelon ekhein* immediately below.

75. Kakrides compares fr. *adesp.* 372 (*TrGF*, ii.114 [Kannicht-Snell]) with vv. 31-4.

76. Kakrides op. cit., 231.

77. Note the assonance of *autorhu[to]us* (v. 11) and *galaktorhutous* (v. 12). The combination of milk and honey, which are consumed separately, *possibly* connotes luxury or wealth: cf. Gow (1952), ii.487 on Theoc. 27.9.

78. For a similar image, cf. the river of wine which flowed through Lucian's fantasy-island (*VH* 7).

79. Spontaneously generated abundance is a motif common to imaginary, idealised ages and landscapes: cf. e.g. Hes. *WD* 117-18 (W).

80. Cf. Hopkinson ad v. 13.

81. 'Bisexuality' was prevalent especially among the leisured class and acceptable so long as one was the active partner vis-à-vis his *paidika*; cf. Dover (1978), 64f., 136f., 149f. As Call. fr. 227.7 (Pf.) shows, the prospect of kissing girls and boys alike after winning at *kottabos* was greatly cherished.

82. Blass-Debrunner-Rehkopf, par. 359.2: 'Wird der Begriff des Wünschens (erfüllbar oder unerfüllbar) durch ein eigenes Verbum ausgedrückt, so steht im NT unterschiedslos *eboulomên* (ohne *an*) [so schon att. Redner ...] oder volkstümlicher *êthelon* [vielleicht in Analogie nach *ôphelon* ...] mit Inf.' Cf. already the classical (colloquial) expression *eboulomên* + inf. at Ar. *Ran.* 866 (= 'I could have wished') and *êthelon* (with inf. implied) at S. *Aj.* 1400: ibid., n. 5.

83. Cf. Mackridge (1985), 9.4.2 on the infinitival function of certain types of *na*-clause in medieval Greek. It is possible to postulate the intermediate stage *êtholon* + *hina* + past indicative.

84. See Chapter IV.

85. The affective force of the dimunitive *glukoutsika* is transferred to the beloved's lips.

86. Cf. Littlewood (forthcoming).

87. On the anonymous *Krasopateras*, see now Eideneier (1988). Cf. the verbal echoes of the medieval poem in two modern drinking-songs printed in *Laogr.* 2 (1910), 184-5, 463-4. Also cf. Eideneier (1983), 126f., 129f.

88. See discussion above.

89. Cf. e.g. St John of the Ladder (sixth/seventh century) *scala paradisi* (*peri gastrimargias*) *PG* 88.864C: *koros brômatôn, porneias patêr*.

90. Personal communication from Dr Maria Diallina of Athens.

91. It may be advisable to recall Dio's comments, quoted above, that songs such as TA59 and TA60 were appropriate to local festivals. On Theocritus' selective realism at the linguistic level see Zanker (1987), esp. 164f. As well, Hellenistic epigrams give an unprecedented emphasis to homely detail: ibid., 161-4.

92. Cf. Version AO, vv. 21-33 (Eideneier), dating from the sixteenth century.

93. Cf. TG66, which effectively is a Type A class 2 wish, and TC17.7-8 and TF19.334-5.

Appendix I

1. So also, coincidentally, do Buxton and Sissa: see Perentidis (1997), 201.

2. He notes that the bride's father also offered *proteleia*.

3. I.e. whose parents were both alive.

4. The chariot pictured in wedding scenes on vases probably was rarely used in real life; in these scenes it was meant to lend an aura of heroic grandeur to the mortal couple: Oakley & Sinos, 30.

5. Following Gernet and Buxton, Perentidis, 191 notes that the invisibility conferred by the veil implied the bride's transient and liminal state. She was a *persona sacra*, moving from one place of residence to another. Cf. ibid. 201.

6. I.e. at least in Ionian society.

7. This rite was performed under the auspices of *Zeus teleios* and *Hera teleia*: ibid., 196-7.

8. See Chapter IV.

9. Perentidis (1995), 345-6.

Appendix IV

1. The ed. notes that he recorded only half of the song.

2. On dawn as an evocative 'signpost' in an agricultural society, cf. Hes. *WD* 581f., discussed in J. Petropoulos (1994), 71, 74-5; on its connection with popular love-songs, see. Appendix V.

Appendix V

1. So Fraenkel (1960 [1922]), 331f., n. 2. Meineke's conjecture *pornôidiôn* in *Ran.* loc. cit. is generally accepted: see Fraenkel ibid. and Dover (1993), 350 ad loc.

2. So West (1982), 148-9; cf. Trenkner and Stephanis below.

3. Songs similar to the Locrian song quoted immediately below were common to the eastern Mediterranean in antiquity: see a thirteenth-century Egyptian song and the Hebrew Song of Songs: Hatto (1965), 105-6, 203-9. For a list of ancient *mimoi*, male and female, many of them active in the Near East, see Stephanis (1988), 592 (table V.24).

4. A woman addresses her illicit lover also in e.g. Meleager lxix (*HE*) (= *AP* 5.8); Phld. vii (*Garland* [Gow-Page]) (= *AP* 5.120). Also cf. n. 10 below.

5. The verb *hiketeuô* sounds pretty colloquial in Ar. *Ran.* 11 and 745 (Dover [1993], 285 on op. cit. 745), and it is common in Menander.

6. Cf. also the admixture of dialects in *carm. conviv.* 904 (*PMG*), discussed in Appendix VII below.

7. West op. cit., 149.

8. Ibid., n. 25.

9. v. 3 = 2 *tr*; v. 4 = 2 *cr* or 2 *ia* (alternatively, 1 *cr* + 1 *mol*); v. 5 = 1 *lk*; v. 6 = 2 *ia*.

10. Sapph. frr. 135 (LP) and 197 (LP), with Page (1955), 145; other testimonia in Fordyce (1961), 258 ad Catullus 62.35; also Meleager xxvii.4136f. (*HE*) (= *AP* 5.172), with note. For a full (if somewhat diffuse) treatment of the 'erotic dawn song' in ancient Greek and early Byzantine literature, see Hatto (above), 28, 255-63; for the song's diachronic attestation in a multitude of other traditions, I-E and non-I-E alike, see ibid. *passim*.

11. The man is regretting the dawn, and the woman's *fear* of her husband's return is surely compatible with regret on her part. For modern Greek examples see Hatto, 264-70 and TG4-5 (discussed in Chapter III) and Appendix IV above.

12. For dialogue (and antiphony) in ancient song see Chapter II section B.10.

13. Full particulars in Peters and Thiersch (1905), 56f. (cited by Powell).

14. For both suppositions see ibid. Hordern (1999), 82, following Thiersch and citing Martial. 1.34.8, etc., notes that a tomb would be an apt trysting-spot, esp. for a prostitute.

15. The end of line 6 is probably corrupt; hiatus is avoided if we emend the line to e.g. *Prâss' hotti*.

16. *Synecphonesis* is not necessary in the first metron, as *dia* is easily analysable as ∪ ∪, yielding an acceptable cretic.

17. Noted by Powell.

18. *eurukhôriên* is an Ionicism.

19. Wilamowitz (1921), 345 found the distich alien to the context and suggested that it belonged either to an earlier part of the song or to a different song. Hordern (above), 81-2 does not question the distribution of speakers nor raise the possibility of interpolation in the song.

20. See LSJ 2, s.v. *krouô*.

21. *psophos* is properly the noise of one thing striking against another, esp. a hard surface: see Arist. *de An.* 420a21; Ar. *Ran.* 604b, of knocking at a door.

Appendix VI

1. Ar. *Eccl.* 938-41 is an exquisite parody of the *scolion*.

2. Campbell (1982 [1967]), 450 ad loc.

3. Ibid.

4. Padel (1992), 32 n. 77, citing Handley on the Aristophanic usage.

5. On *nous* see immediately below; on the concrete use of *phrên* / *phrenes* in ancient Greek poetry, particularly tragedy, see Padel (above), esp. 20-4.

6. As at e.g. *Il.* 13.732 (cf. *en stêthessi*), this song locates the *nous* within the chest. On *splankhna* as organs of consciousness see Padel, esp. 13-18; on *nous* as *splankhna*: ibid., 32-3.

7. Noted by Sullivan (1988), 32.

8. Cited by Eustathius *Od.* 1574.16, where he preserves and comments on this *scolion*.

9. *Loci similes* from the *Od.* in Sullivan (above), 32 n. 28; Thgn., too, explicitly links *phrenes* with deceptive behaviour: Sullivan, 32 n. 29.

10. Noted in Barrett (1964), 340 ad loc.

11. See Page (1952), 110-11 ad E. *Med.* 516f.; further on this *topos* in trag.: Padel, 14 with n. 8. For a similar sentiment cf. E. *IA* 345-8 (Günther) (not found in Page, Padel or Barrett).

12. Padel, 14. The final act of closing up the other person's chest (cf. *kleisanta*) is bizarre and suggests that the song as a whole is meant as a joke; cf. ibid., 32: 'This [the *scolion*] is a joke ...'

13. So Eustathius (n. 8 above). Similarly *CFA* no. 211 (Hausrath & Hunger i.2.32) underlies *carm. conviv.* 892 (*PMG*), as Bowra (1961), 421 notes.

14. Padel, 16-17.

Appendix VII

1. Discussed above in Appendix V.

2. Note also the neat parallelism, with repeition: A ~ B yet C (v. 1) A' ~ B' yet C' (v. 2).

3. In connection with this epigram it may be noted that Alcm. fr. 1, esp. 70-3 (Davies) also features a catalogue of female intimates and their charming aspects.

4. I.e. assuming that the modern singer's revulsion is capricious.

Appendix VIII

1. Cited in Burnett, 148.

2. Bowra, 382.

3. A favourite parlour game in rural Greece and in other cultures; discussion of the modern Greek genre with bibliography in Loukatos (1978), 116-21.

Appendix IX

1. So also Dover (1993), 271-2.

Bibliography

A. *Ag.* (Fraenkel) = *Aeschylus: Agamemnon*, Fraenkel, E. (ed.), i-iii (Oxford, 1950).

A. *Supp.* (FJW) = *Aeschylus: The Suppliants*, Friis, J.H. & Whittle, E.W. (eds), i-iii (Denmark, 1980).

A. *Th.* (Hutchinson) = *Aeschylus: Septem contra Thebas ...*, Hutchinson, G.O. (ed.) (Oxford, 1985).

Abbott, G.F. (1903), *Macedonian folklore* (Cambridge).

Abbott, T.K. (1897), *A critical and exegetical commentary on the Epistles to the Ephesians and to the Colossians* (Edinburgh).

Achilleïs (Hesseling) = *L'Achilléïde Byzantine*, avec une introduction, des observations et un index, Hesseling, D.C. (ed.) (Amsterdam, 1919).

Ach. Tat. (Garnaud) = *Achille Tatius d'Alexandrie: le roman de Leucippé et Clitophon*, Garnaud, J.-P. (ed. & tr.) (Paris, 1991).

Achmetis Oneirocriticon (Drexl) = *Achmetis Oneirocriticon*, Drexl, F. (ed.) (Bibliotheca ... Teubneriana, 1925).

ActaSS = *Acta Sanctorum*, 71 vols (Paris, 1863-1940).

Adams, J.N. (1982), *The Latin sexual vocabulary* (Baltimore & London).

Aesop. (P) = *Aesopica ...*, Perry, B.E. (ed.) (Urbana, 1952).

AIS, iv (Papadopoulos-Kerameus) = *Analekta ierosolymitikis stachyologias ...*, Papadopoulos-Kerameus, A. (ed.), iv (St Petersburg, 1897).

Alc. (LP) = *Poetarum Lesbiorum fragmenta*, Lobel, E. & Page, D. (eds) (Oxford, 1955).

Alc. (V) = *Sappho et Alcaeus: fragmenta*, Voigt, E.-M. (ed.) (Amsterdam, 1971) [to be used in conjunction with Alc. (LP) above].

Alcm. (Calame) = *Alcman: fragmenta ...*, Calame, C. (ed.) (Lyricorum Graecorum quae exstant, vi, 1983).

Alcm. (Davies) *see* Davies (1991)[b].

Alexakis, E.P. (1984), *I exagora tis niphis* (Athens).

—— (1990), *I simaia sto gamo: teletourgia, exaplôsi, proelefsi* (Athens).

Alexiou, M.K. (1974), *The ritual lament in Greek tradition* (Cambridge).

—— (1975), 'The lament of the Virgin in Byzantine literature and modern Greek folk-song', *BMGS* 1: 116-21.

—— (1978), 'Modern Greek folklore and its relation to the past: the evolution of Charos in Greek tradition', in Vryonis (1978) 221-36.

—— (1986), 'The poverty of écriture and the craft of writing: towards a reappraisal of the Prodromic poems', *BMGS* 10: 1-40.

—— (1999), 'Ploys of the performance: games and play in the Ptochoprodromic poems', *DOP* 53: 91-109.

Alexiou, S. (1975) *see Voscopoula* (S. Alexiou).

—— (1990) see *Dig. Akr.* (S. Alexiou).

—— (1992) (ed.), *Erotocritos* (3rd rev. rp., Athens).

Ameling, W. (1985), 'PHAGÔMEN KAI PIÔMEN: Griechische Parallelen zu zwei Stellen aus dem Neuen Testament', *ZPE* 60: 35-43.

Anacreont. (West) = *Carmina Anacreontea*², West, M.L. (ed.), corr. edn (Bibliotheca ... Teubneriana, 1993).

Antzoulatou-Retsila, E. (1980), *Ta stephana tou gamou sti neôteri Ellada* (Athens).

Ar. *Av.* (Dunbar) = *Aristophanes: Birds*, edited with introduction & commentary, Dunbar, N. (ed.) (Oxford, 1995).

Ar. *Av.* (Ph. Kakrides) = *Aristophanous Ornithes, ermineftiki ekdosi*, ed. Kakrides, Ph.I. (Athens, 1974).

Ar. *Av.* (Sommerstein) = *Birds*, Sommerstein, A.H. (ed.) (Warminster, 1987).

Ar. *Eccl.* (Sommerstein) = *Aristophanes Ecclesiazusae*, Sommerstein, A.H. (ed., tr. & comm.) (Warminster, 1998).

Ar. *Eccl.* (Ussher) = *Aristophanes: Ecclesiazusae*, Ussher, R.G. (ed.) (Oxford, 1973).

Ar. *Nub.* (Dover) = *Aristophanes: Clouds*, Dover, K.J. (ed.) (Oxford, 1968).

Ar. *Pax* (Olson) = *Aristophanes:Peace*, edited with introduction & commentary, Olson, S.D. (ed.) (Oxford, 1998).

Ar. *Pax* (Sommerstein) = *Peace*, Sommerstein, A.H. (ed.) (Warminster, 1985).

Ar. *Ran.* (Dover) = *Aristophanes: Frogs*, edited with introduction & commentary, Dover, K.J. (ed.) (Oxford, 1993, rp. 1994).

Ar. *Ran.* (Stanford) = *Aristophanes: Frogs*², Stanford, W.B. (ed.) (London, 1963).

Ar. *Vesp.* (Sommerstein) = *Aristophanes: Wasps*, edited with translation & notes, Sommerstein, A.H. (ed.) (Warminster, 1983).

Aravantinos, P. (1880) (ed.), *Sillogi dimôdôn asmatôn* (Athens).

Archer, W.G. (1974), *The hill of flutes: life, love and poetry in tribal India* (Pittsburgh).

Aristaenet. (Mazal) = *Aristaeneti epistularum libri ii*, Mazal, O. (ed.) (Bibliotheca ... Teubneriana, 1971).

Artem. (Pack) = *Artemidori Daldiani Onirocriticon libri v*, Pack, R.A. (ed.) (Bibliotheca ... Teubneriana, 1963).

Averincev, S. (1979), 'L'or dans le système des symboles de la culture protobyzantine', *StMed*³ 20: 47-67.

Bakker, W.F. (1978), *The sacrifice of Abraham: the Cretan biblical drama I thysia tou Avraam and western European and Greek tradition* (Centre for Byzantine Studies, Univ. of Birmingham).

────── & van Gemert, A.F. (1996) (eds), V*itzentzou Kornarou: I Thysia tou Avraam* (Herakleion).

Baldwin, B. (1984), 'Dioscuros of Aphrodito: The worst poet of antiquity?', in *Atti del XVII Congresso internazionale di papirologia*, ii (Naples).

Bancroft-Marcus, R. (forthcoming) (ed.), *The plays of Georgios Chortatsis: introduction, text, translation* (Oxford).

Barrett (1964) *see* E. *Hipp.* (Barrett).

Baud-Bovy, S. (1935-8), i-ii = *Chansons du Dodécanèse*, Baud-Bovy, S. (ed.) (Archives musicales de folklore, I, Athens).

────── (1936), *La chanson populaire grecque du Dodécanèse: les textes*, i (Paris).

────── (1979-85), 'Archaia kai nea Ellada', *Epist. Epet. Philos. Sch. Pan. Ath.* 28: 549-59.

────── (1983), 'Chansons populaires de la Grèce antique', *Rev. de la Musicologie* 69: 5-20.

────── (1988), 'La canzone popolare della Grecia moderna e la musica antica', in B. Gentili & R. Pretagostini (eds), *La musica in Grecia* (Storia e società) 218-27.

Bausinger, H. (1961), *Volkskultur in der technischen Welt* (Stuttgart).

────── & Brückner, W. (1969) (eds), *Kontinuität? Geschichtlichkeit und Dauer als volkskundliches Problem* (Berlin).

Beaton, R. (1980)ᵃ, *Folk poetry of modern Greece* (Cambridge).

────── (1980)ᵇ, 'Modes and roads: factors of change and continuity in Greek musical tradition', *ABSA* 75: 1-11.

―――― (1986), 'Byzantine historiography and modern Greek oral poetry: the case of Rapsomatis', *BMGS* 10: 41-50.

―――― (1988) (ed.), *The Greek novel AD 1-1986* (Kent).

―――― (1996), *The Medieval Greek romance*[2], rev. and exp. edn (London & N.Y.).

―――― & Ricks, D. (1993) (eds), *New approaches to Byzantine heroic poetry* (Centre for Hellenic Studies, King's College London, 2).

Beck, H.-G. (1959), *Kirche und theologische Literatur im Byzantinischen Reich* (*HAW*, xii.2.1).

―――― (1971), *Geschichte der Byzantinischen Volksliteratur* (*HAW*, xii.2.3).

―――― (1984), *Byzantinisches Erotikon: Orthodoxie – Literatur – Gesellschaft* (*SBAW*, v).

Beckh (1895) *see Geoponica* (Beckh).

Belon du Maus, P. (1555), *Les observations du plusieurs singularitez ...* (Anvers).

Belthandros & Chrysantza (Kriaras) *see* Kriaras (1955).

Bergk iii = *Poetae lyrici Graeci*[4], Bergk, T. (ed.), iii (Bibliotheca ... Teubneriana, 1882; rp. 1914).

Bidez-Cumont *see* Jul. *Or.*

Biehl (1970) *see* E. *Tr.* (Biehl).

Bieler, L. (1935-6), *THEIOS ANÊR: das Bild des 'göttlichen Menschen' in Spätantike und Frühchristentum*, i-ii (Vienna; rp. in 1 vol., Darmstadt, 1967).

Bion *Epitaph on Adonis* (Reed) = *Bion of Smyrna: the fragments and the Adonis*, Reed, J.D. (ed., tr. & comm.) (Cambridge, 1997).

Blass-Debrunner-Rehkopf = Blass, F., Debrunner, A. & Rehkopf, F. (eds), *Grammatik des neutestamentlichen Griechisch*[16] (Göttingen, 1984).

Bloch, M. (1982), 'Death, women and power', in Bloch & Parry (1982) 211-30.

―――― & Parry, J. (1982) (eds), *Death and the regeneration of life* (Cambridge).

Bond, G.W. (1981), *Euripides, Heracles*, with introduction and commentary (Oxford).

Bouvier, B. (1960) (ed.), *Dimotika tragoudia apo cheirographo tis Monis tôn Ivirôn* (Collection de l'Institut français d'Athènes, Archives musicales de folklore, 120ᶜ).

Bowersock, G.W. (1990), *Hellenism in late antiquity* (Jerome lectures, 18, Ann Arbor, MI).

Bowie, A.M. (1981), *The poetic dialect of Sappho and Alcaeus* (N.Y.).

Bowie, E.L. (1986), 'Early Greek elegy, symposium and public festival', *JHS* 106: 13-35.

Bowra, C.M. (1961), *Greek lyric poetry from Alcman to Simonides*[2] (Oxford).

Bramble, J.C. (1970), 'Structure and ambiguity in Catullus LXIV', *PCPS*[2] 16: 22-41.

Braudel, F. ([1963] 1994), *A history of civilizations* (Engl. tr. Harmondsworth).

Brazda, M.-K. (1977), *Zur Bedeutung des Apfels in der antiken Kultur* (Bonn).

Bremmer, J.N. (1987), 'The old women of ancient Greece', in J. Blok & P. Mason (eds), *Sexual asymmetry: studies in ancient society* (Amsterdam) 191-215.

―――― (1994), *Greek religion* (*G & R* Survey, xxiv).

Brown, C.G. (1992), Review of Contiades-Tsitsoni (1990), in *CR*[2] 42.i: 201.

Brown, P. (1988), *The body and society: men, women and sexual renunciation in early Christianity* (London).

Browning, R. (1983)[a], *Medieval and modern Greek*[2], rev. edn (Cambridge).

―――― (1983)[b], 'The continuity of Hellenism in the Byzantine world: appearance or reality?', in T. Winnifrith & P. Murray (eds), *Greece old and new* (London & Basingstoke) 111-28.

―――― (1995), 'Tradition and originality in literary criticism and scholarship', in A.R. Littlewood (ed.), *Originality in Byzantine literature, art and music: a collection of essays* (Oxford) 17-28.

Bruce, F.F. (1984), *The Epistles to the Colossians, to Philemon, and to the Ephesians* (Grand Rapids).

Burnett, A.P. (1983), *Three archaic poets: Archilochus, Alcaeus, Sappho* (London).

Buxton, R. (1994), *Imaginary Greece: the contexts of mythology* (Cambridge).

Bybilakis, G. (1840), *Neugriechisches Leben verglichen mit dem Altgriechischen, zur Erläuterung beider* (Berlin).

Cairns, D.L. (1993), *Aidôs: the psychology and ethics of honour and shame in ancient Greek literature* (Oxford).

Calame, C. (1977), *Les choeurs de jeunes filles en Grèce archaïque*, i-ii (Filologia e critica, xxi-xxii).

—— (1983) *see* Alcm. (Calame).

Call. (Pf.) = *Callimachus*, Pfeiffer, R. (ed.), i-ii (Oxford, 1949; rp. 1985).

Callicles (Sternbach) = *Nicolai Callicles carmina*, Sternbach, L. (ed.) (Cracow, 1903).

Callimachos & Chrysorrhoë (Kriaras) *see* Kriaras (1955).

Callimachos & Chrysorrhoë (Pichard) = *Le roman de Callimaque et de Chrysorrhoë*, Pichard, M. (ed.) (Paris, 1956).

Cameron, Alan (1974), 'Demes and factions', *BZ* 57: 74-91.

—— (1985), *Literature and society in the early Byzantine world* (Variorum CS, 209).

Cameron, Averil (1986), 'New and old in Christian literature', in *17th International Congress of Byzantine Studies* (Washington, D.C., August 3-8, 1986): major papers (New Rochelle, N.Y.).

Campbell, D.A. ([1967] 1982) (ed. & comm.), *Greek lyric poetry*[2], enlarged & corr. edn (London).

Campbell i = *Greek lyric I: Sappho, Alcaeus*, Campbell, D.A. (ed. & tr.) (Cambridge, MA, 1982).

Campbell ii = *Greek lyric II: Anacreon, Anacreontea, choral lyric from Olympus to Alcman*, Campbell, D.A. (ed. & tr.) (LCL, 143, 1988).

Campbell iii = *Greek lyric III: Stesichorus, Ibycus, Simonides, and others*, Campbell, D.A. (ed. & tr.) (LCL, 476, 1991).

Campbell iv = *Greek lyric IV*, Campbell, D.A. (ed. & tr.) (LCL, 461).

Campbell v = *Greek lyric V: the new school of poetry and anonymous songs and hymns*, Campbell, D.A. (ed. & tr.) (LCL, 1993).

Campbell, J. (1964), *Honour, family and patronage: a study of institutions and moral values ...* (Oxford).

Carey, C. (1981), *A commentary on five odes of Pindar ...* (Monogr. in Class. Studies).

carm. anacreont. (W) *see* Anacreont. (West).

Carmina (Miller) = *Manuelis Philae carmina ...*, Miller, E. (ed.), ii (Paris, 1857).

Cataudella, Q. (1940), 'Giovanni Crisostomo, "imitatore" di Aristofane', *Athenaeum*[2] 18: 236-43.

Cecaumenos *Strategicon* (Litavrin) = *Sovety i rasskazy Kekavmena*, Litavrin, G.G. (ed.) (Moscow, 1972).

CEG I = *Carmina Epigraphica Graeca, Saeculorum VIII-V a. Chr. n.*, Hansen, P.A. (ed.) (Berlin & New York, 1983).

CFA (Hausrath & Hunger) = *Corpus fabularum Aesopicarum*, Hausrath, A. & Hunger, H. (eds), i, fasc. 1, 2nd edn (Bibliotheca ... Teubneriana, 1970); i, fasc. 2 (1959).

Chansons populaires (Pernot) = *Chansons populaires grecques des XV et XVI siècles*, Pernot, H. (ed.) (Collection de l'Institut néo-Hellénique de l'Univ. de Paris, viii, 1931).

Chantraine, P. (1968), *Dictionnaire étymologique de la langue grecque: histoire des mots*, i-ii (Paris).

CHCL, i = *Cambridge history of classical literature*, Easterling, P.E. & Knox, B.M.W. (eds), i: *Greek literature* (Cambridge, 1985).

(Nicetas) Choniates *Historia* (van Dieten) = *Nicetae Choniatae Historia*, van Dieten, J.-L. (ed.) (*CFHB*, xi.1, 1975) [also cf. *N.C.O.E.* (van Dieten) below].

Chor. (FR) = *Choricii Gazaei opera*, Foerster, R. & Richsteig (eds) (Bibliotheca ... Teubneriana, 1929; rp. 1972).

Chryssanthopoulou-Farrington, V. (1999), 'To kako mati stous Ellines tis Afstralias', in J. Petropoulos (1999)[c] 22-30.

CMH = *Cambridge Medieval History*, iv.1, 2nd edn (Cambridge, 1966).

Colonna (1951) *see* Him. (Colonna).

Conca = *Il romanzo bizantino del XII secolo: Teodoro Prodromo – Niceta Eugeniano, Eustazio Macrembolita – Constantino Manasse*, Conca, F. (ed.) (Torino, 1994).

—— (1990) (ed.), *Nicetas Eugenianus: De Drosillae et Chariclis amoribus* (London Stud. in Class. Philol., 24 [Amsterdam]).

Const. Porphyr. *De Caerem.* (Reiske) = *Constantini Porphyrogeniti imperatoris De ceremoniis aulae byzantinae ...*, Reiske, J.J. (ed.), i-ii (*CSHB* [Bonn], i: Bks 1.1-2.56, 1829; ii: Commentary, 1830).

Const. Porphyr. *De Caerem.* (Vogt) = *Constantin VII Porphyrogénète: le livre des cérémonies*, Vogt, A. (ed.), 4 vols (Bk 1, chs 1-92 [83], with Fr. tr.) (Paris, 1935-40) [corr. by, among others, Festugière (1971) 240-57].

Constantelos, D.J. (1978), 'Byzantine religiosity and ancient Greek religiosity', in Vryonis (1978) 135-51.

Contiades-Tsitsoni, E. (1990), *Hymenaios und Epithalamion: Das Hochzeitslied in der frühgriechischen Lyrik* (Beiträge zur Altertumskunde, xvi).

Coulton, M. (1983), 'Imagery in Greek folk songs: the wedding farewells and related songs' (Univ. of Birmingham, M.Litt. thesis).

CPG (Leutsch-Schneidewin) = *Corpus paroemiographorum Graecorum*, Leutsch, E.L. von & Schneidewin, F.G. (eds), i (Göttingen, 1839; rp. Hildesheim, 1958); Leutsch, E.L. von (ed.), ii (Göttingen, 1851; rp. Hildesheim, 1959).

Cunningham (1971) *see* Herod. (Cunningham).

Curtius, E.R. (1953), *European literature and the Latin Middle Ages*, tr. W.R. Trask (London).

Cypria (Davies) = *Epicorum Graecorum fragmenta*, Davies, M. (ed.) (Göttingen, 1988).

Danforth, L. (1982), *The death rituals of rural Greece* (Princeton).

Davidson, J. (1997), *Courtesans and fish cakes: the consuming passions of classical Athens* (UK, 1997).

Davies, M. (1984), Review of Burnett (1983), in *CR*[2] 34.ii: 169-73.

—— (1988) *see Cypria* (Davies).

—— (1991)[a] = S. *Trach.* (Davies).

—— (1991)[b] = *Poetarum melicorum graecorum fragmenta*, i: *Alcman, Stesichorus, Ibycus* post D.L. Page, Davies, M. (ed.) (Oxford).

Davisson, M.H.T (1993), '*Quid moror exemplis?*: mythological *exempla* in Ovid's pre-exilic poems and the elegies from exile', *Phoenix* 57: 213-37.

D. Chr. (von Arnim) = *Dionis Prusaensis ... omnia*, Arnim, J. von (ed.), i (Berlin, 1893).

de Boor (1885) *see* Theophanis *Chronographia* (de Boor).

de Cuenca (1976) *see* Euphorion (de Cuenca).

Demianczuk = *Supplementum comicum ...*, Demianczuk, I. (ed.) (Kracow, 1912).

Denniston, J.D., *The Greek particles*[2] (Oxford, 1954; rp. with corr. 1959).

Devereux, G. (1967), 'Greek pseudo-homosexuality and the "Greek miracle"', *SO* 42: 69-92.

—— (1970), 'The nature of Sappho's seizure in fr. 31 LP as evidence of her inversion', *CQ*[2].i 20: 17-31.

Diehl ii = *Anthologia lyrica Graeca*, Diehl, E. (ed.), ii (Bibliotheca ... Teubneriana, 1942).

Dig. Akr. (S. Alexiou) = *Vasileios Digenis Akritis*, Alexiou, S. (ed.) (Ermis, Athens, 1990).

Dig. Akr. (E. Jeffreys) = *Digenis Akritis: the Grottaferrata and Escorial versions*, Jeffreys, E. (ed. & tr.) (Cambridge Medieval Classics, 7, 1998).

Dig. Akr. (Trapp) = *Digenes Akrites: synoptische Ausgabe der ältesten Versionen*, Trapp, E. (ed.) (WByzSt, viii, 1971).

Diggle (1970) *see* E. *Phäeth.* (Diggle).

Diller, I. (1977), 'Märchenmotive in Kallimachus und Chrysorrhoë', *Fol. Neohell.* 2: 25-40.

Dillon, M. (1994), 'Margites: a lost Greek trickster type' (unpubl. paper, 126th Annual Meeting of the APA, Atlanta, GA).

―――― (1999), 'Post-nuptial sacrifices on Kos (Segre, *ED* 178) and ancient Greek marriage rites', *ZPE* 124: 63-80.

Dirichlet, G.L. (1914) = *De veterum macarismis* (Giessen).

Dodds (1960) *see* E. *Ba.*

Dornseiff, F. (1936), 'Aegyptische Liebeslieder, Hoheslied, Sappho, Theokrit', *ZDMG* 90: 589-601.

Dover, K.J. (1968) *see* Ar. *Nub.* (Dover).

―――― (1971) = Theoc. (Dover).

―――― (1974), *Greek popular morality in the time of Plato and Aristotle* (Oxford; rp. with corr. Indianapolis, 1994).

―――― (1978), *Greek homosexuality* (London).

―――― (1980) = Pl. *Smp.* (Dover).

―――― (1987), *Greek and the Greeks, Collected papers*, i: *Language, poetry, drama* (Oxford).

―――― (1988), *The Greeks and their legacy: collected papers*, ii: *Prose literature, history, society, transmission, influence* (Oxford).

―――― (1993) *see* Ar. *Ran.* (Dover).

―――― (1997), *The evolution of Greek prose style* (Oxford).

Drexl, F. (1925)[a] *see* Achmetis *Oneirocriticon* (Drexl).

―――― (1925)[b], 'Das anonyme Traumbuch des Cod. Paris. Gr. 2511', *Laogr.* 8: 347-75.

Dunbar (1995) *see* Ar. *Av.* (Dunbar).

E. *Alc.* (Garzya) = *Euripides, Alcestis*, Garzya, A. (ed.) (Bibliotheca ... Teubneriana, 1980) [to be used in conjunction with OCT].

E. *Andr.* (Garzya) = *Euripides: Andromache*, Garzya, A. (ed.) (Bibliotheca ... Teubneriana, 1978) [to be used in conjunction with OCT].

E. *Ba.* (Dodds) = *Euripides, Bacchae*[2], Dodds, E.R. (ed. & comm.) (Oxford).

E. *Cyclops* (Seaford) = *Euripides: Cyclops, with introduction and commentary*, Seaford, R. (ed.) (Oxford, 1984).

E. *Hel.* (Kannicht) = *Euripides, Helena*, Kannicht, R. (ed.), i-ii (Heidelberg, 1969).

E. *Hipp.* (Barrett) = *Euripides, Hippolytos*, Barrett, W.S. (ed.) (Oxford, 1964).

E. *IA* (Günther) = *Euripides, Iphigeneia Aulidensis*, Günther, H.-C. (ed.) (Bibliotheca ... Teubneriana, 1988).

E. *Med.* (Page) = *Euripides, Medea ...*, Page, D.L. (ed.) (Oxford, 1938; rp. with corr. 1952).

E. *Phäeth.* (Diggle) = *Euripides, Phaëthon*, Diggle, J. (ed.) (Cambridge, 1970).

E. *Tr.* (Biehl) = *Euripides: Troades*, Biehl, W. (ed.) (Bibliotheca ... Teubneriana, 1970) [to be used in conjunction with OCT].

Easterling, P.E. (1982), *Sophocles: Trachiniae* (Cambridge).

Eideneier, H. (1977) (ed.), *Spanos: eine Byzantinische Satire in der Form einer Parodie* (Suppl. Byz., 5).

—— (1983) 'Leser-order Hörerkreis? Zur Byzantinischen Dichtung in der Volks-sprache', *Hellenika* 34: 119-50.

—— (1988) (ed.), *Krasopateras: kritische Ausgabe der Versionen des 16.-18. Jahrhunderts* (Neograeca medii aevi, 3 [Cologne]).

—— (1991) (ed.), *Ptochoprodromos: Einführung, kritische Ausgabe ...* (Neograeca medii aevi, 5 [Cologne]).

Eisenberger, H. (1956), 'Der Mythos in der äolischen Lyrik' (Doctoral thesis, Frankfurt).

Epi. Gr. = *Epigrammata Graeca ex lapidibus conlecta*, Kaibel, G. (ed.) (Berlin, 1878).

Erôphili (S. Alexiou & M. Aposkiti) = *Erôphili: Tragôdia Geôrgiou Chortatsi*, Alexiou, S. & Aposkiti, M. (eds) (Stigmi, Athens, 1988).

Erotocritos (S. Alexiou) = *Erôtokritos: Vitsentzos Kornaros*, Alexiou, S. (ed.) (Ermis, Athens, 1985).

Erôtopaignia (H.-P.) = *Erôtopaignia: chansons d'amour*, Hesseling, D.C. & Pernot, H. (eds) (Bibl. gr. vulgaire, 10, 1913).

Eub. (Hunter) = *Eubulus: the fragments*, Hunter, R.L. (ed. & comm.) (Cambridge, 1983).

Euphorion (de Cuenca) = *Euforion de Calcis: fragmentos y epigramas*, de Cuenca, L.A. (ed.) (Madrid, 1976).

Euphorion (van Groningen) = *Euphorion*, van Groningen, B.A. (ed.) (Amsterdam, 1977).

Eustathii Metropolitae: Thessalonicensis Opuscula, Tafel, G.L.F. (ed.) (Frankfurt am Main, 1832; rp. Amsterdam, 1964).

Evans, E.C. (1969), *Physiognomics in the ancient world* (Trans. Amer. Philos. Society [Philadelphia], 59).

Evans-Pritchard, E.E. (1965), *The position of women in primitive societies and other essays in social anthropology* (London).

Faraone, C.A. (1985), 'Aeschylus' *hymnos desmios* (*Eum.* 306) and Attic judicial curse tablets', *JHS* 105: 150-4.

—— (1990), 'Aphrodite's KESTOS and apples for Atalanta: aphrodisiacs in early Greek myth and ritual', *Phoenix* 44: 219-43.

Fedeli, P. (1983), *Catullus' Carmen 61* (London Stud. in Class. Philol., 9).

Fehling, D. (1972), 'Erysichthon oder das Märchen von der mündlichen Überlie-ferung', *RhM* 115: 173-96.

—— (1977), *Amor und Psyche: die Schöpfung des Apuleius und ihre Einwirkung auf das Märchen ...* (*AAWM*, 9).

Fehrle, E. (1920), *Richtlinien zur Textgestaltung der griechischen Geoponica* (Heidelberg).

Festugière, A.-J. (1971), 'Observations grammaticales sur le *De Caeremoniis* de Constantin Porphyrogénète', *RPhil* 45: 240-57.

—— (1974), *Observations stylistiques sur l'Évangile de s. Jean* (Études et com-mentaires, 84)

F Gr Hist (Jacoby i) = *Die Fragmente der griechischen Historiker ...*, Jacoby, F. (ed.), i (Leiden, 1957).

Field = *Sancti Patris nostri Joannis Chrysostomi ... interpretatio omnium epistu-larum Paulinarum ...*, Field, F. (ed.), i-vii (Oxford, 1849-62).

Finnegan, R. (1977), *Oral poetry: its nature, signficance, and social context* (Cam-bridge).

Foerster (1903-27) *see* Lib. (Foerster).

Fordyce, C.J. (1961), *Catullus: a commentary* (Oxford).

Fortunatos (Vincent) = Markou Antôniou Foscolou *Fortunatos ...*, Vincent, A.L. (ed.) (Etair. krit. istorikôn meletôn, iii, 1980).

Fowler, B.H. (1994) (tr.), *Love lyrics of ancient Egypt* (Chapel Hill & London).

Fraenkel, E. (1950) *see* A. *Ag.* (Fraenkel).
――― (1955), '*Vesper adest* (Catullus LXII)', *JRS* 45: 1-8.
――― (1960), *Elementi Plautini in Plauto* (1st German edn, 1922; enlarged edn, Florence).
Fraser, L. (1985), 'Wedding scenes on Attic vases' (D.Phil. thesis, Oxford).
Friedl, E. (1962), *Vasilika, a village in modern Greece* (N.Y.).
Friis & Whittle (1980) *see* A. *Supp.* (FJW).
Frontisi-Ducroux, F. & Vernant, J.-P. (1997), *Dans l'oeil du miroir* (Paris).
Gager, J.G. (1992) (ed.), *Curse tablets and binding spells from the ancient world* (N.Y. & Oxford).
Garland (Gow-Page) = *The Greek Anthology: the Garland of Philip and some contemporary epigrams*, Gow, A.S.F. & Page, D.L. (eds), i-ii (Cambridge, 1968).
Garland, L. (1985), 'Conventions of love and marriage in late Byzantine literature' (DPhil thesis, Oxford).
――― (1990), ' "Be amorous, but be chaste ...": sexual morality in Byzantine learned and vernacular romance', *BMGS* 14: 62-120.
Garnaud (1991) *see* Ach. Tat. (Garnaud).
Garzya (1978) *see* E. *Andr.* (Garzya).
――― (1980) *see* E. *Alc.* (Garzya).
Gazis, G. (1828), *Viographia ... Markou Botsari kai Karaïskaki ...* (Aigina).
Geanakoplos, D.J. (1976), *Interaction of the 'sibling' Byzantine and western cultures in the Middle Ages and Italian Renaissance (330-1600)* (New Haven & London).
Geffcken, J. (1916), *Griechische Epigramme* (Heidelberg).
Geoponica (Beckh) = *Geoponica sive Cassiani Bassi ... De re rustica eclogae*, Beckh, H. (ed.) (Bibliotheca Teubneriana, 1895).
Gleason, M.W. (1990), 'The semiotics of gender: physiognomy and self-fashioning in the second century CE', in Halperin et al. (1990) 389-414.
Goodwin = Goodwin, W.W., *Syntax of the moods and tenses of the Greek verb* (enlarged edn, rp. London, 1965).
Goody, J. (1968) (ed.), *Literacy in traditional societies* (Cambridge).
Gow (1952) *see* Theoc. (Gow), ii.
――― (1965) *see* Machon (Gow).
――― & Page (1965) *see* HE.
――― & Page (1968) *see* Garland (Gow-Page).
Greg. Nyss. = *Grégoire de Nysse: Vie de sainte Macrine*, Maraval, P. (ed.) (SC, 178, 1971).
Gregory, T.E. (1986), 'The survival of paganism in Christian Greece: a critical essay', *AJP* 107.ii: 229-41.
Griffiths, A. (1972), 'Alcman's *Partheneion*: the morning after the night before', *QUCC* 14: 7-30.
――― (1995), 'Non-aristocratic elements in archaic poetry,' in A. Powell (ed.), *The Greek world* (London) 85-103.
Günther (1988) *see* E. *IA* (Günther).
Guthrie, W.K.C. (1950), *The Greeks and their gods* (London).
Guys, P.A. (1783), *Voyage littéraire de la Grèce ...*[3], i (Paris).
Hägg, T. (1983), *The novel in antiquity* (Oxford).
Hague, R. (1983), 'Ancient Greek wedding songs: the tradition of praise', *Journal of Folklore Research* 20: 131-43.
――― (1985), 'Marriage in Greek tradition', unpublished paper, joint APA-MGSA conference, Washington DC.
Hall, E. (1989), *Inventing the barbarian: self-definition through tragedy* (Oxford).
Halliwell, S. (1986), *Aristotle's Poetics* (London).
――― (1991), 'The uses of laughter in Greek culture', CQ^2 41.ii: 279-96.

Halperin, D.M. et al. (1990) (eds), *Before sexuality: the construction of erotic experience in the ancient world* (Princeton).

Hansen *see CEG* I

Haslam, M.W. (1981), 'Narrative about Tinouphis in prosimetrum', in *Papyri Greek and Egyptian edited by various hands in honour of Eric Gardner Turner* (London) 35-45.

Hatto, A.T. (1965) (ed.), *Eos: an enquiry into the theme of lovers' meetings and partings at dawn in poetry* (London, The Hague & Paris).

Hausrath & Hunger (1959) *see CFA* (Hausrath & Hunger).

h. Cer. (Richardson) = *The Homeric Hymn to Demeter*, Richardson, N.J. (ed.) (Oxford, 1974, 1979).

HE = *The Greek Anthology: Hellenistic epigrams* ..., Gow, A.S.F. & Page, D.L. (eds), i-ii (Cambridge, 1965).

Headlam (1922) *see* Herod. (Headlam).

Heisenberg, A. (1920), 'Aus der Geschichte und Literatur der Palaiologenzeit', *SBAW* 10: 100-5.

Heitsch = *Die Griechischen Dichterfragmente der Römischen Kaiserzeit*[2], Heitsch, E. (ed.), i (Abh. Götting., Phil.-hist. Kl., 49, 1963).

Henderson, J. (1975), *The maculate muse: obscene language in Attic comedy* (New Haven & London).

Henrichs, A. (1980), 'Riper than a pear: Parian invective in Theokritos', *ZPE* 39: 7-27.

Henry (1962) *see* Photius *Bibliotheca*.

Herod. (Cunningham) = *Herodas: mimiambi*, Cunningham, I.C. (ed.) (Oxford, 1971).

Herod. (Headlam) = *Herodas: the mimes and fragments*, with notes by Walter Headlam, Knox, A.D. (ed.) (Cambridge, 1922).

Herzfeld, M. (1972), 'The "khelidonisma": A study in textual and ritual variation' (MA thesis, Univ. of Birmingham).

—— (1973), 'Prophoriki paradosi kai koinôniki synecheia stis anoixiatikes teletes tôn notioroditikôn chôriôn', *Dôdekanisiaka Chronika* 2: 1-19.

—— (1993), 'In defiance of destiny: the management of time and gender at a Cretan funeral', *American Ethnologist* 20.ii: 241-55.

Hes. fr. (MW) = *Fragmenta Hesiodea*, Merkelbach, R. & West, M.L. (eds) (Oxford, 1967).

Hes. *WD* (W) = *Hesiod: Works and Days*, West, M.L. (ed.) (Oxford, 1978).

Hesseling (1919) *see Achilleïs* (Hesseling).

—— & Pernot (1910) *see* 'Ptocho-Prodromos' (H.-P.).

Higgins, R.A. (1980), *Greek and Roman jewellery*[2] (London).

Him. (Colonna) = *Himerii declamationes et orationes* ..., Colonna, A. (ed.) (Rome, 1951).

Holton, D. (1988), '*Erotokritos* and Greek tradition', in Beaton (1988) 144-55.

—— (1991) (ed.), *Literature and society in Renaissance Crete* (Cambridge).

Hooker, J.T. (1977), *The language and text of the Lesbian poets* (Innsbrucker Beitr. zur Sprachwiss., 26).

Hopkinson = *A Hellenistic anthology*, Hopkinson, N. (ed.) (Cambridge, 1988).

Hörandner (1974) *see* Prodromos.

Hordern, J. (1999), 'An erotic inscription from Marisa, Judaea (I.U. Powell, Collectanea Alexandrina 184)', *ZPE* 126: 81-2.

Horrocks, G. (1997), *Greek: a history of the language and its speakers* (London & N.Y.).

Hoskins, J. (1987), 'Complementarity in this world and the next: gender and agency in Kodi mortuary ceremonies', in Strathern (1987) 174-208.

Hunger, H. (1973), *Byzantinische Grundlagenforschung: gesammelte Aufsätze* (Variorum Rp. C21).

——— (1978)[a], 'Stilstufen in der Byzantinischen Geschichtsschreibung des 12. Jahrhunderts: Anna Komnene und Michael Glykas', *EtByz* 5: 139-70.

——— (1978)[b], *Die hochsprachliche profane Literatur der Byzantiner*, i-ii (*HAW* xii.5).

——— (1980) *Antiker und Byzantinischer Roman* (Sitzungsb., Heidelberger Akad. der Wiss., phil.-hist. Kl., iii).

——— (1981), 'The importance of rhetoric in Byzantium', in M. Mullett & R. Scott (eds), *Byzantium and the classical tradition* (Birmingham) 176-91.

Hunter, R.L. (1983), *A study of Daphnis and Chloe* (Cambridge).

Hutchinson (1985) *see* A. *Th.* (Hutchinson).

Hyphantes, N.T. (1972) (ed.), *O Pôgônisios gamos* (Athens).

Ibyc. (Davies) *see* Davies (1991)[b].

ICUR X = *Inscriptiones Christianae urbis Romae, Coemeteria viae Salariae ...*, Mazzoleni, D. & Carletti, C. (eds), n.s. X (Rome & Vatican, 1992).

IE, i-ii (W) = *Iambi et elegi Graeci ...*[2], West, M.L. (ed.), i-ii (Oxford, 1989-92).

IG = *Inscriptiones Graecae.*

IGSK = *Inschriften griechischer Städte aus Kleinasien* (Bonn, 1972-).

Ioannes Geometres = *The progymnasmata of Ioannes Geometres*, Littlewood, A.R. (ed.) (Amsterdam, 1972).

Ioannou, G. (1966) (ed.), *Ta dimotika mas tragoudia ...* (Athens).

Jacobi (1957) *see F Gr Hist* (Jacoby i).

Jannaris, A.N. (1897), *An historical Greek grammar, chiefly of the Attic dialect ...* (London & New York).

Jeffreys, E.M. (1968), 'The question of western influence on the Greek popular verse romances, with particular reference to the garden-castle theme' (DPhil thesis, Oxford).

——— (1981), 'The later Greek verse romances: a survey', in E.M. Jeffreys & A. Moffatt (eds), *Byzantine Papers* (Byzantina Australiensia, 1) 116-27.

——— (1998) *see Dig. Akr.* (E. Jeffreys).

Jeffreys, M.J. (1974), 'The nature and origins of the political verse', *DOP* 28: 176-91.

——— (1981), 'Byzantine metrics: non-literary strata', *JÖB* 31: 313-34.

Jouanno, C. (1987), 'L'ekphrasis dans la littérature byzantine d'imagination' (Doctoral thesis, Univ. de Paris IV).

Jul. *Or.* (Bidez-Cumont) = *L'empereur Julien: Oeuvres complètes*, 1,i *Discours de Julien César*, Bidez, J. (ed. & tr.) rev. Cumont, F. (Budé 1932).

Just, R. (1985), 'Freedom, slavery and the female psyche', in P.A. Cartledge & F.D. Harvey (eds), *Crux: essays presented to G.E.M. de Ste. Croix ...* (Exeter) 169-88.

——— (1989), *Women in Athenian law and life* (London & N.Y.).

Kaibel, G. (1878) *see Epi. Gr.*

——— (1892), 'Theokrits *Helenês Epithalamion*', *Hermes* 27: 249-59.

Kakrides, J.Th. (1949), *Homeric researches* (Skrifter ... Lund, xlv).

——— (1970), 'Nausikaa', *WHB* 12: 24-34.

——— (1971)[a], *Homer revisited* (Skrifter ... Lund, lxiv).

——— (1971)[b], *Xanagyrizontas ston Omiro* (Thessalonica).

——— (1979), *Oi archaioi sti neoelliniki laïki paradosi*[2] (Athens).

——— (1983), *Ela, Aphroditi, anthostephanômeni ...* (Athens).

Kakrides, Ph. (1974) *see Ar. Av.* (Ph. Kakrides).

Kambouroglous, G. (1896), *Istoria Athinaiôn*, iii (Athens).

Kannicht (1969) *see E. Hel.* (Kannicht).

Karapatakis, C. (1960) (ed.), *O gamos tou paliou kairou ...* (Athens).

Karayiannis, V. (1983) (ed.), *Ta adiantropa* (Athens).

Karlin-Hayter, P. (1992), 'Further notes on Byzantine marriage: raptus-*arpagê* or *mnêsteiai*?', *DOP* 46: 133-54.

Kassel, R. & Austin, C. *see PCG*.

Kazavis, G. (1940) (ed.), *Nisyrou laographika* (N.Y.).

Kazhdan, A.P. & Franklin, S. (1984), *Studies on Byzantine literature of the eleventh and twelfth centuries* (Cambridge).

────── & Epstein, A.W. (1985), *Change in Byzantine culture in the eleventh and twelfth centuries* (Berkeley & Los Angeles).

Kehayioglou, G. (1984), 'Nea stoicheia yia ellinika entypa', *Epist. Epet. Philos. Sch. Pan. Thes/nikis* 22: 233-50.

────── (1988), 'Translations of eastern "novels" and their influence on late Byzantine and modern Greek fiction (eleventh-eighteenth centuries)', in Beaton (1988) 156-66.

Kennedy, G.A. (1983), *Greek rhetoric under Christian emperors* (Princeton, N.J.).

Kilmer, M.F. (1993), *Greek erotica* (London).

King, H. (1983), 'Bound to bleed: Artemis and Greek women', in A. Cameron & A. Kuhrt (eds), *Images of women in antiquity* (London & Canberra) 109-27.

Knös, B. (1970), 'Une version grecque de l'histoire du faux Démétrius, tzar de la Russie', *Delt. Et. Ell.* 16: 240-50.

Kopidakis, M.Z. (1989), 'Sapphô, Aposp. 111 Voigt', *Ariadni* 5: 45-54.

Kost (1971) *see* Musae. (Kost).

Koukoules = Koukoules, Ph., *Vyzantinôn vios kai politismos*, i-vi, with supplement (Collection de l'Institut français d'Athènes, 1948-55).

Kourkoulas, C.C. (1957), *I theôria tou kirygmnatos kata tous chronous tis Tourkokratias* (Athens).

Kovacs iv = *Euripides IV: Trojan women, Iphigenia among the Taurians, Ion*, Kovacs, D. (ed. & tr.) (LCL, 10, 1999).

Kriaras, E. (1955) (ed.), *Vyzantina ippotika mythistorimata* (Vasiki vivliothiki, ii, 1955).

────── (1975) *see Panôria* (Kriaras).

Krikos, K.H. (1976), 'Moira at birth in Greek tradition' (MA thesis, Univ. of Birmingham).

Kurtz (1903) *see* Mityl. (Kurtz).

────── & Drexl (1936) *see* Psellos (Kurtz & Drexl).

Kyriakides, S. (1951), 'Gamilion dimôdes vyzantinon asma', *AIPhO* 11: 179-83.

────── (1978), *To dimotiko tragoudi: synagôgi meletôn* (Athens).

Kyriakidou-Nestoros, A. (1978), *I theôria tis neoellinikis laographias: kritiki kai analysi* (Vivliothiki genikis paideias, vi).

Laiou, A.E. ([1985] 1992), *Gender, society and economic life in Byzantium* (CS 370).

────── (1992), *Mariage, amour et parenté à Byzance, XIème-XIIIème siècles* (Paris).

────── (1993), 'Sex, consent, and coercion in Byzantium', in A.E. Laiou (ed.), *Consent and coercion to sex and marriage in ancient and medieval societies* (Washington, D.C.) 109-221.

Lambert, J.A. (1935) (ed.), *Le roman de Libistros et Rhodamné* (Amsterdam, 1935).

L.A. Ms. = *Laographikon Archeion*, Kentron erevnis tis ellinikis laographias, Akademia Athinôn.

Lane, E.N. (1988), 'PASTOS', *Glotta* 66.i-ii: 100-23.

Lane Fox, R. (1986), *Pagans and Christians* ... (Harmondsworth).

Lattimore, R. (1942), *Themes in Greek and Latin epitaphs* (Illinois studies in lang. and literature, xxvii.1-2).

Lefkowitz, M.R. (1986), *Women in Greek myth* (London).

Lelekos, M. (1888) (ed.), *Epidorpion*, i (Athens).

Leutsch & Schneidewin (1958) *see CPG* (Leutsch-Schneidewin).

Leutsch (1959) *see CPG* (Leutsch).

189

Lib. (Foerster) = *Libanii opera*, Foerster, R. (ed.), i-xii (Bibliotheca ... Teubneriana, 1903-27).

Litavrin (1972) *see* Cecaumenos *Strategicon* (Litavrin).

Littlewood, A.R. (1967), 'The symbolism of the apple in Greek and Roman literature', *HSCP* 72: 147-81.

——— (1972) *see* Ioannes Geometres (Littlewood) .

——— (1974), 'The symbolism of the apple in Byzantine literature', *JÖB* 22: 33-59.

——— (1978), 'The apple in the sexual imagery of Kazantzakis: a study in the continuity of a Greek tradition', *Neo-Hellenika* 3: 37-55.

——— (1979), 'Romantic paradises: the role of the garden in the Byzantine romance', *BMGS* 5: 95-114.

——— (1993), 'The erotic symbolism of the apple in late Byzantine and meta-Byzantine demotic literature', *BMGS* 17: 83-103.

——— (forthcoming), 'From Homer to Seferis: the continuity of the tradition of the erotic symbolism of the apple in classical Greek, Roman, Byzantine and modern Greek literature', in H. Temporini (ed.), *Aufsteig und Niedergang der Römischen Welt* (Berlin).

Lloyd-Jones (1994) *see* S. *Ph.* / S. *Trach.* (Lloyd-Jones).

——— (1996) *see* S. frr. (Lloyd-Jones).

——— & Parsons (1983) *see SH* (Lloyd-Jones and Parsons)

Lobel & Page (1955) *see* Alc. (LP).

Longus (Reeve) = *Longus, Daphnis et Chloe*^{2}, Reeve, M.L. (ed.) (Bibliotheca ... Teubneriana, 1986).

Lorimer, H.L. (1936), 'Gold and ivory in Greek mythology', in C. Bailey et al. (eds), *Greek poetry and life: essays presented to Gilbert Murray* ... (Oxford & N.Y.) 14-38.

Loukatos, D.S. (1978), *Eisagôgi stin elliniki laographia*^{2} (MIET, Athens).

——— (1988), 'Ta teletourgika tragoudia tou ellinikou gamou: I magiko-thriskeftiki, psychologiki kai koinôniki simasia tous', in *SYNDEIPNON: Timitiko aphierôma ston kathigiti Dimitrio S. Loukato* ... (Ioannina) 57-70.

Loutzaki, R. (1983-5), 'O gamos ôs choreftiko drômeno. I periptôsi tôn prosphygôn tis Anatolikis Rômylias sto Mikro Monastiri Makedonias', *Ethnographika* 4-5: 3-50.

Maas & Trypanis (1963) *see* Romanos (Maas-Trypanis)

MacCoull, L.S.B. (1988), *Dioscorus of Aphrodito: his work and his world* (Berkeley & London).

Machon (Gow) = *Machon: the fragments* ..., Gow, A.S.F. (ed.) (Cambridge, 1965).

Mackridge, P. (1985), *The modern Greek language: a descriptive analysis of standard modern Greek* (Oxford).

——— (1993), ' "None but the brave deserve the fair": abduction, elopement, seduction and marriage in the Escorial *Digenis Akrites* and modern Greek heroic songs', in Beaton & Ricks (1993) 150-60.

——— (1999), Review of Horrocks (1997), in *Dialogos* 6: 77-82.

Maehler (1989) *see* Pi. (M).

Maguire, H. (1981), *Art and eloquence in Byzantium* (Princeton).

Mair (1928) *see* 'Oppian' *Cynegetica* (Mair).

MAMA I = *Monumenta Asiae Minoris Antiqua*, Calder, W.M. (ed.), i (Manchester & London).

Mango, C. (1954), 'Quelques remarques sur la Chanson de Daskaloyannis', *Kr. Chron.* 8: 44-54.

——— (1980), *Byzantium: the empire of New Rome* (London).

Manusakas, M.I. & Puchner, W. (1984), *Die vergessene Braut: Bruchstücke einer unbekannten kretischen Komödie des 17. Jahrhunderts* ... (Österreich. Akademie d. Wissenschaften, philos.-histor. Kl., Sitzungsberichte, 436).

Maspero, J. (1911), 'Un dernier poète grec d'Égypte, Dioscore fils d'Apollôs', *REG* 24: 426-81.

Mastrodemetres, P.D. (1983), *Eisagôgi sti neoelliniki philologia* (Athens).

Matranga, *AG* ii = *Anecdota Graeca* ..., Matranga, P. (ed.), ii (Rome, 1850).

Mazal (1971) *see* Aristaenet. (Mazal).

MB, v (Sathas) = *Mesaiôniki vivliothiki* ..., Sathas, C.N. (ed.), v: *Michail Psellou istorikoi logoi* ... (Paris, 1876; rp. Athens, 1972).

McCail, R. (1971), 'The erotic and ascetic poetry of Agathias Scholasticus', *Byzantion* 41: 205-67.

Megas, G. (1956), 'Kallimachou kai Chrysorrhois ypothesis', in *Mélanges Merlier* (Coll. de l'Institut français d'Athènes, 93) 47-72.

Men. Rh. (RW) = *Menander Rhetor* ..., Russell, D.A. & Wilson, N.G. (eds) (Oxford, 1981).

Meraklis, M.G. (1985), *Pente laographika dokima yia ti glossa kai tin poiisi* (Athens).

Mercati = Mercati, S.G., *Collectanea Byzantina*, Longo, A.A. (ed.), i (Bari, 1970).

Merkelbach & West (1967) *see* Hes. fr. (MW).

Merlier, M.O. (1931) (ed.), *Tragoudia tis Roumelis* (Kentro Mikrasiatikôn Spoudôn, 12).

Methodius, *Banquet* (Musurillo-Débidour) = *Méthode d'Olympe, Le banquet* ..., Musurillo, H. & Débidour, V.-H. (eds) (SC, 85, 1963).

Meyendorff, J. (1975), *Marriage: an Orthodox perspective*[2] (N.Y.).

Miller ii *see Carmina* (Miller).

Miller, E. (1883), 'Poésies inédites de Théodore Prodrome', *Annuaire de l'Association des études grecques* 17: 18-64.

Minotou, M. (1934), 'Omilies: tritos tomos Laographias Zakynthou', *Ionios Anthologia* 87-9: 139-60.

Mioni, E. (1973), *Codices Graeci manuscripti Bibliothecae Divi Marci Venetiarum* (Rome).

Miranda = *Iscrizioni Greche d'Italia*, Miranda, E. (ed.), ii: Napoli (Rome, 1995).

Mitchell, S. (1993), *Anatolia: land, men and gods in Asia Minor*, ii: *The rise of the Church* (Oxford, 1993; pback 1995).

Mitsakis, C. (1971), *Vyzantini ymnographia*, i (Christianiki grammatologia, i).

Mitteis-Wilcken (1912), i = *Grundzüge und Chrestomathie der Papyruskunde*, Mitteis, L. & Wilcken, U. (eds), i-iv (Leipzig & Berlin, 1912).

(Christoph.) Mityl. (Kurtz) = *Die Gedichte des Christophoros Mytilenaios*, Kurtz, E. (ed.) (Leipzig, 1903).

Monaco, G. (1963), *Paragoni burleschi degli antichi* (Palermo).

Moravcsik, G. (1931), 'Il Caronte Bizantino', *Studi Biz. e Neoell.* 3: 45-68.

Morgan, G. (1960), 'Cretan poetry: sources and inspiration', *Kr. Chron.* 14: 7-68, 203-70, 379-434.

Morwood, J. (1997) (tr.), *Euripides: Medea, Hippolytus, Electra, Helen* (Oxford).

Mullett, M. & Scott, R. (1981) (eds), *Byzantium and the classical tradition* (Birmingham).

Murgatroyd, P. (1987), 'Sappho 110a LP: A footnote', *CQ*[2] 37.i: 224.

Murray, O. (1982), 'Symposion and Männerbund', in P. Oliva & A. Frolikova (eds), *Concilium Eirene* 16.i (Prague) 47-52.

———— (1990) (ed.), *Sympotica: a symposium on the symposion* (Oxford).

Murray-Dimock i-ii = *Homer Odyssey Books 1-12*[2], Murray, A.T. (tr.), (rev.) Dimock, G.E. (1919; LCL, 104, 1995); *Homer Odyssey Books 13-24*[2] (1919; LCL, 105, 1995).

Murray-Wyatt i-ii = *Homer Iliad Books 1-12*[2], Murray, A.T. (tr.), (rev.) Wyatt, W.F. (1924; LCL, 170, 1999); *Homer Iliad Books 13-24*[2] (1925; LCL, 171, 1999).

Musae. (Kost) = *Musaios: Hero und Leander*, Einleitung, Text, Übersetzung und Kommentar, Kost, K. (ed.) (Bonn, 1971).

Musurillo, H. (1958) (tr.), *St. Methodius: The Symposium, a treatise on chastity* (Westminster, MD & London).

—— & Débidour (1963) *see* Methodius.

Muth, R. (1954), ' "Hymenaios" und "Epithalamion" ', *WS* 67: 5-45.

Nagy, A. (1999), 'Archaioi magikoi polytimoi lithoi', in J. Petropoulos (1999)[a] 34-7.

Nagy, G. (1999 [1979]), *The best of the Achaeans: concepts of the hero in archaic Greek poetry*[2], rev. edn (Baltimore & London).

—— (1990), *Pindar's Homer: the lyric possession of an epic past* (Baltimore & London).

—— (1996), *Poetry as performance: Homer and beyond* (Cambridge).

Nauck = *Tragoricorum Graecorum fragmenta*, recensuit Augustus Nauck – Supplementum ..., adiecit Bruno Snell, Nauck, A. (ed.) (Hildesheim, 1964).

NCOE (van Dieten) = *Nicetae Choniatae orationes et epistulae*, van Dieten, J.-L. (ed.) (*CFHB*, iii [Berlin & N.Y.], 1972).

Nisbet & Hubbard i-ii = Nisbet, R.G.M. & Hubbard, M., *A commentary on Horace: Odes Book I* (Oxford, 1970); *A commentary on Horace: Odes Book II* (Oxford, 1978).

Nissen, T. (1940), *Die byzantinischen Anakreonteen* (Munich).

Nock, A.D. (1986 [1972]), 'SUNNAOS THEOS', in Z. Stewart (ed.), *Essays on religion and the ancient world*[2], i (Oxford, rp. with corr.) 202-51.

Norden, E. (1958), *Die antike Kunstprosa vom VI Jahrhundert v. Chr. bis in die Zeit der Renaissance*[5], ii (Darmstadt).

Oakley, J.H. (1982), 'The anakalypteria', *AA* 97: 113-18.

—— & Sinos, R.H. (1993), *The wedding in ancient Athens* (Madison, WI & London).

Od. (Stanford) = *The Odyssey of Homer*, i, Stanford, W.B. (ed. & comm.) (London, 1950).

Oeri, H.G. (1948), *Der Typ der komischen Alten in der Komödie, seine Nachwirkungen und seine Herkunft* (Basel).

Oikonomides, A.C. (1881) (ed.), *Tragoudia tou Olympou* (Athens).

Olson (1998) *see* Ar. *Pax* (Olson).

'Oppian' *Cynegetica* (Mair) = *Oppian, Colluthus, Tryphiodorus*, Mair, A.W. (ed. & tr.) (LCL, 1928, rp. 1958).

OSB = The Orthodox Study Bible, New Testament and Psalms, New King James version (Nashville, Tenn., 1993).

Pachtikos, G.D. (1905) (ed.), *260 dimôdi ellinika asmata ... syllegenta kai parasimanthenta (1888-1904)* ..., i (Athens).

Pack (1963) *see* Artem. (Pack).

Padel, R. (1992), *In and out of the mind: Greek images of the tragic self* (Princeton).

Page, D.L. (1938) *see* E. *Med.* (Page).

—— (1955), *Sappho and Alcaeus: an introduction to the study of ancient Lesbian poetry* (Oxford).

—— (1962) *see PMG* (Page).

—— (1978) *see* Rufin. (Page).

—— (1981) (ed.) , *Further Greek epigrams* ... (Cambridge).

Panôria (Kriaras) = Georgiou Chortatsi, *Panôria, kritiki ekdosi* ..., Kriaras, E. (ed.) (Vyzantini kai neoell. vivliothiki, ii, 1975).

Papacharalambous, G.C. (1945-6), 'Apo tin Paidiophraston diigisin tôn tetrapodôn zôôn', *Kypriaka Grammata* 10: 262-3.

Papachristodoulou, C.I. (1966), 'Katalogia – stichoi peri erôtos kai agapis', *Laogr.* 24: 14-93.

Papadakis, M.M. (1979-81), 'To archaio laographiko stoicheio sti "Lysistrati" tou Aristophani', *Laogr.* 32: 227-86.

Papadatos, S.G. (1984), *Peri tis mnisteias eis to Vyzantinon dikaion* (Pragmateiai tis Akademias Athinon, 50).

Papadopoulos-Kerameus (1897) *see AIS*, iv (Papadopoulos-Kerameus).

Papadopoullos, T. (1975), *Dimôdi Kypriaka asmata ex anekdotôn tou ITh' aiônos* (Dimosievmata Kentrou Epistimonikôn Erevnôn, 5).

—— (1977), 'Cheirographoi parallagai lyrikôn asmatôn', *Kypr. Spoudai* 41: 191-210.

Papamichaël, A. (1962-3), 'Chrisis tôn metallôn eis magikas, deisidaimonas kai allas energeias eis ton koinônikon vion tou laou', *Ep. Laogr. Arch.* 15-16: 62-91.

Pashley, R. (1837), *Travels in Crete*, i-ii (Cambridge).

Pasquato, O. (1976), *Gli spettacoli in s. Giovanni Crisostomo* (*OCA*, 201).

Passow, A. (1860) (ed.), *Tragoydia rômaiïka: popularia carmina Graeciae recentioris* (Bibliotheca ... Teubneriana).

PCG, ii (K.-A.) = *Poetae comici Graeci* (*PCG*), Kassel, R. & Austin, C. (eds), ii (Berlin & N.Y., 1991).

PCG, v (K.-A.) = *Poetae comici Graeci* (*PCG*) Kassel, R. & Austin, C. (eds), v (Berlin & N.Y., 1986).

PCG, vii (K.-A.) = *Poetae comici Graeci* (*PCG*), Kassel, R. & Austin, C. (eds), vii (Berlin & N.Y., 1989).

Pearson ii = *The fragments of Sophocles*, Pearson, A.C. (ed.), ii (Cambridge, 1917; rp. Amsterdam, 1963).

Peek = *Griechische Vers-Inschriften*, Peek, W. (ed.), i (Berlin, 1955).

Peek, W. (1965), 'Die Penelope der Ionerinnen', *Ath. Mitt.* 80: 160-9.

Pellegrino, M. (1958) (ed.), *L'inno del Simposio di S. Metodio Martire* (Univ. di Torino, pubbl. della fac. di lett. e filos., x. 1).

Perentidis, S. (1995), 'DIAPARTHENIA: une correction sur le Liddell-Scott', *Philologus* 139: 345-6.

—— (1997), '*Apaulia – Epaulia – Anakalyptèria*: définition et fonction des rites et des dons nuptiaux', in G. Thür & J. Vélissaropoulos-Karakostas (eds), *Symposion 1995: Vorträge zur griechischen und hellenistischen Rechtsgeschichte* (Korfu, 1.-5. September 1995) (Köln, Weimar, Wien) 179-204.

Pernot, H. (1931), *Chansons populaires grecques de XVe et XVIe siècles* (Paris).

Perry (1952) *see* Aesop. (P.).

Peters, J.P. & Thiersch, H. (1905), *Painted tombs in the necropolis of Marisa* (London).

Petropoulos, D.A. (1958), 'Isiodeioi prolipseis kai deisidaimoniai', *Ep. Laogr. Arch.* 19: 3-26.

—— (1959), 'Theokritou eidyllia ypo laographikin epopsin erminevomena', *Laogr.* 18: 5-93.

Petropoulos, J.C.B. (1988), 'The erotic magical papyri', in B. Mandilaras (ed.), *Proceedings of the XVIIIth International Congress of Papyrology*, i (Athens) 215-22.

—— (1989), 'The Church Father as social informant: St John Chrysostom on folk-songs', in E.A. Livingstone (ed.), *Studia Patristica*, xxii (Leuven) 159-64.

—— (1994), *Heat and lust: Hesiod's midsummer festival scene revisited* (Lanham, MD & London).

—— (1999)[a] (ed.), *Mageia: Elliniki archaiotita* [special issue], in *Archaiologia kai Technes* 70 (Athens).

—— (1999)[b] (ed.), *I mageia sto Vyzantio* [special issue], ibid. 71.

—— (1999)[c] (ed.), *I mageia sti neoteri Ellada* [special issue], ibid. 72.

Pfeiffer (1949) *see* Call. (Pf.).

Philogelos (Thierfelder) = *Philogelos, der Lachfreund*, Thierfelder, A. (ed.) (Munich, 1968).

Photius *Bibliotheca*, iii = *Photius, Bibliothèque*, Henry, R. (ed. & tr.), iii (Paris, 1962).

Pichard (1956) *see Callimachos & Chrysorrhoë* (Pichard).

Pickard-Cambridge, A.W. (1968), *The dramatic festivals of Athens*[2] (Oxford).

Pilitsis, G. (1987), 'Apotropaic and other magical devices in Greek wedding rituals', *Journal of the Hellenic Diaspora* 14. iii-iv: 91-114.

Pi. (M.) = *Pindari carmina cum fragmentis, Pars II: Fragmenta. Indices*, Maehler, H. (ed.) (Bibliotheca ... Teubneriana, 1989).

Pi. (S.-M.) = *Pindari carmina cum fragmentis, Pars I: Epinicia*[8], post B. Snell, Maehler, H. (ed.) (Bibliotheca ... Teubneriana, 1987).

Pi. (van Groningen) = *Pindare au banquet, les fragments des scolies*, van Groningen, B.A. (ed.) (Leyden, 1960).

Pl. *Smp.* (Dover) = *Plato, Symposium*, Dover, K.J. (ed. & comm.) (Cambridge, 1980).

PMG (Page) = *Poetae melici Graeci*, Page, D.L. (ed.) (Oxford, 1962).

Politis, *Paroimiai* = *Meletai peri tou viou kai tis glôssis tou ellinikou laou: Paroimiai*, Politis, N.G. (ed.), i-iv (Athens, 1899-1902).

Politis, N.G. (1931), *Laographika symmeikta*, iii (Dimosievmata Laogr. Archeiou Akad. Athinôn, vi).

——— (1932) (ed.), *Eklogai apo ta tragoudia tou ellinkou laou*[3] (Athens).

——— (1975), *Laographika summeikta*, ii[2] (Athens).

Pollard, J. (1977), *Birds in Greek life and myth* (London).

Poulianos, A.I. (1964) (ed.), *Laïka tragoudia tis Ikarias* (Athens).

Pouqueville, F.C.H.L. (1826-7), *Voyage de la Grèce*[2], i-vi (Paris).

Powell = *Collectanea Alexandrina*, Powell, J.U. (ed.) (Oxford, 1925).

Preisendanz-Heinrichs = *Papyri Graecae magicae, die griechischen Zauberpapyri*, Preisendanz, K. & Henrichs, A. (eds), i-ii (Samml. wiss. Comm., 1973-4).

(Theodore) Prodromos (Hörandner) = *Theodore Prodromos: historische Gedichte*, Hörandner, W. (ed.) (WByzSt, xi, 1974).

(Michael) Psellos (Kurtz & Drexl) = *Michaelis Pselli scripta minora*, i: *Orationes et dissertationes*, Kurtz, E. & Drexl, F. (eds) (Orbis Romanus, v, 1936).

pseudo-Lucian *Timarion* (Romano) = *Pseudo-Luciano, Timarione*, Roberto, R. (ed.) (Univ. di Napoli, Collana di studi e testi, ii, 1974).

Psychoyiou, E. (1993), 'Mageia kai elliniki laographia', in *Mageia kai Christianismos* (I. Mitropolis Ileias, Athens) 7-136.

'Ptocho-Prodromos' (H.-P.) = *Poèmes Prodromiques en grec vulgaire*, Hesseling, D.C. & Pernot, H. (eds) (Amsterdam, 1910).

'Ptocho-Prodromos' (Eideneier) *see* Eideneier (1991).

Puchner, W. (1983), 'I Erôphili sti dimôdi paradosi tis Kritis', *Ariadni* 1: 173-235.

Quinn, K. (1970), *Catullus: the poems* (London & Basingstoke).

Race i = *Pindar I: Olympian Odes, Pythian Odes*, Race, W.H. (ed. & tr.) (LCL, 56, 1997).

Race ii = *Pindar II: Nemean Odes, Isthmian Odes, fragments*, Race, W.H. (ed. & tr.) (LCL, 485, 1997).

Radcliffe-Brown, A.R. ([1924] 1952), *Structure and function in primitive society* (London).

——— ([1950] 1960) (co-ed.) *African systems of kinship and marriage* (Oxford).

RE = *Paulys Real-Encyclopädie der klassischen Altertumswissenschaft*, Wissowa, G. (ed.) (Stuttgart, 1893-).

Reardon, B.P. (1989) (ed.), *Collected ancient Greek novels* (Berkeley, Los Angeles & London).

Redfield, J. (1982), 'Notes on the Greek wedding', *Arethusa*, 15.i-ii: 181-201.

Reed, J.D. (1997) *see* Bion *Epitaph on Adonis*.

Reeve (1968) *see* Longus (Reeve).

Regas, G.A. (1958) (ed.), *Skiathou laïkos politismos*, Dimôdi asmata, i (Thessalonica).

Rehm, R. (1994), *Marriage to death: the conflation of wedding and funeral rituals in Greek tragedy* (Princeton).

Reiske *see* Const. Porphyr. *De Caerem.*

Renehan, R. (1983), 'The early Greek poets: Some interpretations', *HSCP* 87: 1-29.

Richardson, N.J. (1974) *see h. Cer.* (Richardson).

———— (1986), 'Classical themes in modern Chian popular poetry', in J. Boardman & C.E. Vaphopoulou-Richardson (eds), *Chios: a conference at the Homereion in Chios 1984* (Oxford) 61-77.

Riesenfeld, H. (1946), 'Remarques sur les hymnes magiques', *Eranos* 44:153-60.

Roberto (1974) *see* pseudo-Lucian.

Robinson, C. (1979), *Lucian and his influence in Europe* (London).

Rodd, R. (1892), *The customs and lore of modern Greece* (London).

Rohde, E. (1960), *Der griechische Roman und seine Vorläufer4* (Hildesheim)

Röhrich, L. (1969), 'Das Kontinuitäts-Problem bei der Erforschung der Volksprosa', in Bausinger & Brückner (1969) 117-33.

Romanos (Maas-Trypanis) = *Santi Romani Melodi cantica genuina*, Maas, P. & Trypanis, C.A. (eds) (Oxford, 1963) [to be consulted in conjunction with *Romanos le mélode: hymnes*, Grosdidier des Matons, J. (ed.), i-v (*SC*, 69-283)].

Roscher ii = *Ausführliches Lexikon der Griechischen und Römischen Mythologie*, Roscher, W.H. (ed.), ii.1-2 (Leipzig, 1890-7).

Rosenmeyer, P.A. (1992), *The poetics of imitation: Anacreon and the Anacreontic tradition* (Cambridge).

Rossi, L.E. (1971), 'Il Ciclope di Euripide come KÔMOS "mancato"', *Maia* 23: 19-20.

Rufin. (Page) = *The epigrams of Rufinus*, Page, D.L. (ed.) (Cambridge, 1978).

Russell, D.A. (1979), 'Rhetors at the wedding,' *PCPhS²* 25: 104-17.

———— & Wilson (1981) *see* Men. Rh. (RW).

Rydén, L. (1974), 'The Andreas Salos Apocalypse: Greek text, translation, and commentary', *DOP* 28: 197-261.

S. frr. (Lloyd-Jones) = *Sophocles: fragments*, Lloyd-Jones, H. (ed. & tr.) (LCL, 483, 1996).

S. *Ph.* (Lloyd-Jones) = *Sophocles: Antigone, The Women of Trachis* ..., Lloyd-Jones, H. (ed. & tr.) (LCL, 21, 1994).

S. *Trach.* (Lloyd-Jones) *see* S.*Ph.* above.

Sachlikis (Wagner) = *Carmina Graeca medii aevi*, Wagner, W. (ed.) (Bibliotheca Teubneriana, 1874).

Sapph. (LP) *see* Alc. (LP).

Sapph. (V) *see* Alc. (V).

Sathas (1876) *see MB*, v (Sathas).

Schissel, O. (1942), *Der byzantinische Garten* (Sitzungsb., Akad. der Wiss. in Wien, phil.-hist. Kl., 222).

Scobie, A. (1983), *Apuleius and folklore* ... (Misseltoe ser., 17).

Seaford, R. (1984) *see* E. *Cyclops* (Seaford).

———— (1987), 'The tragic wedding', *JHS* 107: 106-30.

SEG = *Supplementum Epigraphicum Graecum.*

Segal, C. (1995), 'Spectator and listener', in J.-P. Vernant (ed.), *The Greeks* (Engl. tr., Chicago & London).

Settas, D. (1976) (ed.), *Evvia, laïkos politismos* (Athens).

Sevcenko, I. (1969-70), 'Poems on the deaths of Leo VI & Constantine VII in the Madrid manuscript of Scylitzes', *DOP* 23-4: 187-228.

SH (Lloyd-Jones & Parsons) = *Supplementum Hellenisticum*, Lloyd-Jones, H. & Parsons, P. (eds) (Berlin & N.Y., 1983).

Shefton, B.B. (1971), 'Persian gold and Attic black-glaze Achaemenid influences in Attic pottery ...', in *Proceedings of the IXth International Congress of Classical Archaeology, Damascus, 1969* (Damascus) 109-11.

—— (1972), [untitled report], *AK* 15: 148-9.

Shipp, G.P. (1979), *Modern Greek evidence for the ancient Greek vocabulary* (Sydney).

Sifakis, G.M. (1988), *Gia mia poiitiki tou ellinikou dimotikou tragoudiou* (Herakleion).

—— (1992), 'Homeric survivals in the medieval and modern Greek folksong tradition?', *G & R* 39.ii: 139-54.

—— (1996), 'Homeric poetry and modern Greek folksongs: a second essay', *Dialogos* 3: 95-110.

—— (1997), 'Formulas and their relatives: a semiotic approach to verse making in Homer and modern Greek folksongs', *JHS* 117: 136-53.

Silk, M. (1974), *Interaction in poetic imagery, with special reference to early Greek poetry* (Cambridge).

—— (1980), 'Aristophanes as a lyric poet', *YCS* 26: 99-151.

SLG (Page) = *Supplementum lyricis Graecis*, Page, D.L. (ed.) (Oxford, 1974).

Snell & Maehler (1987) *see* Pi. (S.-M.).

Sommerstein (1983) *see* Ar. *Vesp.* (Sommerstein).

—— (1985) *see* Ar. *Pax* (Sommerstein).

—— (1987) see Ar. *Av.* (Sommerstein).

—— (1998) *see* Ar. *Eccl.* (Sommerstein).

Spyridakis-Petropoulos = *Ellinika dimotika tragoudia (eklogi)*, Megas, G.A., Petropoulos, D.A. & Spyridakis, G.C. (eds), i (Dimosievmata Laogr. Archeiou Akad. Athinôn, vii, 1962).

Stanford (1950) *see Od.* (Stanford).

—— (1963) *see* Ar. *Ran.* (Stanford).

Stauffer, A. (1995), *Textiles of late antiquity*, Metropolitan Museum of Art (N.Y.).

Steiner, D. (1986), *The crown of song: metaphor in Pindar* (London).

Stephanis, I.E. (1988), *Diosynisiakoi technitai: symvoles stin prosôpographia tou theatrou kai tis mousikis tôn archaiôn Ellinôn* (Herakleion).

Stephens, S.A. & Winkler, J.J. (1995) (eds), *Ancient Greek novels: the fragments* (Princeton).

Sternbach (1903) *see* Callicles (Sternbach).

Stesich. (Davies) *see* Davies (1991)[b].

Stevens, P.T. (1976), *Colloquial expressions in Euripides* (Hermes Einzelschr., 38).

Stewart, C. (1991), *Demons and the Devil: moral imagination in modern Greek culture* (Princeton).

Stigers, E.S. (1977), 'Retreat from the male: Catullus 62 and Sappho's erotic flowers', *Ramus* 6.i: 83-102.

Strathern, M. (1987) (ed.), *Dealing with inequality* (Cambridge).

Sullivan, S.D. (1988), 'An analysis of *phrenes* in the Greek lyric poets (excluding Pindar and Bacchylides)', *Glotta* 66.i-ii: 26-62.

Sutton, D.F. (1980), *The Greek satyr play* (Beitr. zur klassischen Philol., 90).

Süss, W. (1910), *Ethos. Studien zur älteren griechischen Rhetorik* (Leipzig).

Syntagma canonôn = *Syntagma tôn theiôn kai ierôn canonôn tôn apostolôn ...*, Rallis, G.A. & Potlis, M. (eds), i-vi (Athens, 1852-9).

S.-W. *see* Stephens & Winkler.

Tafel (1832) *see Eustathii ... Opuscula.*

Taplin, O. (1993), *Comic angels and other approaches to Greek drama through vase-paintings* (Oxford).

Tarsouli, A. (1947-50) (ed.), *Dôdekanisa*, i-iii (Athens).

Terzopoulou, M. & Psychoyiou, E. (1993), 'Roloi phylôn kai scheseis syngeneias mesa apo ta gamilia tragoudia', *Revue des Études Néo-Hélléniques.* 2.i-ii: 89-124.

—— (1984)ᵃ, 'Apo ta tragoudia stis koinônikes domes', *Diavazô* 108: 119-22.

—— (1984)ᵇ, 'Gynaika-koinônia sto dimotiko tragoudi', *Antitheseis* 17: 50-67.

Theoc. (Dover) = *Theocritus, select poems ...*, Dover, K.J. (ed. & comm.) (Basingstoke & London, 1971).

Theoc. (Gow) = *Theocritus*², Gow, A.S.F. (ed. & comm.), i-ii (Cambridge, 1952).

Theophanis *Chronographia* (de Boor) = *Theophanis Chronographia*, de Boor, C. (ed.), ii: Theophanis vitae, etc. (Leipzig, 1885; rp. Hildesheim & N.Y., 1980).

Thierfelder (1968) *see* Philogelos (Thierfelder).

Thompson, *Motif-Index* = *Motif-Index of folk-literature ...*, Thompson, S. (ed.), i-vi, with index (rev. and enlarged edn, Copenhagen, 1955-8).

Thomson, G. (1966) (ed. & comm.), *The Oresteia of Aeschylus ...*, ii (rev. edn, Prague, 1966).

Thumb, A. (1928), *Grammatik der Neugriechischen Volkssprache*² (Berlin & Leipzig, 1928).

Tomadakis ii (1965) = Tomadakis, N.B., *Eisagôgi eis tin vyzantinin philologian*³, ii (Athens).

Trapp *see* *Dig. Akr.* (Trapp).

Trask i-ii = *The unwritten song: poetry of the primitive and traditional peoples of the world*, Trask, W.R. (ed. & re-tr.), i-ii (N.Y. & London, 1966-7).

TrGF, ii (Kannicht-Snell) = *Tragicorum Graecorum fragmenta*, Kannicht, R. & Bruno, S. (eds), ii: *Fragmenta adespota*, etc. (Göttingen, 1981).

TrGF, iii (Radt) = *Tragicorum Graecorum fragmenta*, Radt, S. (ed.), iii (Göttingen, 1985).

Trenkner, S. (1958), *The Greek novella in the classical period* (Cambridge).

Trypanis, C.A. (1958) (tr.), *Callimachus, Aetia, Iambi ...* (LCL, 421; rp. 1968, 1975).

Tsetsos, T.L. (1981) (ed.), *Tragoudia apo t'Agrapha* (Athens).

Tsironi, N. (forthcoming), *The lament of the Virgin Mary in the iconoclastic period* (Oxford).

Tuffin, P.G. (1975), 'The *adynaton* in the Greek tradition' (Ph.D. thesis, Univ. of Birmingham).

(Ioannes) Tzetzes *Historiae* (Leone) = *Ioannis Tzetzae Historiae*, Leone, P.A.M. (ed.) (Pubbl. Inst. di filol. class., Univ. di Napoli, i, 1968).

Ussher (1973) *see* Ar. *Eccl.* (Ussher).

Vance, J.M. (1907), *Beiträge zur Byzantinischen Kulturgeschichte am Ausgange des IV. Jahrhunderts aus den Schriften des Johannes Chrysostomos* (Jena).

van Dieten (1972) *see* *NCOE* (van Dieten).

van Gennep, A. (1960 [1909]), *The rites of passage* (orig. Paris; tr. London).

van Groningen (1960) *see* Pi. (van Groningen).

—— (1977) *see* Euphorion (van Groningen).

Vavoules, P. (1950) (ed.), *O Kritikos tragoudistis* (Chania).

Vernant, J.-P. (1974), *Mythe et société en Grèce ancienne* (Paris).

Viljamaa, T. (1968), *Studies in Greek encomiastic poetry of the early Byzantine period* (Comm. human. litt., Soc. sci. Fenn., 42).

Vincent (1980) *see* *Fortunatos* (Vincent).

Vodoklys, E.J. (1992), *Blame-expression in the epic tradition* (N.Y. & London).

Vogt, A. (1935-40) *see* Const. Porphyr. *De Caerem.*

Voight (1971) *see* Alc. (V).

von Arnim (1893) *see* D. Chr. (von Arnim).

(anon.) *Voscopoula* (S. Alexiou) = Anonimo Cretese, *La Voskopula*, Alexiou, S. et al. (eds) (Univ. di Padova, Istituto di Studi Biz. e Neogrec., 9, 1975).

Vrontis, A. (1932), *Roditikos gamos* (Rhodes).

Vryonis, S., Jr (1971), *The decline of medieval Hellenism in Asia Minor and the process of Islamization from the eleventh tnrough the fifteenth century* (Berkeley, Los Angeles & London).

—— (1978) (ed.), *The 'past' in medieval and modern Greek culture* (Malibu, CA).

—— (1978), 'Recent scholarship on continuity and discontinuity of culture: classical Greeks, Byzantines, Modern Greeks', in Vryonis (1978), 237-56.

Wagner (1874) *see* Sachlikis (Wagner).

Walcot, P. (1970), *Greek peasants, ancient and modern: a comparison of social and moral values* (Manchester).

Wehrli = Wehrli, F. (ed. & comm.), *Die Schule des Aristoteles: Texte und Kommentar*, iii: *Klearchos*[2] (enlarged & rev. edn, Basel & Stuttgart, 1969).

Wellesz, E. (1961), *A history of Byzantine music and hymnography*[2] (Oxford).

West, M.L. (1965), 'Alcmanica', *CQ*[2] 15.ii: 188-202.

—— (1969),'Near Eastern material in Hellenstic and Roman literature', *HSCP* 73: 113-14.

—— (1978) *see* Hes. *WD* (W).

—— (1981), 'Tragica V', *BICS* 28: 61-78.

—— (1982), *Greek metre* (Oxford).

—— (1989-92) *see IE*, I-ii (W).

—— (1993)[a] (tr.), *Greek lyric poetry: the poems and fragments of the Greek iambic, elegiac, and melic poets (excluding Pindar and Bacchylides) down to 450 BC* (Oxford).

—— (1993)[b] *see* Anacreont. (West).

—— (1997), *The east face of Helicon: West Asiatic elements in Greek poetry and myth* (Oxford).

Westermarck, E. (1914), *Marriage ceremonies in Morocco* (London).

Whitman, C. (1964), *Aristophanes and the comic hero* (Cambridge, MA).

Wilamowitz-Moellendorf, U. von (1921), *Griechische Verskunst* (Berlin).

Wilhelm, A. (1931), 'Lesefrüchte', *Byzantion* 6.i: 459-68.

Wilson, N.G. (1983), *Scholars of Byzantium* (London).

Winkler, J.J. (1990), *The constraints of desire: the anthropology of sex and gender in ancient Greece* (N.Y. & London).

Wirth, P. (1963), 'Neue Spuren eines Sappho Bruchstücks', *Hermes* 90: 115-17.

Yatromanolakis, D (1999), 'Alexandrian Sappho revisited', *HSCP* 99: 179-95.

Zagagi, N. (1986), 'Mythological hyperboles and Plautus', *CQ*[2] 36.i: 267.

Zanker, G. (1987), *Realism in Alexandrian poetry: a literature and its audience* (London, Sydney, Wolfeboro, New Hampshire).

Zervou, A. (1993), '*Nausikaa parthenos admês*: le récit de l'adolescence féminine', in M. Païzi-Apostolopoulou (ed.), *Spondes ston Omiro* ... (Ithaka, Kentro Odysseiakôn Spoudôn) 149-75.

Zevgoli-Glezou, D. (1963), *Paroimies apo tin Apeirantho tis Naxou* (Laogr. ser., vi).

Zora, P. (1994), *Elliniki techni: Laïki techni* (Athens).

Index

The pages of the main text cited in this index often refer to relevant notes.

199